R. Gupta's®

Legal & Regulatory Aspects

of

BANKING

For JAIIB and Diploma in Banking & Finance Examination

by

Abinash Kumar Mandilwar

M.Sc., MBA (Finance), M.Phil. (Management), CAIIB, Certified Credit Professional,
PGDFA, Diploma in Micro Finance, Diploma in Home Loan Advising

**Chief Manager & Faculty, Bank of India,
Staff Training College, Bhopal**

Updated Upto
JANUARY 2019

Ramesh Publishing House, New Delhi

Published by
O.P. Gupta *for* Ramesh Publishing House

Admin. Office
12-H, New Daryaganj Road, Opp. Officers' Mess,
New Delhi-110002 ℑ 23261567, 23275224, 23275124

E-mail: info@rameshpublishinghouse.com
Website: www.rameshpublishinghouse.com

Showroom
● Balaji Market, Nai Sarak, Delhi-6 ℑ 23253720, 23282525
● 4457, Nai Sarak, Delhi-6, ℑ 23918938

First Edition : February, 2019

Book Code: R-2031

ISBN: 978-93-88642-24-8

HSN Code: 49011010

समर्पण

ॐ भूर्भुवः स्व तत्सवितुर्वरेण्यं भर्गो
देवस्य धीमहि धियो यो नः प्रचोदयात्।।

मेरी यह पुस्तक वेदमाता माँ गायत्री,
हमारे परम पूज्य गुरुदेव पंडित श्रीराम
शर्मा आचार्य, परम वन्दनीया माता
भगवती देवी शर्मा, मेरे पूज्य पिताजी
स्व॰ विश्वनाथ प्रसाद एवं मेरी परम
आदरणीय माँ स्व॰ चन्द्रकान्ता देवी
के चरणों में सादर समर्पित।

Preface

A young generation of bankers are joining the banking industry in huge number due to mass retirements and super annuation of existing staff. Banking sector in India is changing rapidly and banking becomes more complex. To meet the requirement of this generation of bankers a need was felt to equip them with the basics of banking. This book has been written keeping this in mind. A keen attempt has been made to make the book useful. Besides, for the preparation of JAIIB Examination, this book is also very useful for day to day banking and all knowledge based examinations. It is with great hope and expectation that the book has been written which will help the young generation of proficient bankers.

A combination of subjective as well as objective material has been comprehensively dealt in this book. There is a need to publish a comprehensive book covering all the aspects so that new recruits get updated without referring to many voluminous books. This book titled "JAIIB - Legal & Regulatory Aspects of Banking" has many unique features to its credit & consists of all topics/syllabus required for JAIIB/DB&F examination with clear concepts & simple language with latest changes (up to January 2019). It has been experienced that students need objective type questions beside subjective matter. This has been taken care of in this book. To prepare the students well, objective questions are also incorporated after every chapter. Two mock tests (100 questions each) for self-evaluation of preparation are given at the end of the book.

During preparation of this book, I have received tremendous support from my family members, friends & colleagues of BOI Staff Training College, especially my wife Mrs. Sumita Taterway (Ruby), my daughters Miss Tanya and Miss Pragya. Special thanks to Shri Anand Mohan Patel, Shri Ajay Kumar Sinha (Faculty Members of Staff Training College, Bhopal) for their support, vetting & compilation of this book.

Any suggestions towards its further improvement will be thankfully acknowledged and incorporated in the next edition.

Date: 10-02-2019   **— Abinash Kr. Mandilwar**

About the Author

The author Abinash Kumar Mandilwar joined 'Bank of India' as Probationary Officer in 1995. A highly experienced banker, has been working in the bank for more than 23 years. He has held several important assignments which include 10 years as branch head before his current posting as Chief Manager and Faculty Member at Bank of India Staff Training College at Bhopal. 

He is a Certified Associate of Indian Institute of Banking & Finance (CAIIB). His academics include Post Graduate in Chemistry, MBA (Finance), M. Phil. (Management), Honours Diploma in Computer Science., Post Graduate Diploma in Financial Advising, Diploma in Micro Finance, Diploma in Home Loan Advising, Diploma in Banking Oriented Paper in Hindi, Certificate in AML & KYC, Certificate in SME Finance, Certificate in Trade Finance, Certificate in Customer Service & Banking Codes and Standard. He was also awarded the Continuing Professional Development (CPD) Certification from IIBF in 2011.

As a faculty for more than 3 years at training college, he is catering to training needs of managers in middle management/Staff. He has vast experience of teaching on banking subject in Bank of India as well as associated Regional Rural Banks. He is also associated as a visiting faculty with other bank training institutes.

His articles have been published in different in house banking journals. His Power Point Presentations (PPTs) on various banking topics are appreciated by bankers on social media and Slideshare.net.

सुदीप रतन श्रीवास्तव
प्राचार्य
बैंक ऑफ इंडिया
स्टॉफ प्रशिक्षण महाविद्यालय, भोपाल

Sudeep Ratan Srivastava
Principal

Bank of India
Staff Training College, Bhopal

Foreword

I am glad to know that the book "JAIIB -Legal & Regulatory Aspects of Banking" is written by Shri A K Mandilwar. He is a practicing banker for more than 24years and had worked in functional areas of the bank. A quick perusal of the book reveals that it is quite comprehensive, exhaustive and suitable for the new practitioners of Banking as well as for those preparing themselves for the exams conducted by IIBF. The Book covers the basic conceptual part of the subject 'Legal and Regulatory Aspects of Banking'. The language of the book is simple and lucid.

The book will be of great help to the new entrants in the banking industry especially for their orientation to the core operational areas of banking. The readers will also be introduced to the entire Legal and Regulatory Aspects of Banking.

I am confident that this book will be of use to all the candidates who are appearing for the JAIIB/DB&F Examination and also to those general banking personal who desire to update their information on the subject. The book will help the new entrants who did not study such subjects in their academic life. The test papers given at the end of each chapter will immensely be beneficial to the new entrants and will help them to prepare themselves for the practical aspects of banking. In short this is a concise text book which will help the readers prepare for their JAIIB/DB&F Exams.

I am sure the book by Shri Mandilwar will serve the purpose of a "Text Book" on Legal and Regulatory Aspects of Banking which will be quite handy for referring to the basics of banking. I wish the readers an interesting reading and a sound initiation into the world of banking.

Bhopal

Date: 12-02-2019

— **Sudeep Ratan Srivastava**

CONTENTS

MODULE B : LEGAL ASPECTS OF BANKING OPERATIONS

MODULE C : BANKING RELATED LAWS

MODULE D : COMMERCIAL LAWS WITH REFERENCE TO BANKING OPERATIONS

30. The Sale of Goods Act, 1930 .... *164-168*

Test Yourself

31. Indian Partnership Act, 1932 .... *169-174*

Test Yourself

32. Definition and Features of a Company
Distinction between Company and Partnership *175-177*

Test Yourself

33. The Companies Act, 1932 .... *178-187*

MOCK TEST

Legal & Regulatory Aspects of Banking

RULES & SYLLABUS

PAPER-3 : LEGAL & REGULATORY ASPECTS OF BANKING

OBJECTIVE

JAIIB aims at providing required level of basic knowledge in banking and financial services, banking technology, customer relations, basic accountancy and legal aspects necessary for carrying out day to day banking operations.

ELIGIBILITY

(i) The examination is open to the ordinary members of the Institute (Any person working in the banking and finance industry whose employer is an Institutional member of the Institute can apply for membership, for details visit IIBF website).

(ii) Candidates must have passed the 12th standard examination in any discipline or its equivalent. The Institute may, however at its discretion, allow any candidate from clerical or supervisory staff cadre of banks to appear at the examination on the recommendation of the Manager of the bank/officer-incharge of the bank's office where the candidate is working, even if he/she is not 12th standard pass or its equivalent.

(iii) Subordinate staff of recognized Banking / Financial Institutions in India, who are members of the Institute, are eligible to appear at the examination, provided they have passed the 12th standard examination or its equivalent.

SUBJECTS OF EXAMINATION

(1) **Principles & Practices of Banking**
(2) **Accounting & Finance for Bankers**
(3) **Legal & Regulatory Aspects of Banking**

There is no exemption in any of the subject/s for prior qualification/s.

PASSING CRITERIA

1. Minimum marks for pass in the subject is 50 out of 100.

2. Candidates securing at least 45 marks in each subject with an aggregate of 50% marks in all subjects of examination in a single attempt will also be declared as having completed the Examination.

3. Candidates will be allowed to retain credits for the subject they have passed in an attempt till the expiry of the time limit for passing the examination as mentioned below.

TIME LIMIT FOR PASSING THE EXAMINATION

1. Candidates will be required to pass the examination within a time limit of 2 years (*i.e.* 4 consecutive attempts).

2. Candidates not able to pass examination within stipulated time period of two years are required to re-enroll themselves afresh. Such candidates will not be granted credit/s for subjects passed, if any, earlier.

3. Time limit of 2 years will start from the date of application for First attempt.

   Attempts will be counted irrespective of whether a candidate appears at any examination or otherwise.

MEDIUM OF EXAMINATION

Candidates are allowed to attempt the examination either in Hindi or English, and should clearly fill in their choice of medium at the time of registration of application. In any case change of medium will not be allowed at a later stage.

PATTERN OF EXAMINATION

(i) Question Paper will contain approximately 120 objective type multiple choice questions for 100 marks including questions based on case studies/case lets. The Institute may, however vary the number of questions to be asked for a subject.

(ii) The examination will be held in Online Mode only.

(iii) There will NOT be negative marking for wrong answers.

DURATION OF EXAMINATION:

The duration of the examination will be of 2 hours.

PERIODICITY AND EXAMINATION CENTRES

a) Examination will be conducted on pre-announced dates published on IIBF Web Site. Institute conducts examination on half yearly basis, however periodicity of the examination may be changed depending upon the requirement of banking industry.

b) List of Examination centers will be available on the website. (Institute will conduct examination in those centers where there are 20 or more candidates.)

SYLLABUS OF JAIIB/DB&F

PAPER-3 : LEGAL & REGULATORY ASPECTS OF BANKING

MODULE A – REGULATIONS AND COMPLIANCE

✦ **Legal Framework of Regulation of Banks**

   Business of Banking; Constitution of Banks; RBI Act, 1934; Banking Regulation Act, 1949; Role of RBI; Govt. as a Regulator of Banks; Control over Co-operative Banks; Regulation by other Authorities.

✦ **Control over Organization of Banks**

   Licensing of Banking Companies; Branch Licensing; Paid up Capital and Reserves; Shareholding in Banking Companies; Subsidiaries of Banking Companies; Board of Directors; Chairman of Banking Company; Appointment of Additional Directors; Restrictions on Employment; Control over Management; Corporate Governance; Directors and Corporate Governance.

✦ **Regulation of Banking Business**

   Power of RBI to Issue Directions; Acceptance of Deposits; Nomination; Loans and Advances; Regulation of Interest Rate; Regulation of Payment Systems; Internet Banking Guidelines; Regulation of Money Market Instruments; Banking Ombudsman; Reserve Funds; Maintenance of CRR, SLR; Assets in India.

MODULE B – LEGAL ASPECTS OF BANKING OPERATIONS

♦ **Laws Relating to Securities and Modes of Charging-II**

Lien; Pledge; Hypothecation; etc.

♦ **Registration and Satisfaction of Charges**

Definition of Charge; Procedure for Registration of Charge; Effect of Non-registration of Charges; Provisions of Law relating to Registration of Charges

♦ **Case Laws on Responsibility of Paying Bank**

Negotiable Instruments Act and Paying Banks; Liability of Paying Banker; Payment in due course; Payment in Good Faith; Whether Payment under Mistake Recoverable

♦ **Case Laws on Responsibility of Collecting Bank**

Statutory protection to Collecting Bank; Duties of Collecting Bank

MODULE C – BANKING RELATED LAWS

♦ **Recovery of Debts due to Banks and Financial Institutions Act, 1993 (DRT Act)**

Objective of the Act, Constitution of Tribunal, Procedure to be followed, Enforcement process

♦ **Securitisation and Reconstruction of Financial Assets and Enforcement of Securities Interest Act (SARFAESI)**

Constitutional Validity; Definitions; Regulation & Reconstruction; Enforcement of Security Interest; Central Registry; Offences & Penalties; Miscellaneous Provisions

♦ **Banking Ombudsmen Scheme**

Purpose; Extent; Definitions; Establishment; Powers; Procedure for Redressal Grievance

♦ **Bankers Books Evidence Act, 1891**

Applicability; Definition; Important Provisions

♦ **The Legal Services Authorities Act, 1987**

Lok Adalats—Organisation; Jurisdiction; Disposal of Cases; Awards

♦ **The Consumer Protection Act, 1986 and CERSAI**

Preamble, Extent & Definitions; Consumer Protection Councils; Consumer Disputes Redressal Agencies; Objectives and important provisions of Central Registry of Securitisation Asset Reconstruction and Security Interest of India

♦ **The Law of Limitation**

Definition; Computation of Limitation; Important Provisions in schedule to the Limitation Act

♦ **Tax Laws**

Income Tax; Commodity Transaction Tax; Service Tax

♦ **Negotiable Instruments Act, 1881**

Applicability; Definition; Important Provisions

♦ **Payment & Settlements Systems Act, 2007**

Applicability; Definition; Important Provisions

MODULE D – COMMERCIAL LAWS WITH REFERENCE TO BANKING OPERATIONS

♦ **Indian Contract Act, 1872**

Meaning and essentials of contract; Contract of Indemnity & Rights of Indemnity Holder; Contract of Guarantee; Contract of Bailment; Contract of Pledge; Contract of Agency

MODULE–A
REGULATIONS AND COMPLIANCE

LEGAL FRAMEWORK OF REGULATION OF BANKS

HISTORY OF BANKING SECTOR IN INDIA

Banking in India, in the modern sense, originated in the last decades of the 18th century. Among the first banks were the Bank of Hindustan, which was established in 1770 and liquidated in 1829-32; and the General Bank of India, established in 1786 but failed in 1791.

The largest bank, and the oldest still in existence, is the State Bank of India. It originated as the Bank of Calcutta in June 1806. In 1809, it was renamed as the Bank of Bengal. This was one of the three banks funded by a presidency government, the other two were the Bank of Bombay in 1840 and the Bank of Madras in 1843. The three banks were merged in 1921 to form the Imperial Bank of India, which after India attained independence, became the State Bank of India in 1955. For many years the presidency banks had acted as quasi-central banks, as did their successors, until the Reserve Bank of India was established in 1935, under the Reserve Bank of India Act, 1934.

In 1960, the State Banks of India was given control of eight state-associated banks under the State Bank of India (Subsidiary Banks) Act, 1959. These were called associate banks of SBI. On 1st April, 2017, State Bank of India, which is India's largest Bank merged with five of its Associate Banks (State Bank of Bikaner & Jaipur, State Bank of Hyderabad, State Bank of Mysore, State Bank of Patiala and State Bank of Travancore) and Bharatiya Mahila Bank with itself. In 1969 the Indian government nationalised 14 major private banks. In 1980, 6 more private banks were nationalised. These nationalised banks are the majority of lenders in the Indian economy. They dominate the banking sector because of their large size and widespread network.

The Indian banking sector is broadly classified into scheduled and non-scheduled banks. The scheduled banks are those which are included under the 2nd Schedule of the Reserve Bank of India Act, 1934. The scheduled banks are further classified into Nationalised banks, State Bank of India, Regional Rural Banks (RRBs), foreign banks, and other Indian private sector banks. The term commercial banks refers to both scheduled and non-scheduled commercial banks regulated under the Banking Regulation Act, 1949.

DEFINITION OF BANKING

Section 5(B) of Banking Regulation Act, 1949 defines banking as "Accepting for the purpose of lending or investment of deposits of money from the public, repayable on demand and withdrawable by cheques, drafts, and orders or otherwise". Banking Company means any company which transacts the business of banking in India. Banks are governed by Reserve Bank of India Act (RBI Act) 1934 and Banking Regulation Act (BR Act) 1949. Nationalised banks are owned by Government of India and governed by directives issued by RBI.

Thus, the core business of the bank is to accept deposit from the public and lending to the public or investment of such deposit. The deposit may be repayable on demand or fixed for a time as agreed by the banker and the customer.

As per Section 49(A) of BR Act, No person other than a banking company, RBI, SBI shall accept from the public deposits of money withdrawable by cheque.

As per RBI directives, Non-Banking Companies, Firms and other unincorporated associations of persons and individuals can accept deposits from the public, which is regulated by RBI under the Non-Banking Financial Companies Acceptance of Public Deposit (Reserve Bank) Directions, 1998 and other directives issued by RBI Act.

Licence of Banking

As per Section 22 of BR Act, No company shall carry on banking business in India unless it holds a licence issued in that behalf by the Reserve Bank and any such licence may be issued subject to such conditions as the Reserve Bank may think fit to impose.

As per Section 7 of BR Act, No company other than a banking company shall use as part of its name any of the words "bank", "banker" or "banking" and no company shall carry on the business of banking in India unless it uses as part of its name at least one of such words.

Permitted Business for Banking Companies

As per Section 6(1) of BR Act, In addition to the business of banking, a banking company may engage in any one or more of the following forms of business, mainly :

  (a) Basic Banking Functions such as:

    (i) The borrowing, raising, or taking up of money;

    (ii) The lending or advancing of money either upon or without security;

    (iii) The drawing, making, accepting, discounting, buying, selling, collecting and dealing in bills of exchange, hundies, promissory notes, coupons, drafts, bills of lading, railway receipts, warrants, debentures, certificates, scrips and other instruments and securities whether transferable or negotiable or not;

    (iv) The granting and issuing of letters of credit, traveller's cheques and circular notes;

    (v) The buying, selling and dealing in bullion and specie;

    (vi) The buying and selling of foreign exchange including foreign bank notes;

    (vii) The acquiring, holding, issuing on commission, underwriting and dealing in stock, funds, shares, debentures, debenture stock, bonds, obligations, securities and investments of all kinds;

    (viii) The purchasing and selling of bonds, scrips or other forms of securities on behalf of constituents or others,

    (ix) The negotiating of loans and advances;

    (x) The receiving of all kinds of bonds, scrips or valuables on deposit or for safe custody or otherwise;

    (xi) The providing of safe deposit vaults;

    (xii) The collecting and transmitting of money and securities;

  (b) Acting as agents for any Government or local authority or any other person or persons; the carrying on of agency business of any description including the clearing and forwarding of goods, giving of receipts and discharges and otherwise acting as an attorney on behalf of customers, but excluding the business of a 1[Managing Agent or Secretary and Treasurer] of a company;

  (c) Contracting for public and private loans and negotiating and issuing the same;

  (d) The effecting, insuring, guaranteeing, underwriting, participating in Managing and carrying out of any issue, public or private, of State, municipal or other loans or of shares, stock, debentures, or debenture stock of any company, corporation or association and the lending of money for the purpose of any such issue;

  (e) Carrying on and transacting every kind of guarantee and indemnity business;

  (f) Managing, selling and realising any property which may come into the possession of the company in satisfaction or part satisfaction of any of its claims;

  (g) Acquiring and holding and generally dealing with any property or any right, title or interest in any such property which may form the security or part of the security for any loans or advances or which may be connected with any such security;

  (h) Undertaking and executing trusts;

  (i) Undertaking the administration of estates as executor, trustee or otherwise;

  (j) Establishing and supporting or aiding in the establishment and support of associations, institutions, funds, trusts and conveniences calculated to benefit employees or ex-employees of the company or the dependents or connections of such persons; granting pensions and allowances and making payments towards insurance; subscribing to or guaranteeing moneys for charitable or benevolent objects or for any exhibition or for any public, general or useful object;

(k) The acquisition, construction, maintenance and alteration of any building or works necessary or convenient for the purposes of the company.

(l) Selling, improving, managing, developing, exchanging, leasing, mortgaging, disposing of or turning into account or otherwise dealing with all or any part of the property and rights of the company;

(m) Acquiring and undertaking the whole or any part of the business of any person or company, when such business is of a nature enumerated or described in this sub-section;

(n) Doing all such other things as are incidental or conducive to the promotion or advancement of the business of the company;

(o) Any other form of business which the Central Government may, by notification in the Official Gazette, specify as a form of business in which it is lawful for a banking company to engage.

Prohibited Business for Banking Companies

As per Section 8 of BR Act, No banking company shall directly or indirectly deal in the buying or selling or bartering of goods, except in connection with the realisation of security given to or held by it, or engage in any trade, or buy, sell or barter goods for others otherwise than in connection with bills of exchange received for collection or negotiation or with such of its business as is referred to in clause (i) of sub-section (1) of section 6.

Disposal of non-Banking Assets

As per Section 9 of BR Act, no banking company can hold any immovable property howsoever acquired, except such as is required for its own use, for any period exceeding 7 years from the acquisition thereof or from the, commencement of this Act, whichever is later or any extension of such period as in this section provided, and such property shall be disposed of within such period or extended period, as the case may be:

The banking company may, within the period of 7 years as aforesaid, deal or trade in any such property for the purpose of facilitating the disposal thereof:

Reserve Bank may in any particular case extend the aforesaid period of 7 years by such period not exceeding 5 years where it is satisfied that such extension would be in the interests of the depositors of the banking company.

Constitution of Banks

An outline of the Indian Banking structure may be presented as follows:

1. Reserve Banks of India
2. Indian Scheduled Commercial Banks :
   a) State Bank of India,
   b) Nationalized banks.
   c) Regional rural banks.
   d) Other scheduled commercial banks.
3. Foreign Banks
4. Non-scheduled Banks
5. Co-operative Banks
6. Small Finance Banks
7. Payments Banks

✦ **Reserve Bank of India:** The reserve bank of India is a central bank and was established in April 1, 1935 in accordance with the provisions of reserve bank of India act 1934. RBI works as a central bank where commercial banks are account holders.

✦ **Indian Scheduled Commercial Banks:** Scheduled Banks in India constitute those banks which have been included in the second schedule of RBI act 1934. "Scheduled banks in India" means the State Bank of India constituted under the State Bank of India Act, 1955, a corresponding new bank constituted under section 3 of the Banking companies (Acquisition and Transfer of Undertakings) Act, 1980, or any other bank being a bank included in the Second Schedule to the Reserve bank of India Act, 1934, but does not include a co-operative bank".

✦ **Regional Rural Bank:** The government of India set up Regional Rural Banks (RRBs) on 2nd October 1975. The banks provide credit to the weaker sections of the rural areas, particularly the small and marginal farmers, agricultural labourers, and small entrepreneurs.

✦ **Foreign Banks:** Foreign banks are banks from a foreign country working in India through branches. RBI has provided rules and guidelines for a foreign bank to establish and operate in India. According to the new rules set by Reserve Bank of India in the new budget, some decisions regarding foreign banks in India have been taken. The steps taken by the central monetary authority provide some extent of liberty to the foreign banks and they are hopeful to grow unshackled. The foreign banks in India are now allowed to set up local subsidiaries in the country.

✦ **Unscheduled Banks:** Unscheduled Bank in India means a banking company as defined in clause (c) of section 5 of the Banking Regulation Act, 1949 (10 of 1949), which is nota scheduled bank.

✦ **Co-operative Banks:** A co-operative bank is a co-operative society registered or deemed to have been registered under any Central Act for the time being in force relating to the multi-state, co-operative society, or any other central or state law relating to co-operative societies for the time being in force. If a co-operative bank is opening in more than one state, the central act applies. In other cases, the state laws apply.

✦ **Small Finance Banks:** The small finance bank, in furtherance of the objectives for which it is set up, shall primarily undertake basic banking activities of acceptance of deposits and lending to unserved and under served sections including small business units, small and marginal farmers, micro and small industries and unorganized sector entities. It can also undertake other non-risk sharing simple financial services activities, not requiring any commitment of own fund, such as distribution of mutual fund units, insurance products, pension products, etc.

✦ **Payments Banks:** There is a need for transactions and savings accounts for the underserved in the population. Also remittances have both macro-economic benefits for the region receiving them as well as micro-economic benefits to the recipients. Higher transaction costs of making remittances diminish these benefits. Therefore, the primary objective of setting up of payments banks will be to further financial inclusion by providing (i) small savings accounts and (ii) payments / remittance services to migrant labour workforce, low income households, small businesses, other unorganized sector entities and other users, by enabling high volume-low value transactions in deposits and payments / remittance services in a secured technology-driven environment.

Reserve Bank of India Act, 1934

The reserve bank of India act, 1934 came into force on 6th March 1934. It extends to the whole of India. The Act has been amended from time to time to meet the demands of changing times. Latest major amendments of the act are Reserve Bank of India (Amendment) Act, 2006 (Act No. 26 of 2006), Securities and Insurance Laws (Amendment and Validation) Act, 2010 (Act No. 26 of 2010), The Factoring Regulation Act, 2011 (Act No. 12 of 2012), The Banking Laws (Amendment) Act, 2012 (Act No. 4 of 2013), and The Finance Act, 2016 (Act No. 28 of 2016).

The act deals with the constitution, powers and functions of the reserve bank. It does not directly deal with regulation of the banking system except for section 42, which provides cash reserve ratio of schedule banks to be kept with the reserve bank, with a view to regulating the credit system and ensuring monetary stability.

Reserve Bank of India

The reserve bank of India is a central bank and was established in 1ST April 1935 in accordance with the provisions of reserve bank of India act 1934. RBI works as a central bank where commercial banks are account holders. The central office of RBI is located at Mumbai since inception. It was inaugurated with share capital of ₹ 5 Crores divided into shares of ₹ 100 each fully paid up. RBI was nationalised on 1st January 1949 on the basis of the Reserve Bank of India (Transfer to Public Ownership) Act, 1948. RBI is fully owned by the Government of India. The Reserve Bank of India has 20 regional offices, most of them in state capitals and 11 Sub-offices.

RBI is governed by a central board (headed by a governor) appointed by the central government of India. The general superintendence and direction of the bank is entrusted to central board consists of

a) One Governor,

b) Not more than four deputy Governors,

c) Two Governmental official from the ministry of Finance,

d) Ten nominated directors from various fields by the government to give representation to important elements in the economic life of the country, and

e) The four nominated director by the Central Government to represent the four local boards with the headquarters at Mumbai, Kolkata, Chennai and New Delhi.

Local Board consists of five members each appointed by the central government for a term of four years to represent territorial and economic interests and the interests of cooperative and indigenous banks.

Role of RBI

Chapter III of the RBI Act, 1934 describes function of the Central Banks (RBI).

✦ **Obligation to Transact Government Business (Section 20):** The Bank shall undertake to accept monies for account of the Central Government and to make payments up to the amount standing to the credit of its account, and to carry out its exchange, remittance and other banking operations, including the management of the public debt of the Union.

✦ **Right to Transact Government Business in India (Section 21):** Central Government shall entrust the Bank, on such conditions as may be agreed upon, with all its money, remittance, and exchange and banking transactions in India, and, in particular, shall deposit free of interest all its cash balances with the Bank.

- **Bank to Transact Government Business of States on Agreement (Section 21A):** RBI may by agreement with the government of any state undertake all its money, remittance, exchange and banking transactions in India, including in particular, the deposit, free of interest, of all its cash balances with the Bank; and the management of the public debt of, and the issue of any new loans by, that State.

- **Right to Issue Bank Notes (Section 22):** RBI shall have the sole right to issue bank notes in India, and may, for a period which shall be fixed by the Central Government on the recommendation of the Central Board, issue currency notes of the Government of India supplied to it by the Central Government, and the provisions of this Act applicable to bank notes shall, unless a contrary intention appears, apply to all currency notes of the Government of India issued either by the Central Government or by the Bank in like manner as if such currency notes were bank notes, and references in this Act to bank notes shall be construed accordingly.

- **Denominations of Notes (Section 24):** Bank notes shall be of the denominational values of 2, 5, 10, 20, 50, 100, 500, 1000, 5000, and 10000 rupees or of such other denominational values, not exceeding ten thousand rupees, as the Central Government may, on the recommendation of the Central Board, specify in this behalf. The Central Government may, on the recommendation of the Central Board, direct the non-issue or the discontinuance of issue of bank notes of such denominational values as it may specify in this behalf.

- **Legal Tender Character of Notes (Section 26):** Every bank note shall be legal tender at any place in India in payment or on account for the amount expressed therein, and shall be guaranteed by the Central Government. On recommendation of the Central Board, the Central Government may, declare that, any series of bank notes of any denomination shall cease to be legal tender save at such office or agency of the bank and to such extent as may be specified in the notification.

- **Recovery of Notes Lost, Stolen, Mutilated or Imperfect (Section 28):** No person shall of right be entitled to recover from the Central Government or the Bank, the value of any lost, stolen, mutilated or imperfect currency note of the Government of India or bank note.

- **Bank Exempt from Stamp Duty on Bank Notes (Section 29):** The Bank shall not be liable to the payment of any stamp duty under the Indian Stamp Act, 1899 (2 of 1899), in respect of bank notes issued by it.

- **Issue of Demand Bills and Notes (Section 31):** No person in India other than the Bank, or, as expressly authorised by this Act the Central Government shall draw, accept, make or issue any bill of exchange, hundi, promissory note or engagement for the payment of money payable to bearer on demand, or borrow, owe or take up any sum or sums of money on the bills, hundis or notes payable to bearer on demand of any such person.

- **Assets of the Issue Department (Section 33):** The assets of the issue department shall consist of gold coin, gold bullion, foreign securities, rupee coin and rupee securities to such aggregate amount as is not less than the total of the liabilities of the issue department. The aggregate value of the gold coin, gold bullion and foreign securities held as assets and the aggregate value of the gold coin and gold bullion so held shall not at any time be less than ₹ 200 cr and ₹ 115 cr, respectively.

- **Transactions in Foreign Exchange (Section 40):** RBI shall self to or buy from any authorised person who makes a demand in that behalf at its office in Bombay, Calcutta, Delhi or Madras or at such of its branches as the Central Government may, by order, determine, foreign exchange at such rates of exchange and on such conditions as the Central Government may from time to time by general or special order determine, having regard so far as rates of exchange are concerned to its obligations to the International Monetary Fund.

RBI as a Regulators of Banks

The RBI Act 1934 provides the statutory basis of the functioning of the bank. The bank was constituted for the need of following:

- To regulate the issues of bank notes.
- To maintain reserves with a view to securing monetary stability
- To operate the credit and currency system of the country to its advantage.

Functions of RBI as a central bank of India are explained briefly as follows:

Monitory Policy: The RBI formulates, implements, and monitors the monitory policy. Its main objective is maintaining price stability and ensuring adequate flow of credit to productive sector.

Regulator-Supervisor of the Financial System: RBI prescribes broad parameters of banking operations within which the country's banking and financial system functions. Their main objective is to maintain public confidence in the system, protect depositor's interest and provide cost effective banking services to the public.

Manage of Foreign Exchange Control: The manager of exchange control department manages the foreign exchange, according to the foreign exchange management act, 1999. The manager's main objective is to facilitate external trade and payment and promote orderly development and maintenance of foreign exchange market in India.

Controller of Credit

RBI performs the following tasks:

- It holds the cash reserves of all the scheduled banks.
- It controls the credit operations of banks through quantitative and qualitative controls.
- It controls the banking system through the system of licensing, inspection and calling for information.
- It acts as the lender of the last resort by providing rediscount facilities to scheduled banks.

Supervisory Functions: In addition to its traditional central banking functions, the Reserve Bank performs certain non-monetary functions of the nature of supervision of banks and promotion of sound banking in India. The Reserve Bank Act 1934 and the banking regulation act 1949 have given the RBI wide powers of supervision and control over commercial and co-operative banks, relating to licensing and establishments, branch expansion, liquidity of their assets, management and methods of working, amalgamation, reconstruction and liquidation. The RBI is authorized to carry out periodical inspections of the banks and to call for returns and necessary information from them. The nationalisation of 14 major Indian scheduled banks in July 1969 has imposed new responsibilities on the RBI for directing the growth of banking and credit policies towards more rapid development of the economy and realisation of certain desired social objectives.

Government as a Regulators of Banks: The Central Government has also been conferred extensive powers under the RBI Act and BR Act over the banks. RBI is fully owned by the Government of India. The Government of India has power to appoints and remove governor and members of the central board of RBI. The Government of India can also issue direction to the RBI whenever considered necessary in the public interest.

As per section 4 and 53 of the BR Act, the Government has the power to suspend the operations of the Banking Regulation Act or to give exemption from any of the provisions of the act on the representation/recommendation of the reserve bank.

Financial Intelligence Unit- India (FIU-IND)

FIU-IND is a central agency. It was set by the Government of India for vide O.M. dated 18th November 2004 for analyzing and disseminating information relating to suspect financial transaction. It is an independent body and report directly to the Economic Intelligence Council headed by Finance Minister. FIU-IND receives CTR, STR, CCR, NPOTR, CBWT reports. It analyzes information received by banks and suggests AML related crime. It monitors and identifies strategic key areas on AML trends, typologies & developments. The Director of FIU-IND is vested with the power of a civil court under the code of civil procedure. He has the power to seize, direct, penalize reporting entities and its employee for breach or violation of PML Act.

Control over Co-operative Banks: A co-operative bank is a co-operative society engaged in the business of banking and may be a primary co-operative bank, a district co-operative bank, or a state co-operative bank. If a co-operative bank is opening in more than one state, the central act applies. In other cases, the state laws apply.

Banking Regulation Act, 1949

The Banking Regulation Act, 1949 is a legislation in India that regulates all banking firms in India. It extends to the whole of India. The act is amended time to time. The last amendment in banking regulation act, 1949 was under the 'Banking Laws (Amendment) Act 2012. Initially, the law was applicable only to banking companies. But, in 1965 it was amended to make it applicable to cooperative banks and to introduce other changes. As per section 3, The Act does not applicable to:

(a) A primary agricultural credit society;

(b) A co-operative land mortgage bank; and

(c) Any other co-operative society, except in the manner and to the extent specified in Part V.

The Act provides a framework using which commercial banking in India is supervised and regulated. The Act gives the Reserve Bank of India (RBI) the power to license banks, have regulation over share holding and voting rights of shareholders; supervise the appointment of the boards and management; regulate the operations of banks; lay down instructions for audits; control moratorium, mergers and liquidation; issue directives in the interests of public good and on banking policy, and impose penalties.

The amending act has introduced the setting up of a Depositor Education and Awareness fund to take over inoperative deposit accounts which has not been claimed or operated 10 years or more, within a period of three months from the expiry of the said period of 10 years.

TEST YOURSELF

1. As per section 5(b) of Banking Regulation Act, which of the following is not an important element of the definition of banking?
   (a) Acceptance of deposit from public
   (b) Issuance of ATM for withdrawal of deposit amount
   (c) Acceptance of deposit for the purpose of lending
   (d) Acceptance of deposit for investment

2. As per section 5(b) of Banking Regulation Act, the amount deposited by the public can be withdrawn by way of:
   (a) Cheque
   (b) Draft
   (c) Otherwise
   (d) All of the above

3. Each bank in its name must include, which of the following words under the provision of banking regulation Act.
   (a) Bank
   (b) Banking company
   (c) Banking
   (d) Any of the above

4. Which among the following is part of the banking business under the provisions of section 6 (1) of B R Act.
   (a) Collecting and transmitting of money
   (b) Negotiating of loans and advances
   (c) Acquiring and holding the investments
   (d) All the above

5. Who issues a banking license to a multi-state cooperative society for undertaking banking business?
   (a) State govt
   (b) Central govt
   (c) RBI
   (d) NABARD

6. As per RBI Act 1934, originally which of the following is not the objective of creation of RBI:
   (a) To regulate the issue of bank notes
   (b) To regulate the banks in India in all their functions
   (c) To keeping reserves for securing monetary stability in India
   (d) To operate the currency and credit system of India to its advantage

7. Who among the following holds the share capital of RBI:
   (a) Central govt
   (b) Central govt. and state govt.
   (c) Central govt. and public
   (d) Central govt, state govt. and public financial institution

8. Regional Rural banks are licensed for banking business under:
   (a) Companies Act
   (b) Cooperative Societies Act
   (c) Banking Regulation Act
   (d) RBI Act

9. Banking regulation Act 1949 was enacted with the objective of:
   (a) Creating banking companies
   (b) Accepting of deposits' and leading
   (c) Regulating banking business
   (d) Regulating the companies

10. RBI functions under the general superintendence and directions of:
    (a) Central govt
    (b) Governor RBI
    (c) Central Board of Directors of RBI
    (d) A to C all

11. Which among the following can give directions to RBI?
    (a) Central govt
    (b) Governor RBI
    (c) Central Board of Directors of RBI
    (d) All the above

12. RBI does not have a local board of directors, at which of the following complete pair of cities:
    (a) Delhi and Kolkata
    (b) Mumbai and Hyderabad
    (c) Chennai and Mumbai
    (d) Delhi and Mumbai

13. The final decision to issue notes of different denomination is taken by:
    (a) Governor RBI
    (b) Central board of directors of RBI
    (c) Issue department of RBI
    (d) Central govt.

14. RBI is under obligation to undertake banking business for the central govt. under the provisions of:
    (a) Section 22 of RBI Act
    (b) Section 21 of RBI Act
    (c) Section 20 of RBI Act
    (d) In public interest

15. In which of the following areas, RBI cannot issue directions to banks:
    (a) Interest rates on deposits
    (b) Interest rates on advances
    (c) Margin on bank loans
    (d) None of the above

16. On which of the following aspects, RBI does not have authority as far as banks are concerned:
    (a) Collection and dissemination of credit information
    (b) Moratorium, amalgamation and winding of the banks
    (c) Imposition of penalties
    (d) None of the above

17. A cooperative bank can be which of the following:
    (a) Primary coop bank
    (b) District central coop bank
    (c) State coop bank
    (d) A to C all

18. While dealing with shares and securities, banks must follow the regulations framed by:
    (a) Company Law Board
    (b) Registrar of companies
    (c) SEBI
    (d) FEDAI

19. Central govt. can exempt a banking company from the provisions of banking regulation Act under which of the following circumstances:
    (a) On recommendations of state govt
    (b) On recommendations of RBI
    (c) On request from the concerned banking company
    (d) It cannot do so

20. The term corresponding new bank, under banking companies (Acquisition and Transfer of Undertakings) Act 1970, stands for
    (a) New private banks
    (b) Old private banks
    (c) Nationalised banks
    (d) Banking companies

21. The State bank of India constituted under:
    (a) Banking Regulation Act, 1949
    (b) State Bank of India Act, 1955
    (c) RBI Act, 1934
    (d) Under special Act of Govt. of India

22. A banking property is prohibited to acquire any immovable property, except for its own use under:
    (a) Section 9 of BR Act
    (b) Section 8 of BR Act
    (c) Section 9 of RBI Act
    (d) Not prohibited

23. Prohibited business of a banking company is defined under:
    (a) Section 9 of BR Act
    (b) Section 8 of BR Act
    (c) Section 8 of RBI Act
    (d) Section 9 of RBI Act

24. The government of India set up Regional Rural Banks (RRBs) on _____________.
    (a) 2nd October 1972
    (b) 1st April 1972
    (c) 2nd October 1975
    (d) 1st April 1975

ANSWER

1	2	3	4	5	6	7	8	9	10
(b)	(d)	(d)	(d)	(c)	(b)	(a)	(c)	(c)	(c)

11	12	13	14	15	16	17	18	19	20
(a)	(b)	(d)	(c)	(d)	(d)	(d)	(c)	(b)	(c)

21	22	23	24
(b)	(a)	(b)	(c)

____

CONTROL OVER ORGANISATION OF BANKS

INTRODUCTION

Banking Regulation Act, 1949 provides a framework using which commercial banking in India is supervised and regulated.The Act gives the Reserve Bank of India (RBI) the power to license banks, have regulation over share holding and voting rights of shareholders, supervise the appointment of the boards and management; regulate the operations of banks; lay down instructions for audits, control moratorium, mergers and liquidation; issue directives in the interests of public good and on banking policy, and impose penalties.

LICENSING OF BANKING COMPANIES

As per section 22 of the BR Act no company shall carry on banking business in India unless it holds a licence issued in that behalf by the Reserve Bank and any such licence may be issued subject of such conditions as the Reserve Bank may think fit to impose.

Condition for Granting License

Before granting any licence, the Reserve Bank may require to be satisfied by an inspection of the books of the company or otherwise that the following conditions are fulfilled, namely :

(a) That the company is or will be in a position to pay its present or future depositors in full as their claims accrue;

(b) That the affairs of the company are not being, or are not likely to be, conducted in a manner detrimental to the interests of its present or future depositors;

(c) That the general character of the proposed management of the company will not be prejudicial to the public interest of its present or future depositors;

(d) That the company has adequate capital structure and earning prospects;

(e) That the public interest will be served by the grant of a licence to the company to carry on banking business in India;

(f) That having regard to the banking facilities available in the proposed principal area of operations of the company, the potential scope for expansion of banks already in existence in the area and other relevant factors the grant of the licence would not be prejudicial to the operation and consolidation of the banking system consistent with monetary stability and economic growth;

(g) Any other condition, the fulfillment of which would, in the opinion of the Reserve Bank, be necessary to ensure that the carrying on of banking business in India by the company will not be prejudicial to the public interest or the interests of the depositors.

FOREIGN BANK

Before granting any licence under this section to a company incorporated outside India, the Reserve Bank may require to be satisfied by an inspection of the books of the company or otherwise that the conditions specified are fulfilled by the company or not. These conditions are :

(i) That the carrying on of banking business by such company in India will be in the public interest;

(ii) That the Government or law of the country in which it is incorporated does not discriminate in any way against banking companies registered in India;

(iii) That the company complies with all the provisions of this Act applicable to banking companies incorporated outside India.

Cancellation of License

The Reserve Bank may cancel a licence granted to a banking company under this section :

(i) If the company ceases to carry on banking business in India; or

(ii) If the company at any time fails to comply with any of the conditions imposed upon it under sub-section (1) of section 22 of BR Act; or

(iii) If at any time, any of the conditions referred to in sub-section (3) of section 22 of BR Act is not fulfilled.

Any banking company aggrieved by the decision of the Reserve Bank cancelling a licence under this section may, within thirty days from the date on which such decision is communicated to it, appeal to the Central Government.

Branch Licensing

Section 23 of BR Act restricts the bank for opening of new branch, and transfer of existing, places of business of the existing branch. Without obtaining the prior permission of the Reserve Bank :

(a) No banking company shall open a new place of business in India or change otherwise than within the same city, town or village, the location of an existing place of business situated in India;

(b) No banking company incorporated in India shall open a new place of business outside India or change, otherwise than within the same city, town or village in any country or area outside India, the location of an existing place of business situated in that country or area:

Before granting any permission under this section, the Reserve Bank may require to be satisfied the following condition by an inspection that:

(i) The financial condition and history of the company,

(ii) The general character of its management,

(iii) The adequacy of its capital structure and earning prospects and that

(iv) Public interest will be served by the opening branch or, change of location, of the place of business.

Paid up Capital and Reserves: As per section 11 of the BR Act, No banking company in existence on the commencement of this Act, shall, after the expiry of 3 years from such commencement or of such further period not exceeding one year as the Reserve Bank, having regard to the interests of the depositors of the company, may think fit in any particular case to allow, carry on business in India, and no other banking company shall, after the commencement of this Act, commence or carry on business in India, unless it complies with such of the requirements of this section as are applicable to it.

Banking Company Incorporated Outside India (Foreign Banks): Under sub-section 2 of section 11 of the BR Act,

(a) The aggregate value of its paid-up capital and reserves shall not be less than ₹ 15 lac and if it has a place or places of business in the city of Bombay or Calcutta or both, ₹ 20 lac; and

(b) The banking company shall deposit and keep deposited with the Reserve Bank either in cash or in the form of unencumbered approved securities, or partly in cash and partly in the form of such securities an amount which shall not be less than the minimum required by clause (a); and an amount calculated at 20% of its profit for that year in respect of all business transacted through its branches in India, as disclosed in the profit and loss account. It can at any time replace any securities so deposited by cash or by any other unencumbered approved securities or partly by cash and partly by other such securities, so however, that the total amount deposited is not affected; OR any cash so deposited by unencumbered approved securities of an equal value.

Central Government 'May, on the recommendation of the Reserve Bank, and having regard to the adequacy of the amounts already deposited and kept deposited by a banking company, in relation to its deposit liabilities in India declare by order in writing that the above provisions shall not apply to such banking company for such period as may be specified in the order.

Other Banking Companies (Indian Banks)

Under sub-section 3 of Section 11 of the BR Act, for other banks, the aggregate value of its paid-up capital and reserves shall not be less than :

(i) If it has places of business in more than one State, ₹ 5 lac, and if any such place or places of business is or are situated in the city of Bombay or Calcutta or both, ₹ 10 lac;

(ii) If it has all its places of business in one State none of which is situated in the city of Bombay or Calcutta, ₹ 1 lac in respect of its principal place of business, plus ₹ 10000 in respect of each of its other places of business, situated in the same district in which it has its principal place of business, plus ₹ 20000 in respect of each place of business situated elsewhere in the State otherwise than in the same district:

No banking company to which this applies shall be required to have paid-up capital and reserves exceeding an aggregate value of five lakhs of rupees. Further no banking company to which this clause applies and which has only one place of business, shall be required to have paid-up capital and reserves exceeding an aggregate value of ₹ 50000: In case of every banking company to which this clause applies and which commences banking business for the first time after the commencement of the Banking Companies (Amendment) Act, 1962 (36 of 1962), the value of its paid-up capital shall not be less than ₹ 5 lac.

(iii) If it has all its places of business in one State, or more of which is or are situated in the city of Bombay or Calcutta, ₹ 5 lac, plus ₹ 25000 in respect of each place of business situated outside the city of Bombay or Calcutta, as the case may be:

No banking company to which this clause applies shall be required to have paid-up capital and reserves exceeding an aggregate value of ₹ 10 lac.

Regulation of Paid-up, Subscribed and Authorised Capital and Voting Rights of Shareholders

(1) No banking company shall carry on business in India, unless it satisfies that the subscribed capital of the company is not less than one-half of the authorised capital and the paid-up capital is not less than one-half of the subscribed capital. Further, that the capital of the company consists of ordinary shares only or of ordinary shares or equity shares and such preferential shares as may have been issued prior to the 1st day of July, 1944:

(2) No person holding shares in a banking company shall, in respect of any shares held by him, exercise voting rights more than 10% of the total voting rights of all the shareholders of the banking company.

Return: Every Chairman, Managing Director or Chief Executive Officer by whatever name called of a banking company shall furnish to the Reserve Bank returns containing full of the extent and value of his holding of shares, whether directly or indirectly, in the banking company and of any change in the extent of such holding or any variation in the rights attaching thereto and such other information relating to those shares as the Reserve Bank may, by order, require.

Restriction on Nature of Subsidiary Companies (Section 19): A banking company shall not form any subsidiary company except for undertaking of any business which, under clause (a) to (o) of sub-section (1) of section 6, is permissible for a banking company to undertake, or with RBI permission, the carrying on of the business of banking exclusively outside India, or such other business, which the Reserve Bank may, with the prior approval of the Central Government, consider to be conducive to the spread of banking in India or to be otherwise useful or necessary in the public interest.

Share holding in Other Companies {Section 19(2)}: No banking company shall hold shares in any company, whether as pledgee, mortgagee or absolute owner, of an amount exceeding 30% of the paid-up share capital of that company or 30% of its own paid-up share capital and reserves, whichever is less. Further a banking company shall not, hold shares, whether as pledge, mortgagee or absolute owner, in any company in the management of which any Managing Director or Manager of the banking company is in any manner concerned or interested.

CONTROL OVER MANAGEMENT

Power of Reserve Bank to Remove Managerial and Other Persons from Office (Section 36AA): Where the Reserve Bank is satisfied that it is necessary so to do, the Reserve Bank may, for reasons to be recorded in writing, by order, remove from office, with effect from such date as may be specified in the order, any Chairman, Director, Chief Executive Officer (by whatever name called) or other officer or employee of the banking company. Such person, within 30 days from the date of communication to him of the order, prefer an appeal to the Central Government. The decision of the Central Government on such appeal, and subject thereto, the order made by the Reserve Bank, shall be final and shall not be called into question in any court. Where an order has been made for removal, the Reserve Bank may, by order in writing, appoint a suitable person in place of the Chairman or Director or Chief Executive Officer or other officer or employee who has been removed from his office, with effect from such date as may be specified in the order.

Any person appointed as Chairman, Director or Chief Executive Officer or other officer or employee under this section, shall hold office during the pleasure of the Reserve Bank and subject thereto for a period not exceeding 3 years or such further periods not exceeding three years at a time as the Reserve Bank may specify;

Power of Reserve Bank to Appoint Additional Directors (Section 36AB): If the Reserve Bank is of opinion that in the interest of banking policy or in the public interest or in the interests of the banking company or its depositors it is necessary so to do, it may, from time to time by order in writing, appoint, with effect from such date as may be specified in the order, one or more persons to hold office as additional Directors of the banking company.

Any person appointed as additional Director in pursuance of this section shall hold office during the pleasure of the Reserve Bank and subject thereto for a period not exceeding 3 years or such further periods not exceeding 3 years at a time as the Reserve Bank may specify and shall not be required to hold qualification-shares in the banking company.

TEST YOURSELF

1. As per section 22 of Banking Regulation Act 1949, a company desire to commence or carry on banking business is required to obtain _________ from RBI.
   - (a) License
   - (b) Certificate
   - (c) Registration
   - (d) Approval

2. When Banking Regulation Act 1949 came into force, the banking companies, which were in existence were required to apply for license within _________.
   - (a) 3 months
   - (b) 6 months
   - (c) 9 months
   - (d) 12 months

3. Which of the following condition is to be satisfied to get license from RBI?
   - (a) Whether the general character of proposed management is not prejudicial to public interest
   - (b) There is a scope of banking operation in the proposed area
   - (c) All the features are in interest of general public
   - (d) All the above

4. If license of a banking company is cancelled by RBI, the company can appeal to:
   - (a) Central Govt.
   - (b) State Govt., where headquarter of company situated
   - (c) Governor RBI
   - (d) Ministry of Finance- Banking Division

5. If license of a banking company is cancelled by RBI, the company can appeal within:
   - (a) 30 days
   - (b) 60 days
   - (c) 45 days
   - (d) 90 days

6. Minimum paid up capital for banking company incorporated outside India, operating in India:
   - (a) ₹ 15 lakh
   - (b) ₹ 20 lakh
   - (c) ₹ 15 lakh & ₹ 20 lakh both, depending upon the place of business
   - (d) None of these

7. For Indian banking company, minimum paid up capital and reserves if operating in a single state are _________.
   - (a) ₹ 1 lakh
   - (b) ₹ 2 lakh
   - (c) ₹ 5 lakh
   - (d) ₹ 10 lakh

8. Shifting of a bank's branch does not require permission if the shifting is in the same _________.
   - (a) State
   - (b) Town or village
   - (c) District
   - (d) No permission requires at all

9. As per section 11 of BR Act, foreign banks are required to deposit certain percentage of their annual profit with RBI, what is the percentage?
   - (a) 10
   - (b) 20
   - (c) 25
   - (d) 30

10. Banking companies are permitted:
    - (a) Only ordinary share
    - (b) Only Equity Share
    - (c) Preference share
    - (d) Both 'a' and 'b'

11. No banking company can pay dividend until:
    - (a) All capitalized expenses are written off
    - (b) All expenses are paid off
    - (c) All bad debts are recovered
    - (d) No such restriction

12. Any person appointed as Chairman, Director or Chief Executive Officer of the banking company shall hold office during the pleasure of the Reserve Bank for

a period not exceeding _____ or such further periods as the Reserve Bank may specify.
(a) 2 years   (b) 4 years
(c) 3 years   (d) 5 years

13. Appeal against the order of RBI for removal of Chairman or the Managing Director can be made within _____________ from the date of communication to him of the order.
(a) 30 days   (b) 60 days
(c) 45 days   (d) 90 days

14. Appeal against the order of RBI for removal of Chairman or the Managing Director can be made prefer an appeal to the _____________.
(a) Central Govt.
(b) President of India
(c) Governor RBI
(d) Ministry of Finance-Banking Division

15. No banking company shall hold shares in any company, whether as pledgee, mortgagee or absolute owner, of an amount exceeding _________ of the paid-up share capital of that company or _________ of its own paid-up share capital and reserves.
(a) 20%, 30%   (b) 30%, 20%
(c) 30%, 30%   (d) 20%, 20%

16. No person holding shares in a banking company shall, in respect of any shares held by him, exercise voting rights more than _____% of the total voting rights of all the shareholders of the banking company.
(a) 10   (b) 20
(c) 25   (d) 30

17. Any banking company which has only one place of business, shall be required to have paid-up capital and reserves exceeding an aggregate value of _________
(a) ₹ 25000   (b) ₹ 50000
(c) ₹ 1 lakh   (d) ₹ 5 lakh

18. Based on which of the following reasons, an additional director is appointed in a banking company?
(a) Public interest
(b) In the interest of banking company
(c) In the public interest
(d) All the above

19. Additional director can be appointed for a period not exceeding
(a) 2 years   (b) 4 years
(c) 3 years   (d) 5 years

20. Which of the following is not included in "Capitalized Expenses"?
(a) Preliminary expenses
(b) Share selling commission
(c) Loss incurred
(d) None of these

ANSWER

1	2	3	4	5	6	7	8	9	10
(a)	(b)	(d)	(a)	(a)	(c)	(a)	(b)	(a)	(d)

11	12	13	14	15	16	17	18	19	20
(a)	(c)	(a)	(a)	(c)	(a)	(b)	(d)	(c)	(d)

REGULATION OF BANKING BUSINESS

INTRODUCTION

The Reserve Bank's regulatory and supervisory domain extends not only to the Indian banking system but also to the development financial institutions (DFIs), non-banking financial companies (NBFCs), primary dealers, credit information companies and select segments of the financial markets. In respect of banks, the Reserve Bank derives its powers from the provisions of the Banking Regulation Act, 1949, while the other entities and markets are regulated and supervised under the provisions of the Reserve Bank of India Act, 1934.

Power to Issue Directions

Section 21 and Section 35A of the BR Act gives the wide power to RBI to regulate banking companies. The Reserve Bank undertakes supervision of banks to monitor and ensure compliance by them with its regulatory policy framework. This is achieved through on-site inspection, off-site surveillance and periodic meetings with top management of banks. The Reserve Bank focused on perception and outlook of bankers on the economy, liquidity conditions, credit outflows, developments in different market segments and the direction of interest rates.

Traditionally, the Reserve Bank's regulatory and supervisory policy initiatives are aimed at protection of the depositors' interests, orderly development and conduct of banking operations, and liquidity and solvency of banks. With the onset of banking sector reforms during the 1990s, various prudential measures were initiated that have, in effect, strengthened the Indian banking system over a period of time. Apart from giving direction, the Reserve bank may also caution or give advice to banking companies.

Acceptance of Deposits

As per Section 5(b) of BR Act, definition of banking business is "Accepting for the purpose of lending or investment, of deposits of money from public, repayable on demand or otherwise, & withdrawal by cheque, draft, order or otherwise".

Bank accepts different types of deposits from public. Deposits may be classified as Demand and Time deposits. The deposit which is paid on demand such as Current Deposit Account and Savings Deposit Accounts are called Demand Deposits. While Time Deposits, like Fixed Deposit and Recurring Deposits are generally repayable after an agreed period. Regarding period of deposit and rate of deposit are the matters to be agreed between bank and depositor, subject to the any direction given by RBI in this regard.

Return of Unclaimed Deposits

As per Section 26 of BR Act, every banking company shall, within thirty days after the close of each calendar year, submit a return in the prescribed form and manner to the Reserve Bank as at the end of such calendar year of all accounts in India which have not been operated upon for ten years. In the case of money deposited for a fixed period the said term of ten years shall be reckoned from the date of the expiry of such fixed period.

ESTABLISHMENT OF DEPOSITOR EDUCATION AND AWARENESS FUND

The amending act has introduced the setting up of a Depositor Education and Awareness Fund to takeover inoperative deposit accounts which have not been claimed or operated for a period of ten years and more, within a period of three months from the expiry of the said period of ten years.

NOMINATION FACILITY IN BANKS

Section 45ZA to 45ZF of BR Act describes nomination facility in banks.

1) **Deposit Accounts:** Section 45ZA of BR Act provides Nomination for payment of depositors' money. Where a deposit is held by a banking company to the credit of one or more persons, the depositor or, as the case may be, all the depositors together, may nominate, in the prescribed manner, one person to whom in the event of the death of the sole depositor or the death of all the depositors, the amount of deposit may be returned by the banking company. Banks may extend the nomination facility also in respect of deposits held in the name of a sole proprietary concern.

2) **Safe Custody:** Section 45ZC of BR Act provides Nomination for return of articles kept in safe custody with banking company. Where any person leaves any article in safe custody with a banking company, such person may nominate, in the prescribed manner, on person to whom, in the event of the death of the person leaving the article in safe custody, such article may be returned by the banking company.

   The banking company shall, before returning any articles under this section to the nominee or the person appointed under sub-section (2), prepare, in such manner as may be directed by the Reserve Bank from time to time, an inventory of the said articles which shall be signed by such nominee or person and shall deliver a copy of the inventory so prepared to such nominee or person. Banks should note that the facility of nomination is not available in case of deposit of safe custody articles by more than one person.

3) **Safety Lockers:** Section 45ZE of BR Act provides Nomination for Release of contents of safety lockers. Where an individual is the sole hirer of a locker from a banking company, whether such locker is in the safe deposit vault of such banking company or elsewhere, such individual may nominate one person to whom, in the event of the death of such individual, the banking company may give access to the locker and liberty to remove the contents of the locker.

   If safety locker is hired by two or more individuals with operational instruction of 'either or survivor', then only one nominee is allowed.

But where any such locker is hired from a banking company by two or more individuals jointly and under the contract of hire, the locker is to be operated under the joint signatures of two or more of such hirers, such hirers may nominate one or more persons (Maximum two as per IBA guideline) to whom, in the event of the death of such joint hirer or hirers, the banking company may give, jointly with the surviving joint hirer or joint hirers, as the case may be, access to the locker and liberty to remove the contents of such locker. Where the nominee is a minor, it shall be lawful for the depositor making the nomination to appoint in the prescribed manner any person to receive the amount of deposit in the event of his death during the minority of the nominee.

a) Unless the nomination is varied or cancelled, the nominee is entitled to all the rights of the depositors. Payment by a banking company in accordance with the provisions of this section shall constitute a full discharge to the banking company of its liability in respect of the deposit:

b) On the removal of the contents of any locker by any nominee or jointly by any nominee and survivors as aforesaid, the liability of the banking company in relation to the contents of the locker shall stand discharged.

c) Rule 2 to 4 of the Banking Companies (Nomination) Rules 1985 provides for the procedure and forms for making nomination in respect of commercial banks. In case of Co-operative banks, similar provisions are incorporated in the Co-operative banks (Nomination) Rules, 1985.

LOANS AND ADVANCES

Banks accept deposit for the lending and investment purpose. Section 21 of the BR Act explained the power of Reserve Bank to control advances by banking companies.

Reserve Bank may determine policy regarding advances and issue suitable direction to the banks in the public interest or in the interests of depositors or in the interest of banking policy. The policy may be determined in relation to advances to be followed by banking companies generally or by any specific bank. All banking companies or the banking company concerned, shall be bound to follow the policy.

The Reserve Bank may give directions to banking companies, either generally or to any banking company or group of banking companies. Every banking company shall be bound to comply with any directions given to it on the following matters.

(a) The purposes for which advances may or may not be made,

(b) The margins to be maintained in respect of secured advances,

(c) The maximum amount limit of advances or other financial accommodation which, may be made by that banking company to any one company, firm, association of persons or individual,

(d) The maximum amount up to which, guarantees may be given by a banking company on behalf of any one company, firm, association of persons or individual, and

(e) The rate of interest and other terms and conditions on which advances or other financial accommodation may be made or guarantees may be given.

Regulation of Interest Rate

The policy rate is the key lending rate which is decided by Reserve bank of India. It is a monetary policy instrument under the control of the Reserve Bank of India (RBI) to regulate the availability, cost and use of money and credit. A change in the policy rate alters all other short term interest rates in the economy, thereby influencing the level of economic growth and inflation.

The Benchmark Prime Lending Rate (BPLR) system which was introduced in 2003 fell short of its original objective of bringing transparency to lending rates in banking industry. This was mainly because under the BPLR system, banks could lend below BPLR. The Base Rate system replaced the BPLR system with effect from July 1, 2010. Base rate was the minimum rate at which bank finance all category loans except (a) DRI advances (b) Loan against their own TDR and (c) loans to bank's own employee.

Marginal Cost of Funds based Lending Rate (MCLR)

The MCLR methodology for fixing interest rates for advances was introduced by the Reserve Bank of India with effect from April 1, 2016. MCLR refers to the minimum interest rate of a bank below which it cannot lend, except in some cases allowed by the RBI. It is an internal benchmark or reference rate for the bank. MCLR describes the method by which the minimum interest rate for loans is determined by a bank-based on marginal cost or the additional or incremental cost of arranging one more rupee to the prospective borrower. MCLR is based on cost of funds for banks and is derived as the sum of marginal cost of funds, negative carry because

of CRR, operating costs of banks and tenor premium. Banks publish MCLR for at least five durations which are overnight MCLR, 1 month MCLR, 3 month MCLR, 6 month MCLR and 1 year MCLR. However, banks may publish MCLR base rates for more than five periods. The banks may revise the MCLR rate every month. Interest rate on each floating rate loan would be reset on based on the duration of the MCLR to which it is linked.

Reasons for Introducing MCLR

RBI decided to shift from base rate to MCLR because the rates based on marginal cost of funds are more sensitive to changes in the policy rates. This is very essential for the effective implementation of monetary policy. Prior to MCLR system, different banks were following different methodology for calculation of base rate/minimum rate–that is either based on average cost of funds or marginal cost of funds or blended cost of funds. Thus, MCLR aims

○ To improve the transmission of policy rates into the lending rates of banks.

○ To bring transparency in the methodology followed by banks for determining interest rates on advances.

○ To ensure availability of bank credit at interest rates which are fair to borrowers as well as banks.

○ To enable banks to become more competitive and enhance their long run value and contribution to economic growth.

Regulation of Money Market Instruments

The Bank may, in public interest, or to regulate the financial system of the country to its advantage, determine the policy relating to interest rates or interest rate products and give directions in that behalf to all agencies or any of them, dealing in securities, money market instruments, foreign exchange, derivatives, or other instruments of like nature as the Bank may specify from time to time.

Regulation of Banking Business Reserve Fund (Section 17): Banks in India are to create a reserve fund out of the balance of profit of each year, before any dividend is declared by transfer to the reserve fund, not less than 20% of such profit. Central Government on the recommendation of the Reserve Bank (after ascertaining adequacy of the paid-up, capital and reserves in relation to its deposit liabilities), allow a bank that these provisions shall not apply. In that case the amount in the reserve fund together with the amount in the share premium account should not be less than the paid-up capital of the banking company.

Appropriated from Reserve Fund: Where a banking company appropriates any sum from the reserve fund or the share premium account, it shall, within 21 days from the date of such appropriation, report the fact, to the Reserve Bank, explaining the circumstances leading to such appropriation. Reserve Bank may extend the period of 21 days by such period as it thinks fit or condone any delay in the making the report.

Cash Reserve for Non-Scheduled Banks (Section 18): Every banking company, not being a scheduled bank, shall maintain in India, by way of cash reserve with itself OR by way of balance in a current account with the Reserve Bank OR by way of net balance in current accounts or in one or more of the aforesaid ways, minimum 3% of the total of its demand and time liabilities in India as on the last Friday of the second preceding fortnight.

Submission of Return: Bank shall submit to the Reserve Bank, before the 20th day of every month, are turn showing the amount so held on alternate Fridays during a month with particulars of its demand and time liabilities in India on such Friday. If any such Friday is a public holiday under the Negotiable Instruments Act, 1881, then; at the close of business on the preceding working day.

Maintenance of a Percentage of Assets (Statutory Liquidity Ratio) (Section 24): Consequent upon amendment to the Section 24 of the Banking Regulation Act, 1949 through the Banking Regulation (Amendment) Act, 2007 replacing the Regulation (Amendment) Ordinance, 2007, effective January 23, 2007, the Reserve Bank can prescribe the SLR for SCBs in specified assets. The value of such assets of a SCB shall not be less than such percentage not exceeding 40 per cent of its total DTL in India as on the last Friday of the second preceding fortnight as the Reserve Bank may, by notification in the Official Gazette, specify from time to time.

SCBs can participate in the Marginal Standing Facility (MSF) Scheme introduced by Reserve Bank with effect from May 09, 2011. Under this facility, the eligible entities may borrow up to two per cent of their respective NDTL outstanding at the end of the second preceding fortnight from April 17, 2012. Additionally, the eligible entities may also continue to access overnight funds under this facility against their excess SLR holdings. In the event, the banks' SLR holding falls below the statutory requirement up to two per cent of their NDTL, banks will not have the obligation to seek a specific waiver for default in SLR compliance arising out of use of this facility in terms of notification issued under sub section (2A) of section 24 of the Banking Regulation Act, 1949.

Within the mandatory SLR requirement, Government securities to the extent allowed by the RBI under Marginal Standing Facility (MSF) are permitted to be reckoned as the Level 1 High Quality Liquid Assets (HQLAs) for computing Liquidity Coverage Ratio (LCR) of banks. In addition to this, banks are permitted to reckon up to another 5 per cent of their NDTL within the mandatory SLR requirement as level 1 HQLA. This is the Facility to Avail Liquidity for Liquidity Coverage Ratio that was notified vide DBR.BP.BC.No.52/21.04.098/2014-15.

Reserve Bank has specified vide notification DBR.No.Ret.BC.69/12.02.001/2014-15 dated February 03, 2015 that w.e.f. the fortnight beginning February 07, 2015, every SCB shall continue to maintain in India assets as detailed below, the value of which shall not, at the close of business on any day, be less than 21.5 per cent of the total NDTL as on the last Friday of the second preceding fortnight valued in accordance with the method of valuation specified by the Reserve Bank of India from time to time:

(a) Cash or (b) in Gold valued at a price not exceeding the current market price, or (c) Investment in the following instruments which will be referred to as "Statutory Liquidity Ratio (SLR) securities":

i. Dated securities issued up to May 06, 2011 as listed in the Annex to Notification DBOD.No. Ret.91/12.02.001/2010-11 dated May 09, 2011;

ii. Treasury Bills of the Government of India;

iii. Dated securities of the Government of India issued from time to time under the market borrowing programme and the Market Stabilization Scheme;

iv. State Development Loans (SDLs) of the State Governments issued from time to time under the market borrowing programme; and

v. Any other instrument as may be notified by the Reserve Bank of India.

If the securities (including margin) referred to above, if acquired under the Reserve Bank- Liquidity Adjustment Facility (LAF), shall not be treated as an eligible asset for this purpose.

Penalties: If a banking company fails to maintain the required amount of SLR, it shall be liable to pay to RBI in respect of that default, the penal interest for that day at the rate of three per cent per annum above the Bank Rate on the shortfall and if the default continues the next succeeding working day, the penal interest may be increased to a rate of five per cent per annum above the Bank Rate for the concerned days of default on the shortfall.

Return in Form VIII: A return in form VIII showing the amounts of SLR held on alternate Fridays during immediate preceding month with of their DTL in India held on such Fridays is to be submitted to RBI before

20th day of every month. In addition, a statement as annexure to form VIII giving daily position of (a) value of securities held for compliance with SLR and (b) the excess cash balances maintained by them with RBI is to be submitted.

Cash Reserve Ratio: In terms of Section 42(1) of the RBI Act, 1934 the Reserve Bank, having regard to the needs of securing the monetary stability in the country, prescribes the CRR for SCBs without any floor or ceiling rate. The SCBs are required to maintain, in addition to the balances prescribed under Section 42(1) of the Act, an additional average daily balance, the amount of which shall not be less than the rate specified by the Reserve Bank in the notification published in the Gazette of India from time to time. Such additional balance will be calculated regarding the excess of the total of DTL of the bank as shown in the Returns referred to in Section 42(2) of the RBI Act, 1934 over the total of its DTL at the close of the business on the date specified in the notification. At present no incremental CRR is required to be maintained by the banks.

Computation of DTL: Liabilities of a bank may be in the form of demand or time deposits or borrowings or other miscellaneous items of liabilities. As defined under Section 42 of the RBI Act, 1934, liabilities of a bank may be towards the banking system or towards others in the form of demand and time deposits or borrowings or other miscellaneous items of liabilities.

Demand Liabilities: Demand Liabilities of a bank are liabilities which are payable on demand. These include current deposits, demand liabilities portion of savings bank deposits, margins held against letters of credit/ guarantees, balances in overdue fixed deposits, cash certificates and cumulative/recurring deposits, outstanding Telegraphic Transfers (TTs), Mail Transfers (MTs), Demand Drafts (DDs), unclaimed deposits, credit balances in the Cash Credit account and deposits held as security for advances which are payable on demand. Money at Call and Short Notice from outside the banking system should be shown against liability to others.

Time Liabilities: Time Liabilities of a bank are those which are payable otherwise than on demand. These include fixed deposits, cash certificates, cumulative and recurring deposits, time liabilities portion of savings bank deposits, staff security deposits, margin held against letters of credit, if not payable on demand, deposits held as securities for advances which are not payable on demand and Gold deposits.

Other Demand and Time Liabilities: It include interest accrued on deposits, bills payable, unpaid dividends, sundries account balances, participation certificates issued to other banks, net credit balance in branch adjustment account, margin held on bills purchased or discounted.

Liabilities, which are not to be included for Computation of DTL / NDTL for CRR and SLR.

a) Paid up capital, reserves, any credit balance in the Profit & Loss Account, amount availed of as refinance from RBI, and apex institutions like Exim Bank, NABARD, NHB, SIDBI etc.

b) Provision for income tax more than actual estimated liabilities.

c) Amount received from DICGC pending adjustments thereof.

d) Amount received from ECGC by invoking the guarantee.

e) Amount received from insurance company on ad-hoc settlement of claims pending Judgment of the Court.

f) Amount received from the Court Receiver.

Maintenance of CRR on Daily Basis: With a view to providing flexibility to banks in choosing an optimum strategy of holding reserves depending upon their intra fortnight cash flows, all SCBs are required to maintain minimum CRR balances up to 95 per cent of the average daily required reserves for a reporting fortnight on all days of the fortnight with effect from the fortnight beginning September 21, 2013.

No Interest Payment on Eligible Cash Balances maintained by SCBs with RBI under CRR: In view of the amendment carried out to RBI Act 1934, omitting sub-section (1B) of Section 42, the Reserve Bank does not pay any interest on the CRR balances maintained by SCBs with effect from the fortnight beginning March 31, 2007.

Fortnightly Return in Form A (CRR): Under Section 42(2) of the RBI Act, 1934, all SCBs are required to submit to Reserve Bank a provisional Return in Form 'A' within 7 days from the expiry of the relevant fortnight which is used for preparing press communique. The final Form 'A' Return is required to be submitted to RBI within 20 days from expiry of the relevant fortnight.

Penalties: From the fortnight beginning June 24, 2006, penal interest is charged as under in cases of default in maintenance of CRR by SCBs:

(i) In case of default in maintenance of CRR requirement on a daily basis which is currently 95 per cent of the total CRR requirement, penal interest will be recovered for that day at the rate of three per cent per annum above the Bank Rate on the amount by which the amount actually maintained falls short of the prescribed minimum on that day and if the shortfall continues on the next succeeding day/s, penal interest will be recovered at the rate of five per cent per annum above the Bank Rate.

(ii) In cases of default in maintenance of CRR on average basis during a fortnight, penal interest will be recovered as envisaged in sub-section (3) of Section 42 of Reserve Bank of India Act, 1934.

SCBs are required to furnish the detail such as on date, amount, percentage, reason for default in maintenance of requisite CRR and action taken to avoid recurrence of such default.

Assets in India

As per section 25 of BR Act, the assets in India of every banking company at the close of business on the last Friday of every quarter or, if that Friday is a public holiday under the Negotiable Instruments Act, 1881 (26 of 1881), at the close of the business on the preceding working day, shall not be less than seventy-five per cent of its demand and time liabilities in India.

Every banking company shall, within one month from the end of every quarter, submit to the Reserve Bank a return in the prescribed form and manner of the assets and liabilities referred to in sub-section (1) as at the close of business on the last Friday of the previous quarter, or, if that Friday is a public holiday under the Negotiable Instruments Act, 1881 (26 of 1881) at the close of business on the preceding working day:

TEST YOURSELF

1. RBI regulates banking companies and issue direction to banks under which of the following provisions:
   (a) Section 21 of BR Act
   (b) Section 22 of BR Act
   (c) Section 35A of BR Act
   (d) Both 'a' and 'c'

2. What is the nature of effect of the direction issued by RBI?
   (a) Effect is only prospective
   (b) Effect is not retrospective
   (c) The directions do not affect legal rights of banks
   (d) All the above

3. Under section 36 of BR Act, what kind of direction can be given by RBI to banks:
   (a) Relating to advances
   (b) Relating to deposits
   (c) Advice, caution and prohibition
   (d) Inspection and supervision

4. With regard to interest on saving bank account what kind of direction is given by RBI to banks?
   (a) What should be minimum interest rate?
   (b) What can be maximum interest rate?
   (c) What should be rate of interest?
   (d) What should be the minimum amount of interest that can be paid?

5. Regarding bank deposit, what kind of direction can be given by RBI to banks?
   (a) Minimum period for which deposit can be accepted
   (b) Maximum period for which deposit can be accepted
   (c) Guidelines relating to payment of interest in deceased accounts
   (d) All the above

6. The term 'unclaimed deposit' stands for which of the following:
   (a) Deposit where the depositor has expired and not claimed
   (b) Deposit which have not been operated for a long time
   (c) Deposit not operated for 10 years
   (d) All the above

7. Which of the following actions are required to be taken by the bank in connection with unclaimed deposit:
   (a) Annual return is required to be submitted to RBI
   (b) Annual return is to be prepared as on Dec 31 for submission to RBI
   (c) Annual return is to be submitted within 30 days of end of each calendar year
   (d) All the above

8. Section 45ZA of BR Act deals with the banking operations:
   (a) Rules regarding preservation of records
   (b) Rules regarding return of paid instruments to customers
   (c) Rules regarding registration of nomination in deposit account
   (d) Rules regarding nomination in safe deposit locker

9. For nomination in case of articles in safe custody, under which of the following, the legal provisions are contained:
   (a) Section 45 C of BR Act
   (b) Section 24 of BR Act
   (c) Section 45 ZC of BR Act
   (d) Section 45 ZD of BR Act

10. Directions on loans and advances are issued by RBI u/s 21 of BR Act, for which of the following aspects:
    (a) Margin to be maintained
    (b) Maximum amount of advances
    (c) Rate of interest
    (d) All the above

11. A banking company is prohibited from entering into any commitment for granting any loans or advances to or on behalf of a director if the said director is _______ for the firm/company.
    (a) Partner
    (b) Manager
    (c) Guarantor
    (d) Any of the above

12. Banks have to transfer atleast ____% out of ____ to a reserve fund, u/s 17 (1) of BR Act.
    (a) 20%, Profits
    (b) 20%, profits before tax
    (c) 25%, Profits before dividend
    (d) 20%, Profits before dividend

13. Non-scheduled banks have to maintain cash reserve u/s ____ of banking regulation Act at ____ % of demand and time liabilities.
    (a) 18, 5%
    (b) 42, 3%
    (c) 18, 3%
    (d) 24, 25%

14. To be a scheduled bank, what is the minimum paid-up capital and reserves requirement of bank?
    (a) ₹ 1 lac
    (b) ₹ 1 lac
    (c) ₹ 5 lac
    (d) ₹ 10 lac

15. A scheduled bank has to maintain cash reserve u/s ____ of ______ Act:
    (a) 24, BR Act
    (b) 42, BR Act
    (c) 42, RBI Act
    (d) 24, RBI Act

16. What is not included in the term net demand and time liabilities for the purpose of maintaining cash reserve ratio:
    (a) Paid up capital & Reserve
    (b) Credit balance in P & L account
    (c) Amount taken from RBI, NHB, IDBI, SBI etc.
    (d) All the above

17. What amount of interest is paid by RBI on cash reserve ratio balances?
    (a) No interest paid
    (b) At saving bank rate
    (c) 3.5% p.a. on eligible balance
    (d) At bank rate

18. What penalty can be imposed by RBI on non-compliance with requirement of cash reserve ratio:
    (a) 3%
    (b) 3% above bank rate for 1st day
    (c) 5% above bank rate for 2nd day onwards
    (d) 'b' and 'c'

19. Banks are required to maintain liquid asset in addition to cash reserve ratio known as SLR, under _________.
    (a) Section 42 of RBI Act
    (b) Section 42 of BR Act
    (c) Section 24 of BR Act
    (d) Section 24 of RBI Act

20. Banks are required to maintain liquid asset in addition to cash reserve ratio. These liquid assets (known as SLR) can be kept in which of the following forms:
    (a) Cash balance
    (b) Investment in gold
    (c) Investment in approved unencumbered securities
    (d) All the above

21. What is the minimum and maximum requirement for maintenance of SLR:
    (a) Minimum 5% and maximum 25%
    (b) No minimum and maximum limit
    (c) Minimum 25% and maximum 35%
    (d) Minimum and maximum 5%

22. SLR is to be maintained as at:
    (a) Close of each month
    (b) Close of each week
    (c) Close of each business day
    (d) None of the above

23. Assets in India, for the purpose of section 25 of BR Act do not include:
    (a) Cash and gold
    (b) Unencumbered approved securities
    (c) Export bill drawn in India
    (d) None of the above

24. Unclaimed deposits are required to be transferred by banks to which of the following:
    (a) As part of other liabilities to scheduled 5 of balance sheet
    (b) Common fund for write off of bad loans
    (c) Depositors' education and awareness fund with RBI
    (d) Customers' welfare fund with RBI

ANSWER

1	2	3	4	5	6	7	8	9	10
(d)	(d)	(c)	(c)	(d)	(c)	(d)	(c)	(c)	(d)

11	12	13	14	15	16	17	18	19	20
(d)	(d)	(c)	(c)	(c)	(d)	(a)	(d)	(c)	(d)

21	22	23	24
(b)	(c)	(d)	(c)

RETURNS INSPECTION, WINDING UP, MERGERS & ACQUISITIONS

INTRODUCTION

All banks must prepare their annual balance sheet, profit & loss statements and accounts as described in Banking Regulation Act as on 31st March of every year. All those statements and returns are audited by duly qualified auditors as prescribed in the act. All the audited returns should submit to RBI and Registrar of companies. Banking company provides inspection and scrutiny of their books as stated in the act. For these inspection and scrutiny of the returns a board for financial supervision was set up.

Annual Accounts and Balance-Sheet

As per Section 29 of Banking Regulation Act, an expiration of each calendar years or at the expiration of a period of 12 months ending with such date as the Central Government may specify (at present being March 31 every year w.e.f. March 1989), every banking company shall prepare a balance-sheet and profit and loss account as on the last working day of the year or the period, in the Forms set out in the Third Schedule (it is Form A for balance sheet and Form B for profit and loss account) or as near thereto as circumstances admit.

While preparing the accounts, the banking company should comply with the direction and instructions issued by the RBI in respect of Income Recognition and Asset Classification, Provisioning etc. norms from time to time. Central Government may amend the Forms from time to time after giving not less than 3 months' notice.

Who is to Sign the Balance Sheet?

The balance-sheet and profit and loss account shall be signed, in the case of a banking company incorporated in India, by the manager or the principal officer of the company and where there are more than three Directors of the company, by at least three of those Directors, or where there are not more than three Directors, by all the Directors, and in the case of a banking company incorporated outside India by the Manager or Agent of the principal office of the company in India.

Audit of Accounts (Section 30): The balance-sheet and profit & loss account prepared in accordance with section 29 shall be audited by a person duly qualified under any law for the time being in force to be an Auditor of companies. Every banking company shall, before appointing, reappointing or removing any Auditor or Auditors, obtain the previous approval of the Reserve Bank.

Special Audit {Section 30(1B)}: Where the Reserve Bank is of opinion that it is necessary so to do, it may direct that the special audit of the banking company's accounts, for any such transaction or class of transactions or for such period or periods, shall be conducted. It may appoint a person duly qualified, to be an Auditor of companies or direct the Auditor of the banking company himself to conduct such special audit. The Auditor shall comply with such directions and make a report of such audit to the Reserve Bank and forward a copy thereof to the company.

Submission of Annual Accounts (Balance Sheet and Profit & Loss Account) (Section 31): The accounts and balance-sheet together with the Auditor's report shall be published in the prescribed manner and three copies thereof shall be furnished as returns to the Reserve Bank within three months from the end of the period to which they refer. Reserve Bank may in any case extend the said period of 3 months by a further period not exceeding 3 months.

Copies of Balance-Sheets and Accounts to Registrar of Companies (Section 32): Where a banking company in any year furnished its accounts and balance-sheet in accordance with the provisions of section 31, it shall at the same time send to the Registrar of Companies, 3 copies of such accounts and balance-sheet and of the Auditor's report.

Display of Audited Balance-Sheet by Companies Incorporated Outside India (Foreign Banks) (Sec 33): Every banking company, incorporated outside India shall, not later than the first Monday in August of any year in which it carries on business, display in a conspicuous place in its principal office and in every branch office in India a copy of its last audited balance-sheet and profit and loss account prepared under section 29. It shall keep the copy so displayed until replaced by a copy of the subsequent balance-sheet and profit and loss account.

Submission of Returns: Every banking company has to furnish several returns to the Reserve Bank under various provision of the Banking Regulation Act and the Reserve Bank of India Act.

a) **Return on Liquid Assets {Section 24(3)}:** Every banking company has to submit a return of its liquid assets within twenty days from the end of the month to which it relates. The return should contain particulars of assets and the demand and term liabilities, as at the close of business of each alternate Friday or when such a Friday is holiday, as at the close of business of the preceding working day.

b) **Monthly Returns and Powers to Call for Other Returns and Information (Section 27) Statement of Assets and Liabilities:** Every banking company shall, before the close of the month succeeding that to which it relates, submit to the Reserve Bank a return showing its assets and liabilities in India as at the close of business on the last Friday of every month or if that Friday is a public holiday, at the close of business on the preceding working day.

c) **Statement of Investments and Classification of Advances {Section 27(2)}:** Reserve Bank may direct a banking company to furnish it within such time as may be specified by the Reserve Bank, information every half-year regarding the investments of a banking company and the classification of its advances in respect of industry, commerce and agriculture.

d) **Accounts and Balance Sheet:** The annual accounts and balance sheet have to be submitted to the Reserve Bank within three months from end of the period to which they relate. The Reserve bank may extend the time by a further period of three months.

e) **Return of Assets in India {Section 25(1)}:** A banking company has to submit to Reserve Bank a quarterly return regarding its assets in India within one month of the end of the quarter.

f) **Return of Unclaimed Deposits:** As per Section 26 of BR Act, every banking company shall, within thirty days after the close of each calendar year, submit a return in the prescribed form and manner to the Reserve Bank as at the end of such calendar year of all accounts in India which have not been operated upon for ten years. In the case of money deposited for a fixed period the said term of ten years shall be reckoned from the date of the expiry of such fixed period.

g) **Return of Cash Reserve of Non-Scheduled Banks {Section 18(1)}:** Every Non-Scheduled Banks has to furnish a return to the Reserve Bank relating to cash reserve. The RBI uses CRR as a tool to control the money flow in the market to control inflation or deflation of the economy.

h) **Return by Scheduled Banks:** Under section 42 of the RBI Act, all scheduled bank have to submit returns to the Reserve Bank of their demand and time liabilities as specified in the act.

Power to Publish Information (Section 28): Reserve Bank or the NABARD, or both, may publish any information obtained by them under this Act in such consolidated form as they think fit.

Preservation of Records and Return of Paid Instruments (Section 45Y): The Central Government may, after consultation with the Reserve Bank and by notification in the Official Gazette, make rules specifying the periods for which—

(a) a banking company shall preserve its books, accounts and other documents; and

(b) a banking company shall preserve and keep with itself different instruments paid by it.

Banks are also required to maintain all necessary information in respect if transactions referred in Prevention of Money Laundering Act 2002 for at least five years from date of transactions.

Return of Paid Instruments to Customers (Section 45Z): Where a banking company is required by its customer to return to him a paid instrument before the expiry of the period specified by rules made under section 45Y, the banking company shall not return the instrument except after making and keeping in its possession a true copy of all relevant parts of such instrument such copy being made by a mechanical or other process which in itself ensures the accuracy of the copy. The banking company shall be entitled to recover from the customer the cost of making such copies of the instrument.

INSPECTION AND SCRUTINY

Inspection of Banks (Section 35): Reserve Bank by itself or on being directed by the Central Government can, conduct an inspection by its officers, of any banking company and books and accounts. Reserve Bank shall supply to the banking company, a copy of its report on such inspection. Reserve Bank, may also conduct a scrutiny by its officers, of the affairs of any banking company and its books and accounts. A copy of the report of the scrutiny shall be furnished to the banking company if the banking company makes a request OR if any adverse action is contemplated against the banking company based on the scrutiny.

Duty to make available Books and Accounts: It shall be the duty of the banking company to produce to the officer inspecting or a scrutiny, all such books, accounts and other documents and to furnish him with any statements and information relating to the affairs of the banking company as the said officer may require.

Inspection on Direction of Central Govt.: Reserve Bank shall, if it has been directed by the Central Government to conduct an inspection shall report to the Central Government in relation to inspection or scrutiny made. Central Government, if it is of opinion after considering the report that, the affairs of the company are being conducted to the detriment of the interests of its depositors, may, after giving such opportunity to the banking company to make a representation by order in writing :

(a) prohibit the banking company from receiving fresh deposits;

(b) direct the Reserve Bank to apply under section 38 for the winding up of the banking company:

Power of the Reserve Bank to give Directions (Section 35 A): Where the Reserve Bank is satisfied that it is necessary to issue direction (to banking companies generally or to any banking company in particular):

❍ In the public interest or

❍ In the interest of banking policy; or

❍ To prevent the affairs of any banking company being conducted in a manner detrimental to the interests of the depositor or

❍ In a manner prejudicial to the interests of the banking company; or

❍ To secure the proper management of any banking company generally;

Reserve Bank may issue directions and the banking company shall be bound to comply with such directions. Reserve Bank may modify or cancel any direction issued, and impose conditions subject to which the modification or cancellation shall have effect. RBI has issued directives relating to Ombudsman, Know Your Customer (KYC) and clean note policy, under these provisions. Further powers and functions of Reserve Bank (Section 36)

Board for Financial Supervision

The Reserve Bank of India performs this function under the guidance of the Board for Financial Supervision (BFS). The Board was constituted in November 1994 as a committee of the Central Board of Directors of the Reserve Bank of India.

Objective: Primary objective of BFS is to undertake consolidated supervision of the financial sector comprising commercial banks, financial institutions and non-banking finance companies.

Constitution: The Board is constituted by co-opting four Directors from the Central Board as members for a term of two years and is chaired by the Governor. The Deputy Governors of the Reserve Bank are ex-officio members. One Deputy Governor, usually, the Deputy Governor in charge of banking regulation and supervision, is nominated as the Vice-Chairman of the Board.

BFS Meetings

The Board is required to meet normally once every month. It considers inspection reports and other supervisory issues placed before it by the supervisory departments.

BFS through the Audit Sub-Committee also aims at upgrading the quality of the statutory audit and internal audit functions in banks and financial institutions. The audit sub-committee includes Deputy Governor as the chairman and two Directors of the Central Board as members.

The BFS oversees the functioning of Department of Banking Supervision (DBS), Department of Non-Banking Supervision (DNBS) and Financial Institutions Division (FID) and gives directions on the regulatory and supervisory issues.

Functions: Some of the initiatives taken by BFS include:

i) Restructuring of the system of bank inspections

ii) Introduction of off-site surveillance,

iii) Strengthening of the role of statutory auditors and

iv) Strengthening of the internal defenses of supervised institutions.

The Audit Sub-committee of BFS has reviewed the current system of concurrent audit, norms of empanelment and appointment of statutory auditors, the quality and coverage of statutory audit reports, and the important issue of greater transparency and disclosure in the published accounts of supervised institutions.

ACQUISITION, AMALGAMATION & LIQUIDATION

Power of Central Government to acquire Banking Undertakings (Section 36 AE): If, upon receipt of a report from the Reserve Bank, the Central Government is satisfied that a banking company has, on more than one occasion, failed to comply with the directions given to it in writing under section 21 or section 35A, or is being managed in a manner detrimental to the interests of its depositors and it is necessary to acquire such banking company, the Central Government may, after consultation with the Reserve Bank, acquire the undertaking of such company with effect from such date as may be specified in this behalf by the Central Government.

Such acquiring shall be after banking company has been given a reasonable opportunity of showing cause against the proposed action.

Power of the Central Government to make Scheme (Section 36 AF): The Central Government may, after consultation with the Reserve Bank, make a scheme in relation to any acquired bank. The scheme may provide for all matters relating to property, assets, liabilities, board of management, service of employees and their term and conditions, payment of compensation to shareholders of acquired bank and other matters. The Central Government may modify or vary any such scheme after consulting the Reserve Bank. The scheme and any subsequent modification thereof is published in the official gazette and laid down before the parliament.

Compensation to be Given to Shareholders of the acquired Bank (Section 36 AG): Every person who, is registered as a holder of shares, shall be given by the Central Government, or the transferee bank, such compensation as is determined in accordance with the principles contained in the Fifth Schedule. If the amount of compensation offered is not acceptable to any person to whom the compensation is payable, such person may, before such date as may be notified by the Central Government in the Official Gazette, request the Central Government in writing, to have the matter referred to the Tribunal.

Constitution of the Tribunal (Section 36 AH):

(1) The Central Government may, constitute a Tribunal which shall consist of a Chairman and two other members.

(2) The Chairman shall be a person who is, or has been, a Judge of a High Court or of the Supreme Court, and, of the two other members, one shall be a person, who, in the opinion of the Central Government, has had experience of commercial banking and the other shall be a person who is a chartered accountant within the meaning of the Chartered Accountants' Act, 1949.

(3) The Tribunal may, choose one or more persons having special knowledge or experience of any relevant matter to assist it in the determination of such compensation.

Powers of the Tribunal (Section 36AI): The Tribunal shall have the powers of a civil court, while trying a suit, under the Code of Civil Procedure, 1908 in respect of summoning and enforcing the attendance of any person and examining him on oath; requiring the discovery and production of documents; receiving evidence on affidavits; issuing commissions for the examination of witnesses or documents.

SUSPENSION OF BUSINESS AND WINDING UP OF BANKING COMPANIES

Suspension of Business (Section 37): The High Court may on the application of a banking company which is temporarily unable to meet its obligations, make an order (a copy of which it shall forward to the Reserve Bank staying the commencement or continuance of all actions and proceedings against the company for a fixed period of time, and may from time to time extend the period. The total period of moratorium shall not exceed 6 months.

Application shall be maintainable only when it is accompanied by a report of the Reserve Bank indicating that in the opinion of the Reserve Bank the banking company will be able to pay its debts if the application is granted.

Role of RBI: Where the Reserve Bank is satisfied that the affairs of a banking company, in respect of which an order has been made by High Court, are being conducted in manner detrimental to the interests of the depositors, may make an application to the High Court for the winding up of the company. Where any such application is made, the High Court shall not make any order extending the period.

Winding up by High Court (Section 38): High Court shall order the winding up of a banking company if the banking company is unable to pay its debts; or if an application for its winding up has been made by the Reserve Bank under section 37 or this section. Reserve Bank may make an application under this section for the winding up of a banking company:

(a) If the banking company

(i) Has failed to comply with the requirements specified in section 11; or

(ii) Has by reason of the provisions of section 22 become disentitled to carry on banking business in India; or

(iii) Has been prohibited from receiving fresh deposits by an order section 35 or section 42 of the Reserve Bank of India, Act, 1934 or

(iv) Having failed to comply with any requirement of this Act other than the requirements laid down in section 11, has continued such failure, or, has continued contravention beyond specified period

(b) If in the opinion of the Reserve Bank

(i) A compromise or arrangement. Sanctioned by a court in respect of the banking company cannot be worked satisfactorily with or without modifications; or

(ii) The returns, statements or information furnished to it under or in pursuance of the provisions of this Act disclose that the banking company is unable to pay its debts; or

(iii) The continuance of the banking company is prejudicial to the interest of its depositors.

When a Banking Company is Deemed to be unable to Pay its Debts: A banking company shall be deemed to be unable to pay its debts

○ If it has refused to meet any lawful demand made at any of its offices or branches within 2 working days if such demand is made at a place where there is an office, branch or agency of the Reserve Bank, or

○ Within 5 working days if such demand is made elsewhere, and

○ If the Reserve Bank certifies in writing that the banking company is unable to pay its debts.

Court Liquidator (Section 38A): There shall be attached to every High Court a court liquidator to be appointed by the Central Government for the purpose of conducting all proceedings for the winding up of banking companies and performing such other duties in reference there to as the High Court may impose.

Reserve Bank as Official Liquidator (Section 39): Where in any proceeding for the winding up by the High Court of a banking company, an application is made by the Reserve Bank, the State Bank of India or any other bank notified by the Central Government or any individual shall be appointed as the official liquidator of the banking company and the liquidator, functioning in such proceeding shall vacate office upon such appointment.

Application of Companies Act to Liquidators (Sec 39A): All the provisions of the Companies Act, 1956, relating to a liquidator, in so far as they are not inconsistent with this Act, shall apply to or in relation to a liquidator appointed under Section 38A or Section 39.

Stay of Proceedings (Section 40): High Court shall make an order staying the proceedings of winding up where it is satisfied that an arrangement has been made whereby the company can pay its depositors in full as their claims accrue.

Preferential Payments to Depositors (Section 43A):

○ Within 3 months from the date of the winding up order, the preferential payments shall be made by the official liquidator or adequate provision for such payments shall be made by him u/s 530 of Companies Act,

○ After preferential payments, depositors of saving bank account up to ₹ 250,

○ Then other depositors up to ₹ 250 (maximum amount to be paid to one person when he is saving bank & other deposit account holder with balance up to ₹ 250, would be ₹ 250).

○ The balance would be utilized to pay to general creditors,

○ Then to the due amount to other depositors.

Where full payment cannot be made, every depositor would be paid on a pro rata basis.

Deposits covered with D1CGC insurance cover are not covered under these rules.

Voluntary Winding Up (Section 44): No banking company may be voluntarily wound up unless the Reserve Bank certifies in writing that the company is able to pay in full all its debts to its creditors as they accrue. High Court, may, make an order that the voluntary winding up shall continue, but subject to the supervision of the Court.

Amalgamation of Banking Companies (Section 44A): No banking company shall be amalgamated with another banking company, unless a scheme containing the terms of such amalgamation has been placed in draft, before the shareholders of each banking company separately, and approved by the resolution passed by a majority in number representing two-thirds in value of the shareholders of each company, present either in person or by proxy at a meeting called for the purpose.

If the scheme is approved, it shall be submitted to the Reserve Bank for sanction. If sanctioned by the Reserve Bank it will be binding on the banking companies concerned and also on all the shareholders thereof.

Any shareholder, who has voted against the scheme or has given notice that he dissents from the scheme, he shall be entitled, to claim from the banking company concerned their value as determined by the Reserve Bank when sanctioning the scheme.

Sanction of Scheme: On the sanctioning of a scheme by the Reserve Bank, the property of the amalgamated banking company shall, be transferred to and the liabilities of the company shall become the liabilities of the banking company.

Where a scheme is sanctioned by the Reserve Bank, it may, direct that the amalgamated banking company will cease to function, shall stand dissolved wef a particular date.

Restriction on Compromise or Arrangement between Banking Company and Creditors (Section 44B): No High Court shall sanction a compromise or arrangement between a banking company and its creditors and its members only when the compromise or arrangement unless the compromise or arrangement or modification, is certified by the Reserve Bank in writing as not being incapable of being worked and as not being detrimental to the interests of the depositors of such banking company.

Power of Reserve Bank to apply to Central Government for Suspension of Business by a Banking Company and to Prepare Scheme of Reconstitution or Amalgamation (Section 45): Where it appears to the Reserve Bank that there is good reason so to do, it may apply to the Central Government for an order of moratorium in respect of a banking company. The Central Government may make an order of moratorium for a fixed period of time and may extend the period. Maximum total period of moratorium shall not exceed six months. The banking company shall not during the period of moratorium make any payment to any depositors or discharge any liabilities or obligations to any other creditors.

During the period of moratorium, if the Reserve Bank is satisfied it may prepare a scheme for the reconstruction of the banking company, or for the amalgamation of the banking company with any other banking institution. Status of the employees: The scheme, inter alia, provide for the continuance of the services of all the employees of the banking company in the transferee bank at the same remuneration and on the same terms and conditions of service, which they were getting or, as the case may be, by which they were being governed, immediately before the date of the order of moratorium:

Penalties for False Statement (Section 46): Whoever in any return, balance-sheet or other document or on any information required or furnished under this Act, wilfully makes a statement, which is false in any or wilfully omits to make a material statement, shall be punishable with imprisonment for a term which may extend to 3 years and shall also be liable to fine, which may extend to one crore rupees (as per Banking Laws Amendment Act 2012) or with both.

Failure to Produce Books: If any person fails to produce any book, account or other documents or to furnish any statement or information which is his duty to produce or furnish, or to answer any question relating to the business of a banking company which he is asked by an officer making inspection or scrutiny under that section, he shall be punishable with fine which may extend to ₹ 250 in respect of each offence, and if he persists in such refusal, to further fine which may extend to ₹ 100 for every day during which the offence continues.

Acceptance of Deposits: If any deposits are received by a banking company in contravention of an order under section 35, every Director or other officer of the banking company, unless he proves that the contravention took place without his knowledge or that he exercised all due diligence to prevent it, shall be deemed to be guilty of such contravention and shall be punishable with a fine which may extend to twice the amount of the deposits so received.

Contravention of Provisions of the Act: If any other provision of this Act is contravened or if any default is made in complying with any requirement of this Act or of any order, rule or direction made or condition imposed there-under, such person shall be punishable with fine which may extend to ₹ 50000 or twice the amount involved in such contravention or default where such amount is quantifiable, whichever is more, and where a contravention or default is a continuing one, with a further fine which may extend to ₹ 2500 for every day, during which the contravention or default continues.

Under Section 47, the offences are cognizable only by a metropolitan magistrate, judicial first class or a court superior thereto on a complaint by an officer of the Reserve bank and in some cases by the national bank.

Under Section 47A, the Reserve Bank is empowered to impose a penalty for default of contravention. If the Reserve Bank exercises that power, no complaint shall be filed in a court in respect of the same contravention or default.

Power to Exempt in Certain Cases (Section 53): The Central Government may, on the recommendation of the Reserve Bank, that any or all of the provisions of this Act shall not apply to any banking company or institution or to any class of banking companies either generally or for such period as may be specified.

TEST YOURSELF

1. Banking companies are required to prepare ___ u/s 29 of BR Act.
   (a) Statutory returns on bank advances
   (b) Annual returns on assets
   (c) Annual accounts and balance sheet
   (d) Annual statement of unclaimed deposits

2. As per Section 29 of BR Act, the balance sheet and profit and loss account is required to be prepared by a banking company as on:
   (a) End of each calendar year
   (b) Expiry of 12 month period ending with any other date which central Govt. may notify
   (c) As on last working day of the year or the period
   (d) All the above

3. Balance sheet and profit and loss account are prepared by a bank as per:
   (a) 3rd Scheduled of RBI Act
   (b) 2nd Schedule of RBI Act
   (c) Schedule VI of Companies Act
   (d) 3rd Scheduled of BR Act

4. Which form is used to prepare balance sheet and profit and loss account by a bank:
   (a) Form A for balance sheet
   (b) Form B for profit and loss account
   (c) Part I for balance sheet and part II for profit and loss account
   (d) 'a' and 'b'

5. Banks are required to publish their balance sheets in ___________:
   (a) In a news paper in circulation at place of principal office of the banking company
   (b) In two news paper in circulation at place of principle of the banking company
   (c) On website of the bank concerned
   (d) None of the above

6. After end of the period, what is the maximum time during which the balance sheet is to be published by the banking company:
   (a) 3 months
   (b) 6 months
   (c) 9 months
   (d) 12 months

7. Each bank has to get its balance sheet audited from qualified auditors appointed by:
   (a) Central govt.
   (b) RBI
   (c) Institute of Chartered Accountants of India
   (d) Bank Board

8. Which of the following is not true in connection with special audit of banks:
   (a) Special audit can be ordered by RBI and SEBI
   (b) Special audit can be ordered in public interest
   (c) Special audit can be ordered to safeguard interest of depositors
   (d) Special audit can relate to any transaction or a class of transactions

9. A customer demands return of certain cheque issued by him and paid by the bank. What options are not available to the bank?
   (a) Paid cheques cannot be returned at all
   (b) Paid cheques can be returned by keeping copy on the instrument
   (c) Customer has to follow the preservation rules of section 45Y of BR Act
   (d) Authority to return the paid instruments is available to banks u/s 45Z of BR Act

10. On the basis of inspection report of a bank, if central Govt. decides to take stern action such as prohibition of acceptance of fresh deposits, what it is required to do:
    (a) Give opportunity to the bank
    (b) Can impose additional terms and condition
    (c) Can publish the report
    (d) All the above

11. Who among the following are not the members of Board of financial Supervision?

(a) Governor RBI
(b) Dy. Governors
(c) 2 Directors from Local Boards of RBI
(d) 4 Directors from Central Board of RBI

12. Which of the following functions are not carried by Board for Financial Supervision?
(a) Inspection of banks
(b) Supervision of banks
(c) Any other function notified by the central govt.
(d) All the above

13. On acquiring a banking undertaking, what is true with regard to the action, to be taken central government?
(a) It can make a scheme
(b) Scheme can provide for all matters relating to property, assets and liabilities
(c) Scheme can cover the compensation to share holder
(d) All the above

14. If a bank intends to amalgamate with the other bank, which of the following is not correct to meet the objective:
(a) A scheme of amalgamation would be prepared
(b) Draft scheme to be approved by the shareholders of both the banks
(c) Notice has to be given to majority of shareholder
(d) Scheme has to be approved by RBI

15. Central Govt. can order amalgamation of two banking companies for which of the following:
(a) The powers are as per Section 396 of companies Act
(b) The powers are vested as per Section 36 of BR Act

(c) The powers can be exercised in consultation with RBI
(d) 'a' and 'c'

16. What is meant by the term 'moratorium' in the context of a bank:
(a) Stopping the bank to accept fresh deposits
(b) Stop further lending by the bank
(c) Stop the bank to make payment to depositors and discharge other obligations
(d) Stop the bank does any kind of banking business

17. On the request of the RBI, who can be a liquidator in case of winding up of a bank?
(a) RBI itself
(b) State bank
(c) Any other bank notified by central bank
(d) Any of the above

18. What is the maximum period for which the moratorium on a bank can be imposed?
(a) 3 months
(b) 6 months
(c) 9 months
(d) 12 months

19. Who makes the appointment of a liquidator as per section 38A of BR Act in case of winding up of a bank?
(a) Reserve Bank
(b) High Court
(c) Supreme Court
(d) Central Govt.

20. If a banking company provides false information to RBI, what is the penalty as per Banking Laws Amendment Act 2012.
(a) It can be fined up to ₹ 50000/-
(b) It can be fined up to ₹ One lakh
(c) It can be fined up to ₹ 10 lakh
(d) It can be fined up to ₹ One crore

ANSWER

1	2	3	4	5	6	7	8	9	10
(c)	(d)	(c)	(d)	(a)	(b)	(d)	(a)	(a)	(d)

11	12	13	14	15	16	17	18	19	20
(c)	(d)	(d)	(c)	(d)	(c)	(d)	(b)	(d)	(d)

PUBLIC SECTOR BANKS AND CO-OPERATIVE BANKS

INTRODUCTION

Banking sector is the pillar of Indian economy. The Public-Sector Banks, namely State Bank of India, Nationalised Banks, and Regional Rural Banks are established by special statutes and these statutes provide the powers, functions and management of these Banks and the BR Act is applicable to them in a limited way. Cooperative Banks are created and governed by laws relating to co-operative societies, if they operate in one state only, the state act and in different states, Central act applies. BR Act is applicable in a Modified manner.

STATE BANK OF INDIA (SBI)

State Bank of India was established under Section 3 of State Bank of India Act 1955. SBI traces its ancestry to British India, through the Imperial Bank of India, to the founding, in 1806, of the Bank of Calcutta, making it the oldest commercial bank in the Indian subcontinent. Bank of Madras merged into the other two "Presidency Banks" in British India, Bank of Calcutta and Bank of Bombay, to form the Imperial Bank of India, which in turn became the State Bank of India in 1955. Government of India owned the Imperial Bank of India in 1955, with Reserve Bank of India (India's Central Bank) taking a 60% stake, and renamed it the State Bank of India. In 2008, the government took over the stake held by the Reserve Bank of India.

SBI is an Indian multinational, public sector banking and financial services company. It is a government-owned corporation with its headquarters in Mumbai, Maharashtra. On 1st April, 2017, State Bank of India, which is India's largest Bank merged with five of its Associate Banks (State Bank of Bikaner & Jaipur, State Bank of Hyderabad, State Bank of Mysore, State Bank of Patiala and State Bank of Travancore) and Bharatiya Mahila Bank with itself. This is the first ever large scale consolidation in the Indian Banking Industry. With the merger, State Bank of India will enter the league of top 50 global banks. SBI's market share will increase to 22 per cent from 17 per cent. It has 198 offices in 37 countries; 301 correspondents in 72 countries. The company is ranked 232nd on the Fortune Global 500 list of the world's biggest corporations as of 2016.

Organisational Structure of State Bank of India

The apex body of the bank, the central office is headed by a chairman who is assisted by a managing directors. The Chairman and the Managing Directors are appointed by the govt, of India. Besides there are positions of Deputy Managing directors, one each for commercial banking, HR and OD, international banking associate banks and planning, industrial rehabilitation, personal and services, Banking and computer system and technology corporate operations, personnel, development banking and treasury and investment management. The activities of the deputy managing director (DMD) are coordinated by the managing director (M.D.) A central Management committee comprising of chairman, MD and DMD's exists for the purpose of taking important policy decisions. The central office is mainly concerned with corporate policy and planning, development of critical resources, large advances, investments and control of foreign offices.

Business of the State Bank

The State Bank shall act as an agent of the Reserve Bank at the place where it has a branch and where

Reserve Bank has no branch, if so required, by the Reserve Bank, for transacting Govt. business and other business entrusted to it by the Reserve Bank. The term and conditions thereof shall be agreed between the Reserve Bank and the State Bank. If agreement is not reached, the term shall be decided by the Central Government.

REGIONAL RURAL BANKS

Regional Rural Banks were established under the provisions of an ordinance passed in September 1975 and the RRB Act 1976 to provide sufficient banking and credit facility for agriculture and other rural sectors. These were set up on the recommendations of the M. Narasimham Working Group during the tenure of Indira Gandhi's government with a view to include rural areas into economic mainstream since that time about 70% of the Indian Population was of Rural Orientation. The development process of RRBs started on 2 October 1975 with the forming of the first RRB, the Prathama Bank with authorised capital of ₹ 5 crore at its starting. Also on 2 October 1975 five regional rural banks were set up with a total authorised capital ₹ 100 crore ($10 million) which later augmented to 500 crore ($50 million).

Sponsor Bank: The Regional Rural Banks were owned by the Central Government, the State Government and the Sponsor Bank (Any commercial bank can sponsor the regional rural banks). Sponsor Bank is a Bank by which an RRB is sponsored and it holds 35% of the issued capital of RRB while the central Govt. holds 50% and the state Govt. holds the remaining 15% of the issued capital. Every RRB is a body corporate with perpetual succession and common seal with power to acquire, hold or dispose of property. Generally an RRB is allotted a compact area of operation comprising a few districts with homogeneous agro-climatic conditions and rural clientele. These Banks may accept all types of deposits from public and engage in the business of Banking.

Management: Consists of chairman appointed by Sponsor Bank. The power vests in the board of directors.

Amalgamation: Currently, RRB's are going through a process of amalgamation and consolidation. 25 RRBs have been amalgamated in January 2013 into 10 RRBs. This counts 67 RRBs till the first week of June 2013. This counts 56 as of March 2015. On 31 March 2016, there were 56 RRBs (post-merger) covering 525 districts with a network of 14,494 branches. All RRBs were originally conceived as low cost institutions having a rural ethos, local feel and pro poor focus. However, within a very short time, most banks were making losses. The original assumptions as to the low cost nature of these institutions were belied. This may be again amalgamated in near future. At present there are 56 RRBs in India.

NATIONALISED BANKS

Nationalised banks dominate the banking system in India. The history of nationalised banks in India dates back to mid-20th century, when Imperial Bank of India was nationalised (under the SBI Act of 1955) and re-christened as State Bank of India (SBI) in July 1955. Then on 19th July 1960, its seven SBI subsidiaries were also nationalised with deposits over 200 crores.

However, the major nationalisation of banks happened in 1969 by the then-Prime Minister Indira Gandhi. The major objective behind nationalisation was to spread banking infrastructure in rural areas and make cheap finance available to Indian farmers. The nationalised 14 major commercial banks were Allahabad Bank, Andhra Bank, Bank of Baroda, Bank of India, Bank of Maharashtra, Canara Bank, Central Bank of India, Corporation Bank, Dena Bank, Indian Bank, Indian Overseas Bank, Oriental Bank of Commerce (OBC), Punjab and Sind Bank, Punjab National Bank (PNB), Syndicate Bank, UCO Bank, Union Bank of India, United Bank of India (UBI), and Vijaya Bank.

In the year 1980, the second phase of nationalisation of Indian banks took place, in which 6 more banks were nationalised with deposits over 200 crores. Reserve Bank of India has, vide its letter no DBOD. BP. 1630/21.04.152/ 2004-05 dated April 15, 2005 confirmed that IDBI Ltd. (since renamed as IDBI Bank Ltd.) may be considered as Government-owned bank. Ministry of Finance has vide its circular no. 7/96/2005-BOA dated December 31, 2007 advised Secretaries of all Ministries/Departments of Government of India that the IDBI bank may be treated on par with Nationalised Banks/State Bank of India by Govt. Departments / Public Sector Undertakings / other entities for all purposes, including deposits / bonds / investments / guarantees etc. and Government business. With this, the Government of India held a control over 91% of the banking industry in India. After the nationalisation of banks there was a huge jump in the deposits and advances with the banks. Originally the entire paid up capital of the Nationalised Banks were held by Central Govt. Some of these Banks have recently made public issues of shares but central Govt. still holds the majority of shares of not less than 51%. Every Nationalised Bank is a body corporate having perpetual succession and common seal and power to acquire, hold and dispose of property and enter into contracts. They can carry all Banking business; they also act as agents of Reserve Bank.

In a move to strengthen the Indian Banking Sector, the Government of India had announced a merger of 3 major banks–Bank of Baroda, Vijaya Bank & Dena Bank. The Union Cabinet has now approved the merger. As per the Gazette dated 2nd January 2019, the merger will be effective from 1st April 2019.

○ **Management:** vests in the Board of Directors. The Central Govt issues directions to the Bank in the discharge of its functions on matters of policy.

○ **Directors:** are nominated by the Central Govt. or elected from the shareholders. RBI may appoint one or more additional directors on the board.

○ **Accounts and Audit:** close its accounts as on 31st March every year. Balance sheet and P & L account to be audited and the audited balance sheet to be submitted to RBI.

CO-OPERATIVE BANKS

A cooperative bank is an institution which is owned by its members. They are the culmination of efforts of people of same professional or other community which have common and shared interests, problems and aspirations. They cater to a services like loans, banking, deposits etc. like commercial banks but widely differ in their values and governance structures. They are usually democratic set-ups where the board of members are democratically elected with each member entitled to one vote each. In India, they are supervised and controlled by the official banking authorities and thus have to abide by the banking regulations prevalent in the country.

Banking Regulation Act Part V (Section 56) describes about the application of co-operative banks. Co-operative banks are registered either under the state laws governing co-operative or under the multi-state Co-operative Societies Act. If the co-operative bank operates only in one state, the state laws applies and in the case of co-operative banks operating in more than one state, the Central Act applies. The Act was made applicable to co-operative societies by the Banking Laws (Application to Co-operative Societies) Act 1965. As defined in Section 5(cci) of BR Act a co-operative bank means a state co-operative bank, a central co-operative bank.

Cash Reserve: For Scheduled Primary Co-operative Banks and State Co-operative Banks, CRR has to maintain as per Section 42 of RBI Act.

Requirement as to minimum paid-up capital and reserves (Section 11): Notwithstanding any law relating to co-operative societies for the time being in force, no co-operative bank shall commence or carry on the business of banking in India unless the aggregate value of its paid-up capital and reserves is not less than one lakh of rupees: Provided that nothing in this sub-section shall apply to :

(a) Any such bank which is carrying on such business at the commencement of the Banking Laws (Application to Co-operative Societies) Act, 1965 (23 of 1965), for a period of three years from such commencement; or

(b) To a primary credit society which becomes a primary co-operative bank after such commencement, for a period of two years from the date it so becomes a primary co-operative bank or for such further period not exceeding one year, as the Reserve Bank, having regard to the interests of the depositors of the primary co-operative bank, may think fit in any particular case to allow.

CORPORATE GOVERNANCE

Corporate Governance is a dynamic concept. It involves promotion of corporate fairness, transparency and accountability in the interest of shareholders, employees, customers and other stakeholders. First major study on Corporate Governance was done by Cadbury Committee in 1992. It can be seen as the way in which boards oversee the running of a company by its managers, and how board members are in turn accountable to shareholders and the company and it has implications for company behaviour towards employees, shareholders, customers, banks and other stakeholders. It also plays a role in ensuring integrity and efficiency of financial markets.

Organisation for Economic Co-operation and Development (OECD) Principles of Corporate Governance, 2004

It provides the six major principles of Corporate Governance.

1. **Ensuring the Basis for an Effective Corporate Governance Framework:** The corporate governance framework should promote transparent and efficient markets, be consistent with the rule of law and clearly articulate the division of responsibilities among different supervisory, regulatory and enforcement authorities.

2. **The Rights of Shareholders and Key Ownership Functions:** The corporate governance framework should protect and facilitate the exercise of shareholders' rights.

3. **The Equitable Treatment of Shareholders:** The corporate governance framework should ensure the equitable treatment of all shareholders, including minority and foreign shareholders. All shareholders should have the opportunity to obtain effective redress for violation of their rights.

4. **The Role of Stakeholders in Corporate Governance:** The corporate governance framework should recognise the rights of stakeholders

established by law or through mutual agreements and encourage active co-operation between corporations and stakeholders in creating wealth, jobs, and the sustainability of financially sound enterprises.

5. **Disclosure and Transparency:** The corporate governance framework should ensure that timely and accurate disclosure is made on all material matters regarding the corporation, including the financial situation, performance, ownership, and governance of the company.

6. **The Responsibilities of the Board:** The corporate governance framework should ensure the strategic guidance of the company, the effective monitoring of management by the board, and the board's accountability to the company and the shareholders.

Corporate Governance and Banks

The Basel Committee on Banking Supervision has issued guidelines in 2006 for promoting the sound practices of Corporate Governance by banks. These guidelines highlight importance of:

1. Role of Board of Directors and Senior Management

2. Effective Management of Conflict of interest

3. Role of internal and external auditors

4. Governing in a transparent manner

5. Role of supervisors in promoting sound corporate governance practices.

Reserve Bank's Approach Committees set up include: A.S. Ganguly Committee in Nov 2001, Advisory Group on corporate governance headed by Dr. R. H. Patilin March 2001, Advisory group on banking supervision headed by M.S. Verma in Jan 2003. RBI guidelines on ownership and governance in private sector banks released on Feb 28, 2005 provide as under:

1. The RBI guidelines on acknowledgement for acquisition or transfer of shares issued on February 3, 2004 will be applicable for any acquisition of shares of 5 per cent and above of the paid up capital of the private sector bank.

2. In the interest of diversified ownership of banks, the objective will be to ensure that no single entity or group of related entities has share holding or control, directly or indirectly, in any bank in excess of 10 per cent of the paid up capital of the private sector bank. Any higher level of acquisition will be with the prior approval of RBI and in accordance with the guidelines of February 3, 2004 for grant of acknowledgement for acquisition of shares.

3. Where ownership is that of a corporate entity, the objective will be to ensure that no single individual/entity has ownership and control in excess of 10 per cent of that entity. Where the ownership is that of a financial entity the objective will be to ensure that it is a well-established regulated entity, widely held, publicly listed and enjoys good standing in the financial community.

4. Banks (including foreign banks having branch presence in India)/FIs should not acquire any fresh stake in a bank's equity shares, if by such acquisition, the investing bank's/FI's holding exceeds 5 per cent of the investee bank's equity capital as indicated in RBI circular dated July 6, 2004.

5. As per existing policy, large industrial houses will be allowed to acquire, by way of strategic investment, shares not exceeding 10 per cent of the paid up capital of the bank subject to RBI's prior approval. Furthermore, such a limitation will also be considered if appropriate, in regard to important shareholders with other commercial affiliations.

6. In case of restructuring of problem/weak banks or in the interest of consolidation in the banking sector, RBI may permit a higher level of shareholding, including by a bank.

Directors and Corporate Governance

1. The Board of Directors should ensure that the responsibilities of directors are well defined and the banks should arrange need-based training for the directors in this regard. While the respective entities should perform the roles envisaged for them, private sector banks will be required to ensure that the directors on their Boards representing specific sectors as provided under the B.R. Act, are indeed representatives of those sectors in a demonstrable fashion, they fulfil the criteria under corporate governance norms provided by the Ganguly Committee and they also fulfil the criteria applicable for determining 'fit and proper' status of Important Shareholders (i.e., shareholding of 5 per cent and above).-as laid down in RBI Circular dated June 25, 2004.

2. As a matter of desirable practice, not more than one member of a family or a close relative (as defined under Section 6 of the Companies Act, 1956) or an associate (partner, employee, director, etc.) should be on the Board of a bank.

3. Guidelines have been provided in respect of 'Fit and Proper' criteria for directors of banks by RBI circular dated June 25, 2004 in accordance with the recommendations of the Ganguly Committee on Corporate Governance. For this purpose a declaration and undertaking is required to be obtained from the proposed/existing directors.

4. Being a Director, the CEO should satisfy the requirements of the 'fit and proper' criteria applicable for directors. In addition, RBI may apply any additional requirements for the Chairman and CEO. The banks will be required to provide all information that may be required while making an application to RBI for approval of appointment of Chairman/CEO.

For public sector banks, principles of corporate governance have been recognized by Banking Companies (Acquisition and Transfer of Undertakings) Act and as per Act, the shareholder directors should be a person having 'fit and proper' status.

Key differences between Commercial and Co-operative Banks

BASIS FOR COMPARISON	COMMERCIAL BANK	CO-OPERATIVE BANK
Meaning	A bank, that offers banking services to individuals and businesses is known as a commercial bank.	A bank set up to provide finance to agriculturists, rural industries and to trade and industry of urban areas (but up to a limited extent).
Governing Act	Banking Regulation Act, 1949	Co-operative Societies Act, 1965
Area of Operation	Large	Small
Motive of Operation	Profit	Service
Borrowers	Account holders	Member shareholders
Main Function	Accepting deposits from public and granting loans to individuals and businesses.	Accepting deposits from members and the public, and granting loans to farmers and small businessmen.
Banking Service	Offers an array of services.	Comparatively less variety of services.
Interest Rate on Deposits	Less	Slightly higher
Borrowers Status	The borrowers of commercial banks are only account holders; they do not have any voting power	Unlike Co-operative banks, the borrowers are members that influence the credit policy by voting power

Conclusion: The bank, which operates for taking deposits from and making loans to the public is a commercial bank. On the other hand, co-operative banks are mainly established to provide financial support to small businessmen and farmers at the low rate of interest. The big difference between these two terms is that while the network of former is very large whereas the network of the latter is confined to a limited area only.

TEST YOURSELF

1. State Bank of India was established under ________.
   (a) Section 3 of State Bank of India Act 1955
   (b) Section 6 of State Bank of India Act 1955
   (c) Section 6 of Banking Regulation Act 1949
   (d) Section 3 of RBI Act 1935

2. State Bank of India was established as a:
   (a) Company   (b) Society
   (c) Body Corporate   (d) Autonomous Body

3. Which of the following appoints Chairman of State Bank of India?
   (a) Reserve Bank   (b) RBI Governor
   (c) Central Govt.   (d) Central Board of SBI

4. Sponsor Bank is a Bank by which an RRB is sponsored and it holds ____% of the issued capital of RRB while the central Govt. holds ____% and the state Govt. holds the remaining ____% of the issued capital.

    (a) 30, 50, 20   (b) 35, 50, 15
    (c) 15, 50, 35   (d) 50, 35, 15

5. The RRB is managed by:
    (a) The Central Govt.
    (b) Their Board of Directors
    (c) The Board of Directors of Sponsored Bank
    (d) The State Govt.

6. Bank of Madras merged into the other two "Presidency Banks" in British India, Bank of Calcutta and Bank of Bombay, to form the _____________.
    (a) Imperial Bank of India
    (b) State Bank of India
    (c) Presidency Bank of India
    (d) Reserve Bank of India

7. Which is the amount of minimum paid up capital and reserves for commencement on business as a co-operative bank?
    (a) ₹ 1 lac   (b) ₹ 2 lac
    (c) ₹ 5 lac   (d) ₹ 10 lac

8. U/s 31 of BR Act, the state co-operative bank and central co-operative banks are required to submit returns to:
    (a) NABARD only
    (b) RBI only
    (c) RBI and NABARD
    (d) RBI, NABARD and State Govt.

9. State Bank and Nationalized banks act as agent of RBI for:
    (a) Carrying out transaction in Govt. business only
    (b) Payment of pension only
    (c) Collection of taxes only
    (d) Govt. business and other business entrusted by RBI.

10. SBI was constituted by taking over the undertaking of:
    (a) Imperial Bank   (b) Presidency Bank
    (c) Bengal Bank Ltd   (d) All of the above

11. In the capital of Nationalized banks, the share of the Central Govt. should not be less than:
    (a) 75%   (b) 65%
    (c) 51%   (d) 49%

12. The authorised share capital of a nationalised bank can be maximum:
    (a) ₹ 2500 cr   (b) ₹ 1500 cr
    (c) ₹ 1000 cr   (d) ₹ 500 cr

13. For opening branches by co-operative banks, the application to RBI is required to be routed through:
    (a) State Govt.   (b) Central Govt.
    (c) SLBC of the state   (d) NABARD

14. Which of the following appoints Chairman of RRB?
    (a) Reserve Bank   (b) Sponsor Bank
    (c) Central Govt.   (d) State Govt.

15. RRB may operate __________.
    (a) A district   (b) Notified area
    (c) Whole state   (d) Anywhere in India

16. Chairman and Managing Director of SBI are appointed for a period not exceeding:
    (a) 2 years   (b) 3 years
    (c) 4 years   (d) 5 years

ANSWER

1	2	3	4	5	6	7	8	9	10
(a)	(c)	(c)	(b)	(b)	(a)	(a)	(c)	(d)	(a)

11	12	13	14	15	16
(c)	(b)	(d)	(b)	(b)	(d)

CHAPTER 6

FINANCIAL SECTOR LEGISLATIVE REFORMS

INTRODUCTION

Financial Sector Legislative Reforms Commission (FSLRC) was set up by the Indian Government in pursuance of the announcement made in Union Budget 2010-11, to help rewriting and harmonizing the financial sector legislation, rules and regulations so as to address the contemporaneous requirements of the sector. The resolution notifying the FSLRC was issued on March 24, 2011. FSLRC had a two-year term.

The Commission was chaired by Supreme Court Justice (Retired) B. N. Srikrishna, and had ten members with expertise in the fields of finance, economics, law and other relevant fields. The secretariat was placed at National Institute of Public Finance and Policy (NIPFP). Secretariat consisted of a Secretary at the level of Joint Secretary to the Government of India and other officials and support staff.

NEED OF THE REFORMS

The establishment of the FSLRC is the result of a realisation that the institutional foundation (laws and organizations) of the financial sector in India needs to be looked afresh to assess its soundness for addressing the emerging requirements in a rapidly changing world. Today, India has over 60 Acts and multiple Rules/ Regulations that govern the financial sector. Many of them have been written several decades back. For example, the RBI Act and the Insurance Act are of 1934 and 1938 vintage respectively and the Securities Contract Regulation Act, which governs securities transactions, was legislated in 1956 when derivatives and statutory regulators were unknown in the financial system. A Large number of amendments were, therefore, made in these Acts and regulations at different points of time to address various needs. But these have also resulted in their fragmentation, often adding to the ambiguity and complexity of regulations in the financial sector.

KEY RECOMMENDATIONS OF THE COMMITTEE

The commission has proposed a sector-neutral Indian Financial Code to replace multiple and old financial sector laws, splitting the regulation between the Reserve Bank of India and a new 'Unified Financial Agency' that will oversee the remaining financial sector. In effect, the proposed unified financial sector regulator would subsume, repeal and basically every existing law that deals with sector regulators like SEBI, IRDAI, PFRDA and at least some functions of the Forward Markets Commission. These laws include principal and main legislations like the Securities and Exchange Board of India Act (SEBI Act), the Reserve Bank of India Act (RBI Act). Even as the RBI Act is separate, all other laws (essentially 20 laws) would get repealed, while there would be amendments in many other laws. In short the Securities and Exchange Board of India (SEBI), Forward Markets Commission (FMC), Insurance Regulatory and Development Authority of India (IRDAI) and Pension Fund Regulatory and Development Authority (PFRDA) should be merged into this new agency.

A Financial Sector Appellate Tribunal will hear appeals against all financial sector regulators and into which the existing Securities Appellate Tribunal will be subsumed and a Resolution Corporation will replace the Deposit Insurance and Credit Guarantee Corporation of India, which assists in closure of distressed financial sector institutions.

According to the report RBI will be divested of its powers over management of public debt, which is currently one of its subsidiary functions. The Debt Management Bill, likely to be considered by the Cabinet, proposes a separate debt management office to be attached to the finance ministry. The report also recommends creation of a public debt management office, a recommendation that was criticized by RBI when the draft report was issued for consultations.

It also recommends empowering the existing Financial Stability and Development Council, by making it a statutory body responsible for managing risk and crises in the financial system. The report also recommends setting up of a financial data cell, which will look out for systemic risk in the financial sector, especially the ones arising out of the financial conglomerates.

In short, seven pillars of the new Law are:

1. **Reserve Bank of India:** Regulator of Banking & Payments monetary policy.

2. **Unified Financial Agency:** Regulator of financial firms and activities other than banking and payments.

3. **Resolution Corporation:** Deals with closure of distress in firms.

4. **Financial Redressal Agency:** Single window complaint mechanism against financial institutions and intermediaries.

5. **Financial Stability & Development Council:** Recast as statutory body. Will manage systematic risks and development.

6. **Public Debt Management Agency:** Government's debt manager.

7. **Financial Sector Appellate Tribunal:** Will hear complaints against all financial regulators.

It is apparent by the report and recommendations, the overarching objective of the panel is to create a uniform legal process for financial-sector regulators, who would all be statutorily adequately empowered and therefore effectively pursue protection for the consumer's interests.

TEST YOURSELF

1. Financial Sector Legislative Reforms Commission (FSLRC) was set up by the Indian Government in pursuance of the announcement made in Union Budget ________.
   (a) 2010-11 (b) 2011-12
   (c) 2013-14 (d) 2014-15

2. The Commission was chaired by Supreme Court Justice (Retired) __________, and had ten members with expertise in the fields of finance, economics, law and other relevant fields.
   (a) R.V. Gupta (b) B.N. Srikrishna
   (c) M. Narsimham (d) S.N. Lal

3. In effect, the proposed unified financial sector regulator would subsume, repeal and basically every existing law that deals with sector regulators like ____________ and at least some functions of the Forward Markets Commission.
   (a) SEBI (b) IRDAI
   (c) PFRDA (d) All of the above

4. Full form of PFRDA is:
   (a) Public Fund Regulatory and Deployment Authority
   (b) Pension Fund Regulatory and Deployment Agency
   (c) Pension Fund Regulatory and Development Authority
   (d) Pension Fund Regulatory and Development Agency

5. As per FSLRC recommendation, the new law has __________ pillars.
   (a) 5 (b) 6
   (c) 7 (d) 8

6. As per FSLRC recommendation, which is not the pillars of the new Law:
   (a) Schedule Commercial Bank
   (b) Financial Stability & Development Council
   (c) Public Debt Management Agency
   (d) Financial Sector Appellate Tribunal

ANSWER

1	2	3	4	5	6
(a)	(b)	(d)	(c)	(c)	(a)

RECENT LEGISLATIVE CHANGES IN RBI ACT

INTRODUCTION

RBI has issued press release on April 05, 2018 regarding 'Statement on Developmental and Regulatory Policies'. This Statement sets out various developmental and regulatory policy measures for strengthening regulation and supervision; broadening and deepening financial markets; improving currency management; promoting financial inclusion and literacy; and, facilitating data management.

I. REGULATION AND SUPERVISION

1. **Mandatory Loan Component in Working Capital Finance:** With a view to promoting greater credit discipline among working capital borrowers, it is proposed to stipulate a minimum level of 'loan component' in fund based working capital finance for larger borrowers. Draft Guidelines are being issued for feedback in this regard.

2. **Countercyclical Capital Buffer:** The framework on countercyclical capital buffer (CCCB) was put in place by the Reserve Bank in terms of guidelines issued on February 5, 2015 wherein it was advised that the CCCB would be activated as and when the circumstances warranted, and that the decision would normally be pre-announced with a lead time of four quarters. The framework envisages the credit-to-GDP gap as the main indicator, which may be used in conjunction with other supplementary indicators, viz., the Credit-Deposit (C-D) ratio for a moving period of three years (given its correlation with the credit-to-GDP gap and GNPA growth), industrial outlook (IO) assessment index (with due note of its correlation with GNPA growth), and interest coverage ratio (noting its correlation with the credit-to-GDP gap). Based on the review and empirical testing of CCCB indicators, it has been decided that it is not necessary to activate CCCB at this point in time.

3. **Deferment of Indian Accounting Standards (Ind AS) implementation:** Scheduled Commercial Banks (SCBs), excluding Regional Rural Banks (RRBs), were required to implement Indian Accounting Standards (Ind AS) from April 1, 2018 vide our Circular dated February 11, 2016. However, necessary legislative amendments – to make the format of financial statements, prescribed in the Third Schedule to Banking Regulation Act 1949, compatible with accounts under Ind AS – are under consideration of the Government. In view of this, as also the level of preparedness of many banks, it has been decided to defer implementation of Ind AS by one year by when the necessary legislative changes are expected.

4. **Storage of Payment System Data:** In recent times, the payment ecosystem in India has expanded considerably with the emergence of new payment systems, players and platforms. Ensuring the safety and security of payment systems data by adoption of the best global standards and their continuous monitoring and surveillance is essential to reduce the risks from data breaches while maintaining a healthy pace of growth in digital payments.

It is observed that at present only certain payment system operators and their outsourcing partners store the payment system data either partly or completely in the country. In order to have unfettered access to all payment data for supervisory purposes, it has been decided that all payment system operators will ensure that data related to payment systems operated by them are stored only inside the country within a period of 6 months. Detailed instructions will be issued in this regard within one week.

II. FINANCIAL MARKETS

5. **Access for Non-residents into the IRS Market:** Rupee Interest Rate Swap (IRS) market, while it is the most liquid among interest rate derivative markets, still lacks depth to enable large banks to manage risks. Thin participation and consequent absence of divergence of views result in pricing inefficiencies, which further discourages participation. At the same time, it is understood that there is an active market for Rupee interest rate swaps offshore. Also, Indian market has witnessed increasing participation from non-resident players like FPIs in debt. With a view to develop a deep IRS market that accommodates divergent participants, it is proposed to permit non-residents access to the Rupee IRS market in India. Detailed draft regulation will be issued for public comments by end of May 2018.

6. **Introduction of Rupee Swaptions:** In December 2016, RBI introduced Rupee Interest Rate Options (IRO), following the recommendations of the P.G. Apte Working Group. Only plain vanilla Interest Rate Options were allowed initially. Subsequently, market participants including corporates have expressed the need for swaptions to effectively manage interest rate risk. Fixed Income Money Market and Derivative Association of India (FIMMDA) has conveyed a similar request on behalf of its members. It is, therefore, proposed to permit interest rate swaptions in Rupees so as to enable better timing flexibility for those seeking to hedge interest rate risk. The directions will be issued by end of April 2018.

7. **Review of Separate Trading of Registered Interest and Principal Securities (STRIPS) directions:** The Reserve Bank introduced the Separate Trading of Registered Interest and Principal Securities (STRIPS) in Government Securities in April, 2010. After some initial interest, the product did not find much favour with the market. With a view to encouraging trading in STRIPS by making it more aligned with market requirements and to meet the diverse needs of the investors, it is proposed to

review these guidelines. The revised directions will be issued by end of April 2018.

8. **Legal Entity Identifier (LEI) for Non-individual Market Participants:** The Legal Entity Identifier (LEI) code has been conceived as a key measure to improve the quality and accuracy of financial data systems for better risk management post the Global Financial Crisis. The LEI is a 20-character unique identity code assigned to entities who are parties to a financial transaction. RBI has already implemented the LEI code for all market participants in Over-the-Counter (OTC) derivative products in interest rate, currency and credit markets. It was also made applicable for large corporate borrowers. Continuing with this endeavour to improve transparency in financial markets, it is proposed to implement the LEI mechanism for all financial market transactions undertaken by non-individuals, in interest rate, currency or credit markets. Draft directions will be issued by end of April 2018.

9. **Introduction of Single Master Form for Reporting of Foreign Direct Investment in India:** Foreign Direct Investment in India, on a repatriable basis, is made by non-residents through eligible instruments such as Equity Shares, Compulsory Convertible Preference shares, Compulsorily Convertible Debentures, Share Warrants etc., issued by the investee company or by contributing to the capital of a Limited Liability Partnership (LLP). At present, the reporting of the above transactions resulting in foreign investment are in a disintegrated manner across various platforms/modes. The Reserve Bank plans to introduce an online reporting by June 30, 2018 via a Single Master Form which would subsume all reporting requirements, irrespective of the instrument through which the foreign investment is made.

10. **Reporting by Authorised Dealers:** Currently, transactions under Liberalised Remittance Scheme (LRS) are being permitted by Authorised Dealer (AD) banks based on the declaration made by the remitter. As such, it is difficult for the AD banks to monitor/ensure that a remitter has not breached the prescribed limit by approaching multiple AD banks. With the objective of improved monitoring and ensuring compliance with the LRS ceilings, it has been decided to put in place a system for daily reporting of individual transactions by banks. This will, inter alia, enable the AD Banks to view the remittances already sent by an individual before allowing further remittance thus obviating the

possibility of a remitter breaching the LRS limit by approaching multiple AD banks.

III. CURRENCY MANAGEMENT

11. **Norms for Cash-in-Transit (CIT) Industry and Promotion of Self-Regulatory Organisation by CIT Industry:** In the Statement on Developmental and Regulatory Policies of February 7, 2018, the Reserve Bank had announced a time frame to implement the recommendations of the two high level inter-agency committees constituted by it to suggest measures for improvement of currency management, including security of movement of treasure. The Committees, inter alia, had recommended stipulation of minimum standards for cash logistics industry and promotion of a Self-Regulatory Organisation (SRO) for the industry.

    i) Under the 'Guidelines on Managing Risks and Code of Conduct in Outsourcing of Financial Services' issued by the Reserve Bank in November 2006, cash management and logistics at the bank level has largely been outsourced to Cash-in-Transit (CIT) companies and Cash Replenishment Agencies (CRAs). There is, however, no regulation or supervision for this industry at present. With a view to promote healthy growth of the sector and mitigate risks associated with movement of currency through these agencies, Reserve Bank will require the banks to ensure that the CIT companies/CRAs engaged by them meet minimum prescribed standards. The instructions to the banks in this regard will be issued within a month.

    ii) In order to ensure compliance with minimum standards for the CIT industry and other applicable laws, the Bank will encourage the cash management industry to promote a Self-Regulatory Organisation (SRO) for undertaking development work along with self-regulation of the industry, till such time that an appropriate legislative structure is put in place.

12. **Central Bank Digital Currency:** Rapid changes in the landscape of the payments industry along with factors such as emergence of private digital tokens and the rising costs of managing fiat paper/metallic money have led central banks around the world to explore the option of introducing fiat digital currencies. While many central banks are still engaged in the debate, an inter-departmental group has been constituted by the Reserve Bank to study and provide guidance on the desirability and feasibility to introduce a central bank digital currency. The Report will be submitted by end-June 2018.

13. **Ring-fencing Regulated Entities from Virtual Currencies:** Technological innovations, including those underlying virtual currencies, have the potential to improve the efficiency and inclusiveness of the financial system. However, Virtual Currencies (VCs), also variously referred to as crypto currencies and crypto assets, raise concerns of consumer protection, market integrity and money laundering, among others.

    Reserve Bank has repeatedly cautioned users, holders and traders of virtual currencies, including Bitcoins, regarding various risks associated in dealing with such virtual currencies. In view of the associated risks, it has been decided that, with immediate effect, entities regulated by RBI shall not deal with or provide services to any individual or business entities dealing with or settling VCs. Regulated entities which already provide such services shall exit the relationship within a specified time. A circular in this regard is being issued separately.

IV. FINANCIAL INCLUSION AND LITERACY

14. **Tailored Financial Literacy Content:** A 'one size fits all' approach for imparting financial education to various target groups is sub-optimal. Financial education contents sought to be delivered to diverse target groups need to be customized to meet their typical target groups. The Reserve Bank is in the process of developing tailored financial literacy contents for five specified target groups' viz. Farmers, Small entrepreneurs, School children, Self Help Groups and Senior Citizens that can be used by the trainers. The contents in the form of five booklets will be released within 15 days.

15. **Revamping of the Lead Bank Scheme:** The Lead Bank Scheme was started to ensure economic development of the districts/states by establishing coordination between the banks and government agencies. The Scheme was last reviewed by a "High Level Committee" under Smt Usha Thorat, erstwhile Deputy Governor of Reserve Bank of India, as the Chairperson in 2009. In view of several changes that have taken place in the financial sector over the years, Reserve Bank of India had constituted a "Committee of Executive Directors" of the Bank to study the efficacy of the Scheme and suggest measures for its improvement. The Committee has since submitted its recommendations and it has been decided to realign the

Lead Bank Scheme based on the recommendations to make it more relevant. Instructions on the revised scheme would be issued to the banks within 15 days.

V. DATA MANAGEMENT

16. **Creation of RBI Data Sciences Lab:** It is critical for a full-service Central Bank, such as the RBI, with diverse responsibilities –inflation management, currency management, debt management, reserves management, banking regulation and supervision, financial inclusion, financial market intelligence and analysis, and overall financial stability – to employ relevant data and apply the right filters for improving its forecasting, now casting, surveillance and early-warning detection abilities that all aid policy formulation. In the backdrop of ongoing explosion in information gathering, computing capability and analytical toolkits, policy making benefits not only from data collected through regulatory returns and surveys but also from large volumes of structured and unstructured real-time information sourced from consumer interactions in the digital world. Accordingly, it has been decided to gainfully harness the power of Big Data analytics by setting up a Data Sciences Lab within the RBI that will comprise experts and budding analysts, internal as well as lateral, who are trained inter alia in Computer Science, Data Analytics, Statistics, Economics, Econometrics and/or Finance. It is envisaged that the unit will become operational by December 2018.

TEST YOURSELF

1. As per recent legislative changes of RBI, counter cyclical capital buffer (CCCB) would be activated as and when the circumstances warranted, and that the decision would normally be pre-announced with a lead time of _________ quarters.
   - (a) two
   - (b) four
   - (c) six
   - (d) eight

2. Scheduled Commercial Banks (SCBs), excluding Regional Rural Banks (RRBs), were required to implement Indian Accounting Standards (Ind AS) from ___________ vide our Circular dated February 11, 2016.
   - (a) April 1, 2016
   - (b) April 1, 2017
   - (c) April 1, 2018
   - (d) April 1, 2019

3. The Reserve Bank is in the process of developing tailored financial literacy contents for five specified target groups' viz. Farmers, and four others that can be used by the trainers. Which is not in the group?
   - (a) Small entrepreneurs
   - (b) College student
   - (c) Self Help Groups
   - (d) Senior Citizens

4. The Reserve Bank plans to introduce an online reporting by ___________ via a Single Master Form which would subsume all reporting requirements, irrespective of the instrument through which the foreign investment is made.
   - (a) June 30, 2018
   - (b) Sept 30, 2018
   - (c) Dec 31, 2018
   - (d) March 31, 2019

5. Fixed Income Money Market and Derivative Association of India (FIMMD(A) has conveyed a similar request on behalf of its members. It is, therefore, proposed to permit interest rate swaptions in Rupees so as to enable better timing flexibility for those seeking to hedge ___________.
   - (a) Interest rate risk
   - (b) Market risk
   - (c) Operational risk
   - (d) Credit risk

6. The Lead Bank Scheme was last reviewed by a "High Level Committee" under ___________, erstwhile Deputy Governor of Reserve Bank of India, as the Chairperson in 2009.
   - (a) R.V. Gupta
   - (b) M. Narsingham
   - (c) B.N. Srikrishna
   - (d) Smt. Usha Thorat

ANSWER

1	2	3	4	5	6
(b)	(c)	(b)	(a)	(a)	(d)

MODULE–B

LEGAL ASPECTS OF BANKING OPERATIONS

CHAPTER 8

DIFFERENT TYPES OF BORROWERS

Bank accepts deposit for lending and investment purpose. During the lending, the banker deals with different types of borrowers. The banker should acquaint himself with various laws governing different types of borrowers.

The borrowers can be classified as follows:

1. Individual
2. Hindu Undivided Family (HUF)
3. Proprietorship Firm
4. Partnership Firm
5. Limited Liability Partnership (LLP)
6. Companies
7. Statutory Corporation
8. Trust
9. Club & Co-operative Societies

1. Individual

Banker should take care and verify the certain fact while lending to individual. As per Indian Contract Act 1872, a person is competent to enter into a valid contract provided:

- ❍ Individual should be major, *i.e.*, of 18 years of age.
- ❍ He should be sound mind,
- ❍ He is otherwise not disqualified by any law,
- ❍ He should not be an insolvent,
- ❍ Drunken person is not legally competent to enter into a contract,
- ❍ He should be in good sense while lending a loan and entering into a contract,

Different types of individual borrowers are as under:

a) **Single Borrower:** This is purely a personal account in the name of an individual and is normally executed by the account holder himself. Banker must verify the identity, character, credential and capacity of the individual borrower. Whether person is capable to repay the loan and ability to enter into valid contract or not.

b) **Joint Borrowers:** Two or more persons or a group of individuals who do not constitute a registered body of association are called joint borrowers. All documents are signed by all jointly & severally. It means all are jointly liable plus each one of them is individually liable for repayment of Bank's dues. In case of death or insolvency of any one or more of joint borrowers, account showing debit balance is broken to determine liability of deceased joint account holder/s.

c) **Illiterate Person:** Illiterate person is a person who cannot read or write. Such persons are competent to enter in to a valid contract. We used thumb impression for entering into an agreement. Normally, Left Hand Thumb impression (LHT) of male & Right Hand Thumb impression (RHT) of female is to be obtained. Thumb impression must be authenticated by bank official. Photograph is essential for identi-fication. While opening account and providing loans, evidence to be created that the person understood terms & conditions beyond doubt.

d) **Loan to Minor:** Person below the age of 18 under Indian Majority Act and 21 years if he is a ward, under the Guardians and Wards Act

1890 is considered a 'Minor' in eyes of law. Under the law a 'Minor' is not capable of entering into contract & such contract entered into by a minor is null & void. It will not stand in law & the assets of the minor are not available to the Bank for appropriation. Even if an advance is granted to the minor against the guarantee of third party who is legally competent to execute guarantee, legal remedy to recover the dues from guarantor is not available to the Bank.

Exception for Financing to Minor: Normally Banks do not finance to the minors. However, there is an *exception* where finance can be made for the benefit of minor. Security documents in such cases are executed by Guardian of the minor. Indian Contract act (Sec. 26) permits "a minor can draw, endorse, deliver & negotiate instruments so as to bind all other parties except himself". Even minor can be a partner & may make an agreement which will be binding on other partners but will not be binding on him.

2. Hindu Undivided Family (HUF)

'Hindu Undivided Family' otherwise known as 'Joint Hindu Family' property, business or ancestral estates and its common possession, enjoyment ownership is the basis of formation of HUF. As per Hindu law, the Hindus, Sikhs & Jains can form HUF.

HUF is governed basically by two schools of thought. In Bengal, it is governed by **Dayabhag law,** in other parts of India, it is governed by **Mitakshara Law.** The law governing Hindu Undivided Family is codified under Hindu Code and now, succession among Hindu is governed by Hindu Succession Act, 1956. Parts of this Act was amended in 2005 by the Hindu Succession (Amendment) Act, 2005. Creation of Hindu Law under which all major members of the family get right by birth in the ancestral property of the family.

HUF property is managed by senior most major male member called 'Manager' or 'Karta'. Upon death of Karta, next senior male coparcener becomes Karta. Joint owner of HUF are known as coparceners. It consists of one common living ancestor and his all male & female (female from Sept. 2005) descendents up to three generations next to him. HUF cannot enter into a partnership as per Supreme Court judgement of 1998.

HUF account is operated by Karta. Karta has authority to borrow money for the family necessities & for ancestral family business. Documents are to be executed by Karta. All major coparceners are to be made guarantors. The liability of the 'Karta' is unlimited, whereas the liability of the coparceners is limited to their shares in the joint family estate.

3. Proprietorship Firm

Business is wholly owned by an individual. In law, there is no difference between proprietor & the firm. In all respects, it is an account in the name of an individual only except that it is operated upon by the proprietor on behalf of firm. The firm should have PAN or TAN. Proprietorship letter in bank's Performa is to be obtained. Proof of proprietorship may be obtained. Creditors have recourse not only against assets of the firm but also against private assets of the proprietor. Bank insists that proprietor should execute the security documents in the capacity as Proprietor on behalf of the firm as well as in his individual capacity. Proprietor can authorize another person to operate the account through Mandate or Power of Attorney.

4. Partnership Firm

Partnership is the relation between persons who have agreed to share profits of business carried on by all or any one them acting for all (Indian Partnership Act 1932). As per RBI instruction now Registration Certificate and Partnership deed to be obtained. As per Indian Companies Act 2013, Maximum number of partner can be up to 100 (excluding minor) in a firm. (Earlier number of partner was restricted to 20 for other businesses & 10 for banking business). Partnership is not a distinct legal person from the partners who have made partnership firm. HUF cannot enter into a partnership as per Supreme Court judgement of 1998.

The firm should have PAN or TAN. Partner in trading firm has power to borrow money on behalf of the firm & implied powers to sell or pledge any of the partnership property. Partners will sign on behalf of firm & also in their individual capacity. A partner cannot delegate his authority to operate the account. A minor cannot be a partner, but he can be admitted for his benefit in an existing partnership firm. The particulars of minor partner, particularly the DOB should be properly recorded.

In case of death/retirement/insolvency of a partner account should be stopped, if the balance is in debit and a fresh account should opened after fresh sanction of limit. In case of dispute when one partner revokes the authority against the other partner, operation in the account should be stopped.

Dissolution of the Partnership firm can takes place by following ways:

a) By mutual consent;

b) Death/insolvency/retirement of a partner;

c) Operation of Law (insolvency of all partners, business becoming unlawful, dissolution by a competent court, and

d) In case of automatic dissolution.

5. Limited Liability Partnership (LLP)

A limited liability partnership (LLP) is a partnership in which some or all partners (depending on the jurisdiction) have limited liabilities. LLP is governed by limited liability partnership Act 2008. Liability is limited to the extent of his contribution in the LLP. Minimum 2 designated partner and no limit on maximum number of Partners. A partner is not liable for another partner's misconduct or negligence, except in certain cases. LLP is a legal entity separate from its partner. It has own assets in his name, sure and be sued. Since LLP contains element of both 'a corporate structure' as well as 'a partnership firm structure' LLP is called a hybrid between a company and a partnership. It has perpetual succession (death of a partner does not affect the existence of LLP). Partners have a right to manage the business directly. Firms and companies can get themselves converted into LLP. LLP cannot raise fund from public.

6. Companies

Companies are defined in Indian Company Act 1956. As per the provision of Company Act 2013 (implemented with effect from 1ˢᵗ April 2014), recognizes a joint Stock Company is a legal person with perpetual entity & is distinct from its members. A company or association of persons can be created at law as legal person so that the company in itself can accept limited liability for civil responsibility. Because companies are legal persons, they also may associate and register themselves as companies otherwise it will be treated as illegal. Address of the registered office is compulsory. It is the address at which all the documents & notices may be served upon the company. Cheques favouring company are not to be credited to the personal accounts of the Directors or other officers of the company.

Following documents are required for account opening and lending to a company:

a) **Certificate of Incorporation:** Issued by Registrar of Companies. It is conclusive proof for incorporation of the company & compliance of all formalities by promoters.

b) **Certificate of Commencement of Business:** A company having share capital cannot commence business until it has obtained the certificate to commence business (COB) from the concerned Registrar of Companies. Certificate of commencement of business is not required by Private Ltd. Co. as its shares are closely held & it can commence business on its incorporation.

c) **Memorandum of Association:** Company's fundamental & unalterable law. Embodies Company's name, Authorized capital, Objectives of the company, Liability of share holders.

d) **Article of Association:** Regulations controlling internal management of the company. Rights & powers of the Directors, rules about conduct of company meetings & business, Procedure for borrowing & limit on borrowing etc.

e) **Copy of Board Resolution:** Certified copy of Board Resolution authorizing to borrow from the Bank with details of limit, security etc., Persons who are authorized to sign the security documents & operate the Bank Account, persons in whose presence Seal of the company will be affixed to the security documents.

f) **Company common Seal:** Common seal, if any of the company available should be embossed on bank's documents. As per RBI instruction Company Common Seal is not necessary, if other documents available during current account opening.

As per Companies (Amendment) Act, 2015, the following proviso regarding Company Common Seal shall be inserted, namely:

"Provided that in case a company does not have a common seal, the authorisation under this sub-section shall be made by two directors or by a director and the Company Secretary, wherever the company has appointed a Company Secretary.";

Different Types of Companies in India:

(i) **Private Company:** Private Company has share-holders with limited liability and its shares may not be offered to the general public. Share-holders of private companies limited by shares are often bound to offer the shares to their fellow share-holders prior to selling them to a third party. Private Limited Company having a no minimum paid-up share capital limitation now. (As per Companies (Amendment) Act, 2015, paid-up share capital of one lakh rupee or such higher paid-up share capital as may be prescribed is omitted now). It has minimum two members and maximum member restricted to two hundred and Minimum two directors and no maximum number of directors is restricted.

(ii) **Public Company:** Public company means a company which is not a private company and has no minimum paid-up share capital limitation now (As per Companies (Amendment) Act, 2015, paid- up share capital of five lakh rupee or such higher paid-up share capital as may be prescribed is omitted now). Shares are offered to the public & are listed on stock exchange. Minimum seven members no limit of maximum number. Minimum

3 director maximum 15 director limit. Provided that a company may appoint more than fifteen directors after passing a special resolution (As per Companies Act 2013, no Central Govt. permission required now). At least one woman director shall be on Board. Certificate of commencement of business is must to do any type of business.

(iii) The public limited company can be further classified as:

    a) Limited Liability Company: Liability of the member is limited to their contribution of capital.

    b) Unlimited Liability Company: An unlimited company is a company having no limit on the liability of its members.

    c) Limited by Guarantee: It is a registered company in which the liability of members is limited to such amounts as they may respectively undertake by the memorandum to contribute to the assets of the company in the event of its being wound up. In the case of such companies the liability of its members is limited to the amount of guarantee undertaken by them.

(iv) Government Company: "Government Company" means any company in which not less than fifty one per cent of paid-up share capital is held by the Central Government, or by any State Government, or partly by the Central Government and partly by one or more State Governments, and includes a company which is a subsidiary company of such a Government company.

(v) One Person Company: The Companies Act 2013 Act introduces a new type of entity to the existing list *i.e.*, apart from forming a public or private limited company, the 2013 act enables the formation of a new entity a 'one-person company' (OPC). An OPC means a company with only one person having a sole member [section 3(1) of 2013 Act]. OPC will be formed as a 'Private Limited Company'. Hence, minimum paid up capital will be ₹ 1,00,000/-. Memorandum of Association of such a company will mandatorily prescribe the name of the other person, who in the event of death or disability of the subscriber shall assume his position. An OPC can be formed only by an Indian Resident and citizen.

(vi) Other Companies: As per Companies act 1956, companies can be classified on the basis of time, place of incorporation and nature of working share capital as follows:

    a) Foreign Company: It means a company incorporated outside India and having a place of business in India whether by itself or through an agent, physically or through electronic mode and conduct any business activity in India in any other manner.

    b) Existing Company: A company which is established before the Company Act 1956 is called Existing Company.

    c) Holding Company: A company is known as the holding company of another company if it has control over another company.

    d) Subsidiary Company: A company is known as subsidiary of another company when control is exercised by the latter over the former called a subsidiary company. A company is to be deemed to be subsidiary company of another.

7. Statutory Corporation

A company may be incorporated by means of a special Act of the Parliament or any state legislature. Such companies are called statutory companies; Instances of statutory companies in India are Reserve Bank of India, The Life Insurance Corporation of India, and The Food Corporation of India etc. These statutory companies are governed by the act under which they are established. The provisions of the Companies Act 1956 apply to statutory companies except where the said provisions are inconsistent with the provisions of the Act creating them. Statutory companies are mostly invested with compulsory powers.

8. Trust

Trusts are governed by the Indian Trust Act, 1882. A trust is created when ownership of a property is transferred to someone for holding or managing it for benefit of another person(s). Trust may be public charitable trust or private trust (for benefit of private individuals). Trusts managed by trustees. Loan can be granted if it is for the purpose of the trust. Trustee is authorised to borrow as per the trust deed. Original Trust Deed to be examined before financing. Certificate of Registration under Public Trust Act to be examined & copy to be kept on record.

Clubs & Societies:

Clubs & Societies are non-profit making organisation and represent a group of persons. These are normally incorporated under Cooperative Society Act. Clubs can be registered under Society Act 1860, or Company Act 1956. These get the status of a legal entity only after their incorporation in their own name. These are governed by rules & regulations (bye laws). Certified true copy of resolution. Cheques favouring society, club, association not to be collected in individual accounts of office bearers or employees.

TEST YOURSELF

1. As per Indian Contract Act 1872, who is not competent to contract?
   - (a) Minor
   - (b) Insolvent
   - (c) Insane
   - (d) All of the above

2. For opening of bank account, registration of a partnership firm is
   - (a) Optional
   - (b) Compulsory
   - (c) Not required
   - (d) As per partnership deed

3. As per Indian Companies Act 2013, Maximum number of partners in a firm can be:
   - (a) 10
   - (b) 20
   - (c) 100
   - (d) 200

4. If partnership deed is silent about operation of the account, then the account will be operated by:
   - (a) Any of the partner
   - (b) All partners jointly
   - (c) First partner as per deed
   - (c) As per instruction of the partners

5. If bank finance to the partnership firm, the liability of a partner for the loan is:
   - (a) Unlimited
   - (b) Limited to their share in the business
   - (c) Limited
   - (d) No liability of partners

6. In a Government company, number of shares held by the Government at least:
   - (a) 50%
   - (b) 51%
   - (c) 75%
   - (d) 100%

7. HUF property is managed by 'Manager' or 'Karta'. Who becomes the 'Manager' or 'Karta'?
   - (a) Senior most major male member
   - (b) Senior most major female member
   - (c) Appointed by all major coparceners
   - (d) Any of the major coparceners

8. If bank finance to the limited liability partnership firm, the liability of a partner for the loan is:
   - (a) Unlimited
   - (b) Limited to their share in the business
   - (c) Limited
   - (d) No liability of partners

9. Embodies Company's name, Authorized capital, Objectives of the company, Liability of share holders are written in:
   - (a) Certificate of Incorporation
   - (b) Memorandum of Association
   - (c) Article of Association
   - (d) None of the above

10. A company which is established before the Company Act 1956 is called ______.
    - (a) Holding Company
    - (b) Subsidiary Company
    - (c) Existing Company
    - (d) Foreign Company

11. Which is the correct statement about 'Public Company:
    - (a) Its share is listed in stock exchange
    - (b) Minimum seven members no limit of maximum number.
    - (c) Minimum three directors maximum no limit
    - (d) All of the above

12. As per Indian Contract Act 1872, a person who is competent to enter into a valid contract:
    - (a) He is otherwise disqualified by any law
    - (b) He should not be a solvent
    - (c) Drunken person is legally competent to enter into a contract
    - (d) He should be in good sense while lending a loan and entering into a contract

13. Which is not correct about Illiterate person?
    - (a) Illiterate persons are competent to enter in to a valid contract
    - (b) Photograph is essential for identification
    - (c) Normally, Left Hand Thumb impression (LHT) of male & Right Hand Thumb impression (RHT) of female is to be obtained
    - (d) None of the above

14. Which is not correct about Proprietor firm?
    - (a) In law, there is no difference between proprietor & the firm.
    - (b) Creditors have recourse not only against assets of the firm but also against private assets of the proprietor.
    - (c) Bank insists that proprietor should execute the security documents in the capacity as Proprietor on behalf of the firm as well as in his individual capacity.
    - (d) Proprietor cannot authorize another person to operate the account through Mandate or Power of Attorney.

15. Which is not correct about limited liability partnership (LLP)?
    - (a) LLP is governed by limited liability partnership Act 2008.

(b) Minimum 3 designated partner and no limit on maximum number of Partners.

(c) LLP is a legal entity separate from its partner.

(d) LLP cannot raise fund from public.

16. Which is not necessary for financing a Private Company?

(a) Memorandum of Association

(b) Article of Association

(c) Certificate of commencement of business

(d) Board resolution

17. A company is known as the __________ of another company if it has control over another company.

(a) Holding company

(b) Existing company

(c) Other company

(d) Foreign company

18. Which is not a statutory companies in India?

(a) Reserve Bank of India

(b) Tata Iron & Steel Company

(c) The Life Insurance Corporation of India

(d) The Food Corporation of India

19. Which is not correct about Trust?

(a) Trusts are governed by the Indian Trust Act, 1982.

(b) Trust may be public charitable trust or private trust (for benefit of private individuals).

(c) Loan can be granted if it is for the purpose of the trust. Trustee is authorised to borrow as per the trust deed.

(d) Certificate of Registration under Public Trust Act to be examined & copy to be kept on record.

20. While giving a loan to a club or society or school the bank should study:

(a) Bye-laws

(b) Copy of Resolution

(c) Rules & Regulation

(d) All of the above

ANSWER

1	2	3	4	5	6	7	8	9	10
(d)	(b)	(c)	(b)	(a)	(b)	(a)	(b)	(b)	(c)

11	12	13	14	15	16	17	18	19	20
(d)	(d)	(d)	(d)	(b)	(c)	(a)	(b)	(a)	(d)

CHAPTER 9

TYPES OF CREDIT FACILITIES

INTRODUCTION

Lending is an important activity of banking industry. Bank invests public deposit in the form of lending and earns profit. Quality of the advances indicates bank's image in the market. A banker should have a thorough knowledge of the requirement of the customer and should be in a position to cater to needs of the customer. Credit facility is an agreement with bank that enables a person or organization to take credit or borrow money when it is needed. The business of lending is carried on by the bank by offering various credit facilities to its customer. On the basis of the security bank credit can be classified two types.

1. **Secured Advance:** The advance which is secured by primary or collateral security is called Secured Advances. In the event of loan default, the lender can take possession of the asset and use it to cover the loan. e.g. Business loan, housing loan etc.

2. **Unsecured Advances:** Unsecured advance don't have asset either primary or collateral. These are also called clean advance. Unsecured loans rely solely on borrower credit history and his income to qualify for the loan. e.g.- Credit Card, Clean personal loan, Education loan (small) etc.

All types of credit facilities may be classified into two groups on the basis of fund out flow:

1. Fund Based Credit
2. Non Fund Based Credit

1. **Fund Based Credit:** Fund Base Credit is the credit facility which involves direct outflow of Bank's fund to the borrower. Various types of Fund Based Credit facilities are as follows :

a) **Loan:** A term/demand loan is simply a loan provided for meeting the capital expenditure need & business purposes that needs to be paid back within a specified time frame along with interest. Loans are given for purchase of machinery, equipments or any fixed assets for starting a business or fulfilling personal needs. Repayment Schedule, period of the loan, mode of disbursement, rate of interest & other terms are predetermined term.

The loan which is repaid up to three years is called 'Demand Loan' & If repayment schedule is more than three years is called 'Term Loan'. Loans can be classified in three types on the basis of repayment period:

I. **Short Term Loan:** Usually short term loans are repayable within one year.

II. **Medium Term Loan:** It is generally repayable between one and three years.

III. **Long Term Loan:** It is repayable in more than three years.

b) **Cash Credit:** For running the business, borrower needs working capital for meet day to day expenses, Stock and book debt. It refers to credit facility in which borrower can borrow any time within the agreed limit for certain period for their working capital need. It is a running account facility where credit and debit both are permitted. It secured by way of Hypothecation of Stock (goods), Debtors (Book Debts) and all other current Assets of the business generated during the course of business. Cash credit can also be secured by way of mortgage of immovable properties (as collateral security).

c) **Over Draft:** An overdraft allows a current account holder to withdraw in excess of their credit balance up to a sanctioned limit. Overdraft may be permitted without any security as 'clean overdraft' for temporary periods to enable the borrower to tide over some emergent financial difficulty. 'Secured overdraft' facility is secured by way of Mortgage of immovable properties and pledge of F.D., Bonds, Shares securities, Gold & silver and all other current assets of the business generated during the course of business.

d) **Credit Card:** Credit cards serve many useful functions, including the ability to pay for purchases when you don't have cash on hand. The credit card issuer essentially loans you the money to make the purchase, and you will be able to repay that loan at a later date while being charged a certain interest rate. The credit limit of the Credit Card depends upon the credit history and regular income of the card holder.

e) **Bridge Loan:** Loans given to businesses who might be in need of instant cash flow to finance a project. Bridge loans are normally obtained while the borrower is waiting for long-term financing to go through. These loans are repaid out of the amount of term loan sanctioned or the fund raised in the capital market.

f) **Composite Loans:** It is a loan which is granted for both buying capital assets and to meet working capital requirements. Composite Loans are usually given to a MSME Unit, cottage industry, artisan, farmers etc.

g) **Retail Loan:** Retail loans are those loans which are given by the banks to meet personal needs, retail loans are smaller in size as compared to corporate loans. Home loan, Vehicle loan, Education loan, personal loan, Vacation purpose, medical purpose etc are categorized as retail loan.

h) **Bill Finance:** Bill discounting is a major activity with some of the Banks. Under this type of lending, Bank takes the bill drawn by borrower on his (borrower's) customer and pays him immediately deducting some amount as discount/commission. The Bank then presents the Bill to the borrower's customer on the due date of the Bill and collects the proceeds. If the bill is delayed, the borrower or his customer pays the Bank a pre-determined interest depending upon the terms of transaction. The transaction is practically an advance against the security of the bill which is due for payment.

i) **Export Finance:** Banks grant export credit on very liberal terms to meet all the financial requirements of exporters. The bank credit for exports can broadly be divided in two groups as under:

- **Pre Shipment Advances/Packing Credit Advances:** It is a credit facility which sanctioned to an exporter in the Pre-Shipment stage. Such credit facilitates the exporter to purchase raw materials at competitive rates and manufacture or produce goods according to the requirement of the buyer and organize to have it packed for onward export.

- **Post-Shipment Finance:** Post shipment credit is a working capital facility granted by a bank to the exporter of goods/services from date of extending credit after shipment of goods/rendering of services to the date of realization of export proceeds. As per the extent instructions, the maximum period prescribed for realization of export proceeds is 12 month from date of shipment.

2. **Non Fund Based Credit:** Non-fund based facilities are such facilities extended by banks which do not involve outgo of funds from the bank when the customer avails the facilities but may at a later date crystallise into financial liability if the customer fails to honour the commitment made by availing these facilities. The banker undertakes a risk to the amount on happening of a contingency. Different types of Non fund based credit facility are as follow:

(i) **Letter of Credit:** Letter of Credit is an undertaking issued by a Bank (Issuing Bank), on behalf of the buyer (the importer), to the seller (the exporter) to pay for goods and services provided that the seller presents documents which comply with the terms and conditions of the Letter of Credit, within a specified time. The banks follow the Uniform Customs & Practices relating to Documentary Credits 600 (UCPDC 600) framed by International Chamber of commerce. LC issued by the banker is irrevocable and shall not cancel without the consent of both the buyer and the seller.

(ii) **Bank Guarantee:** A Bank guarantee is a promise from a bank that the liabilities of a debtor will be met in the event that debtor fails to fulfil your contractual obligations. It is a promise from a bank or other lending institution that if a particular borrower defaults on a loan, the bank will cover the loss. It may be Financial Guarantee, Performance Guarantee or Deferred Payment Guarantee.

(iii) Derivative Products: In addition to the traditional non-fund facilities, banks are now offering the derivative products to their clients to enable them to hedge their currency and interest rate risks.

(iv) Buyer Credit: It is a short term credit available to an importer (buyer) from overseas lenders such as banks and other financial institution for goods they are importing. The overseas banks usually lend the importer (buyer) based on the letter of comfort (a bank guarantee) issued by the importer's bank.

First let us try to understand it from a layman's perspective: Suppose I have to buy a certain high end mobile phone from Delhi, but I am not able to go to Delhi, for this purpose. I live in Patna, but one of my friends Mr. Sanjay studies there in JNU. I will ask the supplier to send me the mobile and I assure him that I will make arrangements to make the payment to him through my friend Sanjay. The shopkeeper couriers the mobile to me. Sanjay pays the bill to the shopkeeper. I, in turn, send an NEFT to Sanjay's account.

Now coming to the exact definition, in order to make the payment of import bills, the importer buyer, say, in India requests his banker, say, Bank of India to arrange credit for him in foreign currency from its correspondent bank, say, Bank of India in New York. Conceding to his request, Indian Bank arranges a loan to him, say, for $ 1 million from Bank of America and makes it available to the importer for making payment of import bills. Sometimes importer himself strikes a deal by negotiating with various banks to get buyer's credit at a very competitive rate, say, LIBOR+0.80 or so. Later on the importer repays this amount either through their EEFC account, realization proceeds of export bills etc. Such arrangements are known as Buyer's Credit.

As the ROI of such loans are cheaper as compared to bill finance rates, now a days, importer customers prefer to adopt the route of Buyer's Credit instead of availing bill negotiating facility under Letter of Credit.

(v) Supplier Credit: Under such credit facility an exporter extends credit to a foreign importer to finance his purchase. Usually the importer pays a portion of the contact value in cash and issues a Promissory note as evidence of his obligation to pay the balance over a period of time. The exporter thus accepts a deferred payment from the importer and may be able to obtain cash payment by discounting or selling such promissory note created with his bank.

Let us first understand the concept from a layman's point of view: The milkman gives us milk daily for all 30/31 days of a month, but he asks for money only at the end of the month. So all these 30 days he has been extending credit to us. Such type of credit extended by the seller or supplier to the purchaser is termed as Supplier's Credit.

Now coming to the precise definition, such types of credit is extended by the exporter supplier to the buyer or importer of the capital goods. The terms can be down payment with the balance payable in installments. To finance the credit given to the importer under such arrangements, the exporter raises a loan from his banker under the export credit scheme in force.

TEST YOURSELF

1. Which is a non-fund based facility?
   (a) Overdraft (b) Bill Finance
   (c) Term Loan (d) Buyer Credit

2. Which is a fund based facility?
   (a) Bank guarantee
   (b) Bridge loan
   (c) Derivative products service
   (d) Supplier Credit

3. Loans based on the periods of repayment are classified into:
   (a) Short term loan (b) Medium term loan
   (c) Long term loan (d) All of the above

4. Loans given to businesses who might be in need of instant cash flow to finance a project. __________ are normally obtained while the borrower is waiting for long-term financing to go through.

(a) Bridge loans   (b) Composite loan
(c) Credit card   (d) Bill finance

5. Usually short term loans are repayable within:
   (a) 3 moths   (b) 6 moths
   (c) 12 months   (d) 36 months

6. Which is not an un-secured loan?
   (a) Bill finance
   (b) Credit card
   (c) Clean personal loan
   (d) Small Education loan

7. Financing against stock and book debt, banks are generally provides:
   (a) Over draft   (b) Cash credit
   (c) Term loan   (d) Bill finance

8. Which is a correct statement regarding export finance?
   (a) Bank finance for both Pre Shipment /packing credit & Post Shipment credit advances
   (b) Packing creditfacilitates to the exporter for purchase raw materials and produce goods
   (c) In the Post Shipment credit advances, maximum period prescribed for realization of export proceeds is 12 month from date of shipment.
   (d) All of the above

9. Which is a correct statement regarding letter of credit?
   (a) It is issued bank on request of the exporter
   (b) As per UCPDC 600, all LC is irrevocable
   (c) It is a non-fund credit facility
   (d) All of the above

10. Limitation period for filling a suit in term loan is _______ years from date of default of instalments.
    (a) 1   (b) 2
    (c) 3   (d) 5

11. Which is not a type of Bank guarantee?
    (a) Financial Guarantee
    (b) Government Guarantee
    (c) Performance Guarantee
    (d) Deferred payment Guarantee

12. Clayton's rule is applicable in which of the following accounts:
    (a) Cash credit   (b) Overdraft
    (c) Term loan   (d) 'a' & 'b'

13. Which is not a type of bill?
    (a) Demand bill   (b) Sight bill
    (c) Usance bill   (d) None of these

14. Which is not a type of Retail loan?
    (a) Home loan   (b) SRTO loan
    (c) Education loan   (d) Personal loan

15. A loan which is granted for both buying capital assets and to meet working capital requirements is called _______.
    (a) Bridge loans   (b) Composite loan
    (c) Credit card   (d) Bill finance

ANSWER

1	2	3	4	5	6	7	8	9	10
(d)	(b)	(d)	(a)	(c)	(a)	(b)	(d)	(a)	(c)

11	12	13	14	15
(b)	(d)	(d)	(b)	(b)

INDEMNITIES

INDEMNITY

The dictionary meaning of the word Indemnity means 'security or protection against a loss or other financial burden'. As per Section 124 of the Indian Contract Act 1872 the definition of the Indemnity is as follows.*'A contract by which one party promises to save the other from loss caused to him by the contract of the promisor himself, or by the conduct of any other person, is called a "contract of indemnity".* Right of indemnity-holder is defined in Section 124 of the Indian Contract Act 1872.

An indemnity is an obligation by a person (indemnitor) to provide compensation for a particular loss suffered by another person (indemnitee).The concept of indemnity is based on a contractual agreement made between two parties, in which one party agrees to pay for potential losses or damages caused by the other party. Indemnifier is the sole person liable. Liability arises only on occurrence of a loss.

Guarantee

A guarantee is a promise to some one that a third party will meet its obligation to them. "If they do not pay you, I will pay you". It is a contract to perform the promise or discharge the liability of a third person in case of his default.

As per Section 126 of the Indian Contract Act 1872 the definition of the Contract of Guarantee is as follows. A "contract of guarantee" is a contract to perform the promise, or discharge the liability, of a third person in case of his default. The person who gives the guarantee is called the "surety", the person in respect of whose default the guarantee is given is called the "principal debtor", and the person to whom the guarantee is given is called the "creditor". A guarantee may be either oral or written.

Difference between Indemnity Contract and Guarantee Contract

Basis of Difference	Indemnity	Guarantee
1. Definition	A contract by which one party promises to save the other from loss caused to him by the conduct of the promisor himself, or by the conduct of any other person. [Section 124 of Indian Contract Act].	A contract to perform the promise, or discharge the liability, of a third person in case of his default. [Section 126 of Indian Contract Act].
2. No. of Parties	Indemnity contract includes two parties namely, Indemnifier (promisor) and the Indemnity holder (promisee).	Guarantee contract includes three parties namely Creditor (The beneficiary), Principal Debtor (The person whose behalf the guarantee is given) and Surety (The person who gives the guarantee).

Basis of Difference	Indemnity	Guarantee
3. **No. of Contracts**	There is only one contract in case of a contract of indemnity, *i.e.*, between the indemnifier and the indemnified.	In a contract of guarantee there are three contracts, between principal debtor and creditor; between creditor and the surety and between surety and principal debtor.
4. **Nature**	As indemnity contract includes two parties and one contract, it can be said that indemnity contract is simple in nature.	Guarantee contract includes three parties and three sub-contracts and hence be said that guarantee contract is complex in nature.
5. **Liability of Parties**	There is no classification and sharing of liability where the absolute liability rests with indemnifier.	There will be two types of liabilities namely; primary and secondary liabilities which will be with principal debtor and surety respectively.
6. **Recovery**	In case of indemnity contract the indemnifier, after compensating indemnity holder's loss, cannot recover that amount from any person.	In contract of guarantee, if surety makes payment to creditor, he (surety) can recover that amount from principal debtor.
7. **Interest of Parties**	Indemnity contract gets formed upon indemnifier's interest.	Guarantee contract gets formed upon principal debtor's interest.
8. **Purpose**	Indemnity compensates for the loss.	Guarantee gives assurance to the promisee.
9. **Maturity of Liability**	When the contingency occurs it is called a contingent risk.	Liability already exists.

Indemnity Contract— Use and Application in Bank

Letters of indemnity are used during various types of banking transactions. Indemnity taken by bank to protect the bank from any loss or damage and for cost incurred. Indemnity contracts are stamped as per stamp act. Some of the important uses of Indemnity contracts in banks are as under:

- ○ In case of loss of Demand Draft, Travellers Cheque etc and to issue a fresh one.
- ○ During issue of duplicate TDR, FDR, Pay order etc.
- ○ When the valuable items are presented to the recipient prior to a bill of lading.
- ○ In case of deceased account claim payment etc.

TEST YOURSELF

1. Indemnity is defined in:
   (a) Section 125 of the Indian Contract Act 1872
   (b) Section 124 of the Indian Contract Act 1872
   (c) Section 124 of the NI Act 1881
   (d) Section 125 of the Companies Act 2013

2. How many parties are there in a contract of Indemnity?
   (a) 2
   (b) 3
   (c) 4
   (d) No limit

3. A person who is giving the promise is called the indemnifier and the person to whom the promise is made is called indemnified:
   (a) True
   (b) False

4. A contract of indemnity and a contract of guarantee are same:
   (a) True
   (b) False

5. Right of indemnity-holder is defined in:
   (a) Section 125 of the Indian Contract Act 1872
   (b) Section 124 of the Indian Contract Act 1872
   (c) Section 124 of the NI Act 1881
   (d) Section 125 of the Companies Act 2013

6. Indemnifier's liability in a contract of indemnity is:
   (a) Primary
   (b) Secondary
   (c) Subsisting
   (d) None of these

7. Which of the following is not a contract of indemnity:
   (a) Obtaining an insurance policy
   (b) Obtaining loan from bank
   (c) Obtaining a saving bank account
   (d) 'b' and 'c'

8. Banks do not obtain indemnity from their customers in which of the following case?
   (a) Re-issue of traveller's cheque
   (b) Issue of duplicate TDR
   (c) Granting a loan without tangible security
   (d) Issue of duplicate demand draft

9. Which of the following is correct as regard to indemnity?
   (a) An indemnity holder cannot act beyond his authority
   (b) Costs over and above of damages cannot be paid
   (c) If it is contrary to the term, indemnified is not entitled to compromise
   (d) 'a' and 'c'

10. For which of the following cases, indemnity bonds are insisted by bankers?
    (a) Issuing duplicate TDR
    (b) Settlement of death claim accounts
    (c) Issuing duplicate DD & Pay Order
    (d) All of the above

11. The risk covered in a contract of indemnity is called:
    (a) A subsisting risk   (b) A matured risk
    (c) A contingent risk   (d) A settlement risk

12. Which of the following is a contract of indemnity?
    (a) Obtaining loan from a bank
    (b) Giving guarantee for a loan
    (c) Opening a bank account with a bank
    (d) Settlement of deceased accounts

13. At what time the loss is required to be made good by the indemnifier in case of indemnity?
    (a) When loss has occurred
    (b) When there is a demand from the indemnified
    (c) When court of law decided the matter
    (d) When 3rd party certifies which has occurred loss

14. Which of the following statement is correct?
    (a) In a contract of indemnity there are three contracts
    (b) In a contract of indemnity there are two contracts
    (c) In a contract of indemnity there is one contract
    (d) None of the above

15. Indemnified cannot recover which of the following from the indemnifier?
    (a) Damages paid by indemnifier
    (b) All costs
    (c) All sums the indemnified had to pay under the contract
    (d) All of the above

ANSWER

1	2	3	4	5	6	7	8	9	10
(b)	(a)	(a)	(b)	(a)	(a)	(d)	(c)	(d)	(d)

11	12	13	14	15
(c)	(d)	(a)	(c)	(d)

BANK GUARANTEES AND DEFERRED PAYMENT GUARANTEES

BANK GUARANTEE

A Bank guarantee is a promise from a bank that the liabilities of a debtor will be met in the event that debtor fails to fulfil your contractual obligations. It is a promise from a bank or other lending institution that if a particular borrower defaults on a loan, the bank will cover the loss.

Contract of Guarantee: As per Section 126 of Indian Contract Act 1872, A "contract of guarantee" is a contract to perform the promise, or discharge the liability, of a third person in case of his default. The person who gives the guarantee is called the "surety", the person in respect of whose default the guarantee is given is called the "principal debtor", and the person to whom the guarantee is given is called the "creditor". A guarantee may be either oral or written.

Guarantee Parties Involved: The parties to the contract of guarantee are:

a) **Applicant:** The principal debtor: The person at whose request the guarantee is executed.

b) **Beneficiary:** The person to whom the guarantee is given and who can enforce it in case of default.

c) **Guarantor:** The person who undertakes to discharge the obligations of the applicant in case of his default.

Thus, a contract of guarantee is a collateral contract, consequential to a main contract between the applicant and the beneficiary. Guarantee issued must be unconditional and for:

○ Definite period   ○ Definite amount
○ Definite purpose

Types Of Bank Guarantees

Guarantee may be based on location of beneficiary, Purpose and Currency:

Inland: Issued within India in favour of beneficiary located in India for any contract or purpose originating within India.

Foreign: Issued in India in favour of beneficiary located in any other country in Foreign Currency.

As per nature of contract, Bank Guarantees are classified in three types :

1) **Financial Guarantee:** Financial Guarantees are issued by bank on behalf of customer's requirement to deposit a cash security or earnest money. Most Government department insist that before contract is awarded to contractor, insist on a Earnest Money Deposit. Issued in respect of Excise/ Custom duties and Octroi under dispute etc. Issued in respect liabilities towards tax, excise duties, custom duties etc. to Govt. authorities in relation of specific transaction; Issued for covering payments for supplies/services favouring Oil Companies, SAIL, Railways etc.

2) **Performance Guarantee:** Performance Guarantees are issued by the bank on behalf of its customer whereby the bank assures a third party, which the customer will perform the contract as per condition stipulated in the contract. These are issued on

behalf of customer, who enters into contracts to do certain things on or before a given date. It involves a contractual obligation.

3) **Deferred Payment Guarantee:** It is issued in favour of suppliers to guarantee payment of installments for capital goods purchased on deferred payment basis. Under this type of guarantee, the banker guarantees payment of instalment spread over a period. It required when goods or machinery are purchase on long term credit and payment is made through cheque or bills of different dates. In this case, generally the payment terms are as under:

- Advance payment of ten to fifteen per cent of the value of goods is made by the borrower.
- Another ten to fifteen per cent of the value of goods is paid on receipt of documents under letter of credit.
- The balance amount is paid in installments spread over a period of one to five years, which is secured by 'Deferred Payment Guarantee'.

Bank issues guarantee of payment of installments on due date, in event of default by buyer. Following terms are mandatory for issuing a deferred payment guarantee.

a) The payment schedule of both the installment and interest,

b) The supply of goods by the seller to the buyer and the seller agreeing to postpone the payment of the price, this being the consideration of a guarantee,

c) The unconditional and irrevocable assurance of the bank that it would make payment on the invocation of the guarantee.

For example: ₹ 50 Lacs is cost of Machinery, ₹ 10 lacs paid in advance and balance amount ₹ 40 lacs is repayable in 5 yearly installments. Guarantee is issued in case of default in payment of installment by the buyer.

Statutory Guarantee: These are guarantees issued by banks favoring Courts and other statutory authorities guaranteeing that the customer will honor his commitments imposed on under law, failing which bank will compensate to the extent of the amount guaranteed.

Invocation of Guarantee

Where guarantees are invoked, payment should be made to the beneficiaries without delay and demur. An appropriate procedure for ensuring such immediate honouring of guarantees should be laid down so that there is no delay on the pretext that legal advice or approval of higher authorities is being obtained. The obligation of a banker, to honour his commitment on a guarantee given by him being primary, casts a duty on the bank to honour it irrespective of the dispute between the beneficiary and the debtor. Invocation has to be made by the same authority in whose favour guarantee is issued. In case the payment is to be refused, controlling authorities' permission must be obtained before refusal.

Guarantee Onerous Clause

Any provision in the guarantee which is likely to give rise to further pecuniary liability like interest or liability which is unlimited in terms of money as well as validity period is considered as an Onerous Clause:

- Auto Renewal / Extension.
- Jurisdiction clause in different places.
- Where time limit is specified for payment say 24 hours, 48 hours etc.
- Payment of interest on invoked amount.

Application: The branch should obtain request letter for issue of guarantee which contains the following:

- Authority to–adjust margin money, appropriate principal or collateral securities on default & recover all charges in respect of issue of guarantee.
- The customer also accepts the responsibility to get back the original guarantee.

Guarantee Limitation Clause

All guarantees must carry limitation clauses invariably. As per RBI guideline in 2014 minimum claim period to be mentioned in the BG is 1 year Limitation clause as to time and amount. The following paragraph must be mention at the end of each guarantee:

"Notwithstanding anything contained herein above our liability under this guarantee is restricted to ₹ _________ (₹ _________) and this guarantee is valid up to _________ and we shall be released and discharged from all liabilities hereunder unless a written claim for payment under this guarantee lodged on us within _________ months from the date of expiry of this guarantee *i.e.,* on or before _________ irrespective of whether or not the original guarantee is returned to us."

Guarantee Confirmation Clause

All guarantees must contain the following clause in the forwarding letter of the guarantee:

"The confirmation of this bank guarantee is available with our controlling office. The beneficiary in his own interest should obtain such confirmation from the controlling office at the following address_________ "

Expired Guarantee

Expired BGs are those BGs, which are outstanding in the Branch Books attract risk weight, hence expired BGs should be cancelled. The Bank should get back the original guarantee after expiry of the guarantee. If the original guarantee has not been received back for cancellation, confirmation from the beneficiary should be obtained. The Branch should send a registered A/D letter to the beneficiary. A copy of the letter should be sent to the customer also. If the expired guarantee or advice of cancellation is not received within one month from the date of the letter, the guarantee should be treated as cancelled and entries should be reversed.

Limitation Period in a Guarantee

Section 28 of the Indian Contract Act 1872 pertaining to limitation clause of the guarantee has been amended w.e.f. 08.01.97. Due to this amendment, even when the period of liability is specified in the guarantee, the beneficiary can enforce his remedies till the limitation period is alive *i.e.,* 30 years where the beneficiary is Govt. and 3 years in other cases from the stipulated expiry date / invocation, whichever is earlier.

Precaution to be Taken while Issuance of Bank Guarantee

Letter requesting for guarantee should be taken each time a guarantee is issued. Guarantees should be serially numbered. Guarantees should be signed by two officers, if the amount of BG is over ₹ 50,0000. The name, designation and code no. of the officers signing the guarantee should be incorporated. Guarantee must be issued after proper stamping of the paper as per State Stamp Act of the issuing state.

Bank Guarantee Beyond 10 years

In terms of RBI circular dated July 1, 2008 on Guarantees, no bank guarantee should normally have a maturity of more than 10 years. In view of the changed scenario of the banking industry where banks extend tong term loans for periods longer than 10 years for various projects, RBI decided (April 22, 2009) to allow banks to issue guarantees for periods beyond 10 years under a policy approved by their Board of Directors.

TEST YOURSELF

1. Guarantees are defined in:
   - (a) Section 125 of Indian Contract Act 1872
   - (b) Section 126 of Indian Contract Act 1872
   - (c) Section 125 of Transfer of Property Act 1882
   - (d) Section 126 of NI Act 1881,

2. Normally a bank guarantee cannot be issued for more than:
   - (a) 3 years
   - (b) 5 years
   - (c) 10 years
   - (d) 15 years

3. If a customer requires to deposit earnest money with government department, which type of guarantee will be issued by bank?
   - (a) Financial guarantee
   - (b) Performance guarantee
   - (c) Deferred Payment guarantee
   - (d) None of the above

4. How many parties are there in the bank guarantee?
   - (a) 2
   - (b) 3
   - (c) 4
   - (d) 5

5. If a bank wants to issue a bank guarantee for periods beyond 10 years, It has to obtain prior approval from:
   - (a) Their Board of Directors
   - (b) GOI
   - (c) RBI
   - (d) IBA

6. A bank guarantee which has given an assurance to the beneficiary of the guarantee that the issuer will complete the work as per term and condition of contract is called:
   - (a) Financial guarantee
   - (b) Performance guarantee
   - (c) Deferred Payment guarantee
   - (d) None of the above

7. On invocation of a guarantee, what amount is payable by the bank?
   - (a) Amount of transaction
   - (b) Amount of interest
   - (c) Amount of other charges
   - (d) Amount as determined in the guarantee bond

8. In case of invocation of guarantee by the beneficiary, bank should make the payment:
   - (a) Immediately without delay and demur
   - (b) After informing the matter to controlling office
   - (c) After consulting the applicant
   - (d) After due verification of terms of contract

9. Bank can refuse to honour his guarantee in which of the following case?
   (a) Injunction order by court
   (b) fraud
   (c) (a) or (b) or both
   (d) Bank cannot refuse to honour

10. Limitation period to enforce the remedies by the beneficiary of a guarantee is:
    (a) 30 years where the beneficiary is Govt. from the stipulated expiry date / invocation
    (b) 3 years in other cases from the stipulated expiry date / invocation
    (c) Both (a) and (b)
    (d) None of the above

11. When goods or machinery are purchased by customer on long term credit and payment is to be made in instalments which type of guarantee is to be issued by the bank?
    (a) Financial guarantee
    (b) Performance guarantee
    (c) Deferred Payment guarantee
    (d) None of the above

12. The confirmation of this bank guarantee is available with:
    (a) Controlling office of the branch
    (b) Guarantee issued branch
    (c) RBI website
    (d) Concerned bank's website

13. As per RBI guideline in 2014 minimum claim period to be mentioned in the bank guarantee is ______ Limitation clause as to time and amount.
    (a) 1 moths   (b) 3 moths
    (c) 6 moths   (d) 1 year

14. When a guarantee is invoked by the beneficiary, normally court can grant stay on encashment when ________?
    (a) Beneficiary does not state the reason for invocation
    (b) Applicant approaches the court for stay
    (c) Bank certifies that the invocation is not proper
    (d) When there is element of fraud

15. If a guarantee is invoked by the beneficiary, the payment is made by the bank when:
    (a) Beneficiary brings order from competent court
    (b) Beneficiary makes demand on the bank
    (c) Bank obtains consent of the applicant
    (d) Sufficient balance is available in the account of applicant

16. What is the validity period of the guarantee?
    (a) Period during which the guarantee can be invoked
    (b) Period during which the applicant get the guarantee cancelled
    (c) Period during which the cause of action for invocation could rise
    (d) Period during which the guarantee bond remains with the beneficiary

17. What is the claim period of the guarantee?
    (a) Period during which the guarantee can be invoked
    (b) Period during which the applicant get the guarantee cancelled
    (c) Period during which the cause of action for invocation could rise
    (d) Period during which the guarantee bond remains with the beneficiary

18. Under deferred payment guarantee, the liability of the bank is:
    (a) Primary   (b) Secondary
    (c) As per contract term   (d) All of the above

19. Claim period in a guarantee is ________ than the validity period.
    (a) Same
    (b) Longer
    (c) Shorter
    (d) Depends upon terms of guarantee

20. How the amount of guarantee to be issued by the bank is determined?
    (a) It is determined on the basis of security available
    (b) It is determined by the beneficiary
    (c) It is as per contract between the beneficiary and the applicant
    (d) Based on the cash margin available

ANSWER

1	2	3	4	5	6	7	8	9	10
(b)	(c)	(a)	(b)	(a)	(b)	(d)	(a)	(c)	(c)

11	12	13	14	15	16	17	18	19	20
(c)	(a)	(d)	(d)	(b)	(c)	(a)	(a)	(b)	(c)

LETTERS OF CREDIT

INTRODUCTION

Letter of Credit is a guarantee letter issued by a bank in international trade in favour of the exporter that a buyer's payment will be paid on time. In the event that the buyer is unable to make payment on the purchase, the bank will be required to cover the full or remaining amount of the purchase. Now in simple words, If LC opened on seller name as beneficiary, seller will receive amount through the buyer's bank (opening bank) on the agreed time.

Advantage of Letter of Credit

Letters of credit are often used in international trans-actions to ensure that payment will be received. Due to the nature of international dealings including factors such as distance, differing laws in each country and difficulty in knowing each party personally, the use of letters of credit has become a very important aspect of inter-national trade. The bank also acts on behalf of the buyer (holder of letter of credit) by ensuring that the supplier will not be paid until the bank receives a confirmation that the goods have been shipped.

All Letters of Credit for export import trade is handled under the guidelines of Uniform Customs and Practice of Documentary Credit of International Chamber of Commerce (UCPDC 600). The ICC Banking Commission approved UCPDC 600 in 25 October 2006, which came into effect from 1st July 2007.

International trade covers very large distance between two countries and exporter and importers are not known to each other. Letter of Credit plays a major role in this transaction. Both exporter and importer are benefited to do business through letter of credit.

Major advantages to buyer (importer) from letter of credit are as follows:

❖ No cash advance payment has to be made to the seller;

❖ Seller is paid only after shipment and delivery of documents within the LC validity;

❖ Possibility to obtain more favourable payment terms;

❖ Shipment schedule ensured.

Major advantages to seller (exporter) from letter of credit are as follows:

❖ Obligation of the buyer's bank for payment;

❖ Payment is assured if credit terms are fulfilled;

❖ Date of receipt of payment can be determined;

❖ Seller need not bother about the fluctuation of currency;

❖ Seller need not bother about the import regulation of buyer country.

❖ A financing possibility by discounting receivables under LC.

Need of the Letter of Credit

Letter of credit is an important tool of international Trade. Exporter and Importer belong to two different countries having different trading environment and different rules and regulation. Letter of credit can resolve the Complications/Complexities/Contradictions arise in international trade due mainly to involvement of two countries separated by differences in :

○ physical barriers-long distances

○ political systems / legal systems

○ currencies

○ trade and exchange regulations
○ markets and marketing conditions
○ trade practices
○ financial and commercial conditions

Parties of Letter of Credit

- **Applicant:** Applicant is the party who opens Letter of Credit. He is the buyer / importer of the goods (generally borrower of the issuing bank). The applicant arranges to open letter of credit with his bank as per the terms and conditions of Purchase order and business contract between buyer and seller. The applicant has to make payment if documents as per LC are delivered, whether the goods are as per contract between the buyer and beneficiary or not.

- **Beneficiary Party:** The seller or exporter is the beneficiary in whose favour the letter of credit is issued. It gets payment against documents as per LC from the nominated bank within validity period for negotiation,

- **Issuing Bank:** Issuing Bank is the bank that opens letter of credit. Letter of credit is created by issuing bank who takes responsibility to pay amount on receipt of documents from supplier of goods (beneficiary under LC).

- **Advising Bank:** Advising bank, as a part of letter of credit takes responsibility to communicate with necessary parties under letter of credit and other required authorities. The advising bank is the party who sends documents under Letter of Credit to opening bank.

- **Confirming Bank:** Confirming bank as a party of letter of credit confirms and guarantees to undertake the responsibility of payment or negotiation acceptance under the credit.

- **Negotiating Bank:** Negotiating Bank, who negotiates documents delivered to bank by beneficiary of LC. Negotiating bank is the bank that verifies documents and confirms the terms and conditions under LC on behalf of beneficiary to avoid discrepancies.

- **Reimbursing Bank:** Reimbursing bank is the party who authorized to honour the reimbursement claim of negotiation/ payment/ acceptance.

Types of Letter of Credit

Different types of LC are as under:

- **Revocable & Irrevocable LCs:** Inrevocable LC, the buyer and the bank that established the LC are able to manipulate the LC or make corrections without informing or getting permissions from the seller. According to the UCPDC 600, all LCs are irrevocable, hence this type of LC is obsolete. Irrevocable LC is a letter of credit that does not allow the issuing bank to make any changes without the approval of the beneficiary, applicant bank and confirming bank, if any.

- **Deferred or Usance LC:** A letter of credit, which ensures payment after a certain period of time. The date of payment is accepted by both buyer and seller. The bank may review the documents early but the payment to the beneficiary is made after the agreed time passes. It is also known as Usance LC.

- **Sight LC:** A letter of credit that demand payment on the submission of the required documents. The bank reviews the documents and pays the beneficiary if the documents meet the conditions of the letter.

- **With & Without Recourse LCs:** Where the beneficiary holds himself liable to the holder of the bill if dishonoured, it is considered with-recourse LC. Where he does not hold himself liable, the credit is said to be without-recourse LC. As per RBI directive (Jan 23, 2003), banks should not open such LCs. Under LC, the Banks can negotiate bills bearing the 'without recourse' clause.

- **A Restricted LC:** It is one wherein a specified bank is designated to pay, accept or negotiate payment will be made. The confirming bank's liability is similar to the issuing bank. The confirming bank has to negotiate documents if tendered by the beneficiary.

- **Transferable LCs:** It is an LC, where the beneficiary is entitled to transfer the LC, in whole or in part, to the 2nd beneficiary/s (supplier of beneficiary). The 2nd beneficiary, however, cannot transfer it further, but it can transfer the unused portion, back to the original beneficiary. It is transferable only once.

- **A Back to Back Credit:** A pair of LCs in which one is to the benefit of a seller who is not able to provide the corresponding goods for unspecified reasons. In that event, a second credit is opened for another seller to provide the desired goods. Back-to-back is issued to facilitate intermediary trade. Intermediate companies such as trading houses are sometimes required to open LCs for a supplier and receive Export LCs from buyer.

- **A Red Clause LC:** It referred to a packing or anticipatory credit, has a clause permitting the correspondent bank in the exporter's country to grant advance to beneficiary at issuing bank's responsibility. These advances are adjusted from proceeds of the bills negotiated.

- **A Green Clause LC:** It permits the advances for storage of goods in a warehouse in addition to preshipment advance. It is an extension of the red clause LC.

- **Standby Credits:** It is similar to performance bond or guarantee, but issued in the form of LC. The beneficiary can submit his claim by means of a draft accompanied by the requisite documentary evidence of performance, as stipulated in the credit.

- **Documentary Credits:** When LC specifies that the bills drawn under LC must - accompany documents of title to goods such as RRs or MIRs or Bills of lading etc. it is termed as Documentary Credit. If any such documents are not called, the credit is said to be Clean Credit.

- **Revolving Credits:** These LCs provide that the amount of drawings made there under would be reinstated and made available to the beneficiary again and again for further drawings during the currency of credit provided the applicant makes the payment of documents earlier negotiated. At times, an overall turnover cap is also stipulated.

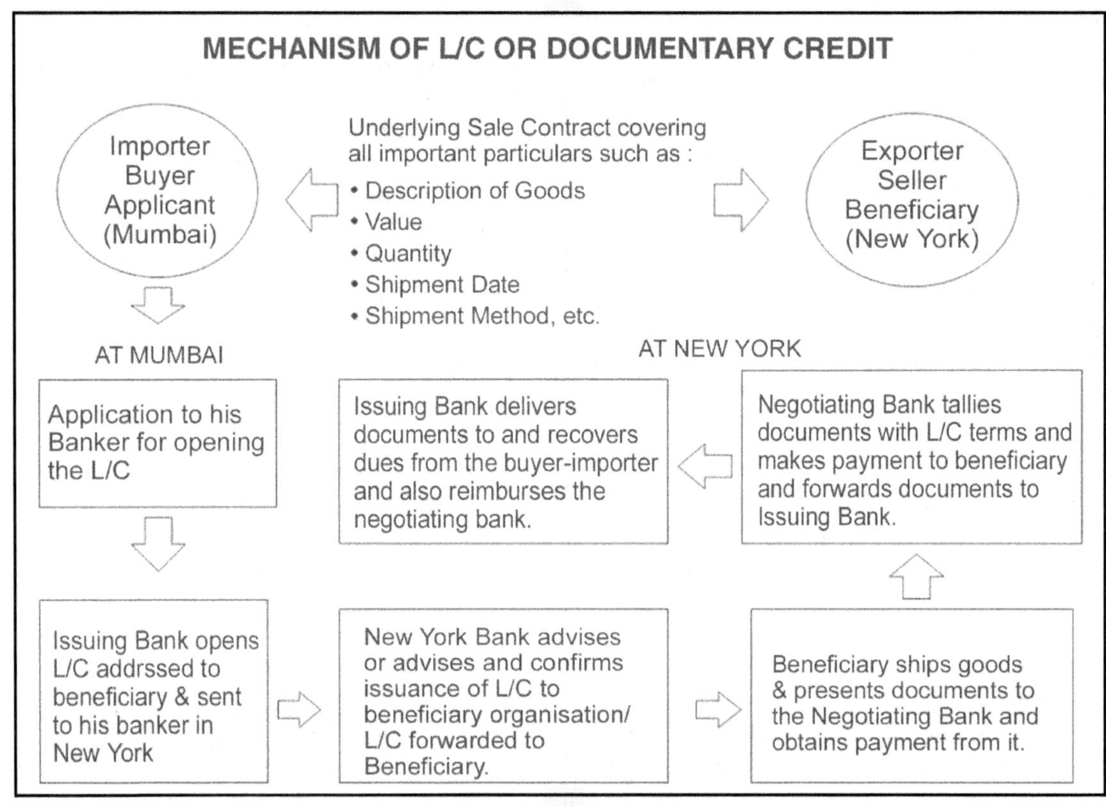

Procedure for Opening Letter of Credit

Buyer entered in to a contract with overseas supplier to import machinery at his factory. As per their contract, buyer needs to open a Letter of credit (LC) in favour of exporter/seller. Banker has to verify the following documents of the buyer/importer:

- ❖ IEC No. of the buyer,
- ❖ Whether Goods/Services under LC is permitted under Foreign Trade Policy or not,
- ❖ Import License of the buyer if applicable,
- ❖ FEMA Guidelines about the items imported.

The customer's financial standing, line of business, frequency of imports, sales, account turnover, satisfactory track record of importer for import of goods, etc. are also scrutinised.

SWIFT Code

SWIFT is the short form of "Society for Worldwide Interbank Financial Telecommunication". In simple terms swift has two main roles in international financial transactions, firstly SWIFT provide a secure communications platform by which financial institutions can communicate each other reliably & fast and secondly SWIFT establishes standard message formats which can be used on secure SWIFT platforms. Today banks use SWIFT platform to communicate each other when sending a wire transfer, issuing a letter of credit, advising a discrepancy message etc. Each of these message formats have a different code, which is called swift message types. For example a bank must use MT700 (MT means Message Type) Issue of a Documentary Credit when issuing a letter of credit and MT 734 advice of a refusal when giving its refusal message.

Important Note: According to the current letters of credit rules, UCP 600, a letter of credit will be deemed to be operative letter of credit, if it is transmitted via an authenticated electronic platform such as SWIFT.

Standard Forms of Documents

When making payment for product on behalf of its customer, the issuing bank must verify that all documents and drafts conform precisely to the terms and conditions of the letter of credit. Although the credit can require an array of documents, the most common documents that must accompany the draft include:

- **Commercial Invoice:** The billing for the goods and services. It includes a description of merchandise, price, FOB origin, and name and address of buyer and seller. The buyer and seller information must correspond exactly to the description in the letter of credit. Unless the letter of credit specifically states otherwise, a generic description of the merchandise is usually acceptable in the other accompanying documents.

- **Bill of Exchange:** This is a financial document. Payment is made on this document. In a letter of credit transaction the right to draw a bill is conferred only on the beneficiary. The bill amount should be within the limit fixed in the letter of credit. The tenor, endorsement and the drawee should be the same as given in the letter of credit.

- **Transport Documents:** The mode of dispatch of goods or the transporting of goods would depend on terms of contract between buyer and seller and the same is incorporated in letter of credit. The two main modes of transport of goods are either by se or by air.

- **Bill of Lading:** A document evidencing the receipt of goods for shipment and issued by a freight carrier engaged in the business of forwarding or transporting goods. The documents evidence control of goods. They also serve as a receipt for the merchandise shipped and as evidence of the carrier's obligation to transport the goods to their proper destination.

- **Airway Bill:** This is a document, which evidences that the goods have been received by an airline company or its agent. Unlike a bill of lading an airway bill does not carry with it the right to the goods, *i.e.*, it is not a document of title to the goods.

- **Postal Parcel Receipt and Courier Receipts:** When the goods to be sent are small in quantity, then they can be sent through post or courier. The document issued by the postal department or courier are similar in nature to the airway bill.

- **Warranty of Title:** A warranty given by a seller to a buyer of goods that states that the title being conveyed is good and that the transfer is rightful. This is a method of certifying clear title to product transfer. It is generally issued to the purchaser and issuing bank expressing an agreement to indemnify and hold both parties harmless.

- **Insurance Document:** The goods shipped, if required to be insured under the terms of the letter of credit should be so insured and the insurance document as required in the letter of credit should be enclosed with the other documents. The type of insurance cover should be the same as specified in the credit.

- **Letter of Indemnity:** Specifically indemnifies the purchaser against a certain stated circumstance. Indemnification is generally used to guaranty that shipping documents will be provided in good order when available.

Risks in Letter of Credit Transactions

Letter of credit transactions are not risks free. The risks inherent in these types of transactions include:

- **Fraud Risks:** The payment will be obtained for non-existent or worthless merchandise against presentation by the beneficiary of forged or falsified documents. Credit itself may be funded.

- **Sovereign and Regulatory Risks:** Performance of the Documentary Credit may be prevented by government action outside the control of the parties.

- **Legal Risks:** Possibility that performance of a documentary credit may be disturbed by legal action relating directly to the parties and their rights and obligations under the documentary credit.

- **Force Majeure Risk:** In which completion of the transaction is prevented by an external force, such as war or natural disaster.

INCOTERMS
(International Commercial Terms) 2000

INCOTERMS introduced by International chamber of commerce in 1936. INCOTERMS or International Commercial Terms are a series of international sales terms widely used throughout the world. INCOTERMS are designed to create a bridge between different members of the industry by acting as a uniform language they can use. From 1st January 2000, the ICC once again updated Incoterms to follow the modern trends in international trade. INCOTERMS 2000 are the standard terms of trade that define the rights and obligations of the parties involved in trade. It specifies the responsibility of the buyer and the seller by defining the transaction and the cost aspects concerning the transaction and especially related to carriage, custom duties as well as Insurance, etc. However it limits itself to the scope of the liability of costs and definition thereof and does not deal with the ownership or transfer of title of goods.

INCOTERMS 2000 are divided into 4 groups namely E, F, C & D.

1. **GROUP-E (Ex Work or Factory Cost):** This group contains only one Incoterm namely EXW.

   EXW (Ex. Works): This term represents minimum liability on the part of the Seller. Seller's responsibility ends with delivering goods at his factory doc. The rest of the risk and expenses involved are borne by the Buyer and would have to be carried out through his agent at origin.

2. **GROUP-F (Freight Unpaid):** Consists of FCA, FAS & FOB terms. Under this category the seller pays for the pre carriage expenses at the origin and the main carriages as well as destination charges are borne by the buyer.

   FCA (Free Carrier): Seller delivers goods to the Buyer's nominated vehicle and his responsibility ceases with delivery. Unloading, transportation as well as Insurance from this point will be borne by the Buyer.

   FAS (Free Alongside Ship): Seller completes export formalities and delivers cargo alongside ship. From this point onwards the risk and costs including transportation and Insurance pass on to the Buyer.

   FOB (Free on Board): Seller is responsible for inland transportation, export clearance as well as delivery cargo on board the Ship. Once on board the Ship the risk and responsibility shifts to the Buyer who pays the transportation, Insurance and destination charges.

3. **GROUP-C (Freight Paid):** Under this group the Seller arranges for and pays for transportation but does not take on the risk.

   CFR (Cost and Freight): Seller pays transportation cost up to destination port. Insurance and risk are with the buyer from the time the seller delivers cargo on board.

CIF (Cost, Insurance & Freight): Seller pays for transportation and insurance but the risk passes to the buyer as soon as the cargo is delivered on board the ship.

CPT (Seller pays Transportation): Seller pays transportation cost. The risk and insurance lies with the buyer from the point of delivery of cargo to the carrier by the seller.

CIP (Carriage & Insurance Paid to): Seller pays transportation and insurance. The risk passes to the buyer when seller delivers cargo to carrier.

4. **GROUP-D (Delivery at Destination):** Under this group the seller assumes all or most of the risk and takes responsibility of delivery at destination upto the agreed point of delivery.

   DAF (Delivered at Frontier): Seller responsible to deliver cargo upto the point of entry at destination. Risk and responsibility further passes on to the buyer.

   DES (Delivered Ex Ship): Seller assumes risk until the ship with the cargo reaches the port of destination. Then the risk shifts to buyer from the point of discharge of vessel onwards.

   DEQ (Delivered Ex. Quay Duty Paid): Seller takes responsibility until the cargo is delivered after import clearance at destination and customs duty paid and delivered to the point on buyers dock.

   DDU (Delivered Duty Unpaid): Seller takes responsibility to deliver cargo at the destination port where the buyer takes on the responsibility for import clearance, Import duties and onward delivery.

   DDP (Delivered Duty Paid): Seller takes responsibility until the cargo reaches destination, clears the customs, pays the duty and delivers cargo at buyer's dock.

INCOTERMS 2000 can be easily explained in the below mention figure:

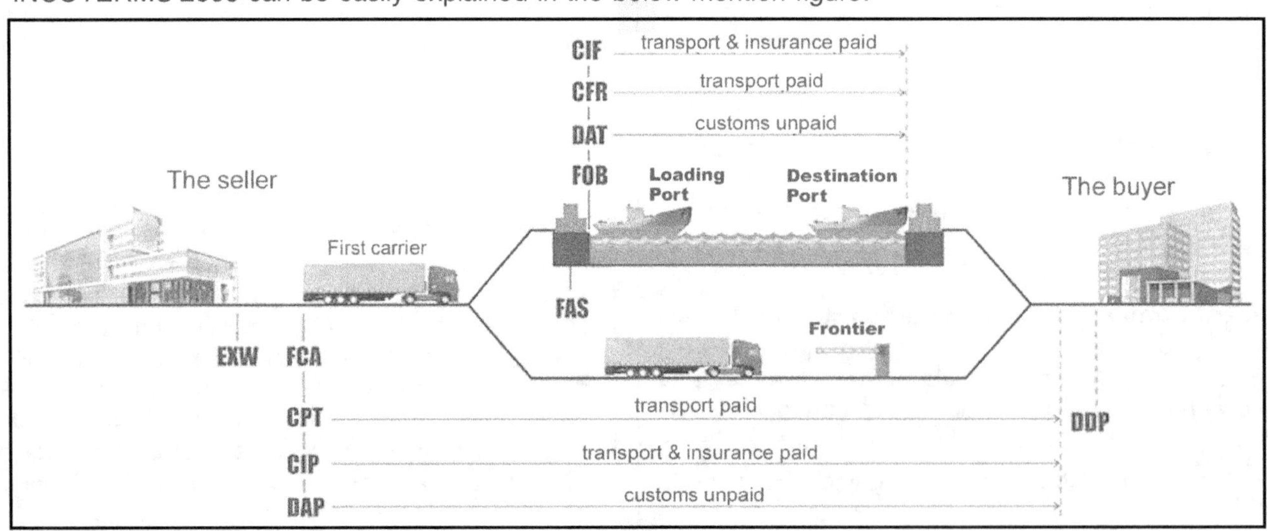

UCPDC (Uniform Customs and Practice for Documentary Credits) 600

This revision of the Uniform Customs and Practice for Documentary Credits (commonly called "UCP") is the sixth revision of the rules since they were first promulgated in 1933. It is the fruit of more than three years of work by the International Chamber of Commerce's (ICC) Commission on Banking Technique and Practice. UCP 600 is the latest revision of the Uniform Customs and Practice that govern the operation of letters of credit. UCP 600 comes into effect on 01 July 2007. The 39 articles of UCP 600 are a comprehensive and practical working aid to bankers, lawyers, importers, and exporters, transport executives, educators, and everyone involved in letter of credit transactions worldwide.

○ **Article-I:** UCPDC-600 apply to any LC when its text expressly indicates that it is subject to these rules. The rules are binding on all parties thereto unless expressly modified or excluded by the credit.

○ **Article-3 Interpretations:** A credit is irrevocable even if there is no indication to that effect.

On or About: Such expression will be interpreted as a stipulation that an event is to occur during a period of 5 calendar days before until 5 calendar days after the specified date, both start and end dates included.

The words **'to', 'until', 'from' and 'between'** when used to determine a period of shipment include the date mentioned and the words 'before' and 'after' exclude the date mentioned.

The words **'from' and 'after'** when used to determine a maturity date exclude the date mentioned.

The terms **'first half' and 'second half'** of a month shall be construed respectively as the 1st to the 15th and the 16th to the last day of the month, all dates inclusive.

The terms **'beginning', 'middle' and 'end'** of a month shall be construed respectively as the 1st to 10th, the 11th to the 20th and the 21st to the last day of the month, all dates inclusive.

Branches in Different Countries are considered to be separate banks.

○ **Article-5: Documents v. Goods:** Banks deal with documents and not with goods, services or performance to which documents relate

○ **Article-9: Advising of Credits and Amendments:** A credit and any amendment may be advised to a beneficiary through an advising bank. An advising bank advises the credit and any amendment without any undertaking to negotiate. By advising the credit, the advising bank signifies that it has satisfied itself as to the apparent authenticity of the credit and the advice accurately reflects the terms and conditions of the credit or amendment received.

○ **Article-10:** Amendment: A credit can neither be amended nor cancelled without the agreement of the issuing bank, the confirming bank and the beneficiary. Partial acceptance is not allowed and will be deemed to be notification of rejection of the amendment.

○ **Article-14:** Standard for Examination of Documents:

(a) A nominated bank and issuing bank shall each have a maximum of 5 banking days following the day of presentation to determine if documents are in order.

(b) A presentation must be made by or on behalf of the beneficiary not later than 21 calendar days after the date of shipment as described in these rules, but in any event not later than the expiry date of the credit.

(c) A document may be dated prior to the issuance date of the credit, but must not be dated later than its date of presentation.

○ **Article-19:** The date of issuance of the transport documents will be deemed to date of despatch, taking in charge or shipped on board and the date of shipment. If the transport document indicates, by stamp or notation, a date of despatch taking in charge or shipped on board, this date will be deemed to the date of shipment.

Trans-shipment means unloading from one means of conveyance and reloading to another means of conveyance (whether or not in different modes of transport) during the carriage, 'from the place of dispatch taking in charge or shipment to the place of final destination stated in the credit.

○ **Article-27:** A clean transport documents is one bearing no clause of notation expressly declaring a defective condition of the goods or their packaging. If there is no indication in the credit about **insurance coverage,** amount of insurance coverage must be at least 110% of CIF or CIP value of the goods.

○ **Article-30:** Tolerance in Credit Amount, Quantity and Unit Prices:

(a) The words "about" or "apprx' used in connection with the amount of LC or the quantity or the unit price stated in the LC are to be construed as allowing a tolerance not to exceed 10% more or 10% less than the amount, the quantity or the unit price to which they refer.

(b) A maximum tolerance of 5% more or 5% less than the quantity of the goods is allowed, where the credit does not state quantity in terms of a stipulated no. of packing units or individual items and the total amount of the drawings does not exceed the amount of LC.

(c) Even when partial shipments are not allowed, a tolerance not to exceed 5% less than the amount of the credit is allowed, provided that the quantity of the goods, if stated in the credit, is shipped in full and a unit price, if stated in the credit, is not reduced or that sub-article 30 (b) is not applicable.

Common Defects in Documentation

About half of all drawings presented contain discrepancies. A discrepancy is an irregularity in the documents that causes them to be in non-compliance to the letter of credit. Requirements set forth in the letter of credit cannot be waived or altered by the issuing bank without the express consent of the customer. The beneficiary should prepare and examine all documents carefully before presentation to the paying bank to avoid any delay in receipt of payment. Commonly found discrepancies between the letter of credit and supporting documents include:

❖ Letter of Credit has expired prior to presentation of draft.

❖ Bill of Lading evidences delivery prior to or after the date range stated in the credit.

❖ Stale dated documents.

❖ Changes included in the invoice not authorized in the credit.

❖ Inconsistent description of goods.

❖ Insurance document errors.

❖ Invoice amount not equal to draft amount.

❖ Ports of loading and destination not as specified in the credit.

❖ Description of merchandise is not as stated in credit.

❖ A document required by the credit is not presented.

❖ Documents are inconsistent as to general information such as volume, quality, etc.

❖ Names of documents not exact as described in the credit. Beneficiary information must be exact.

❖ Invoice or statement is not signed as stipulated in the letter of credit.

When a discrepancy is detected by the negotiating bank, a correction to the document may be allowed if it can be done quickly while remaining in the control of the bank. If time is not a factor, the exporter should request that the negotiating bank return the documents for corrections.

TEST YOURSELF

1. Who request his banker to open a LC?
   a) Buyer
   (b) Seller
   (c) Exporter
   (d) Any one

2. Which of the followings are advantage of the buyer or importer?
   (a) No cash advance payment has to be made to the seller
   (b) Possibility to stipulate favourable terms and condition to protect his interest
   (c) Shipment schedule ensured
   (d) All of the above

3. Which of the followings are advantage of the seller or exporter?
   (a) Obligation of the buyer's bank for payment and payment is assured if credit terms are fulfilled
   (b) Date of receipt of payment can be determined and seller need not bother about the fluctuation of currency
   (c) A financing possibility by discounting receivables under LC
   (d) All of the above

4. Letter of credit can resolve the Complications/ Contradictions arise in international trade due mainly to involvement of two countries separated by differences in:
   (a) Physical barriers–long distances
   (b) Currencies
   (c) Trade and exchange regulations
   (d) All of the above

5. The LC issuing bank is also called:
   (a) Importer's bank or the opening bank
   (b) Negotiating bank
   (c) Advising Bank
   (d) Confirming bank

6. Who is entitled to receive the payment on delivering of documents stipulated in a LC?
   (a) Beneficiary
   (b) Negotiating bank
   (c) Advising Bank
   (d) Confirming bank

7. Which is the role of Negotiating Bank?
   (a) The bank that hands over the LC to the beneficiary

(b) Negotiates documents delivered to bank by bene-ficiary of LC.

(c) The bank that opens the LC

(d) None of the above

8. Which is the role of Reimbursing Bank?
   (a) It reimburse the payment to the seller
   (b) It reimburse the payment to the applicant bank
   (c) It reimburse the payment to the advising bank
   (d) It reimburse the payment to the negotiating bank

9. The letter of credit where documents are paid imme-diately are called:
   (a) Sight credit   (b) Usance credit
   (c) Revocable credit   (d) Demand credit

10. The letter of credit where packing or anticipatory credit is available against the LC is called:
    (a) Transferable LC   (b) Red clause LC
    (c) Back to back LC   (d) Revolving LC

11. Transferable letter of credit can be transferred:
    (a) Any number of times
    (b) Only once
    (c) 2 times
    (d) As per instruction of issuer

12. When a seller undertakes to make the goods available for export, at his factory, such arrangement is called:
    (a) Ex-works   (b) FOB
    (c) CIF   (d) CFR

13. Back to back letter of credit means:
    (a) A revolving credit
    (b) Another credit behind the credit issued
    (c) Issuance of another credit on the security of the original letter of credit
    (d) LC which is backed by a tangible security

14. The confirming bank is:
    (a) The issuing bank when it confirms the issue of the LC
    (b) The negotiating bank when it confirms the negotiation of the bills
    (c) The advising bank when it confirms the LC
    (d) None of the above

15. Which of the following documents are necessarily accompany by letter of credit?
    (a) Bill of exchange   (b) Invoice
    (c) Transport document   (d) All of the above

16. INCOTERMS 2000 are divided into 4 groups namely __________.
    (a) A, B, C & D   (b) W, X, Y & Z
    (c) E, F, C & D   (d) 1, 2, 3 & 4

17. What time is available to the opening for scrutiny of documents?
    (a) 3 working days   (b) 3 calendar days
    (c) 5 working days   (d) 5 calendar days

18. If a letter of credit is silent about the expiry date of presentation of documents, documents are to be presented within how many days:
    (a) 14 days   (b) 21 days
    (c) 30 days   (d) 7 days

19. A letter of credit is a:
    (a) Negotiable Instrument
    (b) Not negotiable Instrument
    (c) Quasi negotiable Instrument
    (d) None of the above

20. A 'Clean Transport Document' means:
    (a) Nothing is mentioned in transport document
    (b) It does not declare any defect in the condition of goods or packaging
    (c) Neatly typed or written
    (d) None of the above

ANSWER

1	2	3	4	5	6	7	8	9	10
(a)	(d)	(d)	(d)	(a)	(a)	(b)	(d)	(a)	(b)

11	12	13	14	15	16	17	18	19	20
(b)	(a)	(c)	(a)	(d)	(c)	(a)	(b)	(b)	(b)

CHAPTER 13

LAWS RELATING TO BILL FINANCE

INTRODUCTION

Bill finance is one of the major activities of the Banks. Under this type of lending, Bank takes the bill drawn by borrower on his (borrower's) customer and pays him immediately deducting some amount as discount/commission. The Bank then presents the Bill to the borrower's customer on the due date of the Bill and collects the proceeds. If the bill is delayed, the borrower or his customer pays the Bank a pre-determined interest depending upon the terms of transaction. The transaction is practically an advance against the security of the bill which is due for payment.

BILL OF EXCHANGE

Section 5 of the NI Act defines, "A bill of exchange is an instrument in writing containing an unconditional order, signed by the maker, directing a certain person to pay a certain sum of money only to, or to the order of a certain person or to the bearer of the instrument".

A bill of exchange, therefore, is a written acknowledgement of the debt, written by the creditor and accepted by the debtor. There are usually three parties to a bill of exchange drawer, acceptor or drawee and payee. Drawer himself may be the payee.

Essential Conditions of a Bill of Exchange

(1) It must be in writing.

(2) It must be signed by the drawer.

(3) The drawer, drawee and payee must be certain.

(4) The sum payable must also be certain.

(5) It should be properly stamped.

(6) It must contain an express order to pay money and money alone.

For example, In the following cases, there is no order to pay, but only a request to pay. Therefore, none can be considered as a bill of exchange:

(a) "I shall be highly obliged if you make it convenient to pay ₹ 1000 to Suresh".

(b) "Mr. Ramesh, please let the bearer have one thousand rupees, and place it to my account and oblige". However, there is an order to pay, though it is politely made, in the following examples:

(i) Please pay ₹ 500 to the order of 'A'.

(ii) 'Mr. A will oblige Mr. C, by paying to the order of 'P'.

(7) The order must be unconditional.

PARTIES TO A BOE

Section 7 of the NI Act defines different parties of bill of exchange.

1. **Drawer:** The maker of a bill of exchange is called the 'drawer'.

2. **Drawee:** The person directed to pay the money is called the 'drawee',

3. **Acceptor:** After a drawee of a bill has signed his assent upon the bill, or if there are more parts than one, upon one of such parts and delivered the same, or given notice of such signing to the holder or to some person on his behalf, he is called the 'acceptor'.

4. **Payee:** The person named in the instrument, to whom or to whose order the money is directed to be paid by the instrument is called the 'payee'. He is the real beneficiary under the instrument.

5. **Endorser:** When the holder transfers or endorses the instrument to anyone else, the holder becomes the 'Endorser'.

6. **Endorsee:** The person to whom the bill is endorsed is called an 'Endorsee'.

7. **Holder & Holder in Due Course:** A person who is legally entitled to the possession of the negotiable instrument in his own name and to receive the amount thereof, is called a 'holder'. 'Holder in Due Course' means any person who for consideration became the possessor of the bill (that is a person to whom the bill is transferred).

8. **Acceptor for Honour:** In case the original drawee refuses to accept the bill or to furnish better security when demanded by the notary, any person who is not liable on the bill, may accept it with the consent of the holder, for the honour of any party liable on the bill. Such an acceptor is called 'acceptor for honour'.

CLASSIFICATION OF BILLS

Bills can be classified as:

(1) Inland and foreign bills (Place wise)

(2) Time and demand bills (Period wise)

(3) Trade and accommodation bills (Nature wise)

(4) Clean and documentary bills (Documents wise)

(1) Inland and Foreign Bills

❖ **Inland bill:** A bill is, named as an inland bill if drawn and made payable in India. A bill drawn or made in India & payable in or drawn upon any persons in India. The necessary requisite for inland bills are:

(a) It must be drawn in India on a person residing in India, whether payable in or outside India, or

(b) It must be drawn in India on a person residing outside India but payable in India.

The following are the example of Inland bills

(i) A bill is drawn by a merchant in Delhi on a merchant in Madras. It is payable in Bombay.

(ii) A bill is drawn by a Delhi merchant on a person in London, but is made payable in India.

(iii) A bill is drawn by a merchant in Delhi on a merchant in Madras. It is accepted for payment in Japan.

❖ **Foreign Bill:** A bill which is not an inland bill is a foreign bill. The following are the foreign bills:

1. A bill drawn outside India and made payable in India.

2. A bill drawn outside India on any person residing outside India.

3. A bill drawn in India on a person residing outside India and made payable outside India.

4. A bill drawn outside India on a person residing in India.

5. A bill drawn outside India and made payable outside India.

Bill of Exchange in Sets: When the bills are in sets, (*i.e.,* first, second or third copy) as in case of foreign trade transactions, the stamp duty is paid only on one part and only one part is required to be accepted.

Bills in Sets (Secs. 132 and 133): The foreign bills are generally drawn in sets of three, and each sets is termed as a 'via'. The stamp duty is paid only on one part and only one part is required to be accepted. As soon as anyone of the set is paid, the others becomes inoperative. These bills are drawn in different parts. They are drawn in order to avoid their loss or miscarriage during transit. Each part is dispatched separately. To avoid delay, all the parts are sent on the same day; by different mode of conveyance.

(2) Time and Demand Bill

❖ **Time or Usance Bills:** A bill payable after a fixed time is termed as a time bill. In other words, bill payable "after date" is a time or usance bill.

❖ **Demand bill:** A bill payable at sight or on demand is termed as a demand bill.

(3) Trade and Accommodation Bill

❖ **Trade Bill:** A bill drawn and accepted for a genuine trade transaction is termed as a "trade bill".

❖ **Accommodation Bill:** A bill drawn and accepted not for a genuine trade transaction but only to provide financial help to some party is termed as an "accommodation bill".

Example: A, is need of money for three months. He induces his friend B to accept a bill of exchange drawn on him for ₹ 1,000 for three months. The bill is drawn and accepted. The bill is an "accommodation bill". A may get the bill discounted from his bankers immediately, paying a small sum as discount. Thus, he can use the funds for three months and then just before maturity he may remit the money to B, who will meet the bill on maturity. In the above example A is the "accommodated party" while B is the "accommodating party".

(4) Clean and Documentary Bills

* ❖ **Clean Bills**: A clean bill is a bill of exchange drawn as per requirements of the NI Act and is not supported by documents of title of goods. Clean bills are drawn normally to effect discharge of a debt or claim.

* ❖ **Documentary Bills**: A bill of exchange accompanying documents of title of goods is called documentary bill. These bills are drawn to claim price of goods supplied. The example of title of goods are Railway receipt, warehouse receipt, bill of lading, dock warrant etc.

* ❖ **Stamp duty on Bills**: The advalorem stamp duty is payable on usance bill (*i.e.*, as per amount and usance period). Following usance bills are exempted from payment of stamp duty (a) with usance period up to 90 days, where bank is a party to the bill since 1989 (b) export bills 2004. On demand bills the stamp duty is exempted.

* ❖ **Acceptance of Bill of Exchange**: The acceptance of a bills means signing by the drawer of a bill, on face with or without the words accepted and delivery thereof or giving notice of signing, to the holder of the bill. There are 2 types of acceptances *i.e.*, general acceptance and qualified acceptance. In cases of several drawees not being partners, each of them can accept it for himself but not others without their authority (Sec 34).

* ❖ **Dishonour of Bill of Exchange**: A bill of exchange is said to be dishonoured either by non-acceptance (when drawee defaults in acceptance) or by non-payment (when the acceptor/drawee makes default in payment). Similarly where the drawee is incompetent to contract or acceptance is qualified, the bill is said to be dishonoured (Section 91 & 92).

* ❖ **Notice of Dishonour**: When a bill is dishonoured, the holder thereof must give notice that the instrument has been so dishonoured to all parties whom the holder seeks to make jointly liable thereon. It is not necessary to give notice to the maker of the dishonoured promissory note, or the drawee or acceptor of the dishonoured bill of exchange or cheque (Section 93).

* ❖ **Presentation for Acceptance**: As per Section 61, a usance bill payable after sight and bills payable on a fixed date (and not demand bills) require to be presented to drawee for acceptance to make him liable and also for calculation of due date.

Rules for Due Date Calculation

* ❍ Demand bill is payable on demand or at sight.

* ❍ Usance bill should be presented for acceptance within a reasonable time.

* ❍ The drawee is allowed 48 hours excluding public holiday to accept the bill.

* ❍ If a usance bill is payable after date, its due date is calculated from date of the bill and if it is payable after sight, its due date is calculated from date of acceptance.

* ❍ 3 days grace period is given to every Usance Promissory Note or BOE.

* ❍ Where the due date is already given by the drawer, no grace period to be given.

* ❍ Instruments payable in installments, the days of grace are to be allowed for each installment.

* ❍ When the maturity date is a public holiday: As per sec 25 of NI Act, such instrument be payable on the next preceding business day *i.e.*, the previous business day.

* ❍ Declaration of Public Holiday : u/s 25 of NI Act 1881, the public holiday includes Sunday and any other day declared by the Central Govt. by notification in the Official Gazette (this power has been delegated to state government).

Date of Bill	Presented on	Accepted on	Payment Terms	Due Date
26.02.16	27.02.16	28.02.16	30 days after acceptance.	01.04.16
26.12.15	26.12.15	28.12.15	45 days after date.	12.02.16
20.12.16	21.12.16	23.12.16	1 month after sight.	25.01.17
26.02.16	27.02.16	28.02.16	3 months after acceptance.	31.05.16
26.12.15	26.12.15	28.12.15	2 months after date.	29.02.16

TYPES OF BILL FINANCE

Basically, a banker offers following types of bill finance:

1. Bill Purchase (B.P.)
2. Bill Discount (B.D.)
3. Advance against Bill for Collection (A.B.C.)

1. **Bill Purchase:** When a bank negotiates bills payable on demand, whether clean or documentary, the facility is known as bill purchase. The face value of the bill is immediately paid to the holder. The bank after purchasing the bill, become holder in due course of the bill and acquires all the right of ownership over the instrument. Bill purchase facility is extended generally in the case of bills payable on demand. However, in a case of usance bills also this is extended when the due date of the bill is not readily known at the time of extending the facility. Such a situation arises when the bill is drawn payable after some days after sight. The due date of such a bill is known when the bill is presented to the drawee and the period of usance commences from date of presentation. In the case of a demand bills the date on which it will be paid is uncertain. The drawee may pay the bill as soon as it is presented to him or he may take a few days to do so. Hence, as in the case of cheque purchase, interest for the estimated time for realization of the bill, say for 15 days, is recovered at the time of purchase. Additional interest is recovered or excess interest refunded on realization of the bill according to the actual number of days taken to realize the bill. In case of dishonour of the bill, the amount is recovered from the customer.

2. **Bill Discount:** In the case of a Usance Bill, the date of payment is certain as it becomes payable after a certain number of days after it is accepted or from the date of the bill. Hence we may be able to calculate the exact amount of interest due on the bill and recover it upfront. Interest recovered at the time of advance is called "discount". When money is against a usance bill for collection, it is called Bill Discounting. In the case of bills purchase also interest is recovered at the time of advance. However, it is only an estimated amount and not the exact amount due. Hence it is called commission and not discount.

3. **Advance Against Bill for Collection:** Banks also give advance against the bills, which are in course of collection is known as advance against bill for collection. Under this facility, a prescribed margin is kept by the bank and the amount, in consideration of this is allowed to the customer. The bill thereafter is sent for collection.

In all cases, the legal effect is that the banker, who lends money, becomes holder in due course for the bill.

Bills Discounting and Purchase are less Risky than CC facility for the following reasons :

❖ **Self-Liquidating:** Bills will be repaid when the buyer pays the bills on the due date.

❖ **Easy to Monitor:** If the bill is not paid on the due date it will be known immediately and the bank can speedily take further action for recovery of the advance.

❖ **More Secure:** The goods covered by demand bills can be taken delivery of by the buyer only after paying the bill. Hence, if the bill is not repaid the bank can take delivery of the goods and sell it to recover the advance. In the case of a usance bill, the bank can proceed against the seller and the buyer for recover. Further, since a bill is a negotiable instrument, on filing a suit, consideration need not be proved.

TEST YOURSELF

1. Bill of exchange is defined in Section ___ of NI Act 1881.
   (a) 3　　　　　　　　(b) 4
   (c) 5　　　　　　　　(d) 6

2. Bill of exchange means:
   (a) An unconditional promise to the drawer to pay moneys
   (b) An unconditional order to the drawer to pay moneys
   (c) An unconditional obligation to the drawer to pay moneys
   (d) An unconditional undertaking to the drawer to pay moneys

3. Maker of the bill of exchange is called:
   (a) Drawer　　　　　(b) Drawee
   (c) Payee　　　　　　(d) None of these

4. The person who is directed to pay the bill of exchange is called:
   (a) Drawer　　　　　(b) Drawee
   (c) Payee　　　　　　(d) None of these

5. 'Drawer' of bill of exchange is the person, who is _____.
   (a) seller of goods
   (b) buyer of goods
   (c) creditor
   (d) (a) & (c)

6. 'Holder in Due Course' means:
   - (a) Any person who for consideration became the possessor of the bill
   - (b) Any person who became the possessor of the bill
   - (c) Any person who holds the bill for some times
   - (d) Any person who pays

7. Which of the following bill can be classified on the basis of 'nature' of bill?
   - (a) Inland bills
   - (b) Usance bills
   - (c) Demand bills
   - (d) Trade bills

8. A 'Documentary bill' of exchange is a bill which accompany with:
   - (a) Documents of title of goods
   - (b) Instruction of payment
   - (c) The detail of contracts
   - (d) KYC documents of the drawer

9. Which of the following is not true for inland bill of exchange?
   - (a) It must be drawn in India
   - (b) It must be payable in India
   - (c) It must be drawn upon some person resident of India
   - (d) None of the above

10. 'Bill purchase' facility is available for:
    - (a) Clean bill
    - (b) Documentary bill
    - (c) Both clean & documentary bill
    - (d) None of the above

11. Bank offers 'Bill discounting' facility on:
    - (a) Demand bill
    - (b) Usance bill
    - (c) Either 'a' or 'b'
    - (d) Neither 'a' nor 'b'

12. What will be due date for a bill dated 15.04.2016, payable 80 days after date:
    - (a) 7th July 2014
    - (b) 4th July 2014
    - (c) 6th July 2014
    - (d) 5th July 2014

13. In case of 'Bill purchase' or 'Bill discounting', bankers becomes:
    - (a) Holder
    - (b) Holder in due course
    - (c) Possessor
    - (d) Negotiator

14. A bill of exchange is not supported by any documents of title of goods is called:
    - (a) Demand documentary bill
    - (b) Clean bill
    - (c) Usance documentary bill
    - (d) Incomplete bill

15. If a bill of exchange, time of payment is not mentioned, it is __________.
    - (a) Payable on demand
    - (b) Invalid bill
    - (c) Incomplete bill
    - (d) Not negotiable

16. Noting or protesting is compulsory in case of:
    - (a) Foreign bill
    - (b) Inland bill
    - (c) Accommodation bill
    - (d) Usance bill of exchange

17. A bill is presented to drawee. What is the period during which he is to give his acceptance?
    - (a) 3 days including holidays
    - (b) 3 days excluding holidays
    - (c) 48 hours including holidays
    - (d) 48 hours excluding holidays

18. A firm supplies material to various Government departments, against payment to be received subsequently. Such bills are called:
    - (a) Usance bill
    - (b) Supply bill
    - (c) Government bill
    - (d) Accommodation bill

19. Which of the following, attached to a bill of exchange makes the bill documentary bill of exchange?
    - (a) Railway receipt, airway bill, bill of lading
    - (b) Railway receipt, warehouse receipt, bill of lading
    - (c) Railway receipt, airway bill, warehouse receipt
    - (d) All of the above

20. Ownership of goods can be transferred by endorsement and delivery of __________.
    - (a) Right to money
    - (b) Obligation to pay
    - (c) Document of title of goods
    - (d) Document of title of immovable property

ANSWER

1	2	3	4	5	6	7	8	9	10
(c)	(b)	(a)	(b)	(d)	(a)	(d)	(a)	(d)	(c)

11	12	13	14	15	16	17	18	19	20
(b)	(a)	(b)	(b)	(a)	(a)	(d)	(b)	(b)	(c)

VARIOUS TYPES OF SECURITIES

INTRODUCTION

An advance made by a bank is generally covered by primary or collateral securities. The effectiveness of the security depend on the nature of security. The securities can be classified in two aspects, economic and legal aspect. Economic aspect covers marketability, valuation and other economic factors of the security. The other legal aspect is the validity and enforceability of the security. As per banking terms, the securities can be classified as Primary and Collateral.

Primary security is the asset created out of the credit facility extended to the borrower and / or which are directly associated with the business / project of the borrower for which the credit facility has been extended. Collateral security is any other security offered for the said credit facility. For example, hypothecation of jewellery, mortgage of house, etc.

Attributes of good security are as follows:

❖ **Title of the Security:** The borrower should have a good title to the security.

❖ **Non Encumbrance:** The security should not have any encumbrance or liability.

❖ **Market Ability:** The security should be easily marketable.

❖ **Ascertain Ability:** The value of security should be easily ascertainable.

❖ **Stability of Value:** The security should not be liable to wide price fluctuation.

❖ **Storability:** Storing of the security should not be difficult.

❖ **Transferability:** The security should be easily and freely transferable.

❖ **Durability:** The security should be durable.

❖ **Transportable:** The security should be easily transportable.

On the basis of security, loan may be classified as follows:

Unsecured Loans

Unsecured advance don't have supported by any collateral. The unsecured loans are given without any tangible security or assets but merely on the strength of the integrity or the "credit worthiness" of the borrower. Unsecured loans rely solely on borrower credit history and his income to qualify for the loan. e.g.- Credit Card, Clean personal loan, Education loan (small) etc. In other words credit worthiness is the confidence of a Banker on the future solvency of a person. They are also called clean loans.

Secured Advance

The advance which is secured by any tangible security is called Secured Advances. A loan or advance made on the security of assets the market value of which is not at any time less than the amount of such loan or advance. In the event of loan default, the lender can take possession of the asset and use it to cover the loan. e.g. Business loan, housing loan etc.

VARIOUS KINDS OF SECURITIES

Bank accepts various kinds of tangible assets as security after creating the charge. Some important types of securities are as under:

1. **Land & Building/Real Estate:** It is a common security accepted by bank. During the lending bank mortgaged the landed property in favour of bank. The advantage of these type of securities is that its value generally increases over the time. It is fixed and cannot be shifted to other place. It can be freehold or leasehold property. Valuation of the property is required for accepting as a security in the loan account.

2. **Term Deposit Receipt:** TDR is most common security accepted by a bank. This security is certainly most valuable, as the money represented by the receipt is already with the bank. It is easy know the present value and liquidation of a TDR. The banker normally grant the advance only to the person in whose name the money is deposited. Banker should not advance against fixed deposit receipt of other bank. If deposit is in the joint names the request for the loan must come from all of them.

   When the deposit receipt is taken as security, the banker should ensure that all the depositors duly discharge it on the back of the instrument. In addition of this, the banker should obtain letter of appropriation which authorises the banker to appropriate the amount of the deposit on maturity or earlier towards the loan amount. Bank has to lien the TDR before disbursement of loan.

3. **Goods/Stocks:** The banker gets a tangible form of security, which in case of default by the borrower, can be realised by sale of pledged goods. Banker acquires a good title to the goods when dealing with customers of repute and standing. Banker should take care while accepting the goods as a security because certain goods are liable to perish or deteriorate in quality over a period of time, thus resulting in reduction of the value of the security.

   Advance are given based on the stocks and their value declared in monthly stock statement. Stock statement must be verified by factory or godown inspection.

4. **Life Insurance Policy:** A life insurance policy is generally taken for both financial security and saving purpose. The assignment of the policy in favour of the banker requires very few formalities and the banker obtains a perfect title. The policy is tangible security and in the custody of the bank. The security can be realised immediately on the borrower's default of payment by surrendering the policy to the insurance company. In the event of the borrower's death, the debt is easily liquidated from the proceeds of the policy.

5. **Book Debts:** Borrowers can take advance by assigning book debt in favour of the bank. The assignment must be in writing and signed by the transferor or his duly authorised agent. The assignment may be absolute or by way of charge. As an actionable claim include future debt, there can be a valid assignment of future debt as well. The value of security depends on the solvency of the debtor and his right of set off, if any. The banker must enquire into both aspects.

6. **Gold Loan:** Banks give loan against gold ornaments for agriculture as well as non-agriculture purpose. Bank pledge the gold and allow loan or overdraft against the security of gold ornaments. Now a days, Bank also accept Gold bond as a security.

7. **Paper Security:** Bank accept various types of deposit receipt such as NSC, KVP, UTI Bond etc as a security and financed against them. Bank must create charge on such paper during the financing.

8. **Share/Debenture:** Banks normally accepted only quoted shares as security. Value of the security can be ascertain easily and creating of charge on share is less expensive. In case of debenture, a charge is created on the assets of the company issuing such debenture in favour of a trustee who is responsible to take care of the interest of individual investors.

9. **Vehicle Financing:** Bank grant loan for purchase of vehicles against security by way of hypothecation of vehicle. The hypothecation charge is required to be registered with the concerned Regional Transport Authority (RTO). In some cases bank accept vehicle as a collateral security after hypothecated with RTO.

Supply Bills

Supply bills arise in relation to transaction with the Government and public sector undertaking. A party might have taken a contract for execution, and he is entitled to progressive payment based on work done, for which he has to submit bills in accordance with the term and condition of the contract. Similarly, parties who have accepted tenders for supply of goods over a period are entitled to payment on the supply of goods, for which they submit bills in accordance with the term of the contract. These bills are known as supply bills. Advance against supply bills should be made only to borrowers who have sufficient experience in Government business and Government regulations. The banker should obtain a power of attorney from the supplier authorising him to receive the money. The same should be registered with appropriate Government department.

TEST YOURSELF

1. Which of the following is a characteristic of good security?
   (a) Marketability   (b) Storability
   (c) Transferability   (d) All of the above

2. Which of the following security is not a self-liquidating security?
   (a) Bank's TDR   (b) LIC policy
   (c) Land & Building   (d) NSC

3. The nature of charge created while granting advance against security of goods is:
   (a) Hypothecation   (b) Pledge
   (c) Lien   (d) 'a' & 'b'

4. Hypothecation is defined in:
   (a) Transfer of property act
   (b) SARFAESI act
   (c) Indian contract act
   (d) It is not defined in any act

5. Charge creation on LIC policy is:
   (a) Assignment   (b) Pledge
   (c) Lien   (d) Hypothecation

6. Which is not a character of a good security?
   (a) The security should have encumbrance or liability.
   (b) The security should be easily marketable.
   (c) The value of security should be easily ascertainable.
   (d) The security should not be liable to wide price fluctuation.

7. Which is an a attributes of a good security?
   (a) The security should be easily and freely transferable.
   (b) The security should be durable.
   (c) The security should be easily transportable.
   (d) All of the above

8. Which of the following value of LIC policy is taken while taking as a security?
   (a) Maturity value   (b) Face value
   (c) Surrender value   (d) Insured value

9. Advance against shares can be made if shares are:
   (a) In physical form   (b) Party paid shares
   (c) Fully paid shares   (d) All of the above

10. _______ arises in relation to transaction of sales of goods, with government and public sector undertaking.
    (a) Supply bills   (b) Accommodation bills
    (c) Trust receipt   (d) Inspection notes

11. Dock warrants, bills of lading, Warehouse receipt are the example of:
    (a) Documents are title to negotiable instrument
    (b) Documents are title to goods
    (c) Documents are title to immovable property
    (d) Documents are title to movable property

12. Charge creation on Land & building and Plant & Machinery permanent fasten with the earth is __________.
    (a) Assignment   (b) Pledge
    (c) Mortgage   (d) Hypothecation

13. Which of the following is preferable security from liquidity point of view:
    (a) Immovable property
    (b) Debenture
    (c) Quoted equity shares
    (d) Stocks

14. The bank is considered to be Pawnee in case of which of the following securities?
    (a) Stocks of goods   (b) Shares
    (c) Immovable property   (d) Debenture

15. On which of the following security, the charge hypothecation, pledge or lien can be created?
    (a) Stocks of goods
    (b) Book debts
    (c) Immovable property
    (d) Bank's TDR

ANSWER

1	2	3	4	5	6	7	8	9	10
(d)	(c)	(d)	(b)	(a)	(a)	(d)	(c)	(c)	(a)

11	12	13	14	15
(b)	(c)	(c)	(a)	(a)

LAWS RELATING TO SECURITIES AND MODES OF CHARGING

INTRODUCTION

Bank accepts different types of securities during the lending and create charge upon them. When land/buildings and fixed assets which is permanently fastened with the earth is offered as a security, it is charged by mortgage in favour of bank. When movable goods are offered as a security, these are charged as pledge or hypothecation. Paper securities are lien or assigned in favour of bank. The law relating to the different types of securities are defined in the concern Acts. Different types of securities, charges and related acts are as under.

Nature of Security	Types of Security	Kind of Charge	Defined in Act	
Immovable Property	Land & Building	Mortgage	Transfer of Property Act (58)	
Actionable Claims (i.e. unsecured debts)	Book debts, FDR, NSC, Life Policies	Assignment	Transfer of Property Act (130, 135)	
Movable Property/Goods	Plant & Machinery, Stocks, Vehicles etc	Pledge or hypothecation or lien as agreed between bank and borrower	Lien	Indian Contract Act (170,171)
			Pledge	Indian Contract Act (172)
			Hypothecation	SARFAESI Act-2(n)
Paper Securities	Shares, debentures, mutual fund units, bonds	Lien		Indian Contract Act (170,171)

MORTGAGE

Mortgage is defined in Transfer of Property Act 1882 Section 58(a). As per the Act:

"A mortgage is the transfer of an interest in specific immoveable property for the purpose of securing the payment of money advanced or to be advanced by way of loan, an existing or future debt, or the performance of an engagement which may give rise to a pecuniary liability".

The transferor is called a 'mortgagor', the transferee a 'mortgagee'; the principal money and interest of which payment is secured for the time being are called the mortgage-money, and the instrument (if any) by which the transfer is effected is called a 'mortgage-deed'.

Interest in the Property & Possession: The mortgagor only parts with the interest in the property and not the ownership. Mortgage is not merely a contract but it is conveyance of interest in the mortgaged property. As regards the possession, except for usufructuary mortgage, the possession remains with the mortgagor.

Essential Features of Mortgages

Essential features of mortgage are as under:

- **Loan Amount:** Mortgages can be created to cover general balances, existing payment as well as future loans or advances.
- **Relationship:** There must be a creditor and debtor relationship (or contract of guarantee) between the bank and the mortgagor at the time of deposit of title deed.
- **Future Debt:** Actual existence of the debit is not necessary. Even an application for debt and its acceptance establishes this relationship.
- **Effective Date:** A registered mortgage (and equitable mortgage) becomes effective from date of mortgage (Section 47 & 48 of Indian Registration Act).
- **Enhanced Limits:** To cover the enhanced bank limits, a supplemental registration deed is required because the mortgage already does not cover the enhanced amount.
- **Repayment of Loan:** On repayment of debt, the mortgage does not remain valid.

Different Types of Mortgage are as under:

Types of mortgage defined in Transfer of Property Act 1882 Section 58(b) to 58(g).

1. **Simple Mortgage: Sec. 58(b)**—Where, without delivering possession of the mortgaged property, the mortgagor binds himself personally to pay the mortgage money, and agrees, expressly or impliedly, that, in the event of his failing to pay according to his contract, the mortgagee shall have a right to cause the mortgaged property to be sold and the proceeds of sale to be applied, so far as may be necessary, in payment of the mortgage-money, the transaction is called a simple mortgage and the mortgagee a simple mortgagee. Features of Simple mortgage are:
   - Mortgagee has no power to sell the property without court intervention.
   - Mortgagee has no right to get any payments out of the rents and produce of the mortgage property.
   - Mortgagee is not put in possession of the property.
   - Registration of the mortgage is compulsory if the principle amount secured is ₹ 100 and above.
   - Mortgagor is personally liable also.

2. **Mortgage by Conditional Sale: Sec. 58(c)**—In this, the mortgagor ostensibly sells the mortgaged property on conditions that on default of payment of the mortgage money, the sale shall become absolute or on such payment being made, the sale shall become *void* or the buyer shall transfer the property to the seller. Features are as under:
   - Sale is ostensible and not real.
   - If money remains unpaid as per agreement, the sale becomes absolute. The mortgagee by applying to court can get decree in his favour where after the mortgagor loses the right of redemption.
   - Mortgagee can sue for foreclosure.
   - No personal liability for repayment of the loan.

3. **Usufructuray Mortgage: Sec. 58(d)**—Where the mortgagor delivers possession or expressly or by implication binds himself to deliver possession of the mortgaged property to the mortgagee, and authorizes him to retain such possession until payment of the mortgage-money, and to receive the rents and profits accruing from the property or any part of such rents and profits and to appropriate the same in lieu of interest, or in payment of the mortgage-money, or partly in lieu of interest or partly in payment of the mortgage money, the transactions called an usufructuary mortgage and the mortgage an usufructuary mortgagee. Features are as under:
   - Mortgagee in actual legal possession of the property, till dues are repaid.
   - Mortgagee has the right to receive rents and profits accruing from the property.
   - No personal liability of the mortgager.
   - No time limit specified
   - Sale is not allowed.

4. **English Mortgage Sec. 58 (e)**—Where the mortgagor binds himself to repay the mortgage-money on a certain date, and transfers the mortgaged property absolutely to the mortgagee, but subject to a proviso that he will re-transfer it to the mortgagor upon payment of the mortgage-money as agree, the transaction is called an English mortgage. Important features are:
   - Personal liability to pay on a specified date
   - Absolute transfer of property to the mortgagee, subject to re-conveying (re-transfer) the property if the debt is repaid

5. **Equitable Mortgage or Mortgage by Deposit of Title Deeds. Sec. 58 (f):** Where the mortgagor delivers (at notified places) to the mortgagee, the documents of title to immovable property with intention to create a security thereon to secure a loan. The transaction is not to be reduced to writing. In case of non-payment, the mortgagee can sue for sale but he cannot foreclose the mortgaged property. According to Section 58 (f) of Transfer of Property Act 1882, where a person delivers to a creditor or his agent documents of title to immovable property, with the intent to create a security thereon, the transaction is called a mortgage by deposit of title deed. However the Act makes the provisions of this Section applicable only to Bombay, Calcutta, Madras and such other towns as may be notified by the State Governments by notification in the Official Gazette. Important features are:

❍ Deposit can be made at Calcutta, Bombay and Madras or at places notified by State government only.

❍ This territorial restriction does not affect the location of the property i.e. property can be located anywhere in India.

❍ There should be deposit of title deed (preferably original) of the property with intention to secure a debt. U/s 96, the provisions which apply to a simple mortgage shall, so far as may be, apply to a mortgage by deposit of title-deeds.

6. **Anomalous Mortgage (Sec. 58g):** A mortgage which is not a simple mortgage, a mortgage by conditional sale, an usufructuary mortgage, an English mortgage or a mortgage by deposit of title deeds within the meaning of this section is called an anomalous mortgage.

Mortgage Type	Defined in Transfer of Property Act	Ownership	Personal Liability of Mortgagor	Registration with Sub Registrar	How the Mortgage Created?
Simple	Section 58(b)	Mortgagor	Yes	Yes	Mortgage Deed
Conditional sale	Section 58(c)	Mortgagor	No	Yes	Mortgage Deed
Usufructuray	Section 58(d)	Mortgagor	No	Yes	Mortgage Deed
English	Section 58(e)	Bank	Yes	Yes	Mortgage Deed
Equitable	Section 58(f)	Mortgagor	Yes	No	Oral Assent

Second Mortgage: A mortgagor after giving 1st mortgage can create 2nd and even subsequent mortgage on the same property. The mortgage will rank in priority according to dates of their creation.

Right of Foreclosure (Sec 67): On default by the mortgagor, the mortgagee in certain types of mortgages, has right to obtain a decree (before decree has been made or money has been paid) from a court to the effect that the former be debarred for ever to get back the mortgage property. Such a right is called the Right of Foreclosure. A suit for foreclosure must be filed within 30 years from date of mortgage money becomes dues.

Right of Redemption (Sec 60): On liquidation of the debt, the mortgagor has the right to get back (redeem) the document relating to mortgaged property, where possession has been given, to get back the possession and where title has been transferred, to get retransferred. This right is known as right of redemption, which can be exercised at any time before the decree for sale or foreclosure has been passed by the court.

Marshalling Securities (Sec 81): If the owner of two or more properties mortgages them to one person and then mortgages one or more of the properties to another person, the subsequent mortgagee is, in the absence of a contract to the contrary, entitled to have the prior mortgage-debt satisfied out of the property or properties not mortgaged to him, so far as the same will extend, but not so as to prejudice the rights of the prior mortgagee or of any other person who has for consideration acquired an interest in any of the properties.

Limitation Period of Mortgage: Limitation period for mortgage is 12 years from date mortgage money becoming due. For right of foreclosure and right of redemption it is 30 years.

ASSIGNMENT AND ACTIONABLE CLAIMS

Assignment: Assignment is another mode of providing security to the lending banker. Assignment means transfer of a right, property or a debt existing or future. The borrower of the bank may assign any of his right, properties, or debt to the banker to secure a loan. Assignment is also transfer of an actionable claim (such as life insurance policy), which may be existing or future, as a security for loan. The transferor of such claim is called the 'assignor' and transferee is called the 'assignee'.

Actionable Claim: Actionable claim means a claim to any debt, other than a debt secured by mortgage of immovable property or by hypothecation or pledge of movable property, or to any beneficial interest inmovable property not in the possession, either actual or constructive, of the claimant, which the civil courts recognise as affording grounds for relief, whether such debt or beneficial interest be existent, accruing, conditional or contingent.

Transfer of Actionable Claim (Sec 130): The transfer shall be effected only by the execution of an instrument in writing signed by the transferor or his duly authorised agent, shall be complete and effectual upon the execution of such instruments, and thereupon all the rights and remedies of the transferor, whether by way of damages or otherwise, shall vest in the transferee, whether such notice of the transfer as is hereinafter provided be given or not. Accordingly, the transferee may sue or institute proceedings for the same in his own name without obtaining the transferor's consent to such suit or proceeding and without making him a party thereto.

For example, 'An' effects a policy on his own life with an insurance company and assigns it to a bank for securing the payment of an existing or future debt. If 'A' dies, the bank is entitled to receive the amount of the policy and to sue on it without the concurrence of executor of 'A', subject to the proviso in sub-section(1) of section 130 and to provisions of section 132.

Notice to be in Writing, Signed (Sec 131): Every notice of transfer of an actionable claim shall be in writing, signed *by* the transferor or his agent duly authorised in this behalf, or, in case the transfer or refuses to sign, by the transferee or his agent, and shall state the name and address of the transferee.

Liability of Transferee of actionable Claim (Sec 132): The transferee of an actionable claim shall take it subject to all the liabilities and equities and.tp which the transferor was subject in respect thereof at the date of the transfer.

PLEDGE

Definition: U/s 172 of Indian Contracts Act, pledge is bailment or delivery of goods as security for payment of a debt or performance of a promise. It may be remembered that only goods (movable assets excluding actionable claims (Sec 2(7) of Sales of Goods Act) can be pledged. The bailor in this case is called the "pawnor or pledger". The bailee is called "pawnee or pledgee". Pledge is different from bailment. Bailment is delivery of goods by one person to another for some purpose while the purpose in pledge is performance of a specific promise or security for a debt. The pledgee can sell the goods pledged after giving notice to the pledger while in bailment the goods can be retained or bailer can be sued for charges.

Authority to Pledge the Goods: The owner of goods, the agent of the owner, the joint owner with the consent of other co-owner and a person having limited interest in the goods (to the extent of his interest), can pledge the securities.

Pledge by Mercantile Agent: U/s 178, where a mercantile agent is, with the consent of the owner, in possession of goods or the documents of title to goods, any pledge made by him, when acting in the ordinary course of business of a mercantile agent, shall be as valid as if he were expressly authorised by the owner of the goods to make the same; provided that the pawnee acts in good faith and has not at the time of the pledge notice that the pawnor has no authority to pledge.

Pledge where Pawnor has only a Limited Interest: As per Section 179, where person pledges goods in which he has only a limited interest, the pledge is valid to the extent of that interest.

Rights of Pledgee

The pledgee gets the rights of a bailee which include:

a) **Right to Retain (Section 173):** The pawnee may retain the goods pledged, not only for payment of the debt or the performance of the promise, but for the interests of the debt, and all necessary expenses incurred by him in respect of the possession or for the preservation of the goods pledged. U/s 174, the pawnee shall not (in the absence of a contract to that effect), retain the goods pledged for any debt or promise of other than the debt or promise for which they are pledged.

b) **Right as to Extraordinary Expenses Incurred (Section 175):** The Pawnee is entitled to receive from the pawnor extraordinary expenses incurred by him for the preservation of the goods pledged.

c) **Right where Pawnor makes Default (Section 176):** If the pawnor makes default in payment of the debt, or performance, at the stipulated time, the pawnee may bring a suit against the pawnor upon the debt or promise and retain the goods pledged as a collateral security; or he may sell the thing pledged, on giving the pawnor reasonable notice of the sale.

If the proceeds of such sale are less than the amount due in respect of the debt or promise, the pawnor is still liable to pay the balance. If the proceeds of the sale are greater than the amount so due, the Pawnee shall pay over the surplus to the pawnor.

d) Defaulting Pawnor Right to Redeem (Section 177): If a time is stipulated for the payment of the debt, or performance of the promise, for which the pledged is made, and the pawnor makes default in payment of the debt or performance of the promise at the stipulated time, he may redeem the goods pledged at any subsequent time before the actual sale of them; but he must, on that case, pay, in addition, any expenses which have arisen from his default.

Duties of the Pledgee

Duties of the pledgee are as follows.

a) To return the goods (along with accretion to goods if any) once the money is paid back by the pledger.

b) To take that much are of the goods, which he would have been taking, had the goods belonged to him.

Banker's Right and Other Dues: Bank's right of pledge prevails over any other dues including Govt. dues (Supreme Court State of Bihar vs Bank of Bihar) except workers' wages.

Law of Limitation: The rights of pledgee are not limited by Law of Limitation.

HYPOTHECATION

Definition: Hypothecation is defined in Securitisation and Reconstruction of Financial Assets and Enforcement of Security Interest (SARFAESI) Act 2002. As per Sec 2(n) of SARFAESI Act 2002, 'Hypothecation means a charge in or upon any movable property, existing or future, created by a borrower in favour of a secured creditor without delivery of possession of the movable property to such creditor, as a security for financial assistance and includes floating charge and crystallisation of such charge into fixed charge on movable property';

Hypothecation is an equitable charge, where the borrower is owner and keeps the possession of the security on behalf of the creditor. In hypothecation on the property the ownership as well as possession of the security remains with the borrower. It is applicable on all movable properties like stock, crop, vehicle, machinery, furniture etc.

Hypothecation is Resorted to in the following cases:

a) When loan is to be raised against work-in-progress, the only way of creating a charge is hypothecation.

b) It is also done in respect of goods which require constant handling in a factory, e.g. rice mills, oil expellers etc.

c) This charge is also convenient, where lending is to be done against goods in a shop or showroom which is required in day to day use.

d) It is easily applicable on vehicle for private or commercial use.

Drawbacks of Hypothecation:

a) The main drawback about this charge is that goods remain in the possession of the borrower and therefore creditor's control over such goods is not practically possible.

b) The borrower may realise and sell the hypothecated stocks and keep only obsolete and slow moving stock.

c) The borrower may hypothecate the same stock for more than on creditor or banker.

d) The realisation of the assets in case of default of payment is a difficult, prolonged and costly affairs.

Precautions to be taken in case of Hypothecation:

a) Banks ensure that firm is not enjoying similar facilities with other banks on the security of same goods.

b) Borrower enjoys facilities from one bank only and an undertaking in writing should be obtained from him.

c) Bank name board should be displayed where the securities are located stating that bank has charge over such goods.

d) Recurring inspection should be conducted by the bank to see that the level of goods being maintained is same as the one declared by the borrower and as per his books.

e) Borrower should submit a stock statement periodically,

f) Such stocks should be insured for fire and other risks.

Legal aspects in Hypothecation Possession & Sale

Hypothecation is an equitable charge, where the borrower keeps the possession of the security on behalf of the creditor. If the borrower fails to return the advance against the hypothecation of securities, the bank can take possession of the securities with consent of the borrower and becomes a pledgee. On becoming pledgee, the bank get all the rights of a pledge including right to sell without intervention of the court. Under Securitisation Act, the bank also has got the right to sell the hypothecated securities without intervention of the court, subject to compliance of certain legal formalities.

LIEN

Definition: Lien is the right of one person to retain goods and securities in his possession belonging to another until certain legal debts due to the person retaining the goods are satisfied. In other words, it is the right of the creditor to retain the goods and securities in his possession, belonging to a debtor, until the debt due is paid. Lien does not give power of sale but only to retain the property.

Particular Lien: Section 170 of Indian Contract Act 1872 defined Particular Lien as 'Where the bailee has, in accordance with the purpose of the bailment, rendered any service involving the exercise of labour or skill in respect of the goods bailed he has in the absence of a contract to the contrary, a right to retain such goods until he receives due remuneration for the services he has rendered in respect of them. Particular lien is that lien which confers the right to retain that particular commodity in respect of which the particular debt arose.

General Lien: Section 171 of Indian Contract Act 1872 defined General Lien as 'Bankers may in the absence of a contract to the contrary, retain as a security for a general balance of account, any goods bailed to them; but no other person have a right retain, as a security for which balance, goods, bailed to them, unless is an express contract to that effect'.

A general lien confers a right to retain goods and securities not only in respect of a particular debt incurred in connection with them but in respect of the general balance due by the owner of the goods and securities, to the person in possession of them.

Banker's Lien: As a general rule, the right of lien does not give the person exercising the right, any power or right to sell or dispose of the securities retained. But in case of a bank, it is otherwise. A banker's lien is more than a general lien.

It is an implied pledge and the banker has a right to sell the property after reasonable notice, provide the property comes into his hands in the ordinary course of his business.

Section 171 of the contract act lays down that a banker's lien can be applied if:
- ❍ The property is in the hands of the banker as the capacity of his customer's bankers;
- ❍ The instruments of the money or goods with the banker are not for a specific purpose inconsistent with lien;
- ❍ The possession of the instruments has been obtained lawfully as a banker;
- ❍ There exists no implied or expressed agreement contrary to the lien.

Negative Lien: At the time the advance is made, the banker sometimes asks a borrower to execute a letter declaring that his assets are free from any sort of charge or encumbrance. The borrower also undertakes that the assets stated in the said declaration shall not be encumbered or disposed of without a bank's permission in writing so long as the advance continues. This undertaking is known as a Negative lien. Usually the arrangement is drafted in the form of an agreement. The banker cannot directly realize his debts from such assets. However, on account of the above restrictions, the interests of the banker are to a certain extent protected.

Set-off: Set-off is the right of a debtor to take into account a debt owing to him by a creditor, when claiming a debt due from him to the creditor. In the case of banker, the right of set-off enables him to adjust a debit balance in a customer's account, with any balance outstanding to his credit in the books of the bank. In other words, the banker can adjust his claim from the amount that is payable to the customer.

TEST YOURSELF

1. Mortgage is defined in:
   - (a) Section 58(b) to 58(g) of Transfer of Property Act 1882
   - (b) Section 57 of Transfer of Property Act 1882
   - (c) Section 57 of Indian Contract act
   - (d) Section 58 of NI act

2. Which of the mortgage is not required to be registered with the registrar of assurance?
   - (a) English Mortgage
   - (b) Equitable Mortgage
   - (c) Simple Mortgage
   - (d) Conditional sale

3. In which of the mortgage, mortgagee cannot sale the property but loan can be recovered from income of the property?
   - (a) English Mortgage
   - (b) Equitable Mortgage
   - (c) Simple Mortgage
   - (d) Usufructuary Mortgage

4. For creation of equitable mortgage, which is the correct statement?
   - (a) An instrument in writing is necessary
   - (b) The mortgager will not sign any documents nor submit any memo in writing at the time of creation of mortgage
   - (c) Mortgage will be registered registrar of assurance
   - (d) Mortgage can be created at any place in India

5. Which charge can be created on the book debts by bank?

(a) Pledge   (b) Assignment
(c) Hypothecation   (d) Lien

6. In which of the mortgage, ownership transfers to the mortgagee?
   (a) English Mortgage
   (b) Equitable Mortgage
   (c) Simple Mortgage
   (d) Usufructuary Mortgage

7. In which of the mortgage, mortgagor create the mortgage by oral assent at any notified place in India in favour of the mortgagee?
   (a) English Mortgage
   (b) Equitable Mortgage
   (c) Simple Mortgage
   (d) Usufructuary Mortgage

8. In case of pledge, relationship between banker and customer is:
   (a) Pledger and Pledgee
   (b) Pledgee and Pledger
   (c) Pawnee and Pawnor
   (d) 'b' or 'c'

9. Assignment is governed by:
   (a) SARFAESI act
   (b) Transfer of Property Act 1882
   (c) Indian Contract act
   (d) NI act

10. Charge created on paper securities such as Shares, debenture, bonds Mutual fund is:
    (a) Hypothecation   (b) Assignment
    (c) Lien   (d) Pledge

11. After the conversion of hypothecation into pledge, the bank will have the same right as that of:
    (a) Pledgee   (b) Pledger
    (c) Hypothecatee   (d) Hypothecator

12. At the time the advance is made, the borrower undertakes that the assets stated in the said declaration shall not be encumbered or disposed of without a bank's permission in writing so long as the advance continues. This undertaking is known as a ________.
    (a) Declaration regarding Hypothecation
    (b) Negative lien
    (c) Declaration regarding assignment
    (d) Mortgage

13. ________ is the right of a debtor to take into account a debt owing to him by a creditor, when claiming a debt due from him to the creditor.
    (a) Set-off   (b) Lien
    (c) Pledge   (d) Assignment

14. ________ is that lien which confers the right to retain that particular commodity in respect of which the particular debt arose.
    (a) Negative lien   (b) General lien
    (c) Particular lien   (d) Banker's lien

15. A pledgee has further pledged the goods and the original pledger has repaid the loan. What is his right?
    (a) Goods can be received by him subject to charge of the 2nd pledgee
    (b) Goods can be delivered to him even when the 2nd pledgee's loan is outstanding
    (c) He is entitle to return the goods
    (d) He is not entitle to return the goods

16. In what respect, a charge hypothecation is different from pledge. The goods are:
    (a) In possession of bank but ownership with borrower
    (b) Both the possession and ownership rest with borrower
    (c) There is no difference in regard of possession

17. The charge on movable assets to be created is known as:
    (a) Set-off   (b) Assignment
    (c) Mortgage   (d) Hypothecation

18. In case of hypothecation, the borrower can:
    (a) Take goods out of godown and use them
    (b) Keep new goods inside the godown in place of old ones
    (c) Sell the goods hypothecated and replenish the stock
    (d) All of the above

19. Bank grants a loan against the security of goods relating to a firm, which kind of charge on goods can be created:
    (a) Pledge   (b) Hypothecation
    (c) Assignment   (d) 'a' or 'b'

20. The person to whom the possession of goods is transferred is called:
    (a) Transferee   (b) Bailee
    (c) Beneficiary   (d) Bailor

ANSWER

1	2	3	4	5	6	7	8	9	10
(a)	(b)	(d)	(b)	(b)	(a)	(b)	(d)	(b)	(c)

11	12	13	14	15	16	17	18	19	20
(a)	(b)	(a)	(c)	(c)	(b)	(d)	(d)	(d)	(b)

REGISTRATION AND SATISFACTION OF CHARGES

CHARGE

The word 'charge' is used to mean any form of security or debt. Sec 125(4) of the Companies Act, 1956 provides the following charges of a Company are to be registered with Registrar of Companies:

a) A charge for the purpose of security debentures,

b) A charge on uncalled capital of the Company,

c) A charge on immovable property;

d) A charge on any book debts of the company,

e) A charge, not being a pledge, on any movable property of the company,

f) A floating charge on the undertaking or any property including stock-in-trade,

g) A charge on a ship or share in a ship

h) A charge on goodwill, on a patent or a trademark or a license under copyright.

As per Chapter VI, Section 77(1) of the Companies Act 2013: 'It shall be the duty of every company creating a charge within or outside India, on its property or assets or any of its undertakings, whether tangible or otherwise, and situated in or outside India, to register the particulars of the charge signed by the company and the charge-holder together with the instruments, if any, creating such charge in such form, on payment of such fees and in such manner as may be prescribed, with the Registrar within thirty days of its creation'.

'Provided that the Registrar may, on an application by the company, allow such registration to be made within a period of three hundred days of such creation on payment of such additional fees as may be prescribed'.

Creation of Charge: Creation of charge by the borrowers on various kinds of securities/assets means creation of a right in favour of the bank. By creation of charge, the ownership is not transferred in favour of the creditor. (Except in few transaction such as English Mortgage).

TYPES OF CHARGE

Charges can be classified into two types:

❖ **Fixed Charge:** Also called 'specific charge'. It extends over a specific property of the company. It gives right to the creditor to sell the property and claim the proceeds towards the dues payable by the Company. It is created on properties such as Land and Building, Plant & Machinery, whose identity does not change during the period of loan.

❖ **Floating Charge:** Means a charge that is general and not specific. It is created on assets which undergone change (stock).

a) Floats over the present and future property of the Company, and it do not attach any specific property.

b) On happening of an event or contingency, crystallizes as a fixed charge. A floating charge is an equitable charge which does not attach on any specific property but covers the whole of the company's property.

Crystallization of Charge

It means the Floating Charge becomes fixed when the company/firm ceases to be a going concern or upon the commencement of winding up or on the appointment of receiver.

Charges can also be classified as under:

1st Charge: Where assets are charged to a creditor on first basis, that creditor has the 1st charge.

2nd Charge: Where assets are already charged to a creditor on 1st basis and subsequently the charge is created in favour of another creditor.

❖ **Pari Passu Charge:** The term is usually used in case of consortium lending. In case of such lending, a number of banks or financial institutions join together to lend to a single borrower in an agreed ratio against some common securities. The securities are charge to all the bankers/financial institutions with the condition that they have priority on proportionate basis in the ratio of their loans. The term that institutions will have a "pari passu charge" over the assets of the borrower means that the lenders are entitled to have equal rights over the assets as per the agreed share.

❖ **Registration of Charge:** All the charge created by the Company shall be filed with the ROC within 30 days of its creation. It can be extended by Registrar of Company for another 270 days.

The registration, modification and satisfaction of charge are to be filed in form No CHG – 1& CHG-4 in MOC21. Recently Government of India has introduced electronic filing of returns.

Effect of non-Registration

As per Chapter VI, Section 78 of the Companies Act 2013: 'Where a company fails to register the charge within the period specified in section 77, without prejudice to its liability in respect of any offence under this Chapter, the person in whose favour the charge is created may apply to the Registrar for registration of the charge along with the instrument created for the charge, within such time and in such form and manner as may be prescribed and the Registrar may, on such application, within a period of fourteen days after giving notice to the company'.

If the charge created is not registered with ROC, the charge would not be valid against the liquidator and any other creditor of the Company in the event of winding up of the company, as against the company itself. So long as the company does not go into liquidation, the mortgage or charge is good and may be enforced.

**Provision of law relating
to the registration of Charges:**

Chapter VI, Section 77 to 87 of the Companies Act 2013 provides for the registration of charges. These sections can be stated briefly as follows:

Section 77: It shall be the duty of every company creating a charge within or outside India, on its property or assets or any of its undertakings, whether tangible or otherwise, and situated in or outside India, to register the particulars of the charge signed by the company.

Sec 142: It empowers ROC to impose penalty on the Company if it fails to comply with the provisions relating to registration of charge.

Sec 144: It provides that any creditor or member of company can inspect the books relating to charges created by the Company and it is the duty of the Company to keep the register of charges open to inspection.

Section 77: This section provides that 'charge' means and includes mortgage/charge over any or all properties of the company within or outside India.

Section 77(1): This section provides that the charge created over the properties of the company shall be registered with registrar of companies within thirty days of creation of charge.

Section 77(2): This section provides that the registrar shall give a certificate under his hand of the registration of any charge registered, stating the amounts thereby secured; and the certificate shall be a conclusive evidence of that the requirements of companies Act as to registration has been complied with.

Section 78: This section provides that in case the charge is not registered by the company, the charge holder may apply for filling of charge in the prescribed manner within a period of 14 (fourteen) days after giving the company a notice in the regard.

Section 79: This section provides that if a company acquires a property charged under section 77, then the company shall declare the same by filing the particulars of the property, so acquired, subject to charge.

Section 80: This section provides that after registration of charge created, any other person acquires such property charged or any party thereof, shall be deemed to have notice of the charge registered and shall take the property subject to such charge.

Section 81: It is provided under this Section that registrar of companies shall keep a register of charges containing particulars of all charges requiring registration. This section further provides that a copy of particulars contained in the register of charges can be obtained by any person on payment of fee.

Section 82: This section provides that the company shall intimate the registrar of any payment satisfaction in full of any charge registered within a period of 30 (thirty) days. The registrar then, upon receipt of such intimation, cause a notice to be sent to the charge-holder to show–cause within a period of 14 (days) as to why they said charge shall not be satisfied. In case no cause is shown, the registrar may order a memorandum of satisfaction shall be entered in the register of charges.

Section 83: Under this section, registrar of companies that on evidence being given to his satisfaction with respect to any registered charge:

a) That the debt for which the charge was given has been paid or satisfied in whole or in part; or

b) That part of the property or undertaking charged has been released from charged has been released from the charge, or has ceased to form part of the company's property or undertaking can record the fact that charge is satisfied or property is released.

Section 84: This Section provides that in case an order for appointment of receiver or manager is obtained by any person, then such person shall give notice of such appointment of receiver/manager within a period of 30 (thirty) days from the date of such order.

Section 85: This section requires the company shall maintain at its registered office, a register of charges in prescribed form and manner.

Section 86: This section provides that contravention of any of the aforesaid provisions shall be punishable with a fine not less than ₹ 100000/- but which may extend to ₹ 1000000/- and every officer in default shall be punishable with imprisonment for a term of upto 6 (six) months.

Section 87: This section provides that the central government may direct that the time for filing charge may be extended upon being satisfied of a few conditions mentioned in the section.

TEST YOURSELF

1. Creation of charge by the borrowers on various kinds of securities/assets means:
   (a) Creation of a right in favour of the bank
   (b) The ownership is not transferred in favour of the creditor normally
   (c) The ownership is transferred in favour of the creditor in case of English Mortgage
   (d) All of the above

2. The term that institutions will have a "Pari Passu charge" over the assets means:
   (a) This term is usually used in case of consortium lending
   (b) In case of such lending, a number of banks or financial institutions join together to lend to a single borrower in an agreed ratio against some common securities
   (c) The lenders are entitled to have equal rights over the assets as per the agreed share
   (d) All of the above

3. Charge created by company shall be registered with:
   (a) Registrar of Assurance
   (b) Registrar of firms
   (c) Registrar of companies
   (d) CERSAI

4. Under Companies Act a charge includes:
   (a) Mortgage   (b) Bill of Exchange
   (c) Promissory Note   (d) Letter of Credit

5. Charge shall be registered within _______ days from the date of creation of charge.
   (a) 15
   (b) 30
   (c) 60
   (d) At discretion of the bank

6. When a floating charge becomes a fixed charge?
   (a) When Debtor Company ceases to carry on a business
   (b) When the company goes into liquidation
   (c) When the creditor intervenes by getting a receiver appointed by court
   (d) All of the above

7. Which of the following is not true in respect of floating charge?
   (a) It is an equitable charge
   (b) It does not attach to any particular or specific property
   (c) Firm or the company, in ordinary course of business, may deal with the charged property in any manner
   (d) None of the above

8. Which of the following is not a part of procedure for registration of charge?
   (a) The company shall file the particulars for creation, modification or satisfaction of charge

(b) A copy of every instrument evidencing any charge is required to be filled with the registrar duly verified and certified

(c) Prescribed fee for registration shall be paid

(d) None of the above

9. Copy of particulars contained in the registrar of charge can be obtained by any person on payment of prescribed fee, this provision is contained in ________ Companies Act 2013.
    (a) Section 81　　　　　(b) Section 82
    (c) Section 83　　　　　(d) Section 84

10. All the charge created by the Company shall be filed with the ROC within 30 days of its creation. It can be extended by Registrar of Company for another _________ days.
    (a) 15　　　　　(b) 60
    (c) 180　　　　　(d) 270

11. As per Chapter VI, Section __________ of the Companies Act 2013: 'Where a company fails to register the charge within the period specified in section 77, without prejudice to its liability in respect of any offence under this Chapter.
    (a) 78　　　　　(b) 79
    (c) 80　　　　　(d) 81

12. What is/are the effect of non-registration of charge?
    (a) Charge would not be valid against the liquidator
    (b) In the event of winding up of the company, charge would not be valid against creditors of the company
    (c) If the company does not go into liquidation, the charge may be enforced
    (d) All of the above

13. Any form of security for debt is called charge:
    (a) True　　　　　(b) False

14. Charges means any form of:
    (i) Security　　　　　(ii) Debt
    (iii) Deposit
    (a) (i)　　　　　(b) (i) and (ii)
    (c) (i) and (iii)　　　　　(d) (i), (ii) and (iii)

15. All the charge created by the Company shall be filed with the ROC. The registration, modification and satisfaction of charge are to be filed in form No ____________.
    (a) CHG–1& CHG-4 in MOC21
    (b) CHG–1& CHG-2 in MOC21
    (c) CHG–1& CHG-4 in MOC22
    (d) CHG–2 & CHG-4 in MOC21

ANSWER

1	2	3	4	5	6	7	8	9	10
(d)	(d)	(a)	(a)	(b)	(d)	(d)	(d)	(a)	(d)

11	12	13	14	15
(a)	(d)	(a)	(b)	(a)

CASE LAWS ON RESPONSIBILITY OF PAYING BANK

INTRODUCTION

Bank has to honour his customer's cheques up to the amount of credit balance in his account or up to the limit of any agreed overdraft. Section 31 of Negotiable Instrument act, 1881 imposes upon bank the obligation to honor the cheques. The text of the act is as follows:

"The drawee of a cheque having sufficient funds of the drawer in his hands properly applicable to the payment of such cheques must pay the cheque when duly required so to do and in default of such payment must compensate the drawer for any loss or damage caused by such default."

The implied duty of a paying banker, however, is dependent on certain other important conditions. Conditions for honouring customer cheques are as under:

1. **The Cheque must be in the Proper Form:** It must be satisfying the condition specified in the Negotiable Instrument Act. As per section 6 a cheque is a bill of exchange drawn on a specified banker and not expressed to be payable otherwise than on demand. It includes electronic image of truncated cheque and also an electronic cheque. RBI decided to prescribe certain benchmark towards achieving standardization of cheques known as 'CTS-2010 standard' specification. No changes/correction should be carried out on the CTS cheques (other than for date validation purpose, if required) for the any change in payee's name; amount etc, fresh cheque forms should be used by customers.

2. **Drawer's Signature must Tally with the Specimen Signature:** In the case of drawer's signature do not tally with the ones on bank record, the banker should obtain fresh set of signatures and should not pay the cheques on which the signatures are different from the bank's record.

3. **The Cheque must not be Either Stale or Post Dated:** The cheque must be presented within the validity period. After the validity period cheque becomes stale cheque, it cannot be paid. As per RBI direction u/s 35A, Banking Regulation Act, validity of the cheque, demand draft and banker's cheque will be valid for 3 months with effect from April 01, 2012. After a cheque becomes stale, it can be revalidated any number of times. A post dated cheque is one which bears date later than which the cheque actually drawn. If cheque is undated, holder can fill the date. A cheque bearing the date prior to actual date of signing or opening of account is called antedated cheque, which is valid and can be paid till it becomes stale.

4. **Sufficient Fund available in Account:** The banker is bound to pay the cheque drawn by his customer. There should be sufficient credit balance available or up to drawing limit which is given by the banker in the customer's account. The fund available in the customer's account should also be properly available for the payment of the cheque. The funds may not be available to pay the cheque if:

   a) The banker has exercised his right of set off for amounts due from the customer or

   b) There is an attachment order from court, Income Tax officer or any other lawful authority restraining the bank from paying the money.

5. **The amount Expressed in Word and Figure should be Matched:** The amount expressed in cheque differ in word and figure, it should not be paid and return with mark 'word and figure differ'. However, Section 18 of NI Act provides that where there is a difference between the amount in words and the amount in figures, the amount in words is the amount payable.

6. **If Mutilated Cheque is Presented for Payment:** A cheque is mutilated when it has been cut or torn or a part of it is missing. Mutilation may be accidental or intentional. When it is accidental, the banker should get the drawer's confirmation before honouring it. If it is intentional, banker should refuse payment with mark 'mutilated cheque' or 'mutilation required confirmation'.

7. **The Cheque must be Properly Endorsed:** In the case of bearer cheque, endorsement is not applicable. In the case of an order cheque, endorsement may be done. An order cheque may be made payable to the bearer by an endorsement in blank. Only a regular endorsed order cheque should be honoured by banker.

A banker justify to refuse payment of a cheque drawn on him in certain circumstances. A banker's obligation to honour the customer's cheques is terminated on the happening of any of the following events:

1. If banker received a notice from the customer to stop payment of a cheque in writing,
2. Notice of the customer's death,
3. Notice of the customer's insanity,
4. Notice of the customer's bankruptcy,
5. Knowledge of any defect in the title of the person presenting the cheque,
6. Notice of a garnishee order

Payment in Due Course

As per Section 10 of N.I. Act. 'payment in due course means payment according to the apparent tenor of the instrument in good faith and without negligence to any person in possession thereof under circumstances which do not afford a reasonable ground for believing that he is not entitled to receive payment of the amount therein mentioned'.

Section 85 of NI Act conditions to be satisfied for being a payment in due course:

a) Payment is in accordance with the apparent tenor of the instrument,
b) Payment must be in good faith and Without negligence,
c) Payment must be made to the person in possession of the instrument,
d) The banker should not have any reasons to "disbelieve" the integrity/honesty of the possessor, i.e. no reasons to think that he is not entitled to receive the payment.
e) Payment must be made in money only.

Various Sections regarding protection to Paying Bankers in Negotiable Instrument Act

10 : Payment to be made in due course.

85-1 : Paying banker protected by payment in due course of order cheque that bears regular endorse-ment. Genuineness of endorsement is not to be ensured by the paying bank.

85-2 : Protection to paying banker in case of a bearer cheque. Endorsement on a bearer cheque has to be ignored.

85-A : Protection to paying banker in case of Bank drafts.

89 : Protection to paying bank for materially altered instrument.

128 : Protection for payment in due course of crossed cheques

131 : Protection to collecting bank for crossed cheques subject to compliance of conditions

131-A : Protection to collecting bank for crossed bank drafts and his position to his detriment, he must repay the money back to the payer.

Banker's Liability in case of Wrongful Dishonour

Before dishonouring a cheque on the ground of customer's credit not being sufficient, or with the remark that the customer has "insufficient fund", the banker should be careful. In this case banker would be liable, if step taken by him proves to be erroneous.

Payment of a Forged Cheque

A cheque with the forged signature of a drawer must not be paid by a banker. The payment of such cheque is deemed as payment without the authority of the customer. The paying banker is not given any protection under law on the payment of a forged cheque. The banker's liability remains even if the signature is cleverly forged and it is difficult to detect it with reasonable care. In case of forged cheque, the banker cannot escape from liability, even if, the customer was negligent in keeping the cheque book under lock and key as required by the rule of the bank.

Cheque Truncation

Cheque truncation means stopping the flow of the physical cheques issued by a drawer to the drawee branch. The physical instrument is truncated at some point en-route the drawee branch and an electronic image of the cheque is sent to the drawee branch along with the relevant information like the MICR fields, date of presentation, presenting banks etc. This would eliminate the need to move the physical instruments across branches, except in exceptional circumstances, resulting in an effective reduction in the time required for payment of cheques, the associated cost of transit and delays in processing, etc., thus speeding up the process of collection or realization of cheques.

TEST YOURSELF

1. A cheque for ₹ 10000/- dated 15/02/2017, presented for the payment on 25/02/2017. It is observed that the cheque book from which the cheque was issued, issued to customer on 20/02/2017. What the bank should do?
   (a) Such cheque cannot be paid
   (b) Upon drawer's confirmation, it can be paid
   (c) Cheque would be paid if otherwise in order
   (d) It should be returned unpaid

2. The duties of paying banker for payment of cheque and protection has been laid down in:
   (a) NI Act
   (b) Indian Contract Act
   (c) RBI Act
   (d) Banking Regulation Act

3. If a cheque is lost, a customer is bound to inform about the lost cheque to
   (a) Payee
   (b) Endorsee
   (c) Drawee Bank
   (d) Collecting bank

4. If one of the signature is forged in case of jointly operated account, who is liable?
   (a) Only the customer
   (b) Only the paying bank
   (c) Both customer and banker
   (d) None

5. A cheque is presented for payment, amount of cheque stated in words and figure differs. What is the proper course of action as per NI Act?
   (a) After making alteration, it can be paid
   (b) Lesser amount can be paid
   (c) Cheque cannot be paid
   (d) As per section 18, amount stated in the words can be paid

6. As per section 129 of NI Act, the paying banker will not get protection:
   (a) If banker makes payment of a cheque crossed generally, otherwise than to the banker
   (b) Crossed special, otherwise than to the banker
   (c) Either (a) or (b)
   (d) Both (a) & (b)

7. If mutilated cheque is presented for payment, what should be the action of a paying banker?
   (a) Cheque must be return unpaid
   (b) Cheque may be paid, when it is accidental, the banker should get the drawer's confirmation before honouring it
   (c) If it is intentional, banker should refuse payment with mark 'mutilated cheque' or 'mutilation required confirmation'
   (d) Both (b) and (c) are correct

8. Find the incorrect Sections regarding Protection to Paying Bankers in NI Act:
   (a) 86-Protection to paying banker in case of Bank drafts
   (b) 89-Protection to paying bank for materially altered instrument
   (c) 128-Protection for payment in due course of crossed cheques
   (d) 131-Protection to collecting bank for crossed cheques subject to compliance of conditions

9. A banker's obligation to honour the customer's cheques is terminated on the happening of any of the following events, which is/are correct answer?
   (a) If banker received a notice from the customer to stop payment of a cheque in writing
   (b) Notice of the customer's death
   (c) Notice of the customer's insanity, or bankruptcy
   (d) All of the above

10. As per RBI direction u/s 35A, Banking Regulation Act, validity of the cheque, demand draft and banker's cheque will be valid for __________ months with effect from April 01, 2012.
    (a) 1   (b) 3
    (c) 6   (d) 12

11. A cheque is presented for payment where amount is written in figure is Hindi and other particulars in English. What the banker should do?
    (a) Bank can pay the cheque as it can be drawn in any language
    (b) All particulars should be in same language
    (c) Request the drawer to reissue the cheque
    (d) None of the above

12. If alteration in the amount of the cheque is authenticated by the drawer:
    (a) It can be paid normally
    (b) It can't be paid, As per RBI direction alteration is only allowed in date for revalidation
    (c) It can be paid normally, if alteration is authenticated by drawer properly
    (d) It can't be paid, As per RBI direction alteration is only allowed in payee name

13. Your branch has received a cheque of ₹ 50,000/- drawn in favour of Lord Krishna or order for payment, across the counter. What would you do with the cheque?
    (a) It will be paid after obtaining the identification of the person obtaining the payment
    (b) It will be paid to a person in whose favour endorsement done by Lord Krishna appears
    (c) It will be paid to a person whose name is stated by the drawer for obtaining payment on behalf of the payee
    (d) It will be returned, as it is drawn in favour of a fictitious name

14. A drawee bank is responsible to one of the following for wrongful dishonour of a cheque:
    (a) The payee, If suffers any loss
    (b) The endorsee, If suffers any loss
    (c) The account holder (drawer), If suffers any loss
    (d) The presenter, If suffers any loss

15. If a bank collects a cheque on which its customer is having a defective title and defect is not in the knowledge of the bank:
    (a) Paying bank is responsible
    (b) Collecting bank is not responsible provided other condition of section 131 are complied with
    (c) Collecting bank is responsible for carelessness
    (d) None of the above

ANSWER

1	2	3	4	5	6	7	8	9	10
(c)	(a)	(c)	(b)	(d)	(d)	(d)	(a)	(d)	(b)

11	12	13	14	15
(a)	(b)	(d)	(c)	(c)

CASE LAWS ON RESPONSIBILITY OF COLLECTING BANK

INTRODUCTION

A banker, who acts as a collecting banker has certain responsibility and he has to take care while collecting cheques and other negotiable instruments. Although collection of cheques and bills of exchange is not legal duty of the bankers, they generally act as collecting bankers for their customers. This function is especially important since crossed cheques can be collected only through a bankers.

A banker (agent) who collects the cheque and credits to his customer's account (Principal) while collecting crossed cheque is given protection under Section 131 of the Negotiable Instrument Act. According to the section: *'A banker who has in good faith and without negligence received payment for a customer of a cheque crossed generally or specially to himself shall not, in case the title to the cheque proves defective, incur any liability to, the true owner of the Cheque by reason only of having received such payment'.*

CONVERSION

Conversion means illegal interference in the property of another person. If a bank collects the cheque for his customer belonging to some other person and the customer has no title to that cheque, bank shall be liable for conversion. Bank will, however be having statutory protection under Section 131 of the Negotiable Instrument Act if certain conditions are satisfied.

The above section protects a collecting banker when it collects a crossed cheques bearing a forged endorsement, or in respect of which a customer has no title or a defective title. It may be noted here that to claim protection, the collecting banker must comply strictly with the provisions of the section. These are as under:

a) **The Collecting Banker should have acted in Good Faith and without Negligence:** The most important point for banker is to remember when he is collecting cheque is that he must act in good faith without negligence. It is deemed to be done in good faith where it is done bonafide and honestly. But section 131 requires him to act without negligence also. Without negligence means with reasonable care (without doubt about the genuineness of the title of the customer to the instrument). The account should be opened with proper KYC. Collection of large amount cheques in new accounts without proper scrutiny means negligence.

b) **Banker should Receive Payment for a Customer:** Customer means having an account in the bank. Section 131 applies only to the crossed cheque collected for a customer. Therefore, if the banker collects cheques for any person other than a customer, he cannot claim protection and he will be held liable to the true owner in case the title of the person for he collects the cheque proves defective.

c) **Examination of Endorsement:** The collecting banker must satisfy himself that all the endorsements on the cheque are regular.

d) Protection only for Crossed Cheque: Protection is not available for an un-crossed cheque. Hence it is always advisable for banker to cross all cheques paid in for collection.

e) Collation of Cheques Crossed 'Not Negotiable': In certain cheques we can see the wording 'Not Negotiable', especially some cheques drawn by LIC. Not Negotiable crossing is only an indication to the collecting banker and it has nothing to do with the paying banker. Not Negotiable crossing does not restrict the transferability of cheques, but the only thing is that the transferee will not get a better title than what the transferor had. In other words, if it is a stolen or forged cheque, the transferee or the "holder in due course" will also get a defective title.

f) Collation of Cheques Crossed 'Not Transferable': A collecting banker is guilty of negligence when he collects a 'Not Transferable' cheque to any person other than the payee.

g) General Crossing and Special Crossing: Before accepting a cheque for collection, the bank should ensure that the cheque is either crossed generally or specially crossed to the collecting bank itself. If the cheque is specially crossed by another bank, then such cheque should not be accepted for collection.

h) Cheque Payable to a Partnership Firm or a Company collected in the Personal Account of the Partner or the Director: The protection is not available when the collecting bank collecting cheques made payable to the partnership firm or the company's cheque for the personal accounts of the partner of the firm or private accounts of the directors of the company.

i) Collection of Cheque Payable to a Customer in his Official Capacity for his Personal Account: The banker should not collect the cheque payable to a customer in his official capacity for his private account. For instance, a cheque payable to 'Mr. XYZ, Income Tax Commissioner' should not be collected for the personal account of Mr. XYZ.

Duties of the Collecting Banker

A banker is bound to show a reasonable care in collection of his customer's cheques and bills. Otherwise, he may be held liable for any loss suffered by the customer. In the case of a cheque entrusted with the banker for collection, he is expected to present it to the drawee banker within a reasonable time. Under Section 84 of the NI Act duties of the collecting banker are as under:

a) He must present the cheque within reasonable time. In determining what a reasonable time is, regard shall be had to the nature of the instrument, the usage of trade and of bankers, and the facts of the particular case.

b) To hand over the proceeds after realisation without delay.

c) Duty to open the account with reference and sufficient documentary proof. RBI has insisted that the bank should open an account of a new customer only after the new account holder has been properly verified. Besides introduction, photograph, sufficient documentary proof for constitution and address to be obtained under the applicable KYC norms.

d) Extra precaution must be taken by a banker while collecting the high value cheque in new open account. In the case of especially new open accounts, the banker should make discreet enquiries as to the source of income, and the banker should desist from handling such cheques.

e) Status of the customer's account should be verified. The collecting banker is required to take into account the status of the customer and the various transactions taking place in his account to observe the standard of living conditions of the customer. If a man of small means and small income tenders cheques for huge amounts, naturally the banker should make discreet enquiries as to the source of income, and the banker should desist from handling such cheques. It may lead to negligence or conversion.

f) Duty of the prudent banker to verify the instrument or any apparent defects in the instrument.

g) The banker has to ensure crossing and special crossing of the cheque prior to send for collection.

RBI's Cheque Collection Policy

Keeping in view the technologically progress in payment and settlement systems and the qualitative changes in operational systems and processes that has been undertaken by the individual banks. As per Cheque Collection Policy, banks are obliged to disclose their liability to customers by way of compensation/interest payments due to delays for non-compliance with the standards set by the banks themselves. The customer has to be compensated by way of compensation/interest payment even if no formal claim is lodged to the effect.

Local Cheques

Local cheques are payable within the jurisdiction of the clearing house and will be presented through the clearing system prevailing at the center. Credit arising out of local cheques shall be given to the customer's account as indicated in the Cheque Collection Policy (CCP) of the concerned collecting bank.

Notwithstanding to the CCP of concerned collecting bank, ideally, in respect of local clearing, banks shall permit usage of the shadow credit afforded to the customers' accounts immediately after closure of the relative return clearing on the next working day or maximum within an hour of commencement of business on the third working day from the day of presentation in clearing, subject to usual safeguards.

Under grid-based Cheque Truncation System clearing, all cheques drawn on bank branches falling within in the grid jurisdiction are treated and cleared as local cheques. The grid clearing allows banks to present/receive cheques to/from multiple cities to a single clearing house through their service branches in the grid location.

If there is any delay in credit, beyond the period specified above, customer is entitled to receive compensation at the rate specified in the CCP of the concerned collecting bank. In case, no rate is specified in the CCP for delay in realisation of local cheques, compensation at savings bank interest rate has to be paid for the corresponding period of delay.

Outstation Cheques

Maximum time frame for collection of cheques drawn on state capitals/major cities/other locations are 7/10/14 days respectively. If there is any delay in collection beyond this period, customer is entitled to receive compensation at the rate specified in the Cheque Collection Policy (CCP) of the concerned bank. In case the rate is not specified in the CCP, interest rate on Fixed Deposits for the corresponding maturity to be paid. Banks' cheque collection policy also indicates the limit up to which outstation cheques are given immediate/instant credit.

Cheque Drop Box Facility

Banks are required to provide both the cheque drop box facility and the acknowledgement facility at their collection counters. No bank branch can refuse to give an acknowledgement to the customer if the latter asks for the same while tendering cheque for collection at the bank branch's counter. No bank can refuse to accept outstation cheques deposited for collection or refuse to offer its products to customers.

TEST YOURSELF

1. During the collection of cheques in customers account, protection is available in the case of:
   (a) un-crossed cheque
   (b) Order cheque
   (c) Crossed cheque
   (d) protection is not available

2. On which of the following a collecting bank will get protection against conversion u/s 131 of NI Act?
   (a) Crossed Draft
   (b) Crossed DP Note
   (c) Crossed Bill of Exchange
   (d) Crossed Cheque

3. Collecting bank is expected to collect the cheque within a reasonable period, else it would be liable to the customer u/s 72 84 of NI Act.
   (a) True   (b) False

4. When a bank is collecting a cheque of a newly opened SB account as first entry in the account, find the correct statement?
   (a) Banker would not get protection because it has not collected the cheque for a customer
   (b) Banker will get protection if the account is opened after complying with KYC requirement
   (c) Banker will not get protection because the first entry in the account is not in cash
   (d) Both (a) & (c)

5. In case of collection of cheque and bills, the relationship of the banker with the customer is that of:
   (a) Banker as agent and customer trustee
   (b) Banker as trustee and customer debtor
   (c) Banker as debtor and customer creditor
   (d) Banker as agent and customer principal

6. A customer of your branch Mahesh, deposited a cheque, which he steals from another person named Mahesh. Your branch collects this cheque without being aware about the defect. Find the correct statement.
   (a) Collecting bank is negligent
   (b) Collecting bank will get protection if it has collected the cheque in good faith and without negligence
   (c) Collecting bank is responsible for conversion
   (d) Collecting bank is negligent but will get protection

7. A cheque is in favour of a Trust. The trustee wants to deposit this cheque in his personal account. The collecting bank:
   (a) Must collect in Trust account only
   (b) Need not enquire before its collection
   (c) May collect in personal account if Trustee requests
   (d) Should know the customer is enough

8. A current account customer of your branch deposited a cheque on 22 May 2017, dated 10 September 2017, issued by Ministry of Rural Development for collection. Find the correct statement.
   (a) Its validity can be 6 months
   (b) Its validity is forever till paid
   (c) Cannot be collected, validity period of cheque is limited to 3 months as per RBI directive
   (d) It can be collected any time

9. As a collecting banker, you receive an un-crossed cheque for collection. What should you do?
   (a) You may request the customer to cross the cheque
   (b) The bank may itself cross the cheque
   (c) You may send un-crossed cheque if customer title is beyond any doubt
   (d) Either (a) or (b)

10. Maximum time frame for collection of cheques drawn on state capitals/major cities/other locations are _____/_____/_____ days respectively.
    (a) 7/10/14   (b) 4/7/10
    (c) 10/14/21   (d) 7/14/21

11. Even if cheque drop box facility is available in the branch, no bank branch can refuse to give an acknowledgement to the customer if the latter asks for the same while tendering cheque for collection at the bank branch's counter.
    (a) True   (b) False

12. If there is any delay in collection beyond this period, customer is entitled to receive compensation at the rate specified in the Cheque Collection Policy (CCP) of the concerned bank.
    (a) True   (b) False

13. The collecting banker need not satisfy himself that all the endorsements on the cheque are regular.
    (a) True   (b) False

14. When a banker receives information that a cheque for collection is lost, the banker should:
    (a) Inform the drawer
    (b) Inform the drawee
    (c) Inform to RBI
    (d) Exercise due caution while collecting the cheque

15. The duties of collecting banker to claim protection has been laid down in:
    (a) NI Act
    (b) Indian Contract Act
    (c) RBI Act
    (d) Banking Regulation Act

ANSWER

1	2	3	4	5	6	7	8	9	10
(c)	(d)	(a)	(b)	(a)	(b)	(a)	(c)	(d)	(a)

11	12	13	14	15
(a)	(a)	(b)	(d)	(a)

MODULE–C
BANKING RELATED LAWS

RECOVERY OF DEBTS DUE TO BANKS AND FINANCIAL INSTITUTIONS ACT, 1993 (DRT ACT)

OBJECTIVE

Banks and financial institutions have been experiencing considerable difficulties in recovering loans and enforcement of securities charge with them. The procedure for recovery of debts due to the banks and financial institutions, which is being followed, has resulted in a significant portion of the funds being blocked.

INTRODUCTION

Mounting of NPA is the major challenges for banking industry. NPA recovery plays a main role for bank's profitability. Recovery of dues from borrower through courts and legal action is major problem for banks and financial institution. It was observed that existing legal actions initiated by banks and FI were not adequate for debt dues recovery.

Undue delay for finalizing banking NPA case in various courts affects the productivity of banking and financial institution. For speedy recovery of bank's dues, Debts Recovery Tribunals have been established by the Government of India under an Act of Parliament (Act 51 of 1993) for expeditious adjudication and recovery of debts due to banks and financial institutions.

Establishment of Tribunal

Recovery of debts due to banks and financial institutions act 1993 came into force on 24th day of June, 1993. The Act is applicable throughout India, except State of Jammu and Kashmir. Presently there are 39 DRTs in India.

List of Amending Acts:

1. The Recovery of Debts Due to Banks and Financial Institutions (Amendment) Act, 1995
2. The Recovery of Debts Due to Banks and Financial Institutions (Amendment) Act, 2000
3. The Enforcement of Security Interest and Recovery of Debts Laws (Amendment) Act, 2004
4. The Enforcement of Security Interest and Recovery of Debts Laws (Amendment) Act, 2012
5. The Enforcement of Security Interest and Recovery of Debts Laws (Amendment) Act, 2016
6. The Enforcement of Security Interest and Recovery of Debts Laws (Amendment) Act, 2018
7. The Enforcement of Security Interest and Recovery of Debts Laws (Amendment) Act, 2018

Language of the Tribunal

The proceedings of the Tribunal shall be conducted in English or Hindi. No reference, application, representation, documents or other matter contained in any language other than English or Hindi shall be accepted by the Tribunal unless the same is accompanied by the true translation thereof in English or Hindi.

Composition of Tribunal

A Tribunal shall consist of one person only (hereinafter referred to as the Presiding Officer) to be appointed by notification of the Central Government for 5 years or till he attains the age of 62 years, whichever is earlier.

Presiding Officer of a tribunal is a person who qualified to be, a District Judge. Presiding Officer of the DRT is called President.

Central Government provides the tribunal one or more recovery officer and such other officers and employees as that Government may think fit.

Establishment of Appellate Tribunal

The Central Government shall, by notification, establish one or more Appellate Tribunals, to be known as the Debts Recovery Appellate Tribunal, to exercise the jurisdiction, powers and authority conferred on such Tribunal by or under this Act.

DRAT is headed by Chair Person is in the rank of High Court Judge is appointed by Central Govt. for 5 years & maximum age 65 years.

Any person aggrieved by order passed by DRT may appeal to DRAT within 45 days of order received. The Tribunal may condone the delay in preferring an appeal beyond 45 days.

For filling appeal, as per Sec. 21 of DRT 50% of the amount to be deposited by the appellant. Provided that the Appellate Tribunal may, for reasons to be recorded in writing, reduce the amount to be deposited by such amount which shall not be less than 25% of the amount of such debt so due.

At present 5 DRATs at Mumbai, Delhi, Kolkata, Chennai & Allahabad are in India. It can transfer, on application, any case from one tribunal to another.

Bar of Jurisdiction: DRT is open only for Banks and Financial Institutions. DRT has Territorial Jurisdiction. As per Section 31 on establishment of a DRT no Civil Court or any other authority is to hear the proceeding of eligible cases. (Not applicable for High Court & Supreme Court). All existing cases are also to be transferred to a DRT.

Application to the Tribunal

Where a bank or a financial institution has to recover any debt from any person, it may make an application to the Tribunal within the local limits of their jurisdiction. DRT has Territorial Jurisdiction.

DRT jurisdiction covers recovery of debts due to banks and financial institutions with amount of ₹ 20.00 lakh (Changed from notification of Ministry of Finance dated 6th September, 2018. Earlier it was ₹ 10.00 lakh) or more (Central Government can reduce the amount to ₹ 1 lakh).

Now therefore, in exercise of the powers conferred by sub-section (4) of section 1 of the Recovery of Debts

Due to Banks and Financial Institutions Act, 1993, the Central Government hereby specifies that the provisions of the said Act shall not apply where the amount of debt due to any bank or financial institution or to a consortium of banks or financial institutions is less than twenty lakh rupees.

If another bank has a claim against the same person, then that bank can join the case before the final order is passed subject to separate fees. They have powers to order Attachment, to appoint a Receiver/ Commissioner for preparation of Inventory or for sale.

On receipt of the application under sub-section (1) or sub-section (2), the Tribunal shall issue summons requiring the defendant to show cause within thirty days of the service of summons as to why the relief prayed for should not be granted.

Counter Claim by Defendant

A defendant in an application may, in addition to his right of pleading a set off as above, set up, by way of counter-claim against the claim of the applicant, any right or claim in respect of a cause of action accruing to the defendant against the applicant either before or after the filing of the application but before the defendant has delivered his defense or before the time limited for delivering his defense has expired, whether such counter-claim is in the nature of a claim for damages or not.

Effect of Counter Claim by Defendant: A counter claim shall have the same effect as a cross-suit so as to enable the Tribunal to pass a final order on the same application, both on the original claim and on the counter-claim.

Answer to Counter-Claim by Applicant Bank/ Financial Institutions: The applicant shall be at liberty to file a written statement in answer to the counter-claim of the defendant within such period as may be fixed by the Tribunal.

Exclusion of Counter Claim from the Main Suit: Where the defendant sets up a counter-claim and the applicant contends that the claim thereby raised ought not to be disposed of by way of counter-claim but in an independent action, the applicant may, at any time before issues are settled in relation to the counter-claim, apply to the Tribunal for an order that such counter-claim may be excluded, the Tribunal may, on the hearing of such application make such order, as it thinks fit.

Procedure for Filing Application in DRT

Every application shall be in such form and accompanied by such documents or other evidence and by such fee as may be prescribed. The application shall be filed by the applicant with the Registrar within whose jurisdiction the applicant is functioning as a bank or financial institution, as the case may be, for time being. Important points for filling an application at DRT are as under:

An application shall be presented in the prescribed Performa. Application can be filled online. An application presented by the applicant in person or by his agent or by an authorised legal practitioner.

An application shall be presented to the registrar of the Bench within jurisdiction his case falls or shall be sent by registered post addressed to the Registrar. If sent by post, it shall be deemed to have been presented to the Registrar the day on receiving date.

The application shall be presented in four sets along with an empty file size envelope bearing full address of the respondent. Envelopes bearing full address of each of the respondents shall be furnished by the applicant.

Documents Required: Every application shall be accompanied by a paper book containing:
a) A statement showing details of the Debt due from a Respondent and the circumstances under which such a debt has become due.
b) All documents relied upon by the applicant and those mentioned in the application.
c) Details of crossed Bank Draft or Indian Postal Order representing the application fee.
d) Index of the documents.

Where the parties to the suit or proceedings are being represented by an agent, documents authorising him to act as such agent/Vakalatnama in case of an advocate shall also be appended to the application.

Application Fee: Every application shall be accompanied with fee provided in sub-rule (2). Fee may be remitted either in the form of crossed demand draft or Postal Order drawn in favour of the Registrar and payable at the Registrar's office is situated.

Presentation & Scrutiny of Application: The registrar or, as the case may be, the officer authorized by him, shall endorse on every application the date on which it is presented or deemed to have been presented under that rule and shall sign endorsement. If on scrutiny the application is found to be in order, it shall be duly registered and give a serial number.

Procedure at DRT
○ Registrar of DRT is responsible for the overall administration of the tribunal.
○ He gives Original Application (OA) number and issues summon after scrutinising the application.

○ He serves a copy of the application and paper book on each of the respondents.
○ The respondent may file 4 complete sets containing the reply to the application along with documents within 1 month (or extended time allowed by the tribunal) of its receipt.
○ The respondent shall also endorse one copy of the reply along with documents to the applicant.
○ If the defendant admits a part of the liability, the bank can request DRT for passing interim order for the admitted amount & pursue the balance dues.
○ The Presiding Officer is responsible for ordering injunction or stay for appointment of Commissioner/ Receiver for issuance of a garnishee order or for passing orders for attachment before judgment.
○ The presiding officer finally issues recovery certificate and sends it to Recovery Officer (RO) for execution.
○ The recovery officer shall, on receipt of the recovery certificate issues notice to certificate debtors and giving 15 day time for payment of the amount specified in the recovery certificate.
○ If the defendant fails to pay the amount , recovery officer will proceed to recover the amount by any one or more of the modes, which are detailed below:
  a) Attachment and sale of movable/immovable property of the defendant
  b) Arrest and detention of the defaulter
  c) Appointment of receiver

Time Limit for Decision: The application made to the Tribunal shall be dealt with by it as expeditiously as possible and endeavour shall be made by it to dispose of the application finally within 180 days from the date of receipt of the application.

Powers of DRAT

On receipt of an appeal, the Appellate Tribunal may, after giving the parties to the appeal, an opportunity of being heard, pass such orders thereon as it thinks fit, confirming, modifying or setting aside the order appealed against. DRAT shall send a copy of every order made by it to the parties to the appeal and to the concerned Tribunal.

Time Limit for Decision: The appeal filed before the Appellate Tribunal shall be dealt with by it as expeditiously as possible and endeavour shall be made by it to dispose of the appeal finally within 6 months from the date of receipt of the appeal.

Appeal against the Order of Recovery Officer: Any aggrieved person can appeal against the order of recovery officer to DRT can be made within 30 days of date of order. On receipt of an appeal, the Tribunal may, after giving an opportunity to the appellant to be heard, and after making such enquiry as it deems fit, confirm, modify or set aside the order made by the Recovery Officer in exercise of his powers under sections 25 to 28 (both inclusive).

Closing of DRT Application: After full recovery of bank dues, application is closed by recovery officer.

The Chairperson of an Appellate Tribunal, the Presiding Officer of a Tribunal, the Recovery Officer and other officers and employees of an Appellate Tribunal and a Tribunal shall be deemed to be public servants within the meaning of section 21 of the Indian Penal Code.

TEST YOURSELF

1. The objective of enactment of DRT Act is:
   (a) For expeditious adjudication and recovery of debts due to banks and financial institutions.
   (b) To increase capital in banks and financial institutions
   (c) To meet the international standard of recovery
   (d) All of the above

2. DRT Act does not cover the loans due to which of the following:
   (a) Commercial banks   (b) Financial institutions
   (c) NBFCs   (d) None of the above

3. Normally DRT Act is applicable to loan with:
   (a) Sanction limit of ₹ 1 lakh and above
   (b) Sanction limit of ₹ 10 lakh and above
   (c) Outstanding balance of ₹ 10 lakh and above
   (d) Outstanding balance of ₹ 20 lakh and above

4. Central Govt. can reduce the amount in DRT Act is applicable to loan with:
   (a) Sanction limit of ₹ 1 lakh and above
   (b) Sanction limit of ₹ 10 lakh and above
   (c) Outstanding balance of ₹ 1 lakh and above
   (d) Outstanding balance of ₹ 20 lakh and above

5. The Presiding Officer of DRT is called:
   (a) Chairman   (b) Chairperson
   (c) President   (d) Judge

6. The Presiding Officer of DRAT is called:
   (a) Chairman   (b) Chairperson
   (c) President   (d) Judge

7. Presiding Officer of DRT is to be appointed by notification of the Central Government for _______ or till he attains the age of _______,
   (a) 5 years, 62 years   (b) 5 years, 65 years
   (c) 3 years, 62 years   (d) 3 years, 65 years

8. Chairperson of DRAT is to be appointed by notification of the Central Government for _______ or till he attains the age of _______,
   (a) 5 years, 62 years   (b) 5 years, 65 years
   (c) 3 years, 62 years   (d) 3 years, 65 years

9. For filing appeal at DRAT against DRT, 50% of the amount to be deposited by the appellant. Provided that the Appellate Tribunal may reduce the amount to be deposited by such amount which shall not be less than _____ of the amount of such debt so due.
   (a) 40%   (b) 25%
   (c) 10%   (d) Nil

10. Any person aggrieved by order passed by DRT may appeal to DRAT within _______ of order received.
    (a) 15 days   (b) 30 days
    (c) 45 days   (d) 60 days

11. Any aggrieved person can appeal against order of recovery officer to DRT can be made within _______ of date of order.
    (a) 15 days   (b) 30 days
    (c) 45 days   (d) 60 days

12. Presiding Officer of a DRT and Chairperson of the DRAT is a person who qualified to be, a _______ judge and _______ judge respectively.
    (a) District, High Court
    (b) District, Supreme Court
    (c) Civil Court, High Court
    (d) Civil Court, Supreme Court

13. The application shall be presented at DRT in _______ sets along with an empty file size envelope bearing full address of the respondent.
    (a) Two   (b) Three
    (c) Four   (d) As per DRT instruction

14. On filing a case, the DRT issues summons to the defendant requires him to show cause for grant of relief to the bank. Defendant is required to show cause within _______.
    (a) 15 days   (b) 30 days
    (c) 45 days   (d) 60 days

15. The recovery officer shall, on receipt of the recovery certificate issues notice to certificate debtors and giving _________ time for payment of the amount specified in the recovery certificate.
(a) 15 days
(b) 30 days
(c) 45 days
(d) 60 days

16. If the defendant fails to pay the amount, recovery officer will proceed to recover the amount by any one or more of the modes, which are the correct actions?
(a) Attachment and sale of movable/immovable property of the defendant
(b) Arrest and detention of the defaulter
(c) Appointment of receiver
(d) All of the above

17. The application made to the Tribunal shall be dealt with by it as expeditiously as possible and endeavour shall be made by it to dispose of the application finally within _________ from the date of receipt of the application.

(a) 90 days
(b) 180 days
(c) 270 days
(d) 1 year

18. After full recovery of bank dues, application at DRT is closed by ___________.
(a) Presiding Officer
(b) Registrar
(c) Recovery Officer
(d) None of the above

19. DRT is established by:
(a) RBI
(b) Central Govt.
(c) Respective State Govt.
(d) Supreme Court

20. In an Appellate Tribunal and a Tribunal who shall be deemed to be public servants within the meaning of section 21 of the Indian Penal Code.
(a) The Chairperson of an Appellate Tribunal
(b) The Presiding Officer of a Tribunal
(c) The Recovery Officer
(d) All of the above

ANSWER

1	2	3	4	5	6	7	8	9	10
(a)	(c)	(d)	(c)	(c)	(b)	(a)	(b)	(b)	(c)

11	12	13	14	15	16	17	18	19	20
(b)	(a)	(c)	(b)	(a)	(d)	(b)	(c)	(b)	(d)

___

SARFAESI ACT, 2002 AND CERSAI

OBJECTIVE

The SARFAESI Act 2002 enables the secured creditors (Banks) to enforce security interest for recovery of its dues without intervention of the Court provided that security interest has been properly created in favour of the bank. It allows banks and other financial institutions to auction residential or commercial properties to recover loans. Under this act secured creditors (banks or financial institutions) have many rights for enforcement of security interest under section 13 of SARFAESI Act, 2002. Under asset securitisation, bank or a financial institution pools and packages individual loans and receivables, creates securities against them, get them rated and sells them to investors in a market. Thus, asset securitisation is nothing but a process of stimulating assets into securities and securities into liquidity on an ongoing basis, increasing thereby turnover of business and profits.

INTRODUCTION

The Securitisation and Reconstruction of Financial Assets and Enforcement of Security Interest Act, 2002 (also known as the SARFAESI Act 2002) is an Indian law. It extends to the whole of India. It shall be deemed to have come into force on the 21st day of June, 2002. The securitisation act amended in 2016. This amended act may be called the Enforcement of Security Interest and Recovery of Debts Laws and Miscellaneous Provisions (Amendment) Act, 2016.

Definitions as per SARFAESI Act 2002

I. **Appellate Tribunal:** Any person aggrieved by the order passed by 'DRT' can file an appeal to the Appellate Tribunal. Appellate Tribunal means a 'Debts Recovery Appellate Tribunal' established under sub-section (1) of section 8 of the Recovery of Debts Due to Banks and Financial Institutions Act, 1993.

II. **Asset Reconstruction:** Asset reconstruction means acquisition of any right or interest of any bank or financial institution in any financial assistance by any securitisation company or reconstruction company for the purpose of realisation of such financial assistance. It is the takeover of advances from banks and financial Institution for recovery purpose.

III. **Bank:** All the banking companies, nationalized banks, State Bank of India, Co-operative Banks, regional rural banks and such other banks which the Central Government may, by notification, specify for the purposes of this Act.

IV. **Board:** Board means the Securities and Exchange Board of India (SEBI) established under section 3 of the Securities and Exchange Board of India Act, 1992.

V. **Borrower:** Borrower means any person,
- Who has been granted financial assistance by any bank or financial institution or
- Who has given any guarantee or
- Who has created any mortgage or pledge as security for the financial assistance granted by any bank or financial institution and
- A person who becomes borrower of a securitisation company or reconstruction company consequent upon acquisition by it of any rights or interest of any bank or financial institution in relation to such financial assistance;
- A person who has raised funds by way of issuance of debt securities (Amendment 2016).

VI. Default: Default means non-payment of any principal debt or interest thereon or any other amount payable by a borrower to any secured creditor consequent upon which the account of such borrower is classified as non-performing asset (NPA) in the books of account of the secured creditor.

Default regarding debt securities. However a 90 days' notice for payment has to be given in such case (Amendment 2016).

VII. Financial Assistance: Financial assistance means any loan or advance granted or any debentures or bonds subscribed or any guarantees given or letters of credit established or any other credit facility extended by any bank or financial institution;

Funds provided for acquisition of tangible assets on hire/financial lease/conditional sale/contract/assignment /purchase of debt securities (Amendment 2016).

VIII. Financial Asset: Financial asset means debt or receivables and includes—

(i) A claim to any debt or receivables or part thereof, whether secured or unsecured; or

(ii) Any debt or receivables secured by, mortgage of, or charge on, immovable property; or

(iii) A mortgage, charge, hypothecation or pledge of movable property; or

(iv) Any right or interest in the security, whether full or part underlying such debt or receivables; or

(v) Any beneficial interest in property, whether movable or immovable, or in such debt, receivables, whether such interest is existing, future, accruing, conditional or contingent; or

(vi) Any financial assistance;

(vii) Any right, title or interest on any intangible asset or license or assignment of such intangible asset, which secures the obligations to pay any unpaid portion of purchase (Amendment 2016).

IX. Financial Institution: The financial institution means—

(i) A public financial institution within the meaning of section 4A of the Companies Act, 1956;

(ii) Any institution specified by the Central Government under the Recovery of Debts Due to Banks and Financial Institutions Act, 1993.

(iii) The International Finance Corporation established under the International Finance Corporation (Status, Immunities and Privileges) Act, 1958;

(iv) Any other institution or non-banking financial company as defined in the Reserve Bank of India Act, 1934, which the Central Government may, by notification, specify as financial institution for the purposes of this Act.

(v) Any ARC and Debenture Trustee appointed for debt securities and registered with board (Amendment 2016).

X. Hypothecation: Hypothecation is defined first time under SARFAESI Act 2002. Earlier, no Indian Law defined it. Hypothecation means a charge in or upon any movable property, existing or future, created by a borrower in favour of a secured creditor without delivery of possession of the movable property to such creditor, as a security for financial assistance and includes floating charge and crystallisation of such charge into fixed charge on movable property.

XI. Non-Performing Asset: Non-performing asset means an asset or account of a borrower, which has been classified by a bank or financial institution as sub-standard, doubtful or loss asset—

(a) In case such bank or financial institution is administered or regulated by any authority or body established, constituted or appointed by any law for the time being in force, in accordance with the directions or guidelines relating to assets classifications issued by such authority or body;

(b) In any other case, in accordance with the directions or guidelines relating to assets classifications issued by the Reserve Bank.

XII. Property: Property means—

(i) Immovable property;

(ii) Movable property;

(iii) Any debt or any right to receive payment of money, whether secured or unsecured;

(iv) Receivables, whether existing or future;

(v) Intangible assets, being know-how, patent, copyright, trade mark, licence, franchise or any other business or commercial right of similar nature (Amendment 2016).

XIII. Qualified Institutional Buyer: Qualified institutional buyer means a financial institution, insurance company, bank, state financial corporation, state industrial development corporation, trustee or securitisation company or reconstruction company which has been granted a certificate of registration under sub-section (4) of section 3 or any asset management company making investment on behalf of mutual fund or pension fund or a foreign institutional investor registered under the Securities and Exchange Board of India Act, 1992 or regulations made thereunder, or any other body corporate as may be specified by SEBI; Any other category of Non-institutional investors specified by RBI (Amendment 2016).

XIV. **Securitisation:** Securitisation means acquisition of financial assets by any securitisation company or reconstruction company from any originator, whether by raising of funds by such securitisation company or reconstruction company from qualified institutional buyers by issue of security receipts representing undivided interest in such financial assets or otherwise.

XV. **Securitisation Company**: Securitisation company means any company formed and registered under the Companies Act, 1956 for the purpose of securitisation.

XVI. **Secured Asset:** Secured asset means the property on which security interest is created.

XVII. **Secured Creditor:** Secured creditor means any bank or financial institution or any consortium or group of banks or financial institutions and includes—

a) Debenture trustee appointed by any bank or financial institution; or

b) Securitisation company or reconstruction company, whether acting as such or managing a trust set up by such securitisation company or reconstruction company for the securitisation or reconstruction, as the case may be; or

c) Any other trustee holding securities on behalf of a bank or financial institution, in whose favour security interest is created for due repayment by any borrower of any financial assistance;

d) Any other institution holding right, title or interest upon financial asset, bank appointed debenture trustee registered with SEBI and appointed by company, any other trustee holding securities on behalf of a Bank (Amendment 2016).

XVIII. **Secured Debt:** Secured debt means a debt which is secured by any security interest.

XIX. **Unpaid Portion** of purchase or any right/title/ interest on unpaid portion (Amendment 2016).

REGISTRATION OF SECURITISATION COMPANIES OR RECONSTRUCTION COMPANIES

Securitisation Company or Reconstruction Company

No securitisation company or reconstruction company shall commence or carry on the business of securitisation or asset reconstruction without—

(a) Obtaining a certificate of registration granted under this section; and

(b) Having the own fund of not less than ₹ 2 crores or such other amount not exceeding 15% of total financial assets acquired or to be acquired by the Securitisation Company or Reconstruction Company, as the Reserve Bank may, by notification, specify. Reserve Bank may, by notification, specify different amounts of owned fund for different class or classes of securitisation companies or reconstruction companies.

Existing Company: Securitisation company or reconstruction company, existing on the commencement of this Act, shall make an application for registration to the Reserve Bank before the expiry of six months from such commencement and notwithstanding anything contained in this sub-section may continue to carry on the business of securitisation or asset reconstruction until a certificate of registration is granted to it or, as the case may be, rejection of application for registration is communicated to it.

Registration with RBI

Every securitisation company or reconstruction company shall make an application for registration to the Reserve Bank in such form and manner as it may specify.

Process to the followed at RBI: The Reserve Bank may, for the purpose of considering the application for registration of a securitisation company or reconstruction company to commence or carry on the business of securitisation or asset reconstruction, as the case may be, require to be satisfied, by an inspection of records or books of such securitisation company or reconstruction company, or otherwise, that the following conditions are fulfilled, namely:

a) That the securitisation company or reconstruction company has not incurred losses in any of the three preceding financial years;

b) That such securitisation company or reconstruction company has made adequate arrangements for realisation of the financial assets acquired for the purpose of securitisation or asset reconstruction and shall be able to pay periodical returns and redeem on respective due dates on the investments made in the company by the qualified institutional buyers or other persons;

c) That the directors of securitisation company or reconstruction company have adequate professional experience in matters related to finance, securitisation and reconstruction;

d) That the board of directors of such securitisation company or reconstruction company does not consist of more than half of its total number of directors who are either nominees of any sponsor or associated in any manner with the sponsor or any of its subsidiaries;

e) That any of its directors has not been convicted of any offence involving moral turpitude;

f) That a sponsor, is not a holding company of the securitisation company or reconstruction company, as the case may be, or, does not otherwise hold any controlling interest in such securitisation company or reconstruction company;

g) That securitisation company or reconstruction company has complied with or is in a position to comply with prudential norms specified by the Reserve Bank.

h) That securitisation company or reconstruction company has complied with one or more conditions specified in the guidelines issued by the Reserve Bank for the said purpose.

Rejection of Application by RBI: Reserve Bank may reject the application made if it is satisfied that the conditions are not fulfilled. Before rejecting the application, the applicant shall be given a reasonable opportunity of being heard.

Change in Management/Location: Every securitisation company or reconstruction company, shall obtain prior approval of the Reserve Bank for any substantial change in its management or change of location of its registered office or change in its name. The decision of the Reserve Bank, whether the change in management of a securitisation company or a reconstruction company is a substantial change in its management or not, shall be final.

Cancellation of Certificate of Registration

The Reserve Bank may cancel a certificate of registration granted to a securitisation company or a reconstruction company, if—

a) The company ceases to carry on the business of securitisation or asset reconstruction; or ceases to receive or hold any investment from a qualified institutional buyer; or

b) The company has failed to comply with any conditions subject to which the certificate of registration has been granted to it; or

c) The company fails to—

   I. Comply with any direction issued by the Reserve Bank under the provisions of this Act; or

   II. Maintain accounts in accordance with the requirements of any law or any direction or order issued by the Reserve Bank under the provisions of this Act; or

   III. Submit or offer for inspection its books of account or other relevant documents when so demanded by the Reserve Bank; or

   IV. Obtain prior approval of the Reserve Bank required under subsection (6) of section 3.

Appeal against Cancellation of Registration: A securitisation company or reconstruction company aggrieved by the order of rejection of application for registration or cancellation of certificate of registration may prefer an appeal, within a period of 30 days from the date on which such order of rejection or cancellation is communicated to it, to the Central Government. Before rejecting an appeal such company shall be given a reasonable opportunity of being heard.

Circumstances when such Companies would Continue Despite Cancellation: A securitisation company or reconstruction company, which is holding investments of qualified institutional buyers and whose application for grant of certificate of registration has been rejected or certificate of registration has been cancelled shall, notwithstanding such rejection or cancellation be deemed to be a securitisation company or reconstruction company until it repays the entire investments held by it (together with interest, if any) within such period as the Reserve Bank may direct.

Acquisition of Rights or Interest in Financial Assets: A securitisation company or reconstruction company may acquire financial assets of any bank or financial institution:

a) By issuing a debenture or bond or any other security in the nature of debenture, for consideration agreed upon between such company and the bank or financial institution, incorporating therein such terms and conditions as may be agreed upon between them;

b) By entering into an agreement with such bank or financial institution for the transfer of such financial assets to such company on such terms and conditions as may be agreed upon between them.

Status of Company on Asset Acquisition: If the bank or financial institution is a lender in relation to any financial assets acquired by the securitisation company or the reconstruction company, such securitisation company or reconstruction company shall, on such acquisition, be deemed to be the lender and all the rights of such bank or financial institution shall vest in such company in relation to such financial assets.

States of Covenants Prior to Purchase: All contracts, deeds, bonds, agreements, powers of attorney, grants of legal representation, permissions, approvals, consents or no-objections under any law or otherwise and other instruments of whatever nature which relate to the said financial asset and which are subsisting or having effect immediately before the acquisition of financial asset and to which the concerned bank or financial institution is a party or which are in favour of such bank or financial institution shall, after the acquisition of the financial assets, be of as full force and effect against or in favour of the securitisation company or reconstruction company, as the case may be, and may be enforced or acted upon as fully and effectually as if, in the place of the said bank or financial institution, securitisation company or reconstruction company, as the case may be, had been a party thereto or as if they had been issued in favour of securitisation company or reconstruction company, as the case may be.

Notice to Obligor and Discharge of Obligation of such Obligor: The bank or financial institution may, if it considers appropriate, give a notice of acquisition of financial assets by any securitisation company or reconstruction company, to the concerned obligor and any other concerned person and to the concerned registering authority (including Registrar of Companies) in whose jurisdiction the mortgage, charge, hypothecation, assignment or other interest created on the financial assets had been registered.

Obligation of Obligor: Where a notice of acquisition of financial asset is given by a bank or financial institution, the obligor, on receipt of such notice, shall make payment to the concerned securitisation company or reconstruction company, as the case may be, and payment made to such company in discharge of any of the obligations in relation to the financial asset specified in the notice shall be a full discharge to the obligor making the payment from all liability in respect of such payment.

Issue of Security Receipts: A securitisation company or reconstruction company, may, after acquisition of any financial asset offer security receipts to qualified institutional buyers (other than by offer to public) for subscription in accordance with the provisions of those Acts.

Raising of Funds by ARC: A securitisation company or reconstruction company may raise funds from the qualified institutional buyers by formulating schemes for acquiring financial assets and shall keep and maintain separate and distinct accounts in respect of each such scheme for every financial asset acquired out of investments made by a qualified institutional buyer and ensure that realisations of such financial asset is held and applied towards redemption of investments and payment of returns assured on such investments under the relevant scheme.

Rights of Qualified Institutional Buyers: In the event of non-realisation of financial assets, the qualified institutional buyers of a securitisation company or reconstruction company, holding security receipts of not less than 75% of the total value of the security receipts issued by such company, shall be entitled to call a meeting of all the qualified institutional buyers and every resolution passed in such meeting shall be binding on the company. These buyers shall, at a meeting follow the same procedure, as nearly as possible as is followed at meetings of the board of directors of the securitisation company or reconstruction company; as the case may be.

Exemption from Registration of Security Receipt: A security receipt issued by the securitisation company or reconstruction company, as the case may be, and not creating, declaring, assigning, limiting or extinguishing any right, title or interest, to or in immovable property except in so far as it entitles the holder of the security receipt to an undivided interest afforded by a registered instrument; or any transfer of security receipts, shall not require compulsory registration.

Measures for Assets Reconstruction: A securitisation company or reconstruction company may, for the purposes of asset reconstruction, having regard to the guidelines framed by the Reserve Bank in this behalf, provide for any one or more of the following measures, namely :

a) The proper management of the business of the borrower, by change in, or takeover of, the management of the business of the borrower;

b) The sale or lease of a part or whole of the business of the borrower;

c) Rescheduling of payment of debts payable by the borrower;

d) Enforcement of security interest in accordance with the provisions of this Act;

e) Settlement of dues payable by the borrower;

f) Taking possession of secured assets in accordance with the provisions of this Act.

Other Functions of Securitisation Company or Reconstruction Company: A securitisation company or reconstruction company may act:

a) As an agent for any bank or financial institution for the purpose of recovering their dues from the borrower on payment of such fees or charges as may be mutually agreed upon between the parties;

b) As a manager referred to in such fee as may be mutually agreed upon between the parties;

c) As a receiver if appointed by any court or tribunal: Provided that no securitisation company or reconstruction company shall act as a manager if acting as such gives rise to any pecuniary liability. However, no securitisation company or reconstruction company granted a certificate of registration shall commence or carry on, without prior approval of the Reserve Bank, any business other than that of securitisation or asset reconstruction.

Resolution of Disputes: Where any dispute relating to securitisation or reconstruction or non-payment of any amount due including interest arises amongst any of the parties, namely, the bank, or financial institution, or securitisation company or reconstruction company or qualified institutional buyer, such dispute shall be settled by conciliation or arbitration as provided in the Arbitration and Conciliation Act, 1996, as if the parties to the dispute have consented in writing for determination of such dispute by conciliation or arbitration and the provisions of that Act shall apply accordingly.

ENFORCEMENT OF SECURITY INTEREST

Enforcement of Security Interest: As per SARFAESI Act any security interest created in favour of any secured creditor (charge created) may be enforced (security may be sold), without the intervention of the court or tribunal, by such creditor in accordance with the provisions of this Act.

Issue of Notice for Payment of Dues: Where any borrower, who is under a liability to a secured creditor under a security agreement, makes any default in repayment of secured debt or any instalment thereof, and his account in respect of such debt is classified by the secured creditor as non-performing asset, then the secured creditor may require the borrower by notice in writing to discharge in full his liabilities to the secured creditor within 60 days from the date of notice failing which the secured creditor shall be entitled to exercise all or any of the rights under this Act. As per amendment in 2016, the demand notice can be served/delivered by hand delivery also and electronic mode of service, apart from the other prescribed mode.

Contents of the Notice: The notice shall give details of the amount payable by the borrower and the secured assets intended to be enforced by the secured creditor in the event of non-payment of secured debts by the borrower.

Failure of the Borrower: In case the borrower fails to discharge his liability in full within the stipulated period, the secured creditor may take recourse to one or more of the following measures to recover his secured debt, namely:

a) Take possession of the secured assets of the borrower including the right to transfer by way of lease, assignment or sale for realizing the secured asset;

b) Take over the management of the secured assets of the borrower including the right to transfer by way of lease, assignment or sale and realise the secured asset; appoint any person (hereafter referred to as the manager), to manage the secured assets the possession of which has been taken over by the secured creditor;

c) Require at any time by notice in writing, any person who has acquired any of the secured assets from the borrower and from whom any money is due or may become due to the borrower, to pay the secured creditor, so much of the money as is sufficient to pay the secured debt.

If Borrower Makes the Payment: Any payment made by any person to the secured creditor shall give such person a valid discharge as if he has made payment to the borrower.

Reply to Representation of the Borrower: (a) After issue of demand notice under sub-section (2) of section 13, if the borrower makes any representation or raises any objection to the notice, the Authorized Officer shall consider such representation or objection and examine whether the same is acceptable or tenable.

After issuance of notice u/s 13(2) by the bank, if any borrower/guarantor makes any representation or raise any objection, then the bank has to consider such objection and serve a revised notice or pass such other suitable orders as deemed necessary, or If bank feels that objection is not acceptable or tenable, he shall communicate the justification for possession within fifteen days (After amendment it was enhanced from seven days to fifteen days) from the date of receipt of the representation or objection.

Effect of Possession by the Secured Creditor: Any transfer of secured asset after taking possession thereof or takeover of management, by the secured creditor or by the manager on behalf of the secured creditor shall vest in the transferee all rights in, or in relation to, the secured asset transferred as if the transfer had been made by the owner of such secured asset.

Costs and Charges: Where any action has been taken against a borrower under the above provisions, all costs, charges and expenses which, in the opinion of the secured creditor, have been properly incurred by him or any expenses incidental thereto, shall be recoverable from the borrower and the money which is received by the secured creditor shall, in the absence of any contract to the contrary, be held by him in trust, to be applied, firstly, in payment of such costs, charges and expenses and secondly, the dues of the secured creditor and the residue of the money so received shall be paid to the person entitled thereto in accordance with his rights and interests.

Payment of Dues after Possession but Before Sale: If the dues of the secured creditor together with all costs, charges and expenses incurred by him are tendered to the secured creditor at any time before the date fixed for sale or transfer, the secured asset shall not be sold or transferred by the secured creditor, and no further step shall be taken by him for transfer or sale of that secure asset.

Sale of Assets in Case of Consortium: In the case of financing of a financial asset by more than one secured creditors or joint financing of a financial asset by secured creditors, no secured creditor shall be entitled to exercise any or all of the rights conferred on him unless exercise of such right is agreed upon by the secured creditors representing not less than 75% in value of the amount outstanding as on a record date and such action shall be binding on all the secured creditors. In the case of a company in liquidation, the amount realised from the sale of secured assets shall be distributed in accordance with the provisions of section 529A of the Companies Act, 1956.

Companies in Liquidation: In case of companies in liquidation, the liquidator shall intimate the secured creditor, the workmen's dues in accordance with the provisions of section 529A of the Companies Act, 1956 and in case such workmen's dues cannot be ascertained, the liquidator shall intimate the estimated amount of workmen's dues under that section to the secured creditor and in such case the secured creditor may retain the sale proceeds of the secured assets after depositing the amount of such estimate dues with the liquidator.

Dues of Workmen: In case the secured creditor deposits the estimated amount of workmen's dues, such creditor shall be liable to pay the balance of the workmen's dues or entitled to receive the excess amount, if any, deposited by the secured creditor with the liquidator. The secured creditor shall furnish an undertaking to the liquidator to pay the balance of the workmen's dues, if any.

Where Liability is not Discharged Fully: Where dues of the secured creditor are not fully satisfied with the sale proceeds of the secured assets, the secured creditor may file an application in the form and manner as may be prescribed to the Debts Recovery Tribunal having jurisdiction or a competent court, as the case may be, for recovery of the balance amount from the borrower. Secured creditor shall be entitled to proceed against the guarantors or sell the pledged assets without first taking any of the measures in relation to the secured assets under this Act.

Who shall Exercise the Rights of Secured Creditor (Sec 12): The rights may be exercised by officers authorised in this behalf in such manner as may be prescribed (Chief Manager in a Public Sector Bank has been prescribed by the Govt.).

Restrictions on the Borrower to Deal with the Assets: No borrower shall, after receipt of notice, transfer by way of sale, lease or otherwise (other than in the ordinary course of his business) any of his secured assets referred to in the notice, without prior written consent of the secured creditor.

Chief Metropolitan Magistrate or District Magistrate to Assist Secured Creditor in Taking Possession of Secured Asset:

(1) Where the possession of any secured assets is required to be taken by the secured creditor or if any of the secured asset is required to be sold or transferred by the secured creditor under the provisions of this Act, the secured creditor may, for the purpose of taking possession or control of any such secured asset, request, in writing, the Chief Metropolitan Magistrate or the District Magistrate within whose jurisdiction any such secured asset or other documents relating thereto may be situated or found, to take possession thereof, and the Chief Metropolitan Magistrate or, as the case may be, the District Magistrate shall, on such request being made to him—

  (a) Take possession of such asset and documents relating thereto; and

  (b) Forward such assets and documents to the secured creditor.

(2) For the purpose of securing compliance with the provisions of sub-section (1), the Chief Metropolitan Magistrate or the District Magistrate may take or cause to be taken such steps and use, or cause to be used, such force, as may, in his opinion, be necessary.

(3) No act of the Chief Metropolitan Magistrate or the District Magistrate done in pursuance of this section shall be called in question in any court or before any authority.

(4) The application before the DM/CMM for physical possession of the charged property must be disposed of within a period of 30 days from the date of application and in any case not later than 60 days. (Amendment 2016).

Restoration of Management: Where the management of the business of a borrower had been taken over by the secured creditor, the secured creditor shall, on realisation of his debt in full, restore the management of the business of the borrower to him.

Compensation to Directors for Loss of Office: No managing director or any other director or a manager or any person in charge of management of the business of the borrower shall be entitled to any compensation for the loss of office or for the premature termination under this Act of any contract of management entered into by him with the borrower.

BIFR cases—the cases already referred to BIFR can be called back if the majority of the lenders (75% in terms of value) agree for that.

Amount Ceiling—Loans with outstanding up to ₹ 1 lac will not be covered under the provisions. Similarly, the security interest created in agriculture land and in those cases where the borrower has already paid 80% of the total dues to secured creditor, are also excluded from the purview.

Receipt of Notice by the Borrower: If, on receipt of the notice from the creditor, the borrower makes any representation or raises any objection, the secured creditor shall consider such representation or objection. If the secured creditor comes to the conclusion that representation or objection is not acceptable or tenable, he shall communicate within 15 days of receipt of such representation or objection, the reasons for non-acceptance of the representation or objection to the borrower.

Application by the Borrower to DRT Against Possession: The borrower may make an application along with such fee as may be prescribed, to DRT, without deposit of any amount.

Action by DRT: On receipt of an application from the borrower DRT shall consider whether any of the measures taken by the secured creditor for enforcement of security are in accordance with the provisions of this Act and fee rules made thereunder. If, DRT comes to the conclusion that any of the measures taken by the secured creditor are not in accordance with the provisions of the Act, it may by, order, declare the recourse to any one or more measures taken by the secured assets as invalid and restore the possession of the secured assets to the borrower.

If, DRT declares the recourse taken by a secured creditor is in accordance with the provisions of this Act and the rules made thereunder, then, notwithstanding anything contained in any other law for the time being in force, the secured creditor shall be entitled to take recourse to one or more of the measures to recover his secured debt.

Appeal to DRAT and Deposit of Amount before Appeal: No appeal shall be entertained by Appellate Tribunal unless the borrower has deposited with Appellate Tribunal 50% of the amount of debt due from him. As claimed by the secured creditors or determined by the DRT, whichever is less. The Appellate Tribunal may reduce the amount to not less than 25% of debt.

(An earlier provision, Borrowers aggrieved by any action of a lender shall be able to approach DRTs but by depositing 75% of dues up front before appeal, has been dispensed with by Supreme Court in its judgement dated April 09, 2004 while up-holding the constitutional validity of the Act).

SALE OF CHARGED SECURITIES

Ministry of Finance notified (during Sept 2002) the rules for taking possession and subsequent sale of assets of defaulters called Securities Interest (Enforcement) Rules, 2002. Under these rules:

Lenders have been permitted to dispose off the assets that have been taken possession of, both through private treaty and public auction including through e-auction mode.

○ **Possession:** Prior to the sale of any immovable secured asset, an authorised officer of the lender would have to take possession of the same by service of a 60 days possession notice.

○ **Sale:** Sale by way of public tenders or through public auction including through e-auction mode has to be backed by public notices in two newspapers.

○ **Minimum Notice Period:** A minimum 30 days' notice to be given to the owner after taking the possession by the authorised officer and the eventual sale of both movable and immovable properties.

○ **Designated Official:** The authorised officer has to be an officer equivalent to a Chief Manager of a PSB or such person specified by the Board of the lenders. The Board can also appoint a manager who would manage the secured assets taken possession of by the lenders.

○ **Reserve Price:** Both for the movable and immovable assets the lenders would have to make proper valuation, prior to sale. The reserve price would have to be arrived at only after the valuation exercise.

○ **Valuation of Securities:** In case of movable secured assets, authorized officer will simply obtain an estimated value, for immovable property valuation to be obtained from a valuer approved by the lenders' Board of Directors.

○ **Offer Price:** In case where a price higher than the reserve price cannot be obtained, the asset can be disposed off at a lower price with the consent of both the borrower and lender except where the assets could have natural decay or where the cost of possession might exceed the value of sale. Sale will be confirmed after deposit of 25% by the highest bidder. Balance within 15 days of confirmation of sale.

Right to Appeal (Sec 17): (1) Any person (including borrower), aggrieved by any of the measures taken by the secured creditor or his authorised officer, may prefer an appeal to the Debts Recovery Tribunal having jurisdiction in the matter within forty-five days from the date on which such measure had been taken.

(2) Where an appeal is preferred by a borrower, such appeal shall not be entertained by the Debts Recovery Tribunal unless the borrower has deposited with the Debts Recovery Tribunal seventy-five per cent of the amount claimed in the notice referred to in sub-section of section 13: Provided that the Debts Recovery Tribunal may, for reasons to be recorded in writing, waive or reduce the amount to be deposited under this section.

Save (3) provided in this Act, the Debts Recovery Tribunal shall, as far as may be, dispose of the appeal in accordance with the provisions of the Recovery of Debts- Due to Banks and Financial Institutions Act, 1993 (51 of 1993) and rules make thereunder.

Appeal to Appellate Tribunal (Sec 18): Any person aggrieved, by any order made by the Debts Recovery Tribunal under section 17, may prefer an appeal to the Appellate Tribunal within 30 days from the date of receipt of the order of Debts Recovery Tribunal. The Appellate Tribunal shall, as far as may be, dispose of the appeal in accordance with the provisions of the Recovery of Debts Due to Banks and Financial Institutions Act, 1993 and rules made thereunder.

Right of Borrower to Receive Compensation and Costs in Certain Cases: If the Debts Recovery Tribunal or the Appellate Tribunal, as the case may be, on an appeal filed under section 17 or section 18 holds the possession of secured assets by the secure creditor as wrongful and directs the secured creditor to return such secured assets to the concerned borrower, such borrower shall be entitled to payment of such compensation and costs as may be determined by such Tribunal or Appellate Tribunal.

ACTION	PERIOD
Notice for possession	60 days
Reply by bank to borrower's representation or objection from date of receipt of such representation or objection	15 days
Borrower can approach DRT against Possession Notice from date of acknowledgement	45 days
Appeal to DRAT against decision of DRT	30 days
Notice before sale of the immovable secured asset	30 days
Period of balance payment of 75% amount by the buyer of the secured assets	15 days

Central Registry of Securitisation Asset Reconstruction and Security Interest of India (CERSAI)

Central Registry of Securitisation Assets Reconstruction & Security Interest of India Govt. of India established the Central Registry of Securitisation Asset Reconstruction and Security Interest of India (CERSAI), a Govt. Company, u/s 25 of Companies Act, 1956 on March 31, 2011. It operates/maintains Central Registry functions as per SARFAESI Act 2002 under the superintendence and direction of Central Registrar. The majority shareholding (51%) is with Central Govt., Public Sector Banks and National Housing Bank. Central Government may, set up a registry to be known as the Central Registry with its own seal for the purposes of registration of transaction of securitization and reconstruction of financial assets and creation of security interest under this Act. Central Government may define the territorial limits within which an office of the Central Registry may exercise its functions. The provisions of this Act pertaining to the Central Registry shall be in addition to any of the provisions contained in the Registration Act, 1908 (16 of 1908), the Companies Act, 1956 (1 of 1956), the Merchant Shipping Act, 1958 (44 of 1958), the Patents Act, 1970 (39 of 1970), the Motor Vehicles Act, 1988 (49 of 1988), and the Designs Act, 2000 (16 of 2000) or any other law requiring registration of charges and shall not affect the priority of charges or validity there of under those Acts or laws.

Central Registrar (Sec 21): Central Government may appoint a person for the purpose of registration of transactions relating to securitisation, reconstruction of financial assets and security interest created over properties, to be known as the Central Registrar. Central Government may appoint such other officers under the superintendence and direction of the Central Registrar.

Register of Securitisation, Reconstruction and Security Interest Transactions (Sec 22): A record called the Central Register shall be kept at the Head Office of the Central Registry (wholly or partly in computer, floppies, diskettes or in any other electronic form) for entering the particulars of the transactions relating to securitisation of financial assets; reconstruction of financial assets; and creation of security interest.

Filing of Transactions of Securitisation, Reconstruction and Creation of Security Interest (Sec 23): The particulars of every transaction of securitisation, asset reconstruction or creation of security interest shall be filed, with the Central Registrar on payment of prescribed fee, within 30 days after the date of such transaction or creation of security, by the securitisation company or Reconstruction Company or the secured creditor, as the case may be. Central Registrar may allow the filing of the particulars of such transaction or creation of security within 30 days next following the expiry of the said period of 30 days on payment of additional fees not exceeding 10 times the amount of such fee.

Modification of Security Interest Registered under this Act (Sec 24): Whenever the terms or conditions, or the extent or operation of any security interest registered under this Chapter are or is reconstruction company or the secured creditors, as the case may be, to send to the Central Registrar, the particulars of such modification, and the provisions of this Chapter as to registration of a security interest shall apply to such modification modified, it shall be the duty of the securitisation company or the of such security interest.

Securitisation Company or Reconstruction Company or Secured Creditors to Report Satisfaction of Security Interest (Sec 25): The securitisation/reconstruction company or the secured creditors, shall give intimation to the Central Registrar of the payment or satisfaction in full within 30 days from the date of such payment or satisfaction. The Central Registrar shall, send a notice to the securitization/reconstruction company or the secured creditors calling to show cause within a time not exceeding fourteen days as to why payment or satisfaction should not be recorded as intimated to the Central Registrar. If no cause is shown, the Central Registrar shall order that a memorandum of satisfaction shall be entered in the Central Register.

Right to Inspect Particulars of Securitisation, Reconstruction and Security Interest Transactions (Sec 26): The particulars of securitisation or reconstruction or security interest entered in the Central register of such transactions kept under section 22 shall be open during the business hours for inspection by any person on payment of such fees as may be prescribed. The Central Register maintained in electronic form, shall also be open during the business hours for the inspection of any person through electronic media on payment of such fees as may be prescribed.

OFFENCES AND PENALTIES

Penalties (Sec 27): If a default is made in filing under section 23, the particulars of every transaction of any securitisation or asset reconstruction or security interest created by a securitisation company or reconstruction company or secured creditors; or in sending under section 24, the particulars of the modification referred to in that section; or in giving intimation under section 25, every company and every officer of the company or the secured creditors and every officer of the secured creditor who is in default, shall be punishable with fine which may extend to ₹ 5000 for every day during which the default continues.

Penalties for Non-compliance of Direction of Reserve Bank (Sec 28): If any securitisation company or reconstruction company fails to comply with any direction issued by the Reserve Bank under section 12, such company and every officer of the company who is in default, shall be punishable with fine which may extend to ₹ 5 lac and in the case of a continuing offence, with an additional fine which may extend to ₹ 10000 for every day during which the default continues.

Offences (Sec. 29): If any person contravenes or attempts to contravene or abets the contravention of the provisions of this Act or of any rules made thereunder, he shall be punishable with imprisonment for a term which may extend to one year, or with fine, or with both. No court inferior to that of a Metropolitan Magistrate or a Judicial Magistrate of the first class shall try any offence punishable under this Act.

Miscellaneous: What kind of loans are not covered (Sec 31): Provisions of this Act not to apply in case of:

(a) A lien on any goods, money or security.

(b) A pledge of movables;

(c) Creation of any security in aircraft;

(d) Creation of security interest in vessel;

(e) Any conditional sale, hire-purchase or lease or any other contract in which no security interest has been created;

(f) Any rights of unpaid seller under section 47 of the Sale of Goods Act, 1930 (3 of 1930);

(g) Any properties not liable to attachment or sale under Section 60 of the Code of Civil Procedure, 1908;

(h) Any security interest for securing repayment of any financial asset not exceeding ₹ 1 lac;

(i) Any security interest created in agricultural land;

(j) Any case in which the amount due is less than 20% of the principal amount and interest thereon.

Capital Civil Court not to have Jurisdiction (Sec 34): No civil court shall have jurisdiction to entertain any suit or proceeding in respect of any matter which a Debts Recovery Tribunal or the Appellate Tribunal is empowered by or under this Act to determine and no injunction shall be granted by any court or other authority in respect of any action taken or to be taken in pursuance of any power conferred by or under this Act or under the Recovery of Debts Due to Banks and Financial Institutions Act, 1993.

Limitation (Sec 36): No secured creditor shall be entitled to take all or any of the measures section 13, unless his claim in respect of the financial asset is made within the period of limitation prescribed under the Limitation Act, 1963.

Power of Central Government to Make Rules (Sec 38): The Central Government may make rules for carrying out the provisions of this Act. Such rules may provide for all or any of the following matters, namely:

(a) The form and manner in which an application may be filed under section 13;

(b) Manner in which the rights of a secured creditor may be exercised by one or more of his officers under section 13;

(c) The safeguards subject to which the records may be kept under section 22;

(d) Manner in which particulars of transaction of securitisation shall be filed under sec 23 and fee for filing such transaction;

(e) The fee for inspecting particulars of transactions kept u/s 22 and entered in Central Register under section 26;

(f) The fee for inspecting the Central Register maintained in electronic form under section 26.

Types of Transactions

The Central Register registers transactions relating to security interest over property and transactions of securitization and asset reconstruction. With registration of these transactions, a public database is created about encumbrances created on properties to secure loans and advances given by banks/FIs, as also transactions of securitization or asset reconstruction undertaken under provisions of the SARFAESI Act.

The following transactions are not covered:

(1) Securitization or asset reconstruction done outside the provisions of the SARFAESI Act; or

(2) Security interest created in favour of any lender not included in the definition, of bank or, FI as per the SARFAESI Act.

SARFAESI Act. Which is Covered

The secured creditors notified under the SARFAESI Act. are to file the details mandatorily which include:

(1) Banks

(2) Financial Institutions

(3) Debenture trustees appointed by any Bank or FIs

(4) Securitization Company or Reconstruction Company

(5) Any other trustee holding securities on behalf of a Bank or FI. Others, not notified can also file their records. Time limit for filing details for registration:

(a) Within 30 days of date of transaction.

(b) For delay up to next 30 days, permission of Central Registrar and thereafter, permission of Central Govt. is required. The right to enforce security u/s 13 of SARFAESI Act is not linked to the registration with the Central Registry and such enforcement can be done even if there is no registration with the Central Registry.

The registration under SARFAESI Act is additional and does not affect the requirement of registration under Companies Act or Indian Registration Act.

Search of Records: The records maintained by the Central Registry are available for search by any lender or any other person, by paying fee of ` 50. Forms:

Act or Indian Registration Act. Search of Records: The records maintained by the Central Registry are available for search by any lender or any other person, by paying fee of ₹ 50.

Forms:

- Form-1: For registration and modification
- Form-2: For satisfaction
- Form-3: For registration and modification of Securitization/Reconstruction transactions
- Form-4: For satisfaction of Securitization/Reconstruction transactions

TEST YOURSELF

1. SARFAESI Act 2002 does not cover which State in India?
   (a) Jammu & Kashmir
   (b) Goa
   (c) Nagaland
   (d) None of the above, It covers whole India

2. SARFAESI Act 2002 does not concern which of the following aspects?
   (a) Securitisation of Financial Assets
   (b) Reconstruction of Assets
   (c) Authority to enforce security without intervention of the court
   (d) Setting up of Central Registry

3. Provision of SARFAESI Act 2002 are applicable to which of the following kinds of securities?
   (a) All type of movable & immovable security
   (b) All kinds of mortgages
   (c) Where security interest is created to secure the loan
   (d) All of the above

4. Under the provision of SARFAESI Act 2002, where a transaction of Securitisation is registered?
   (a) Registrar of companies
   (b) Registrar of assurance
   (c) Registrar of firms
   (d) Registrar of Central Registry

5. Which of the following type of charge has been defined only under the SARFAESI Act 2002?
   (a) Pledge
   (b) Mortgage
   (c) Hypothecation
   (d) Assignment

6. Under the provision of SARFAESI Act 2002, which among the following is a borrower?
   (a) A person who has obtained financial assistance from bank
   (b) A person who has created mortgage or any other charge over assets
   (c) A person who has given guarantee
   (d) All of the above

7. If on issue of notice the borrower does not pay in __________ days, the secured creditor under the provision of SARFAESI Act 2002, can _______ the security.
   (a) 60 days, take possession of
   (b) 60 days, sell
   (c) 30 days, file a suit for possession of
   (d) 30 days, sell

8. Which of the following is a correct statement under the provision of SARFAESI Act 2002?
   (a) Possession of security can be taken by Distt. Magistrate only
   (b) Possession of security can be taken by CJM only
   (c) Possession of security can be taken when account is classified as NPA as per RBI directives only
   (d) All of the above

9. What norm has to be followed by Securitisation Company regarding owned fund and the acquired financial assets i.e. owned fund as ___ % of acquired assets.
   (a) 20   (b) 15
   (c) 12.5   (d) 10

10. Where registration of a securitisation company is cancelled, what are the provision of appeal?
    (a) Appeal to Company Law Board within 30 days
    (b) Appeal to ROC within 45 days
    (c) Appeal to Central Govt. within 30 days
    (d) No appeal is available

11. When the securitisation company fails to realize the securitized assets, the qualified institutional buyers holding _________% of total value of the security receipts can force the securitisation company for a particular decision.
    (a) 75   (b) 60
    (c) 50   (d) 25

12. Powers available to Securitisation Company can be exercised by it as per guideline framed by _______ only.
    (a) RBI   (b) SEBI
    (c) RoC   (d) Central Registry

13. What is the maximum period allowed to a securitisation company for recovery of reconstructed financial assets?
    (a) 2 years   (b) 3 years
    (c) 4 years   (d) 5 years

14. Direction issued RBI under the provision of SARFAESI Act 2002 are __________ on the parties concerned and have __________ effect.
    (a) Binding, Moral
    (b) Compulsory, Statutory
    (c) Binding, Statutory
    (d) Binding, Compulsory

15. How much time is given to the borrower to make the payment of the dues under the provision of

SARFAESI Act 2002, before taking possession of the assets?

(a) 60 days   (b) 50 days

(c) 45 days   (d) 30 days

16. In case, there is any objection from the borrower, which of the following action required to be taken by the secured creditor:
    (a) Must apply his mind to the objection
    (b) The objection should be replied within 15 days
    (c) The reply should contain the reasons for not accepting the objection
    (d) (a) to (c)

17. In which of the following provisions at which SARFAESI Act 2002 are not applicable?
    (a) Where security interest is in agriculture land
    (b) In any in which the amount due is less than 20% of the principal + interest
    (c) The contractual dues is below ₹ 10 lac
    (d) All of the above

18. As per SARFAESI Act 2002 the authorized officers should be:
    (a) Of the level equivalent to at least a Chief Manager (Scale IV) of the public sector bank
    (b) Of the level equivalent to at least a AGM (Scale V) of the public sector bank
    (c) Of the level equivalent to at least a Senior Manager (Scale III) of the public sector bank
    (d) Any officer posted at administrative office

19. If a borrower fails to make payment of the dues of a secured creditor, which of the following options are not available to the secured creditor under the provision of SARFAESI Act 2002.
    (a) Take possession of the secured assets or lease the secured assets
    (b) Take over management of the secured assets
    (c) Appoint another person to manage the secured assets
    (d) None of the above

20. Before sale of the security, the authorized officer is required to publish the possession notice in _______ newspapers.
    (a) 1   (b) 2
    (c) 3   (d) Not required

21. What time period is to be given to the borrower as a notice before sale of the secured assets?
    (a) 60 days   (b) 50 days
    (c) 45 days   (d) 30 days

22. What is the minimum price at which security can be sold by the secured creditor?
    (a) Market Price   (b) Cost Price
    (c) Reserve Price   (d) Acquisition Cost

23. When offer of sale of property is accepted by the purchaser and secured creditor, the purchaser has to immediately deposit _____% of the offer price.
    (a) 10   (b) 20
    (c) 25   (d) 50

24. On sale of the immovable property as security by the creditor, which of the following document is executed.
    (a) Sale Certificate
    (b) Sale Agreement
    (c) Sale Deed
    (d) Conveyance Certificate

ANSWER

1	2	3	4	5	6	7	8	9	10
(d)	(b)	(d)	(d)	(c)	(d)	(a)	(c)	(b)	(c)

11	12	13	14	15	16	17	18	19	20
(a)	(a)	(d)	(c)	(a)	(d)	(d)	(a)	(d)	(b)

21	22	23	24
(d)	(c)	(c)	(a)

CHAPTER 21

BANKING OMBUDSMAN SCHEME

OBJECTIVE

The Scheme is introduced with the object of enabling resolution of complaints relating to certain services rendered by banks and to facilitate the satisfaction or settlement of such complaints. Resolution of complaints relating to banking services through conciliation & mediation between the bank and the aggrieved parties or by passing an award.

INTRODUCTION

For the improvement of customer service in banking industry, RBI has provided a platform to customer for redressal of banking related dispute. RBI notified the Banking Ombudsman Scheme 2006 u/s 35A of Banking Regulation Act 1949. The scheme came into force effective from 01st Jan 2006. It covers all commercial banks, RRB's & scheduled primary Co-operative Banks. Presently the Banking Ombudsman Scheme 2006 (As amended up to July 1, 2017) is in operation.

Definitions as per Banking Ombudsman Scheme:

1. 'Award' means an award passed by the Banking Ombudsman in accordance with the Scheme.

2. 'Appellate Authority' means the Deputy Governor in charge of the department of the Reserve Bank implementing the scheme.

3. 'Authorised Representative' means a person duly appointed and authorised by a complainant to act on his behalf and represent him in the proceedings under the Scheme before a Banking Ombudsman for consideration of his complaint.

4. 'Banking Ombudsman' means any person appointed under Clause 4 of the Scheme.

5. 'Bank' means all 'Scheduled Commercial Banks', a 'Regional Rural Bank', 'State Bank of India' or a 'Primary Co-operative Bank'

6. 'Complaint' means a representation in writing or through electronic means containing a grievance alleging deficiency in banking service as mentioned in clause 8 of the Scheme

7. 'Settlement' means an agreement reached by the parties either by conciliation or mediation under Clause 11 of the Scheme.

Eligibility of Ombudsman: The Reserve Bank may appoint one or more of its officers in the rank of Chief General Manager or General Manager for maximum period not exceeding 3 Years at a time.

Location of Office: The office of the Banking Ombudsman shall be located at such places as may be specified by the Reserve Bank. At present, twenty Banking Ombudsmen have been appointed with their offices located mostly in state capitals. All costs of the office are borne by RBI.

Jurisdiction: The Reserve Bank shall specify the territorial limits to which the authority of each Banking Ombudsman. A person makes a complaint to the Banking Ombudsman within whose jurisdiction the branch or office of the bank complained against is located. For Credit card, the jurisdiction is with reference to Ombudsman having jurisdiction over the billing address of the card holder. For other accounts, it is as per location of the branch.

Grounds of Complaint

Any person may file a complaint with the Banking Ombudsman having jurisdiction on any one of the following grounds alleging deficiency in banking including internet banking or other services.

(a) Non-payment or inordinate delay in the payment or collection of cheques, drafts, bills etc.

(b) Non-acceptance, without sufficient cause, of small denomination notes or coins;

(c) Non-payment or delay in payment of inward remittances;

(d) Failure to issue or delay in issue of drafts, pay orders or bankers' cheques;

(e) Non-adherence to prescribed working hours;

(f) Failure to provide or delay in providing a banking facility (other than loans and advances) promised in writing by a bank or its direct selling agents;

(g) Delays, non-credit of proceeds to parties' accounts, non-payment of deposit or non-observance of the Reserve Bank directives;

(h) Complaints from Non-Resident Indians having accounts in India in relation to their remittances from abroad, deposits and other bank-related matters;

(i) Refusal to open deposit accounts without any valid reason for refusal;

(j) Levying of charges without adequate prior notice to the customer;

(k) Non-adherence to the instructions of Reserve Bank on ATM /Debit Card and Prepaid Card operations in India by the bank or its subsidiaries on any of the following:

    i. Account debited but cash not dispensed by ATMs

    ii. Account debited more than once for one withdrawal in ATMs or for POS transaction

    iii. Less/Excess amount of cash dispensed by ATMs

    iv. Debit in account without use of the card or details of the card

    v. Use of stolen/cloned cards

(l) Non-adherence by the bank or its subsidiaries to the instructions of Reserve Bank on credit card operations on any of the following:

    i. Unsolicited calls for Add-on Cards, insurance for cards etc.

    ii. Charging of Annual Fees on Cards issued free for life

    iii. Wrong Billing/Wrong Debits

    iv. Threatening calls/inappropriate approach of recovery by recovery agents including non-observance of Reserve Bank guidelines on engagement of recovery agents

    v. Wrong reporting of credit information to Credit Information Bureau

    vi. Delay or failure to review and correct the credit status on account of wrongly reported credit information to Credit Information Bureau.

(m) Non-adherence to the instructions of Reserve Bank with regard to Mobile Banking / Electronic Banking service in India by the bank on any of the following:

    i. Delay or failure to effect online payment / Fund Transfer,

    ii. Unauthorized electronic payment / Fund Transfer,

(n) Non-disbursement or delay in disbursement of pension (to the extent the grievance can be attributed to the action on the part of the bank concerned, but not with regard to its employees);

(o) Refusal to accept or delay in accepting payment towards taxes, as required by Reserve Bank/ Government;

(p) Forced closure of deposit accounts without due notice or without sufficient reason;

(q) Non-adherence to the provisions of the Code of Bank's Commitments to Customers issued by Banking Codes and Standards Board of India and as adopted by the bank ;

(r) Non-adherence to Reserve Bank guidelines on para-banking activities like sale of insurance/mutual fund /other third party investment products by banks with regard to following:

    i. Improper, unsuitable sale of third party financial products,

    ii. Non-transparency/lack of adequate transparency in sale,

    iii. Non-disclosure of grievance redressal mechanism available,

    iv. Delay or refusal to facilitate after sales service by banks.

(s) Any other matter relating to the violation of the directives issued by the Reserve Bank in relation to banking or other services.

(t) A complaint on any one of the following grounds alleging deficiency in banking service in respect of loans and advances may be filed with the Banking Ombudsman having jurisdiction:

I. non-observance of Reserve Bank Directives on interest rates;

II. delays in sanction, disbursement or non-observance of prescribed time schedule for disposal of loan applications;

III. Non-acceptance of application for loans without furnishing valid reasons to the applicant; non-adherence to the provisions of the fair practices code for lenders as adopted by the bank or Code of Bank's Commitment to Customers, as the case may be;

IV. Non-observance of Reserve Bank guidelines on engagement of recovery agents by banks; and

V. Non-observance of any other direction or instruction of the Reserve Bank as may be specified by the Reserve Bank for this purpose from time to time.

(u) The Banking Ombudsman may also deal with such other matter as may be specified by the Reserve Bank from time to time in this behalf.

Procedure for Filing Complaint

Any person who has a grievance against a bank on any one or more of the grounds mentioned in the Scheme may, himself or through his authorised representative (other than an advocate), make a complaint on paper or through electronic media (e-mail), or forwarded by RBI or Central Govt. to the Banking Ombudsman.

The complaint in writing shall be duly signed by the complainant or his authorized representative and shall be, as far as possible, in the form specified in Annexure 'A' or as near as thereto as circumstances admit, stating clearly:

I. The name and the address of the complainant,

II. The name and address of the branch or office of the bank against which the complaint is made,

III. The facts giving rise to the complaint,

IV. The nature and extent of the loss caused to the complainant, and

V. The relief sought for.

Conditions for Complaint

○ Complaint was made to the Bank and Bank had rejected or no reply was received within a month or complainant is not satisfied with the reply given by the bank.

○ The complaint is made not later than one year after the complainant has received the reply of the bank to his representation or, where no reply is received, not later than one year and one month after the date of the representation to the bank;

○ Complaint is not for issues already settled by Ombudsman or for which proceeding before court or any other forum is pending or a decree or order has been passed.

○ The complaint is not frivolous or vexatious in nature.

○ The complaint is within limitation period under Indian limitation Act 1963.

Power to Call for Information

(1) Banking Ombudsman may require the bank against whom the complaint is made or any other bank concerned with the complaint to provide any information or furnish certified copies of any document relating to the complaint which is or is alleged to be in its possession.

Provided that in the event of the failure of a bank to comply with the requisition without sufficient cause, the Banking Ombudsman may, if he deems fit, draw the inference that the information if provided or copies if furnished would be unfavourable to the bank.

(2) The Banking Ombudsman shall maintain confidentiality of any information or document that may come into his knowledge or possession in the course of discharging his duties and shall not disclose such information or document to any person except with the consent of the person furnishing such information or document.

Provided that nothing in this Clause shall prevent the Banking Ombudsman from disclosing information or document furnished by a party in a complaint to the other party or parties to the extent considered by him to be reasonably required to comply with any legal requirement or the principles of natural justice and fair play in the proceedings.

Process of Redressal of Grievance

Banking Ombudsman sent a copy of the complaint to the bank and endeavour shall be made for a settlement by agreement through conciliation or mediation. The proceedings shall be summary in nature.

Award by the Ombudsman

Where a complaint is not settled by agreement within a period of one month from the date of receipt of the complaint, Ombudsman may pass an Award or reject the complaint, on the basis of evidence, the principles of banking law and practice, directions and guidelines issued by RBI.

Amount of Award: Award shall specify the amount, to be paid by bank as compensation, not more than actual loss suffered as direct consequence of act of omission or commission of the bank or ₹ 20 lac (As amended up to July 1, 2017) earlier it was ₹ 10 lac, whichever is lower.

The Banking Ombudsman may award compensation not exceeding ₹ 1 lakh to the complainant for mental agony and harassment. The Banking Ombudsman will take into account the loss of the complainant's time, expenses incurred by the complainant, harassment and mental anguish suffered by the complainant while passing such award.

Effect of Award: A copy of the Award shall be sent to the complainant and the bank. An award shall lapse and be of no effect unless the complainant furnishes to the bank concerned within a period of 30 days from the date of receipt of copy of the Award, a letter of acceptance of the Award in full and final settlement of his claim. The bank shall, unless it has preferred an appeal within one month from the date of receipt by it of the acceptance in writing of the Award by the complainant, comply with the Award and intimate compliance to the Banking Ombudsman.

Implementation: Customer has to send acceptance of the award within 30 days of date of receipt of the award. Bank is to implement the award within one month from the date of receipt of the acceptance from the complainant and intimate compliance to the Banking Ombudsman.

Rejection of the Complaint

The Banking Ombudsman may reject a complaint at any stage if it appears to him that the complaint made is;

   (a) Not on the grounds of complaint referred to in clause 8; or

   (b) Otherwise not in accordance with Sub Clause (3) of clause 9; or

   (c) Beyond the pecuniary jurisdiction of Banking Ombudsman prescribed; or

   (d) Requiring consideration of elaborate documentary and oral evidence and the proceedings before the Banking Ombudsman are not appropriate for adjudication of such complaint; or

   (e) Without any sufficient cause; or

   (f) That it is not pursued by the complainant with reasonable diligence; or

   (g) In the opinion of the Banking Ombudsman there is no loss or damage or inconvenience caused to the complainant.

The Banking Ombudsman, shall, if it appears at any stage of the proceedings that the complaint pertains to the same cause of action, for which any proceedings before any court, tribunal or arbitrator or any other forum is pending or a decree or Award or order has been passed by any such court, tribunal, arbitrator or forum, pass an order rejecting the complaint giving reasons thereof.

Appeal

Customer can appeal to appellate authority within 30 days of receipt of rejection to Dy. Governor RBI. Customer or bank can file the appeal to appellate authority (Dy. Governor RBI) against the award or decision of the Banking Ombudsman rejecting the complaint within 30 days of the date of receipt of the Award. Provided further that appeal may be filed by a bank only with the prior sanction of the Chairman or, in his absence, the Managing Director or the Executive Director or the Chief Executive Officer or any other officer of equal rank.

The Appellate Authority may, if he/she is satisfied that the applicant had sufficient cause for not making an application for appeal within time, also allow a further period not exceeding 30 days. The appellate authority may dismiss/allow the appeal or set aside the award or refer the matter to Ombudsman for fresh disposal or modify the award or pass any order as it may deem fit.

Banks to Display Salient Features of the Scheme for Common Knowledge of Public

The banks covered by the Scheme shall ensure that the purpose of the Scheme and the contact details of the Banking Ombudsman to whom the complaints are to be made by the aggrieved party are displayed prominently in all the offices and branches of the bank in such manner that a person visiting the office or branch has adequate information of the Scheme.

The banks covered by the Scheme shall appoint Nodal Officers at their Regional/Zonal Offices and inform the respective Office of the Banking Ombudsman under whose jurisdiction the Regional/Zonal Office falls. The Nodal Officer so appointed shall be responsible for representing the bank and furnishing information to the Banking Ombudsman in respect of complaints filed against the bank.

TEST YOURSELF

1. RBI notified the Banking Ombudsman Scheme 2006 u/s _______________.
   - (a) 34A of Banking Regulation Act 1949
   - (b) 35A of Banking Regulation Act 1949
   - (c) 34A of RBI Act 1934
   - (d) 35A of RBI Act 1934

2. The scheme came into force effective from _______.
   - (a) 01ˢᵗ Jan 2006
   - (b) 01ˢᵗ April 2006
   - (c) 01ˢᵗ Jan 2007
   - (d) 01ˢᵗ April 2007

3. Banking Ombudsman Scheme 2006 covers:
   - (a) Commercial Banks
   - (b) RRB's
   - (c) Scheduled primary Co-operative Banks
   - (d) All of the above

4. The Reserve Bank may appoint one or more of its officers in the rank of __________.
   - (a) Chief General Manager
   - (b) General Manager
   - (c) Dy. Governor
   - (d) (a) or (c)

5. The Reserve Bank may appoint one or more of its officers for maximum period not exceeding _______ at a time.
   - (a) 3 Years
   - (b) 4 Years
   - (c) 5 Years
   - (d) 6 Years

6. All costs of the Banking Ombudsman office are borne by _______________.
   - (a) State Bank of India
   - (b) All Commercial Banks of the area
   - (c) RBI
   - (d) All Commercial Banks & RRB of the area

7. Which is correct statement about Jurisdiction of Banking Ombudsman? A person makes a complaint to the Banking Ombudsman within whose jurisdiction?
   - (a) For Credit card, the jurisdiction is with reference to Ombudsman having jurisdiction over the billing address of the card holder.
   - (b) For other accounts, it is as per location of the branch.
   - (c) For other accounts, it is as per location of the administrative office of the bank.
   - (d) (a) and (b)

8. Which is correct about grounds of Complaint for Banking Ombudsman?
   - (a) Non-payment or inordinate delay in the payment or collection of cheques, drafts, bills etc.
   - (b) Failure to provide or delay in providing a banking facility (other than loans and advances) promised in writing by a bank or its direct selling agents.
   - (c) Delays, non-credit of proceeds to parties' accounts, non-payment of deposit or non-observance of the Reserve Bank directives.
   - (d) All of the above

9. Any person who has a grievance against a bank on any one or more of the grounds mentioned in the Scheme may, make a complaint ___________.
   - (a) Himself
   - (b) Through his authorised representative
   - (c) Through an advocate
   - (d) (a) or (b)

10. Which is correct statement about complaint at Banking Ombudsman?
    - (a) Any person who has a grievance makes a complaint on paper to the Banking Ombudsman.
    - (b) Any person who has a grievance makes a complaint through electronic media (e-mail) to the Banking Ombudsman.
    - (c) Any person who has a grievance makes a complaint forwarded by RBI or Central Govt. to the Banking Ombudsman.
    - (d) All of the above

11. Who is the appellate authority for Banking Ombudsman under the scheme?
    - (a) Dy. Governor of RBI
    - (b) Governor of RBI
    - (c) High Court
    - (d) Supreme Court

12. Conditions for complaint at Banking Ombudsman under the scheme is:
    - (a) Complaint was made to the Bank and Bank had rejected or no reply was received within a month or complainant is not satisfied with the reply given by the bank.
    - (b) The complaint is made not later than one year after the complainant has received the reply of the bank.
    - (c) Complaint is not for issues already settled by Ombudsman or for which proceeding before court or any other forum is pending or a decree or order has been passed.
    - (d) All of the above

13. The maximum amount of the Banking Ombudsman award as compensation is:
    - (a) ₹ 5 lac
    - (b) ₹ 10 lac
    - (c) ₹ 20 lac
    - (d) No limit

14. Which is the major amendment in 2017 in Banking Ombudsman Scheme 2006?
  (a) The maximum amount of the award as compensation increased from ₹ 5 lac to ₹ 10 lac.
  (b) The maximum amount of the award as compensation increased from ₹ 10 lac to ₹ 20 lac.
  (c) The maximum amount of the award as compensation increased from ₹ 5 lac to ₹ 20 lac.
  (d) None of the above

15. The Banking Ombudsman may reject a complaint at any stage if it appears to him that the complaint made is:
  (a) Not pursued by the complainant with reasonable diligence.
  (b) Requiring consideration of elaborate documentary and oral evidence and the proceedings before the Banking Ombudsman are not appropriate for adjudication of such complaint.
  (c) In the opinion of the Banking Ombudsman there is no loss or damage or inconvenience caused to the complainant.
  (d) Any of the above

16. What is the limitation period for filling an appeal against the order of Banking Ombudsman?
  (a) 30 days   (b) 45 days
  (c) 60 days   (d) 90 days

17. The Banking Ombudsman may award compensation not exceeding _______ to the complainant for mental agony and harassment.
  (a) ₹ 1 lac   (b) ₹ 5 lac
  (c) ₹ 10 lac   (d) ₹ 20 lac

18. Appeal against the order of Banking Ombudsman may be filed by a bank only with the prior sanction of the _______ or any other officer of equal rank.
  (a) Chairman   (b) MD or CEO
  (c) ED   (d) Any of the above

19. Customer and bank have to send acceptance of the award within _____ of date of receipt of the award.
  (a) 15 days   (b) 30 days
  (c) 60 days   (d) 90 days

20. Bank is to implement the award within _________ from the date of receipt of the acceptance from the complainant and intimate compliance to the Banking Ombudsman.
  (a) One month
  (b) Three month
  (c) Six month
  (d) Decided by Banking Ombudsman

ANSWER

1	2	3	4	5	6	7	8	9	10
(b)	(a)	(d)	(d)	(a)	(c)	(d)	(d)	(d)	(d)

11	12	13	14	15	16	17	18	19	20
(a)	(d)	(c)	(b)	(d)	(a)	(a)	(d)	(b)	(a)

BANKERS' BOOKS EVIDENCE ACT, 1891

INTRODUCTION

Banks maintain all its transactions, statements and other important records in the form of ledgers, registers, files and documentary evidence. These are stored in ledgers, files or printout of the report in physical form or in soft copy in floppy, CD or any other form of electromagnetic data storage device. These can be produced before the court as evidence. These are required to be produced in original. These evidence and records are guided by the act called 'The Bankers' Books Evidence Act, 1891'. It extends to the whole of India except the State of Jammu and Kashmir.

Definitions

Some important definition as per the Act:,

1) "Company" means any company as defined in section 3 of the Companies Act, 1956, and includes a foreign company within the meaning of section 591 of that Act;

2) "Corporation" means anybody corporate established by any law for the time being in force in India and includes the Reserve Bank of India, the State Bank of India.

3) "Bank" and "banker" means—
   a) any company or corporation carrying on the business of banking;
   b) any partnership or individual to whose books the provisions of this Act shall have been extended as hereinafter provided;
   c) any post office savings bank or a money order office;

4) "Bankers' books" include ledgers, day-books, cash-books, account-books and all other books used in the ordinary business of a bank whether kept in the written form or as printouts of data stored in a floppy, disc, tape or any other form of electro-magnetic data storage device. Such record can be either 'on site'or at 'off site' location and includes a back-up or disaster recovery site.

5) "Legal proceeding" means—
   a) any proceeding or inquiry in which evidence is or may be given;
   b) an arbitration; and
   c) any investigation or inquiry under the Code of Criminal Procedure, 1973, or under any other law for the time being in force for the collection of evidence, conducted by a police officer or by any other person (not being a magistrate) authorised in this behalf by a magistrate or by any law for the time being in force;

6) "The Court" means the person or persons before whom a legal proceeding is held or taken;

7) "Judge" means a Judge of a High Court;

8) "Trial" means any hearing before the Court at which evidence is taken;

Certified Copy

Certified copy means when the books of a bank—

(a) If maintained in written form, a copy of any entry in such books together with a certificate written at the foot of such copy that it is a true copy of such entry, that such entry is contained in one of the ordinary books of the bank and was made in the usual and ordinary course of business and that such book is still in the custody of the bank, and where the copy was obtained by mechanical or other process which in itself ensured the accuracy of the copy, a further certificate to that effect, but where the book from which such copy was prepared has been destroyed in the usual course of the bank's business after the date on which the copy has been so prepared, a further certificate to that effect, each such certificate being dated and subscribed by the principal accountant or manager of the bank with his name and official title; and

(b) If consists of printouts of data stored in a floppy, disc, tape or any other electro-magnetic data storage device, a printout of such entry or a copy of such printout together with such statements certified in accordance with the provisions of section 2A.

Conditions in the Printout (2A)

A printout of entry or a copy of printout shall be accompanied by the following, namely:

A. A certificate to the effect that it is a printout of such entry or a copy of such printout by the principal accountant or branch manager; and

B. A certificate by a person in-charge of computer system containing a brief description of the computer system and the particulars of:

a) The safeguards adopted by system to ensure that data is entered or any other operation performed only by authorised persons;

b) The safeguards adopted to prevent and detect unauthorised change of data;

c) The safeguards available to retrieve data that is lost due to systemic failure or any other reasons;

d) The manner in which data is transferred from the system to removable media like floppies, discs, tapes or other electro-magnetic data storage devices; the mode of verification in order to ensure that data has been accurately transferred to such removable media;

e) The mode of identification of such data storage devices;

f) The arrangements for the storage and custody of such storage devices;

g) The safeguards to prevent and detect any tampering with the system; and

h) Any other factor which will vouch for the integrity and accuracy of the system.

C. A further certificate from the person in-charge of the computer system to the effect that to the best of his knowledge and belief, such computer system operated properly at the material time, he was provided with all the relevant data and the printout in question represents correctly, or is appropriately derived from, the relevant data.

Power to Extend Provisions of Act (Sec 3)

The State Government may, from time to time, by notification in the Official Gazette, extend the provisions of this Act to the books of any partnership or individual carrying on the business of bankers within the territories under its administration, and keeping a set of not less than three ordinary account books, namely, a cash book, a day-book or journal, and a ledger, and may in like manner rescind any such notification.

Mode of Proof of Entries in Bankers' Books (Sec 4)

A certified copy of any entry in a banker's books shall in all legal proceedings be received as prima facie evidence of the existence of such entry, and shall be admitted as evidence of the matters, transactions and accounts therein recorded in every case where, and to the same extent as, the original entry itself is now by law admissible, but not further or otherwise.

Case in which Officer of Bank not Compellable to Produce Books (Sec 5)

No officer of a bank shall in any legal proceeding to which the bank is not a party be compellable to produce any banker's book the contents of which can be proved under this Act, or to appear as a witness to prove the matters, transactions and accounts therein recorded, unless by order of the Court or a Judge made for special cause.

Inspection of Books by Order of Court or Judge

(1) On the application of any party to a legal proceeding the Court or a Judge may order that such party be at liberty to inspect and take copies of any entries in a banker's book for any of the purposes of such proceeding, or may order the bank to prepare and produce, within a time to be specified in the order, certified copies of all such entries accompanied by a further certificate that no other entries are to be found in the books of the bank relevant to the matters in issue in such

proceeding, and such further certificate shall be dated and subscribed in manner herein before directed in reference to certified copies.

(2) An order under this or the preceding section may be made either with or without summoning the bank, and shall be served on the bank three clear days (exclusive of bank holidays) before the same is to be obeyed, unless the Court or Judge shall otherwise direct.

(3) The bank may at any time before the time limited for obedience to any such order as aforesaid either offer to produce their books at the trial or give notice of their intention to show cause against such order, and thereupon the same shall not be enforced without further order.

Costs (Sec 7)

(1) The costs of any application to the Court or a Judge under or for the purposes of this Act and the costs of anything done or to be done under and order of the Court or a Judge made under or for the purposes of this Act shall be in the discretion of the Court or Judge, who may further order such costs or any part thereof to be paid to any party

by the bank if they have been incurred inconsequence of any fault or improper delay on the part of the bank.

(2) Any order made under this section for the payment of costs to or by a bank may be enforced as if the bank were a party to the proceeding.

(3) Any order under this section awarding costs may, on application to any Court of Civil Judicature de signated in the order, be executed by such Court as if the order were a decree for money passed by itself provided that nothing in this sub-section shall be construed to derogate from any power which the Court or Judge making the order may possess for the enforcement of its or his directions with respect to the payment of costs.

Order of Court to be Construed to be Order Made by Specified Officer (Sec 8)

In the application of sections 5, 6 and 7 to any investigation or inquiry, the order of a court or a Judge referred to in the said sections shall be construed as referring to an order made by an officer of a rank not lower than the rank of a Superintendent of Police as may be specified in this behalf by the appropriate Government.

TEST YOURSELF

1. 'The Bankers' Books Evidence Act' passed in the year __________. It extends to the whole of India except the State of __________.
   (a) 1891 & Jammu and Kashmir
   (b) 1991 & Jammu and Kashmir
   (c) 1891 & Tamil Nadu
   (d) 1991 & Tamil Nadu

2. Which of the following in part of banker's book under 'The Bankers' Books Evidence Act'?
   (1) Ledgers
   (2) Day books
   (3) Cash book
   (4) Account book
   (a) 1 to 4 all   (b) 1 to 3 only
   (c) 2, 3, 4 only   (d) 3 and 4 only

3. A certified copy under provision of 'The Bankers' Books Evidence Act' is considered to be:
   (a) Original record
   (b) Prima facie evidence
   (c) Provisional evidence
   (d) None

4. Certificate under 'The Bankers' Books Evidence Act' on the copy of a banker's book, is to be given at:
   (a) Foot of such copy
   (b) Top of such copy
   (c) Middle of such copy
   (d) Foot and top of such copy

5. Instead of submission of original documents in the court of law, which of the following can be submitted?
   (a) Photo copy of the original documents
   (b) Typed version of originals
   (c) Copy certified under Bankers' Books Evidence Act
   (d) Copy certified under Indian Evidence Act

6. 'Legal Proceedings' under Bankers' Books Evidence Act means:
   (a) Any proceeding or inquiry in which evidence is or may be given
   (b) An Arbitration
   (c) Any investigation or inquiring under the court of criminal procedure 1973
   (d) All of the above

7. Banks maintain all their transactions, statements and other important records in the form of ledgers,

registers, files and documentary evidence. These are stored in:

(a) Ledgers, files or printout of the report in physical form

(b) In soft copy in floppy, CD

(c) Any other form of electromagnetic data storage device

(d) All of the above

8. As per 'The Bankers' Books Evidence Act' Section __________, certified copy of any entry in a banker's books shall in all legal proceedings be received as prima facie evidence of the existence of such entry.

(a) 3   (b) 4

(c) 5   (d) 6

9. As per 'The Bankers' Books Evidence Act "Judge" means:

(a) A Judge of a High Court

(b) A Judge of a Civil Court

(c) A Judge of a Supreme Court

(d) A Judge of a DRT

10. Unless the court otherwise directs, bank officer cannot be compelled to produce original books to prove any Banker's Books contents when copy is produced.

(a) True   (b) False

ANSWER

1	2	3	4	5	6	7	8	9	10
(a)	(a)	(b)	(a)	(c)	(d)	(d)	(b)	(a)	(a)

CHAPTER 23

THE LEGAL SERVICES AUTHORITIES ACT, 1987
(LOK ADALATS)

OBJECTIVE

The mounting of NPAs in the Bank and tardy recovery process of the dues is important concern for the Banks. Lok Adalat is one of the forum which has been playing an important role in settlement of disputes. Lok Adalat is a process of administering justice without resorting to courts. Its process is voluntary and works on the principle that both parties to the dispute are willing to sort out their disputes amicably. Through this mechanism, disputes can be settled in a simpler, quicker and cost-effective way. It is for the Banks to make use of this forum and speed up recovery of NPAs.

INTRODUCTION

Lok Adalat is one of the alternative dispute redressal mechanisms, it is a forum where disputes/cases pending in the court of law or at pre-litigation stage are settled/ compromised amicably. Lok Adalats have been given statutory status under the Legal Services Authorities Act, 1987. Under the said Act, the award (decision) made by the Lok Adalats is deemed to be a decree of a civil court and is final and binding on all parties and no appeal against such an award lies before any court of law.

Proceedings in Lok Adalat

Salient features in Lok Adalat are as under:

i) No Court Fee is involved.

ii) Lok Adalats to settle banking disputes involving amount up to ₹ 20 lakh.

iii) It can take cognizance of any existing suit pending in Civil Court/DRT court.

iv) If no settlement is arrived at, the parties can continue with Court/DRT proceedings.

v) Decrees passed by it have legal status and are binding on all the parties to the dispute and no appeal shall lie to any Court against the Award.

vi) Settlement of cases through Lok Adalat will reduce the expenses and time in pursuing the cases before the Court/DRT which is a time consuming affair.

Organisation of Lok Adalats

Every State Authority or District Authority or the Supreme Court Legal Services Committee or every High Court Legal Services Committee or, as the case may be, Taluk Legal Services Committee may organise Lok Adalats at such intervals and places and for exercising such jurisdiction and for such areas as it thinks fit.

Every Lok Adalat organised for an area shall consist of such number of—

(a) Serving or retired judicial officers; and

(b) Other persons, of the area as may be specified by the State Authority or the District Authority or the Supreme Court Legal Services Committee or the High Court Legal Services Committee, or as the case may be, the Taluk Legal Services Committee, organising such Lok Adalat.

Establishment of Permanent Lok Adalats

The Central Authority or, as the case may be, every State Authority shall, by notification, establish Permanent Lok Adalats at such places and for exercising such jurisdiction in respect of one or more public utility services and for such areas as may be specified in the notification.

Cognisance of Case by Lok Adalats:

1. Both the parties to the suit may agree to refer their dispute to Lok Adalat, or

2. One of the parties there of makes an application to the Court/DRT for referring the case to the Lok Adalat for settlement, or

3. The court is satisfied that the matter is an appropriate one to be taken cognizance of by the Lok Adalat, the court shall refer the case to the Lok Adalat.

4. Where any case is referred to a Lok Adalat, it shall proceed to dispose of the case or matter and arrive at a compromise or settlement between the parties.

Disposal of Case in Lok Adalat

Every Lok Adalat while determining any reference shall be guided by the principles of justice, equity, fair play and other legal principles. Where no award is made by the Lok Adalat on the ground that no compromise or settlement could be arrived at between the parties, the record of the case shall be returned by it to the court from which reference has been received, and advice the parties to seek remedy in Court. Where the record of the case is returned, such court shall proceed to deal with such case from the state which was reached before such reference.

Every award made by a Lok Adalat shall be deemed to be a decree of Civil Court or as the case may and shall be final and binding on all the parties to the dispute and no appeal shall lie to any Court against the award.

Powers of Lok Adalat

For the purpose of determination of the dispute referred to it, the Lok Adalat shall have the following powers:

○ to summon and enforce the attendance of any witness and examine him on oath.

○ to discovery and production of documents.

○ to receive evidence on affidavits.

○ to requisition of public record or copy of the record.

How to Organise Lok Adalats

For organising Lok Adalat respective banks can approach the district legal services authority. The authorities agree for organising Lok Adalat exclusively for the Banks and exclusively for a particular Bank also.

Lok Adalats identify the area taking into consideration conglomeration of the bank's branches. Number of cases pending in the courts or before DRT, irregular/sticky accounts. Where there is a likelihood of a compromise or a settlement & amount involved.

TEST YOURSELF

1. Lok Adalats have been given statutory status under the __________.
   (a) Legal Services Authorities Act, 1987
   (b) Payment and Settlement System Act 2007
   (c) Recovery of debts due to banks and financial institutions act 1993
   (d) Bank's NPA Recovery Act

2. Salient features in Lok Adalat are as under:
   (a) No Court Fee is involved.
   (b) Lok Adalats to settle banking disputes involving amount up to ₹ 50 lakh.
   (c) It cannot take cognizance of any existing suit pending in Civil Court/DRT court.
   (d) All of the above

3. Which is the correct statement regarding Lok Adalat?
   (a) It can take cognizance of any existing suit pending in Civil Court/DRT court, if no settlement is arrived at, the parties can continue with Court/DRT proceedings.
   (b) Decrees passed by it have legal status and are binding on all the parties to the dispute and no appeal shall lie to any Court against the Award.
   (c) Settlement of cases through Lok Adalat will reduce the expenses and time in pursuing the cases before the Court/DRT which is a time consuming affair.
   (d) All of the above

4. Who can organise Lok Adalats?
   (a) Every State Authority or District Authority
   (b) The Supreme Court Legal Services Committee
   (c) Every High Court Legal Services Committee
   (d) Any of the above

5. Every Lok Adalat organised for an area shall consist of such number of:
   - (a) Serving or retired judicial officers; and
   - (b) Other persons, of the area as may be specified by the State Authority or the District Authority or the Supreme Court Legal Services Committee or the High Court Legal Services Committee, or as the case may be, the Taluk Legal Services Committee, organising such Lok Adalat.
   - (c) Both of the above
   - (d) Only (b)

6. Monetary ceiling of amount regarding which Civil Disputes can be settled under the Lok Adalats is:
   - (a) ₹ 10 lac
   - (b) ₹ 20 lac
   - (c) ₹ 50 lac
   - (d) No limit

7. Who can establish Permanent Lok Adalats at such places and for exercising such jurisdiction in respect of one or more public utility services and for such areas as may be specified in the notification.
   - (a) The Central Authority
   - (b) Every State Authority shall
   - (c) Both of the above
   - (d) None of the above

8. Who will decide cognisance of case by Lok Adalats:
   - (a) Both the parties to the suit may agree to refer their dispute to Lok Adalat.
   - (b) One of the parties there of makes an application to the Court/DRT for referring the case to the Lok Adalats for settlement.
   - (c) The court is satisfied that the matter is an appropriate one to be taken cognizance of by the Lok Adalat, the court shall refer the case to the Lok Adalat.
   - (d) Any of the above

9. For the purpose of determination of the dispute referred to it, the Lok Adalat shall have which of the following powers:
   - (a) To summon and enforce the attendance of any witness and examine him on oath.
   - (b) To discovery and production of documents and to receive evidence on affidavits.
   - (c) To requisition of public record or copy of the record.
   - (d) All of the above

10. How to organise Lok Adalat? Find the correct statement.

(a) For organising Lok Adalat respective banks can approach the district legal services authority.
(b) The authorities agree for organising Lok Adalat exclusively for the Banks and exclusively for a particular Bank also.
(c) The authorities identify the area taking into consideration conglomeration of the bank's branches. Number of cases pending in the courts or before DRT, irregular/sticky accounts. Where there is a likelihood of a compromise or a settlement & amount involved.
(d) Any of the above

11. Award of the Lok Adalat has the status of order of:
   - (a) Civil Court
   - (b) High Court
   - (c) Supreme Court
   - (d) District Collector

12. Lok Adalats are supposed to be guided by the principal of:
   - (a) Justice
   - (b) Equity and fair play
   - (c) Legal Principles
   - (d) All of the above

13. Under the Legal Services Authorities Act, Which is the correct statements?
   - (a) The award (decision) made by the Lok Adalats is deemed to be a decree of a High Court.
   - (b) The award is final but not binding on all parties.
   - (c) No appeal against such an award lies before any court of law.
   - (d) Any of the above

14. Lok Adalat is one of the alternative dispute redressal mechanisms. Find the correct statements.
   - (a) It is a forum where disputes/cases not pending in the court of law or at pre-litigation stage are settled.
   - (b) Award is passed amicably by consent of both parties.
   - (c) If amicably compromise not possible, Lok Adalat passed the award which is binding on both parties.
   - (d) All of the above

15. If a matter pending with the court is referred to Lok Adalat and is not settled:
   - (a) It will be treated as dismissed.
   - (b) It will be decided by Lok Adalat only.
   - (c) It will be referred back to the court that had referred the matter to Lok Adalat.
   - (d) Any of the above at discretion of Lok Adalat.

ANSWER

1	2	3	4	5	6	7	8	9	10
(a)	(a)	(d)	(d)	(c)	(b)	(c)	(d)	(d)	(d)

11	12	13	14	15
(a)	(d)	(c)	(b)	(c)

THE CONSUMER PROTECTION ACT, 1986

INTRODUCTION

An Act to provide for better protection of the interests of consumers and for that purpose to make provision for the establishment of consumer councils and other authorities for the settlement of consumers' disputes and for matters connected therewith.

The Consumer Protection Act (COPRA) was initially enacted in 1986 and implemented from April 15, 1987. A comprehensive amendment (The Consumer Protection (Amendment) Act 2002) has been passed on Dec 17, 2002 (implemented effective from March 15, 2003, the 'World Consumer Rights Day'). Further, it was amended in 2011 as 'The Consumer Protection (Amendment) Bill, 2011'. It extends to the whole of India except the State of Jammu and Kashmir.

Consumer Protection Council

To promote and protect the right of the consumers, councils are established. Their scope is not regarding directly dealing with the consumer complaints at initial or appellate scope but to promote and protect the rights of consumer.

1. **Central Consumer Protection Council:** The Central Government has established a council known as the Central Consumer Protection Council, called the Central Council. The Central Council consists of the following:

    a) The Minister-in-charge of the Consumer Affairs in the Central Government shall be the Chairman of the council, and

    b) Such member of other official or non-official members representing such interests as may be prescribed.

The Central Council shall meet as and when necessary but at least once in a year.

2. **State Consumer Protection Council:** The State Government has established a council known as the State Consumer Protection Council, called the State Council. The State Council consist of the following:

    a) The Minister-in-charge of the Consumer Affairs in the State Government shall be the Chairman of the council,

    b) Such member of other official or non-official members representing such interests as may be prescribed by the State Government, and

    c) Such member of other official or non-official members not exceeding ten as may be nominated by Central Government.

The State Council shall meet as and when necessary but at least twice in a year.

3. **District Consumer Protection Council:** The State Government has established a council known as the District Consumer Protection Council in every district, called the District Council. The District Council consists of the following:

    a) The Collector of the District shall be the Chairman of the council,

    b) Such member of other official or non-official members representing such interests as may be prescribed by the State Government, and

The State Council shall meet as and when necessary but at least twice in a year.

Objectives of the Councils

The objectives of the Councils under Consumer Protection Act (COPRA) is to promote and protect the rights of the consumers such as:

1. The right to be protected against the marketing of goods and services which are hazardous to life and property.

2. The right to be informed about the quality, quantity, potency, purity, standard and price of goods or services, as the case may be so as to protect the consumer against unfair trade practices;

3. The right to be assured, wherever possible, access to a variety of goods and services at competitive prices;

4. The right to be heard and to be assured that consumer's interest will receive due consideration at appropriate forums;

5. The right to seek redressal against unfair trade practices or restrictive trade practices or unscrupulous exploitation of consumers; and

6. The right to consumer education.

Definition of a Consumer

Consumer means any individual who:

1. Buys any goods for a consideration which has been paid or promised or partly paid and partly promised, or

2. Hires or avail of any services for a consideration which has been paid or promised or partly paid and partly promised, or under any system of deferred payment and,

3. Includes any user of such goods other than the person who buys such goods or hires of any services for consideration paid or

4. Promised or partly paid or partly promised, or under any system of deferred payment when such use is made with the approval of such person.

Who is not a Consumer?

1. Person buying goods for resale.

2. Person buying goods for any commercial purpose.

3. Person receiving goods/services free or gifts.

4. Person enjoying personal service under a contract (service by employees/maid servants) etc.

Coverage: All goods and services including banking, insurance, transport, processing, electricity, professional such as physicians etc. in private, public and cooperative sectors are covered under this Act. All banking services are covered due to their being essential services.

Who Can File a Complaint? A consumer (individually or jointly) himself or through any voluntary consumer Organisation, Central or State Governments can file a complaint. Limitation period is 2 years from the date of cause of action i.e. purchase of goods/hiring of services.

Procedure to File a Complaint: A simple written complaint in duplicate with full name and address of opposite party narrating facts of the complaint along with copies of the supporting documents and details of relief sought. No Court Fee is charged.

Engaging of Lawyer is not necessary. Consumer or anyone can represent his case. To protect his rights, a consumer should obtain proper receipt/cash memo for purchase made and guarantee/warranty card duly stamped and signed by the seller, wherever applicable.

Consumer can fill his complaint in the following consumer forum:

1) **District Forum:** a Consumer Disputes Redressal Forum to be known as the "District Forum" established by the State Government in each district of the State by notification. Subject to the other provisions of this Act. The District Forum shall have jurisdiction to entertain complaints where the value of the goods or services and the compensation, if any, claimed does not exceed ₹ 20 lakh.

Each District Forum shall consist of a person who is, or has been, or is qualified to be a District Judge, who shall be its President and two other members, one of whom shall be a women. They shall have the following qualifications, be persons of ability, integrity and standing, and have adequate knowledge and experience of at least ten years, in dealing with problems relating to economics, law, commerce, accountancy, industry, public affairs or administration.

Every member of the District Forum shall hold office for a term of 5 years or up to the age of 65 years, whichever is earlier.

2) **State Commission:** Each State Commission shall consist of a person who is or has been a Judge of a High Court, appointed by the State Government, who shall be its President and not less than two, and not more than such number of members, as may be prescribed, and one of whom shall be a woman. They will be not less than thirty-five years of age. They will be the persons of ability, integrity and standing, and have adequate knowledge and experience of at least ten years in dealing with problems relating to economics, law, commerce, accountancy, industry, public affairs or administration.

Every member of the State Commission shall hold office for a term of 5 years or up to the age of 67 years, whichever is earlier.

3) **National Commission:** The National Commission shall consist of a person who is or has been a Judge of the Supreme Court, to be appointed by the Central Government, who shall be its President and not less than four, and not more than such number of members, as may be prescribed, and one of whom shall be a woman. They will be not less than thirty-five years of age. They will be the persons of ability, integrity and standing, and have adequate knowledge and experience of at least ten years in dealing with problems relating to economics, law, commerce, accountancy, industry, public affairs or administration.

District Forum	Up to ₹ 20 lakh	Headed by President (qualified to be a District Judge) & 2 other members (1 Woman).
State Commission	More than ₹ 20 lakh up to ₹ 100 lakh	Headed by President (has/had been HC Judge) & 2 other members (1 Woman). They will be not less than thirty-five years of age.
National Commission	Above ₹ 100 lakh	Headed by President (has/had been Judge of Supreme Court) & 4 members (1 Woman). They will be not less than thirty-five years of age.

Relief by COPRA

If, after the proceeding conducted the Forum is satisfied about the complaint, it shall issue an order to the opposite party directing him:

- ○ To remove the defect pointed out from the goods,
- ○ To removal of deficiencies in services,
- ○ To replacement by new goods free from defects,
- ○ To refund of price/charges etc.
- ○ To pay such amount as may be awarded by it as compensation to the consumer for any loss or injury suffered by the consumer, due to the negligence of the opposite party.

PENALTY: Penalty for non-compliance of order is imprisonment for not less than one month and up to 3 years/fine not less than ₹ 2,000/- and up to ₹ 10,000/- or both. If the complaint is found to be of frivolous nature, fine up to ₹ 10,000/- or imprisonment for not less than one month but up to 3 years.

APPEAL: Any person aggrieved by an order made by the District Forum may appeal against the order to the State Commission within 30 days from the date of order in all cases. Appeal to State Commission against the award of District Forum will be accepted after Deposit amount is 50% of the Claim amount or ₹ 25,000/- whichever is less.

Any person aggrieved by an order made by the State Commission may appeal against the order to the National Commission within 30 days from the date of order in all cases. Appeal to National Commission against the award of State Commission will be accepted after Deposit amount is 50% of the Claim amount or ₹ 35,000/- whichever is less.

Any person aggrieved by an order made by the National Commission may appeal against the order to the Supreme Court within 30 days from the date of order in all cases. Appeal to Supreme Court against the award of National Commission will be accepted after Deposit amount is 50% of the Claim amount or ₹ 50,000/- whichever is less.

Time Limits for Disposal: Endeavour is made to decide the complaint within the following time frame:

A: Admissibility of the complaint from date of receipt of the complaint: within 21 days.

B: Decision on complaint: Without analysis or testing of commodities: 3 months

C: With analysis or testing of commodities: 5 months

ACTION	TIME
Admission of complaint from the date of receipt of the complaint	21 days
Disposal without analysis or testing of commodities	3 months
Disposal with analysis or testing of commodities	5 months
Disposal should be done at State/National Commission	3 months
Decision should be taken on Appeals for admission/rejection	90 days

TEST YOURSELF

1. A comprehensive amendment (The Consumer Protection (Amendment) Act 2002) has been passed on Dec 17, 2002 implemented effective from March 15, 2003. The day March 15 is celebrated as:
   (a) World Consumer Day
   (b) World Consumer Rights Day
   (c) India Consumer Rights Day
   (d) COPRA Establishment Day

2. The objectives of the Consumer Protection Act (COPRA) is to promote and protect the rights of the consumers such as:
   (a) The right to be protected against the marketing of goods and services which are hazardous to life and property.
   (b) The right to be informed about the quality, quantity, potency, purity, standard and price of goods or services, as the case may be so as to protect the consumer against unfair trade practices.
   (c) The right to consumer education.
   (d) All of the above

3. As per Consumer Protection Act (COPRA), Consumer means any individual who:
   (a) Buys any goods for a consideration which has been paid or promised or partly paid and partly promised.
   (b) Hires or avail of any services for a consideration which has been paid or promised or partly paid and partly promised, or under any system of deferred payment.
   (c) Promised or partly paid or partly promised, or under any system of deferred payment. when such use is made with the approval of such person.
   (d) All of the above

4. As per Consumer Protection Act (COPRA), who is not a consumer?
   (a) Person buying goods for resale, or Person buying goods for any commercial purpose.
   (b) Person receiving goods/services free or gifts.
   (c) Person enjoying personal service under a contract (service by employees/maid servants).
   (d) All of the above

5. As per Consumer Protection Act (COPRA), which are covered under this Act.
   (a) All goods and services including banking & insurance.
   (b) Professional such as physicians etc.
   (c) All of the above
   (d) None of the above

6. Consumer Protection Act has been enacted in bank with which of the following main objectives?
   (a) Protection of interest of banks
   (b) Protection of interest of consumers that include bank customers also
   (c) Create tribunals to deal with bank recovery purpose
   (d) All of the above

7. As per Consumer Protection Act (COPRA), who can file a complaint?
   (a) A consumer (individually or jointly) himself
   (b) Through any voluntary consumer organisation,
   (c) Through Central or State Governments can file a complaint.
   (d) All of the above

8. For filing a complaint under COPRA, Limitation period is ________ from the date of cause of action i.e. purchase of goods/hiring of services.
   (a) 2 years
   (b) 1 years
   (c) 6 months
   (d) No time limitation

9. Which is the correct statement about COPRA?
   (a) A simple written complaint in duplicate with full name and address of opposite party narrating facts of the complaint along with copies of the supporting documents required.
   (b) Prescribed Court Fee is charged.
   (c) Engaging of Lawyer is necessary.
   (d) All of the above

10. The terms 'goods' as per COPRA means which of the following?
    (a) Movable and immovable property
    (b) Actionable claim
    (c) Goods as stated in Indian Contract Act
    (d) Goods as stated in Sale of Goods Act

11. Consumer can fill his complaint in which the following consumer forum?
    (a) District Forum
    (b) State Commission
    (c) National Commission
    (d) All of the above

12. Which is the correct statement about consumer forums?
    (a) Complaint can be filed at District Forum, if claim does not exceed ₹ 20 lakh.

(b) Complaint can be filed at State Commission, if claim does not exceed ₹ 20 lakh but up to ₹ 50 lac

(c) Complain can be filed at National Commission, if claim exceeds ₹ 50 lakh

(d) All of the above

13. Under Consumer Protection Act, the Central Government has established a council known as:
(a) National Commission
(b) State Commission
(c) Central Consumer Protection Council
(d) All of the above

14. Who acts as the chairman of State Consumer Protection Council?
(a) The Minister-in-charge of the Consumer Affairs in the Central Government
(b) The Minister-in-charge of the Consumer Affairs in the State Government
(c) Secretary of the Consumer Affairs in the State Government
(d) Chief Justice of High Court

15. Who makes the appointment of the member of District Forum?
(a) Supreme Court   (b) High Court
(c) State Govt.   (d) Central Govt.

16. Which of the following is correct with regard to term of office of the member of district forum?
(a) 3 years or up to age of 60 years
(b) 3 years or up to age of 65 years
(c) 5 years or up to age of 60 years
(d) 3 years or up to age of 65 years

17. On receipt of complaint by district forum and after a direction to the opposite party, it is to submit its version within _______.
(a) 15 days   (b) 30 days
(c) 45 days   (d) 60 days

18. If, after the proceeding conducted the Forum is satisfied about the complaint, it shall issue an order to the opposite party directing him:
(a) To remove the defect pointed out from the goods, or to removal of deficiencies in services.
(b) To replacement by new goods free from defects, or to refund of price/ charges etc.
(c) To pay such amount as may be awarded by it as compensation to the consumer for any loss or injury suffered by the consumer, due to the negligence of the opposite party.
(d) All of the above

19. Penalty for non-compliance of order of the forum is:
(a) Imprisonment for not less than one month and up to 3 years/fine not less than ₹ 2,000/- and up to ₹ 10,000/- or both.
(b) Imprisonment for not less than one month and up to 2 years/fine not less than ₹ 2,000/- and up to ₹ 10,000/- or both.
(c) Imprisonment for not less than one month and up to 3 years/fine not less than ₹ 5,000/- and up to ₹ 10,000/- or both.
(d) Imprisonment for not less than one month and up to 3 years/fine not less than ₹ 2,000/- and up to ₹ 100,000/- or both.

20. Any person aggrieved by an order made by the State Commission may appeal against the order to the National Commission within 30 days from the date of order in all cases. Appeal to National Commission against the award of State Commission will be accepted after Deposit amount is:
(a) 50% of the Claim amount or ₹ 25,000/- whichever is less.
(b) 50% of the Claim amount or ₹ 35,000/- whichever is less.
(c) 50% of the Claim amount or ₹ 50,000/- whichever is less.
(d) 25% of the Claim amount or ₹ 35,000/- whichever is less.

ANSWER

1	2	3	4	5	6	7	8	9	10
(b)	(d)	(d)	(d)	(c)	(b)	(c)	(a)	(a)	(d)

11	12	13	14	15	16	17	18	19	20
(d)	(a)	(c)	(b)	(c)	(d)	(b)	(d)	(a)	(b)

CHAPTER 25

THE LAW OF LIMITATION

INTRODUCTION

Banks and financial institutions finance to the borrower after executing the security documents. On default of the loan, bank and FI have to initiate recovery action and file suit against the borrower. The recovery act and court only permit action if the claim is within the period of limitation. Limitation act defines the limitation period of various security documents. This Act may be called the Limitation Act, 1963. It extends to the whole of India except the State of Jammu and Kashmir.

Period of Limitation

It is related to documents which entitle the holder to take action in the court of law. Period of limitation prescribed for any suit, appeal or application by the Schedule, and prescribed period means the period of limitation computed in accordance with the provisions of this Act.

Bar of Limitation

It defines that, every suit instituted, appeal preferred, and application made after the prescribed period shall be dismissed although limitation has not been set up as a defense.

Expiry of Prescribed Period when Court is Closed

Where the prescribed period for any suit, appeal or application expires on a day when the court is closed, the suit, appeal or application may be instituted, preferred or made on the date when the court reopens.

Extension of Prescribed Period in Certain Cases

Any appeal or any application, other than an application under any of the provisions of Order XXI of the Code of Civil Procedure, 1908, may be, admitted after the prescribed period, if the appellant or the applicant satisfies the court that he had sufficient cause for not preferring the appeal or making the application within such period.

Computation of Period of Limitation

a) In computing the period of limitation for any suit or application for the execution of a decree, the institution or execution of which has been stayed by injunction or order, the day on which it was issued or made, and the day on which it was withdrawn, shall be excluded.

b) In computing the period of limitation for any suit of which notice has been given, or for which the previous consent or sanction of the Government or any other authority is required, in accordance with the requirements of any law for the time being in force, the period of such notice or, as the case may be, the time required for obtaining such consent or sanction shall be excluded.

c) In computing the period of limitation for any suit the time during which the defendant has been absent from India and from the territories outside India under the administration of the Central Government, shall be excluded.

Extension of Limitation Period:

a) Period of limitation can be extended by Acknowledgement of debt or part payment. In both cases, limitation period will start from the date of acknowledgement or part payment.

b) The acknowledgment or part payment should be by the borrower himself or his agent specifically authorized for this purpose.

c) Acknowledgement or part payment should be before the expiry of limitation period.

d) Once the limitation expires it cannot be extended by part payment or acknowledgement of debt.

e) The stamped acknowledgement of debt by the borrower before the expiry of documents does not automatically extend the period of limitation against the guarantor.

f) Similarly, the acknowledgement of debt signed by the principal debtor and a surety does not bind another surety who has not joined in signing the acknowledgement / revival letter of debt.

g) An admission of debt in the balance sheet filed by a firm before the I.T. Authority also extends the period of limitation from the date of (signing) the balance sheet. Such an acknowledgement does not require to be stamped. The balance sheet constitutes sufficient acknowledgement of debt in writing,

In case limitation expires in a particular case, the liability can be revived by obtaining fresh promise to pay the outstanding debt. As per section 25 (3) of Indian Contract Act, a time barred debt is a valid consideration.

Limitation period of various documents is given below:

Description of Suits	Period of Limitation	Time from which Period Begins to Run
Demand Loan	3 Years	From the date of loan
Demand Promissory Note	3 Years	From the date of DPN
Bill of Exchange payable on demand	3 Years	From the date of BoE
Usance Bill	3 Years	From the due date of bill
TOD without DP Note	3 Years	From the date of loan
Term Loan	3 Years	From the due date of each instalment
Arrear of rent	3 Years	From the date of arrear become due
Surety (guarantor) against the principal debtor	3 Years	From the date when the notice is given
Specific performance of contract	3 Years	From the date fixed for performance
To enforcement payment of money secured by a mortgage	12 Years	When the money sued for become due
Execution of Decree	12 years	From date of decree
Right of foreclosure by a mortgage	30 Years	From the date when money become due
Right of redemption	30 Years	From the date when the right to recover accrues
Any suit by State/Central Government	30 Years	From the date when limitation would start
Any suit for which no period of limitation is provided elsewhere in this schedule	30 Years	From the date when the right to sue accrues
Money deposited payable on demand like SB, Current Account	3 Years	From the date of demand
Appeal to be filled to High court against the judgement of lower court	90 days	From date of decree
Appeal to be filled to other court on decree of lower court	30 days	From date of decree
Recovery of loss caused by fraud	3 years	From date of detection of fraud

TEST YOURSELF

1. What is a period of limitation?
   (a) A fixed period within which a person can enforce his legal rights through a court
   (b) Limit of documentation
   (c) Period during which the sanction limit shall be a valid limit
   (d) All of the above

2. Limitation period for right of foreclosure by a mortgage is _________ years from the date when money become due.

(a) 3
(b) 12
(c) 30
(d) No limitation period

3. In which of the following the limitation period is 3 years?
(a) Foreclosure of a mortgage
(b) Enforcing payments of money secured by a mortgage
(c) For specific performance of a contract
(d) Money secured by Demand Promissory Note

4. In which of the following the limitation period is not 3 years?
(a) Equitable Mortgage
(b) Demand Promissory Note
(c) Agreement of hypothecation of movable assets
(d) All of the above

5. Which of the following instance give rise to fresh period of limitation?
(a) Acknowledgement of liability by the borrower before expiry of limitation
(b) Part payment of debt by the borrower or his duly authorised agent on his behalf before expiry of limitation
(c) Both of the above
(d) None of the above

6. The limitation period for guarantor starts:
(a) From the date of execution of deed of guarantee
(b) From the date of execution of D.P. Note by the borrower
(c) From the date of notice of demand is given to the guarantor by the bank
(d) There is no limitation for guarantor

7. Which of the following is not a method for extending the limitation period?
(a) Execution of fresh documents
(b) Execution of letter of acknowledgement by the borrower before expiry
(c) Requesting the court for extension of limitation
(d) None of the above

8. Documents in respect of a borrower's account expired by a week, what are the options before the bank:
(a) No option lies before the bank
(b) Bank has to look for payment made by the borrower during last 3 years for fresh limitation period
(c) Bank has to look whether the borrower has acknowledged the debt in his audited balance sheet during immediately preceding 3 years
(d) (b) & (c)

9. What are the rights that the banks loose once the documents/debt is time barred under limitation act 1963?
(a) Right to file suit for recovery of dues/debt in a court of law
(b) Right to file application for recovery for recourse in DRT
(c) Right to proceed for recovery from secured assets charged security under SARFAESI Act 2002
(d) All of the above

10. Limitation period for mortgage suit is:
(a) 3 years
(b) 12 years
(c) 30 years
(d) No limitation period

11. For an execution of a decree, an application can be moved within _______ years.
(a) 3
(b) 12
(c) 30
(d) No limitation period

12. Under the Law of limitation, limitation period for a term loan is __________.
(a) 5 years from the date of loan
(b) 3 years from the date of DP Note
(c) 3 years from the due date of each instalment
(d) 3 years from the date of loan

13. Under the Law of limitation, limitation period for recovery of loss caused by fraud is ________.
(a) 3 years from the date of detection of fraud
(b) 3 years from the date of fraud
(c) 5 years from the date of detection of fraud
(d) 5 years from the date of fraud

14. Appeal to be filled to High court against the judgement of lower court to be filled within ________ days from date of decree.
(a) 30
(b) 60
(c) 90
(d) 180

15. Under the Law of limitation, limitation period for a bill of exchange payable on demand is _________.
(a) 5 years from the date of demand
(b) 3 years from the date of bill of exchange
(c) 3 years from the date of demand
(d) 3 years from the date of bill of exchange

16. Under the Law of limitation, limitation period for TOD without DP Note is __________.
(a) 3 months from the date of TOD
(b) 6 months from the date of loan
(c) 1 year from the date of loan
(d) 3 years from the date of loan

ANSWER

1	2	3	4	5	6	7	8	9	10
(a)	(c)	(d)	(a)	(c)	(c)	(d)	(d)	(d)	(b)

11	12	13	14	15	16
(b)	(c)	(a)	(c)	(b)	(d)

TAX LAWS

INTRODUCTION

Banks and FIs have to follow tax laws applicable in India. Banks have to implement the provision of tax law and deduct TDS before paying interest on TDR and salary paid to the staff etc. and crediting the TDS to income tax authorities. Banks have to also implement the provision related to Goods and Services Tax (GST), in their day to day operations.

INCOME TAX IN INDIA

The Constitution of India has given the power to the Central Government to levy a tax on any income other than agricultural income, which is defined in Section 10(1) of the Income Tax Act, 1961. The Income Tax Law consists of Income Tax Act 1961, Income Tax Rules 1962, Notifications and Circulars issued by Central Board of Direct Taxes (CBDT), Annual Finance Acts and judicial pronouncements by the Supreme Court and High Courts.

The government imposes a tax on taxable income of all persons who are individuals, Hindu Undivided Families (HUFs), companies, firms, LLPs, association of persons, body of individuals, local authority and any other artificial juridical person. Levy of tax on a person depends upon his residential status. The CBDT administers the Income Tax Department, which is a part of the Department of Revenue under the Ministry of Finance, Govt. of India. Income tax is a key source of funds that the government uses to fund its activities and serve the public.

Meaning of Income

Income includes all types of income from Agriculture, business, salary, and income from property or from any other source of income. Thus, there is no precise definition as what constitutes income.

ASSESSEE

Assessee means a person by whom any tax or any other sum of money is payable under this Act, and includes:

(a) Every person in respect of whom any proceeding under this Act has been taken for the assessment of his income or assessment of fringe benefits or of the income of any other person in respect of which he is assessable, or of the loss sustained by him or by such other person, or of the amount of refund due to him or to such other person;

(b) Every person who is deemed to be an assessee under any provision of this Act;

(c) Every person who is deemed to be an assessee in default under any provision of this Act.

Assessment Year

Means the period of twelve months commencing on the 1st day of April every year. The income arising in the previous year is taxed in the assessment year.

PERMANENT ACCOUNT NUMBER (PAN)

What is PAN?

A PAN is a 10 character alphanumeric number allotted by the Income Tax Deptt, to a taxpayer who is eligible to file the income tax return. First 3 characters are Alphabetic series, 4th is status of PAN holder, 5th is the 1st character of PAN holder's name, Next 4 are special sequential numbers and the last one is alphabetic check.

Who must have a PAN?

(i) All existing assessees or taxpayers or persons who are required to furnish a return of income, even on behalf of others,

(ii) Any person, who intends to enter into financial transaction where quoting PAN is mandatory (details given below). The Assessing Officer may allot PAN to any person either on his own or on a specific request from such person.

The Central Board of Direct Taxes (CBDT) made it mandatory to quote PAN or General Index Number (GIR) on specified transactions (specified as per Rule 114B) with a view to ensure voluntary compliance of the income tax procedures. The quoting PAN became mandatory with effect from 01.11.1998.

Permanent Account Number (PAN): IT Act rule 114B has made it mandatory PAN (Form 60/61 in the absence of PAN) for certain banking transactions:

1. Opening of an account (other than basic saving);
2. An application for issuing Credit/Debit card;
3. Opening of Demat account;
4. Deposit/payment of cash exceeding ₹ 50,000/day;
5. Amount exceeding ₹ 50,000/- or aggregating more than ₹ Five lac in a financial year;
6. Payment of cash by way of DD/PO aggregating more than ₹ 50,000/- in a financial year.

Tax Deducted at Source (TDS) for Assessment Year 2019-2020 (Financial Year 2018-2019)

1. Interest paid on Deposits with Banks:

❍ No tax is deducted at source on interest payable on saving bank deposits.

❍ **Deposits on which tax to be Deducted:** Fixed deposit /Time Deposit including Recurring Deposit. (TDS is applicable on Recurring Deposit w.e.f. 01.06.2015).

❍ TDS on interest on deposits will be deducted only if the interest paid or payable credited or to be credited in a financial year exceeds ₹ 10,000 from bank and ₹ 5000 from others.

❍ Rate of TDS: 10%

❍ Interest paid on NRE, FCNR accounts is exempt from income tax and therefore no deduction of tax at source.

❍ **Submission of Form No.15G/15H:** No deduction shall be made in the case of individual who is resident in India who furnishes a declaration in writing in duplicate in the prescribed form 15G (in the case of other than senior citizens) or on 15H in the case of senior citizens and satisfy the following conditions:

a) Depositor is a person other than a company or Firm.

b) Tax on the estimated income of the depositor for the financial year will be NIL.

c) The amount of interest on securities, dividends, Interest other than interest on securities, payment in respect of deposits under National Savings Scheme and income in respect of units credited or paid during the previous year does not exceed the maximum amount, which is not chargeable to income-tax.

❍ In cases where the deductee who furnishes Form No. 15G or 15H but does not provide PAN, TDS will be deductible @ 20% w.e.f 01.04.2010.

❍ Declaration obtained on Form 15G or 15H is to be obtained at the beginning of the every financial year or before the deduction of Tax at source. The declaration will remain valid only for one Assessment year. One copy of form 15G/15H is to be delivered by the branch/office to the Income Tax Office on or before the seventh day of the succeeding month. In case the Forms are dispatched through post or courier or through any other medium, the same should reach the Assessing Officer latest by seventh day of succeeding month.

❍ In case of joint account, and in the absence of any information to the contrary, both the persons can be treated as payees for the purposes of TDS. In such cases, the interest on a joint account may be aggregated with the interest on deposits in the individual account that has higher interest income.

❍ Where the depositor submits certificate from the Income Tax Assessing Officer for deducting tax at a lower rate or for not deducting tax at all, then, the bank will act as per the certificate issued by the Assessing Officer. The certificate is valid only for the person named therein and will remain valid for A.Y. so specified in certificate.

❍ **Quarterly Return:** As per amendment made in section 194 A (3) (1), the quarterly return u/s 206A shall have to be furnished if the payment of interest to a resident does not exceed ₹ 10,000/- where the payer is a banking company or a co-operative society.

2. Payment to Resident Contractors:

(a) The deduction will be made only where the amount of any sum credited or paid or likely to be credited or paid to the account of, or to, the contractor or sub-contractor exceeds ₹ 30,000/- or more in a single payment or ₹ 1,00,000/- in the aggregate during the financial year.

(b) Rate of TDS: 1% if the payment is to an individual or a HUF and 2% for payment to others. TDS is not deductible if contractor is engaged in transport business if PAN is furnished.

3. Brokerage/Commission Other than Insurance Commission

(a) Tax will be deducted at source if the amount credited or paid or likely to be credited or paid exceeds ₹ 15,000/- in a financial year.

(b) Rate of TDS: 5%

4. Rent:

(a) Tax will be deducted at source if the amount of rent credited/paid during the financial year exceeds ₹ 1,80,000 per taxpayer.

(b) **Rate of TDS:**
   (i) Rent of plant or machinery or equipment: 2%;
   (ii) Rent of land, building furniture or fittings: 10%

(c) If there are a number of payees each having definite and ascertainable share in the property, the limit of ₹ 1,80,000/- will apply to each of the payee/co-owner separately.

(d) The Tax Deducted at source under this section shall be required to be made on the amount of rent paid/payable without including service tax.

5. Fees for Professional or Technical Services or Royalty:

(a) Tax will be deducted at source if the payment in a financial year is more than ₹ 30,000.

(b) Rate of Tax: 10%, (If person engaged only in the business of operation of call center 2%)

(c) If a consolidated bill is given by a professional/consultant for his fees as well as out of pocket expenditure, then the entire amount is subject to TDS. If a separate bill is given for reimbursement of out of pocket expenditure, then reimbursement of expenditure is not subject to tax deduction.

6. Time Limit for Depositing of TDS, Issuing TDS Cert. and Filing of Quarterly Return:

(a) Tax deducted should be deposited within one week from the last day of the month in which tax is deducted.

(b) However, if interest or amount of rent or commission or payment to contractor is credited to the account of the payee during March then TDS can be deposited upto 30th April.

(c) The statement of TDS should be sent on form 24Q in the case of salaries, on form 26Q in all other payments to residents and on form 27Q for all payments to non-residents.

(d) The statement of TDS should be sent within 15 days from the end of quarter i.e. 15th July, 15th October, 15th January. In the case of last quarter of financial year, the return can be sent within 45 days i.e. by 15th May.

(e) The TDS certificate except in the case of salary should be issued in form No. 16A within 15 days from the due date of the quarterly statement. In the case of TDS on salary, the same should be issued on Form No. 16 and 12BA by 31st May immediately following the financial year in which the Income was paid and tax deducted.

(f) Quarterly TDS return should be submitted in electronic form. Form No. 27A is to be furnished in paper form by deductor along with the e-TDS Return. It is a summary of e-TDS Returns which contains control totals of amount paid and income tax deducted at source. A separate form No. 27A is to be furnished for each e-TDS Return i.e. one each for Form Nos. 24Q, 26Q and 27Q.

7. Consequence of Failure to Deduct and Pay (Sec. 201)

As per Section 201 of the Income Tax Act, if a person who is required to deduct tax at source does not deduct the same or after deducting fails to pay the tax, then, such person shall be deemed to be an assessee in default in respect of such tax and shall be liable to pay simple interest at the rate of 18% per annum w.e.f. financial year 2010-11 on the amount of such tax from the date on which such tax was deductible to the date on which such tax is actually paid. Further, such person shall be liable to pay, by way of penalty, a sum equal to the amount of tax which such person failed to deduct or pay as aforesaid.

8. Failure to Comply with Provisions Regarding TAN

If the person required to deduct tax at source, fails to apply for TAN or after allotment of such number fails to quote such number wherever required then he shall be liable for penalty of a sum which may extend upto ₹ 10,000/-.

9. Failure to Issue Certificate, or Submit Return, Statement, etc.

If any person fails to furnish in due time annual return for tax deducted; or furnish certificate of tax deducted at source; or furnish in due time quarterly statement of TDS deposited, then, he shall be liable for penalty which shall be ₹ 100 for every day during which the failure continues subject to a maximum of the amount of tax deductible.

10. Prosecution Under Section 276B:

If a person fails to pay to the credit of the Central Government, the tax deducted at source by him, then he shall be punishable with rigorous imprisonment for a term which shall not be less than three months but which may extend to seven years and with fine.

11. TDS on Payment of Interest on Non-Resident (Ordinary) Account

India has entered into Double Taxation Avoidance Agreement (DTAA) with many countries, in order to grant relief in the tax payable on the same income in both the countries (i.e. the country of residence of the non-resident as well as India). As per Section 90 of the Income Tax Act, the tax should be deducted at the rate provided in the Finance Act of the relevant year or the rate provided in the DTAA with that country, whichever is more beneficial to the assessees.

Annual Information Return (AIR)

Annual Information Return of 'high value financial transactions' is required to be furnished under section 285BA of the Income-tax Act, 1961 by 'specified persons' in respect of 'specified transactions' registered or recorded by them during the financial year. The due date of filing of the return is the 31st of August of the following year. AIR is a mechanism through which the Income Tax Dept. is looking to ensure automatic flow of information on the material financial transactions entered into by the taxpayers with other persons. The information is to be utilized by the Revenue dept. for widening/deepening of tax base. CBDT has specified 7 categories of persons who are required to file AIR with the Income Tax depts., which include:

- Banks—on cash deposits aggregating to ₹ 10 lac or more in a year in any savings account of a person.
- Companies, banks or institutions issuing credit cards—payments made by any person against bills raised in respect of a credit card issued to that persons, aggregating to ₹ 2 lac or more in a year.
- Mutual Funds—receipt of an amount of ₹ 2 lac or more for acquiring units of that fund.
- Companies for shares—transactions where company has received from any person an amount of ₹ 1 lac or more for acquiring shares issued by the company.
- Companies or institutions for bonds—receipt of an amount of ₹ 5 lac or more for acquiring bonds or debentures issued by the company or institution. Sub-registrar—purchase or sale, by any person, of immovable property valued at ₹ 30 lac or more.
- RBI—receipt of an amount aggregating to ₹ 5 lac or more in a year for bonds issued by RBI.

TDS at Lower Rates

If a depositor submits certificate from the Income Tax Assessing Officer for deducting tax at a lower rate or for not deducting tax at all, then, the bank will act as per the certificate issued by the Assessing Officer.

Issue of TDS Certificate

Banks are to issue TDS certificate within one month from the end of the quarter in which credit is given or the amount is paid.

INCOME TAX SLABS FOR TAXPAYERS FOR FINANCIAL YEAR 2019-20 (AY 2020-21)

Incomes up to extent of ₹ 5 lakh will be exempt from tax. In addition to that, the standard deducation has also been increased to the extent of ₹ 50,000 now, as opposed to the previously prevalent amount of ₹ 40,000.

General Category (Up to 60 years of age)		Senior Citizens (60-80 years)		Super Senior Citizens (Above 80 years)	
Income	*Tax*	*Income*	*Tax*	*Income*	*Tax*
Up to ₹ 2.5 lakh	Nil	Up to ₹ 3 lakh	Nil	Up to ₹ 5 lakh	Nil
₹ 2,50,001—₹ 5 lakh	5%	₹ 3,00,001—₹ 5 lakh	5%	₹ 5,00,001—₹ 10 lakh	20%
₹ 500,001—₹ 10 lakh	20%	₹ 5,00,001—₹ 10 lakh	20%	Above ₹ 10 lakh	30%
Above ₹ 10 lakh	30%	Above ₹ 10 lakh	30%		

Surcharge of 10% for income between ₹ 50 lakh and ₹ 1 crore with marginal relief.

Surcharge of 15% for income above ₹ 1 crore with marginal relief.

The health & education cess at the rate of 4% shall be computed on aggregate of Income-Tax and Surcharge.

₹ 40,000 Standard Deduction for salaried employees and pensioners in lieu of transport and medical expenses.

For senior citizens, exemption of interest income on bank deposits raised to ₹ 50,000 from the current ₹ 10,000.

Deduction allowed under section 80D for payment of Medical Insurance Premium increased from ₹ 30000 to ₹ 50000 for senior citizens.

GOODS AND SERVICES TAX (GST)

Introduction

The introduction of Goods and Services Tax (GST) would be a very significant step in the field of indirect tax reforms in India. By amalgamating a large number of Central and State taxes into a single tax, it would mitigate cascading or double taxation in a major way and pave the way for a common national market. From the consumer point of view, the biggest advantage would be in terms of a reduction in the overall tax burden on goods, which is currently estimated to be around 25%-30%. Introduction of GST would also make Indian products competitive in the domestic and international markets. Studies show that this would have a boosting impact on economic growth. Last but not the least, this tax, because of its transparent and self-policing character, would be easier to administer.

Goods and Services Tax (GST)

GST is an indirect tax which was introduced in India on 1 July] 2017 and was applicable throughout India which replaced multiple cascading taxes levied by the central and state governments. It was introduced as The Constitution (One Hundred and First Amendment) Act 2017, following the passage of Constitution 122nd Amendment Act Bill. The GST is governed by a GST Council and its Chairman is the Finance Minister of India. Under GST, goods and services are taxed at the following rates, 0%, 5%, 12%, 18% and 28%. There is a special rate of 0.25% on rough precious and semi-precious stones and 3% on gold. In addition a cess of 22% or other rates on top of 28% GST applies on few items like aerated drinks, luxury cars and tobacco products. GST replaced a slew of indirect taxes with a unified tax and is therefore set to dramatically reshape the country's 2 trillion dollar economy.

Launch: The Goods and Services Tax was launched at midnight on 1 July 2017 by the President of India, Shri Pranab Mukherjee, and Prime Minister of India, Shri Narendra Modi. The launch was marked by a historic midnight (30 June–1 July) session of both the houses of parliament convened at the Central Hall of the Parliament. It is one of the few midnight sessions that have been held by the parliament—the others being the declaration of India's independence on 15 August 1947, and the silver and golden jubilees of that occasion.

GST RATES: The GST Council in its 23rd meeting on November 10, 2017 recommended widespread changes in the Goods and Services Tax (GST). The council has decided to keep the highest 28% tax on luxury and sinful items as a result 177 items have been shifted to the 18% bracket. GST on many items have also been reduced.

TEST YOURSELF

1. GST is an indirect tax which was introduced in India on _______ and is applicable throughout India.
   (a) 1 July, 2016
   (b) 1 June, 2017
   (c) 1 July, 2017
   (d) 1 Sept., 2017

2. The Constitution of India has given the power to the Central Government to levy a tax on any income other than agricultural income, which is defined in _________ of the Income Tax Act, 1961.
   (a) Section 10(1)
   (b) Section 11(1)
   (c) Section 10(2)
   (d) Section 11(1)

3. A PAN is a ______ character alphanumeric number allotted by the Income Tax Deptt, to a tax payer who is eligible to file the income tax return.
   (a) 5
   (b) 7
   (c) 9
   (d) 10

4. IT Act rule 114B has made it mandatory to quote PAN (Form 60/61 in the absence of PAN) for certain banking transactions.
   (a) An application for issuing Credit/Debit card;
   (b) Opening of Demat Account;
   (c) Deposit/payment of cash exceeding ₹ 50,000/- day;
   (d) All the above

5. The Central Board of Direct Taxes (CBDT) made it mandatory to quote PAN or General Index Number (GIR) on specified transactions (specified as per Rule 114(B)) with a view to ensure voluntary compliance of the income tax procedures. Quoting PAN became mandatory with effect from _________.
   (a) 01.11.1998
   (b) 01.04.1998
   (c) 01.11.1999
   (d) 01.04.1999

6. Assessee means a person by whom any tax or any other sum of money is payable under this Act, and includes:
   (a) Every person in respect of whom any proceeding under this Act has been taken for the assessment of his income or assessment of fringe benefits or of the income of any other person in respect of which he is assessable, or of the loss sustained by him or by such other person, or of

the amount of refund due to him or to such other person;

(b) Every person who is deemed to be an assessee under any provision of this Act;

(c) Every person who is deemed to be an assessee in default under any provision of this Act;

(d) All of above

7. TDS is applicable on Recurring Deposit w.e.f. _______.
(a) 01.04.2015 (b) 01.06.2015
(c) 01.09.2015 (d) 01.06.2016

TDS is applicable for A/Y 2018-2019 (Financial Year 2017-2018) in the following questions

8. TDS on interest on deposits will be deducted only if the interest paid or payable credited or to be credited in a financial year exceeds ___________ from bank and ________ from others.
(a) ₹ 10,000, ₹ 10,000
(b) ₹ 10,000, ₹ 5,000
(c) ₹ 10,000, ₹ 15,000
(d) ₹ 5,000, ₹ 10,000

9. TDS on interest on deposits will be deducted at the Rate of:
(a) 10% (b) 20%
(c) 10% (d) 15%

10. In cases where the deductee who furnishes Form No. 15G or 15H but does not provide PAN, TDS will be deductible @ ________ w.e.f 01.04.2010.
(a) 10% (b) 20%
(c) 12% (d) 15%

11. The deduction will be made only where the amount of any sum credited or paid or likely to be credited or paid to the account of, or to, the contractor or sub-contractor exceeds ______ or more in a single payment or ________ in the aggregate during the financial year.
(a) ₹ 20,000, ₹ 75,000
(b) ₹ 30,000, ₹ 50,000
(c) ₹ 30,000, ₹ 75,000
(d) ₹ 10,000, ₹ 50,000

12. Rate of TDS: ___ if the payment is to an individual or a HUF and ___ for payment to others. TDS is not deductible if contractor is engaged in transport business if PAN is furnished.
(a) 1%, 10% (b) 2%, 10%
(c) 2%, 20% (d) 1%, 2%

13. Brokerage/Commission other than Insurance Commission, Tax will be deducted at source if the amount credited or paid or likely to be credited or paid exceeds ________ in a financial year.
(a) ₹ 10,000 (b) ₹ 15,000
(c) ₹ 25,000 (d) ₹ 50,000

14. Brokerage/Commission other than Insurance Commission, Tax will be deducted at source if the amount credited or paid or likely to be credited or paid exceeds the amount @ Rate of TDS:
(a) 5% (b) 10%
(c) 20% (d) 15%

15. Tax will be deducted at source if the amount of rent credited/paid during the financial year exceeds ________ per taxpayer.
(a) ₹ 1,00,000 (b) ₹ 1,50,000
(c) ₹ 1,80,000 (d) ₹ 2,00,000

16. There is a special GST rate of ______ on rough precious and semi-precious stones and ______ on gold.
(a) 0.25%, 3% (b) 0.50%, 1%
(c) 0.25%, 1% (d) 1%, 3%

ANSWER

1	2	3	4	5	6	7	8	9	10
(c)	(a)	(d)	(d)	(a)	(d)	(b)	(b)	(c)	(b)

11	12	13	14	15	16
(c)	(d)	(b)	(a)	(c)	(a)

CHAPTER 27

NEGOTIABLE INSTRUMENTS ACT, 1881

Introduction

In India, the Negotiable Instruments Act was passed during 1881 which came into force from March 01, 1882. Originally, it had 137 Sections. Sections 138 to 142 were added in 1988, and Sections 143 to 147 were added during December 2002. At present it has 147 Sections and 17 Chapters. It extends to the whole of India. According to Section 13 (a) of the Act, Negotiable Instruments means Promissory Note (PN), Bill of Exchange (BOE) and Cheque.

Features of Negotiable Instruments are as under:

- A negotiable instrument is one which is freely used by the parties in their business deal as a medium of payment.
- The word 'negotiable' means the transfer of ownership of the instrument from one person to another person for the purpose of consideration.
- Transfered Negotiable Instruments will further transfer without any restriction.
- Transferee taking the instrument for value and in good faith, gets better and absolute title despite any defect in the title of the transferor.
- The property in a negotiable instrument, i.e. the complete right of ownership, and not merely the possession passes, in the case of bearer instruments, by mere delivery, and in case of order instruments, by endorsement and delivery.
- The holder in due course is not, in any way, affected by the defect of the title of his transferor or of any prior party.
- The holder in due course can sue against the negotiable instrument in his own name.
- The transferee of a negotiable instrument is known as 'holder in due course.' A bona fide transferee for value is not affected by any defect of title on the part of the transferor or of any of the previous holders of the instrument.
- The instrument may be defined as a written document which creates a right in favour of some person.
- Negotiable instrument means Promissory Note (PN), Bill of Exchange (BE), and Cheque payable to order or bearer.

Different types of Negotiable Instruments

Promissory Notes: Section 4 of the Act defines, "A promissory note is an instrument in writing (note being a bank-note or a currency note) containing an unconditional undertaking, signed by the maker, to pay a certain sum of money to or to the order of a certain person, or to the bearer of the instruments." Example- A writes "I promise to pay B or order, the sum of ₹ 5000".

An instrument to be a promissory note must possess the following elements:

1. It must be in writing,
2. It must certainly be an express promise or clear understanding to pay a certain sum of money,
3. The promise should be to pay money and money only,
4. Promise to pay must be unconditional,
5. It should be signed by the maker,
6. The maker & payee must be certain.

Bill of Exchange: Section 5 of the Act defines, "A bill of exchange is an instrument in writing containing an unconditional order, signed by the maker, directing a certain person to pay a certain sum of money only to, or to the order of a certain person or to the bearer of the instrument".

A bill of exchange, therefore, is a written acknowledgement of the debt, written by the creditor and accepted by the debtor. There are usually three parties to a bill of exchange drawer, acceptor or drawee and payee. Drawer himself may be the payee.

For example, Mahesh directed to Ramesh for payment of ₹ 1000 to Suresh : "I shall be highly obliged if you make it convenient to pay ₹ 1000 to Suresh".

Essential Conditions of a Bill of Exchange

(1) It must be in writing.

(2) It must be signed by the drawer.

(3) The drawer, drawee and payee must be certain.

(4) The sum payable must also be certain.

(5) It should be properly stamped.

(6) It must contain an express order to pay money and money alone.

Cheques: Section 6 of the Act defines : "A cheque is a bill of exchange drawn on a specified banker, and not expressed to be payable otherwise than on demand".

A cheque is bill of exchange with two more qualifications, namely,

a) It is always drawn on a specified banker, and

b) It is always payable on demand.

Consequently, all cheque are bill of exchange, but all bills are not cheque. A cheque must satisfy all the requirements of a bill of exchange; that is, it must be signed by the drawer, and must contain an unconditional order on a specified banker to pay a certain sum of money to or to the order of a certain person or to the bearer of the cheque. It does not require acceptance.

Other Negotiable Instruments: The following are also considered as negotiable instruments:

- ○ Demand Draft,
- ○ Hundi,
- ○ Traveller Cheque,
- ○ Gift Cheque,
- ○ Dividend Warrant,
- ○ Interest Warrant,
- ○ Bankers' Cheque,
- ○ Pay Order,
- ○ Commercial Paper.

Not Negotiable Instruments: The following are not Negotiable Instruments:

- ○ Deposit Receipt,
- ○ NSC,
- ○ Postal Order,
- ○ Share Certificate,
- ○ Bill of Lading,
- ○ Lorry Receipt,
- ○ Airway Bill,
- ○ Railway Receipt,
- ○ Stock Invest,
- ○ Dock Warrant

Parties to Negotiable Instruments:

- ○ **Drawer:** The maker of a bill of exchange or a cheque is called the 'drawer'.

- ○ **Drawee:** The person directed to pay the money by the drawer is called the 'drawee.'

- ○ **Payee:** The person named in the instrument, to whom or to whose order the money is directed to be paid by the instrument is called the 'payee'. He is the real beneficiary under the instrument.

- ○ **Endorser:** When the holder transfers or endorses the instrument to anyone else, the holder becomes the 'endorser'.

- ○ **Endorsee:** The person to whom the bill is endorsed is called an 'endorsee'.

- ○ **Holder:** A person who is legally entitled to the possession of the negotiable instrument in his own name and to receive the amount thereof, is called a 'holder'. He is either the original payee, or the endorsee. In case the bill is payable to the bearer, the person in possession of the negotiable instrument is called the 'holder'.

- ○ **Holder in Due Course:** Defined in Section 9 of the NI Act. Holder in due course is a person who became possessor of a NI for valuable consideration, in good faith, before becoming due, and without having any reason to believe that the person transferring the instrument was not entitled thereto. If before the amount mentioned in it became payable, and without having sufficient cause to believe that any defect existed in the title of the person from whom he derived his title.

CLASSIFICATION OF BILLS

Bills can be classified as:

(1) Inland and Foreign Bills (Place wise)

(2) Time and Demand Bills (Period wise)

(3) Trade and Accommodation Bills (Nature wise)

(1) Inland and Foreign Bills

Inland Bill: A bill is, named as an inland bill if drawn and made payable in India. A bill drawn or made in India & payable in or drawn upon any persons in India. The necessary requisite for inland bills are:

(a) It must be drawn in India on a person residing in India, whether payable in or outside India, or

(b) It must be drawn in India on a person residing outside India but payable in India.

Foreign Bill: A bill which is not an inland bill is a foreign bill. The following are the foreign bills:

1. A bill drawn outside India and made payable in India.
2. A bill drawn outside India on any person residing outside India.
3. A bill drawn in India on a person residing outside India and made payable outside India.
4. A bill drawn outside India on a person residing in India.
5. A bill drawn outside India and made payable outside India.

(2) Time and Demand Bill

Time or Usance Bills: A bill payable after a fixed time is termed as a time bill. In other words, bill payable "after date" is a time or usance bill.

Demand Bill: A bill payable at sight or on demand is termed as a demand bill.

(3) Trade and Accommodation Bill

Trade Bill: A bill drawn and accepted for a genuine trade transaction is termed as a "trade bill".

Accommodation Bill: A bill drawn and accepted not for a genuine trade transaction but only to provide financial help to some party is termed as an "accommodation bill".

Example: A is in need of money for three months. He induces his friend B to accept a bill of exchange drawn on him for ₹ 1,000 for three months. The bill is drawn and accepted. The bill is an "accommodation bill". A may get the bill discounted from his bankers immediately, paying a small sum as discount. Thus, he can use the funds for three months and then just before maturity he may remit the money to B, who will meet the bill on maturity. In the above example A is the "accommodated party" while B is the "accommodating party".

Acceptance of Bill of Exchange: The acceptance of a bill means signing by the drawer of a bill, on face with or without the words accepted and delivery thereof or giving notice of signing, to the holder of the bill. There are 2 types of acceptances i.e. general acceptance and qualified acceptance. In cases of several drawees not being partners, each of them can accept it for himself but not others without their authority (Sec 34).

Dishonour of Bill of Exchange: A bill of exchange is said to be dishonoured either by non-acceptance (when drawee defaults in acceptance) or by non-payment (when the acceptor/drawee makes default in payment). Similarly where the drawee is incompetent to contract or acceptance is qualified, the bill is said to be dishonoured (Section 91 & 92).

Presentation for Acceptance: As per Section 61, a usance bill payable after sight and bills payable on a fixed date (and not demand bills) require to be presented to drawee for acceptance to make him liable and also for calculation of due date.

Negotiation: When a promissory note, bill of exchange or cheque is transferred to any person so as to constitute that person the holder thereof, the instrument is said to be negotiated.

Negotiation of a Bearer Instruments: A bearer instrument is negotiated by mere delivery and no endorsement is required.

Negotiation of an Order Instrument: An order instrument can be negotiated by endorsement followed by delivery. It may be noted that legal heirs cannot complete the negotiation of a negotiable instrument with endorsement by the deceased merely by delivery.

ENDORSEMENT

Signing of an instrument on the back or on a slip of paper annexed thereto for the purpose of negotiation is called endorsement (Section 15). The person who transfers the instrument is called endorser and the person to whom it is transferred is called endorsee. Various types of endorsements are as under:

a) **Blank Endorsement:** In a blank endorsement the endorser just signs his name without indicating endorsee. It can be converted into full by writing name of a person above signatures. The effect of an endorsement in blank is that it makes an instrument drawn originally payable to order to bearer instrument for the purpose of negotiation which can be further negotiated by mere delivery.

b) **Endorsement in Full:** When, the endorser indicates the name of the endorsee it is called full endorsement.

c) **Sans Recourse Endorsement:** An endorsement in which endorser excludes his liability is termed 'sans recourse' or 'without recourse' endorsement. In case of dishonour of instrument, the amount cannot be recovered from such endorser.

d) **Facultative:** An endorsement in which endorser waives the notice of dishonour is called Facultative endorsement But this is not applicable to other parties to the instrument.

e) **Restrictive Endorsement:** An endorsement which restricts further right of negotiation is called as restrictive endorsement. For example if it is written in the endorsement as "Pay to Hari for my use" it is restrictive endorsement.

f) Conditional Endorsement: When along with endorsement, condition is imposed by endorser. For example, pay to C on completion of studies. Paying bank not to ensure compliance of condition. Condition binds endorser and endorsee only.

g) Back to Back Endorsement: An endorsement in which the endorser himself becomes endorsee is called as back to back endorsement and in such a case, the endorsee can recover the amount only from parties prior to his own endorsement.

h) Negotiation Back: When the drawer of a cheque himself becomes endorsee, it is called "Negotiation Back" and this cheque is treated as satisfied.

i) Partial Endorsement: The endorsement can be made only for full amount but in case part payment has been received and a note to that effect is made on the instrument, then the same can be endorsed for the balance amount.

j) Forged Endorsement: When endorsement is made by a person other than Holder by forging signatures of Holder Title does not pass to any person on the basis of such endorsement. A person getting instrument after such endorsement does not become holder.

k) Regularity of Endorsement: Paying bank gets protection u/s 85(1) only when endorsement is regular (may not be genuine).

Payment in Due Course

As per Section 10 of NI Act, 'payment in due course means payment according to the apparent tenor of the instrument in good faith and without negligence to any person in possession thereof under circumstances which do not afford a reasonable ground for believing that he is not entitled to receive payment of the amount therein mentioned'.

Section 85 of NI Act conditions to be satisfied for being a payment in due course.

○ Payment is in accordance with the apparent tenor of the instrument,

○ Payment must be in good faith and without negligence,

○ Payment must be made to the person in possession of the instrument,

○ The banker should not have any reasons to "disbelieve" the integrity/honesty of the possessor, i.e. no reasons to think that he is not entitled to receive the payment.

○ Payment must be made in money only.

Inchoate Instruments: As per section 20 of the NI Act, an instrument on which date, payee or amount is not mentioned is called as inchoate or incomplete instrument. Incomplete cheque can be completed by the Holder and the completion so made will not be treated as material alteration.

An instrument without signatures is not treated as an instrument at all.

Ambiguous Instruments: Where the instrument is drawn in such a manner that it can be construed both as PN or BE.

In the following cases, the instrument is taken as ambiguous;

    (a) Where drawer and drawee are the same person.

    (b) Where drawee is a fictitious person e.g., Lord Krishna etc

    (c) Where drawee is a person incapable of entering into a contract.

The Amount Expressed in Words and Figures should be Matched: The amount expressed in cheque differ in words and figures, it should not be paid and returned with mark 'words and figures differ'. However, Section 18 of NI Act provides that where there is a difference between the amount in words and the amount in figures, the amount in words is the amount payable.

If Mutilated Cheque is Presented for Payment: A cheque is mutilated when it has been cut or torn or a part of it is missing. Mutilation may be accidental or intentional. When it is accidental, the banker should get the drawer's confirmation before honouring it. If it is intentional, banker should refuse payment with mark 'mutilated cheque' or 'mutilation required confirmation'.

CROSSING OF A CHEQUE

Section 123 to 131 of the NI Act with the crossing of cheque. When two angular parallel lines are drawn on the face of the cheque with or without words, then the cheque is said to be crossed. Two types of crossing such as 'General Crossing' and 'Special Crossing' are defined in the act.

General Crossing

Where a cheque bears across its face an addition of the words "& company" or any abbreviation thereof, between two parallel transverse lines, or of two parallel transverse lines simply, either with or without the words "not negotiable," that addition shall be deemed a crossing, and the cheque shall be deemed to be crossed generally.

The effect of general crossing of the cheque is that the same should not be paid over the counter and only paid through a bank account only.

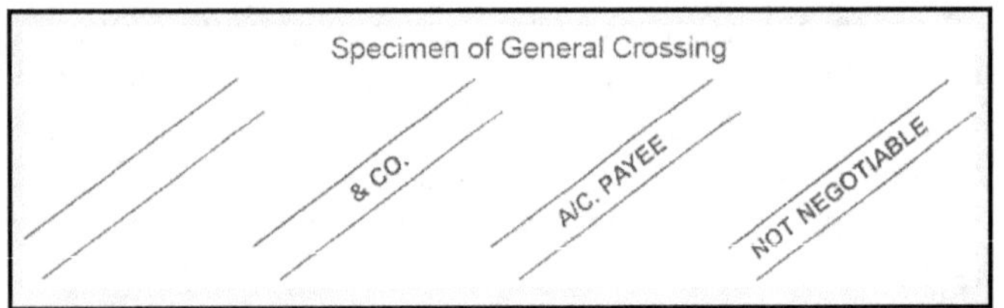

Special Crossing

If the cheque bears across its face, in addition of the crossing, the name of the banker, the cheque is deemed to have been crossed specially to that banker.

The effect of this crossing is that, the proceeds of the cheque should be paid only to that banker. Because of this reason, the banks put the crossing stamp on the cheques received by them for collection.

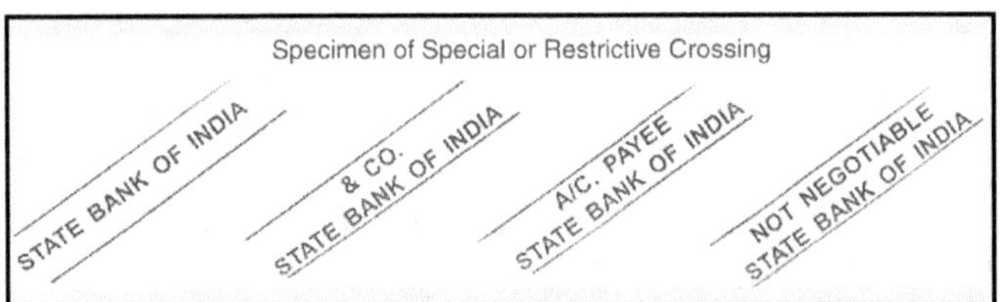

Not Negotiable Crossing: This type of crossing would remove the negotiable characteristic of the instrument and the transferee cannot have a better title than what the transferor had. Section 130 of the NI Act define that "A person taking a cheque crossed generally or specially, bearing in either case the words "not negotiable," shall not have, and shall not be capable of giving, a better title to the cheque than that which the person from whom he took it had."

Account Payee Crossing: In order to add more protection, to the cheque sometimes the word like "A/c Payee" or "Payee's A/c only" are added to the crossing. This type of crossing has not been provided for the Negotiable Instrument Act but it is a practice widely followed. These words constitute a direction to the collecting bank to collect proceeds in the payee's account only and such instruction do not take away characteristic of negotiability.

Crossing after Issue of the Cheque:

○ If the cheque is not crossed, the holder of the cheque may cross it either generally or specially.

○ If the cheque is crossed generally, the holder may cross it specially.

○ The holder may add the words "Not Negotiable" to the crossing.

Protection Only for Crossed Cheque: Protection is not available for an un-crossed cheque. Hence it is always advisable for a banker to cross all cheques before/prior send for collection.

Banker's Liability in Case of Wrongful Dishonour: Before dishonouring a cheque on the ground of customer's credit not being sufficient, or with the remark that the customer has "insufficient fund", the banker should be careful. In this case banker would be liable, if step taken by him proves to be erroneous.

Payment of a Forged Cheque: A cheque with the forged signature of a drawer must not be paid by a banker. The payment of such cheque is deemed as payment without the authority of the customer. The paying banker is not given any protection under law on the payment of a forged cheque. The banker's liability remains even if the signature is cleverly forged and it is difficult to detect it with reasonable care. In case of forged cheque, the banker cannot escape from liability, even if, the customer was negligent in keeping the cheque book under lock and key as required by the rule of the bank.

SOME IMPORTANT SECTIONS OF NEGOTIABLE INSTRUMENTS ACT:

- **01** Indian Paper Currency Act 1871 not to be affected by the provisions of this Act.
- **04** Promissory note defined
- **05** Bill of exchange defined
- **06** Cheque defined (also include electronic cheque and truncated cheque)
- **07** Drawer, drawee in case of need, acceptor, acceptor for honour, payee defined
- **08** Holder defined
- **09** Holder in due course defined
- **10** Payment in due course: Paying banker's protection if payment is made in due course
- **11** Inland instruments defined—drawn and made payable in India
- **12** Foreign instruments defined.
- **13** Negotiable instruments defined indirectly
- **14** Negotiation defined.
- **15** Endorsement and endorser defined

- **16** Endorsement in blank and in full and endorsee defined
- **17** Ambiguous instruments
- **18** Difference in amount in words and figures. Amount in words to be paid
- **20** Inchoate stamped instruments—Holder has implied authority to complete the instrument
- **22** 3 days of grace are allowed on an usance Bill of Exchange/Promissory note
- **25** When a BOE/PN matures on a holiday—due date on the next preceding working day
- **26** A minor can draw, endorse and deliver and negotiate a negotiable instrument so as to bind all parties except himself
- **31** Banker's obligation to pay cheque & compensate drawer for wrongful dishonour
- **65** Presentment for acceptance to be made during the usual business hours
- **80** If no interest rate mentioned in the Promissory Note interest @ 18% p.a. is to be paid
- **85-1** Paying banker protected by payment in due course of an order cheque which is properly endorsed by the payee or his agent
- **85-2** Protection to paying banker in case of a bearer cheque
- **85-A** Protection to paying banker in case of Bank drafts
- **87** Material alteration renders NI renders void
- **89** Protection to paying banker for materially altered instrument
- **99** Noting—must for foreign instruments
- **100** Protest—must for foreign instruments
- **105-107** Reasonable time—for presentment, dishonour and transmission of notice
- **123** General crossing
- **124** Special crossing
- **125** Who can cross-holder, banker
- **126-127** Payment of cheque crossed generally or specially
- **128** Payment in due course of crossed cheques
- **129** Paying banker liable to the true owner for loss when payment not made in due course
- **130** 'Not Negotiable' crossing—transferee does not get better title than that of transferor
- **131** Protection to collecting bank for crossed cheques subject to compliance of conditions
- **131-A** Protection to collecting bank for crossed bank drafts
- **138** Drawer's liability for cheque returned unpaid for insufficient funds
- **139** Unless proved otherwise, it will be presumed that the cheque has been issued for the discharge of a debt/liability
- **140** The drawer cannot plead that he did not expect the cheque to be dishonoured
- **141** Offences by companies
- **147** Offences to be compoundable

TEST YOURSELF

1. In India, the Negotiable Instruments Act was passed during 1881 which came into force from:
   (a) March 01, 1881
   (b) March 01, 1882
   (c) January 01, 1881
   (d) January 01, 1882

2. Originally, it had 137 Sections, five Sections were added in 1988, and again five Sections were added during December 2002. At present it has _________.
   (a) 147 sections and 17 Chapters
   (b) 149 sections and 17 Chapters
   (c) 149 sections and 18 Chapters
   (d) 147 sections and 18 Chapters

3. The Negotiable Instruments Act extends to the:
   (a) Whole of India, except the state of J & K
   (b) Whole of India, except NE states
   (c) Whole of India
   (d) Whole of India, except the state of Tamilnadu

4. According to Section 13 (a) of the Act, Negotiable Instruments means:
   (a) Promissory Note (PN),
   (b) Bill of Exchange (BOE)

(c) Cheque
(d) All of the above

5. Bill of exchange is defined under which section of the NI Act?
   (a) Section 4
   (b) Section 5
   (c) Section 6
   (d) Section 7

6. Which of the following elements must possess in a Promissory Note?
   (a) It must be in writing
   (b) It must certainly be an express promise or clear understanding to pay a certain sum of money
   (c) Promise to pay must be unconditional
   (d) All of the above

7. Maker of the bill of exchange is also referred to as:
   (a) Payee
   (b) Drawee
   (c) Drawer
   (d) None

8. An Inchoate instrument is the one in which ________.
   (a) Amount is left blank
   (b) Name of the payee is left blank
   (c) Date is not filled
   (d) Any or all of the above

9. Negotiation in an order cheque is completed by:
   (a) Only delivery
   (b) Endorsement only
   (c) Endorsement & Delivery
   (d) Order cheque is not negotiable

10. Which of the following is a characteristic of payment in due course under negotiable instrument act 1881?
    (a) Payment in good faith
    (b) Payment without negligence
    (c) Payment as per apparent tenor of the instrument
    (d) All of the above

11. A negotiable instrument can be endorsed by:
    (a) Signing on the back of the instrument
    (b) Signing on a separate piece of paper is insufficient at the back of the instrument
    (c) Both (a) & (b)
    (d) Neither (a) nor (b)

12. If a cheque is payable to Anil or order and Anil only signs on the back of the instrument, such a chain of endorsement is_____________.
    (a) Partial endorsement
    (b) Blank endorsement

(c) Full endorsement
(d) Conditional endorsement

13. Who can cross a cheque?
    (a) Drawer of the cheque
    (b) Holder of the cheque
    (c) A banker who receives the cheque for collection
    (d) All of the above

14. What constitutes special crossing?
    (a) Drawing two parallel transverse lines on the face of the cheque
    (b) Writing a/c payee only on the face of the cheque
    (c) Drawing two parallel transverse lines on the face of the cheque and writing the name of the bank in between
    (d) Writing the words not negotiable on the face of the cheque

15. Which of the following does not constitute a material alteration?
    (a) Change in date
    (b) Conversion of order cheque to bearer cheque
    (c) Conversion of a bearer cheque to a crossed cheque
    (d) All of the above

16. Number of parties in a bill of exchange is:
    (a) 2
    (b) 3
    (c) 4
    (d) None

17. Which of the following bills is/are allowed grace period under section 22 of NI Act?
    (a) Usance bill
    (b) Demand bill
    (c) Both
    (d) None of the above

18. Present validity period of cheque, as per RBI and w.e.f. 01.04.2012 is:
    (a) 2 months
    (b) 3 months
    (c) 4 months
    (d) 6 months

19. 'Pay to Alok only'. Such Endorsement is:
    (a) Partial endorsement
    (b) Restrictive endorsement
    (c) Full endorsement
    (d) Conditional endorsement

20. If the cheque is dishonoured wrongly, the drawer banker is liable for damages to whom?
    (a) Payee
    (b) Drawer
    (c) Holder
    (d) None

ANSWER

1	2	3	4	5	6	7	8	9	10
(b)	(a)	(c)	(d)	(b)	(d)	(c)	(d)	(c)	(d)

11	12	13	14	15	16	17	18	19	20
(c)	(b)	(d)	(c)	(c)	(b)	(a)	(b)	(b)	(b)

CHAPTER 28

PAYMENT & SETTLEMENTS SYSTEMS ACT, 2007

OBJECTIVE

The PSS Act, 2007 provides for the regulation and supervision of payment systems in India and designates the Reserve Bank of India as the authority for that purpose and all related matters. The Reserve Bank is authorized under the Act to constitute a Committee of its Central Board known as the Board for Regulation and Supervision of Payment and Settlement Systems (BPSS), to exercise its powers and perform its functions and discharge its duties under this statute. The Act also provides the legal basis for "netting" and "settlement finality".

INTRODUCTION

Payment and Settlement Systems Act, 2007 (PSS Act, 2007) received the assent of the President on 20th December 2007 and it came into force with effect from 12th August 2008. It extends to the whole of India.

Regulations made under the PSS Act

Two Regulations have been made by RBI w.e.f. Aug 12, 2008. *(1)* The Board for Regulation and Supervision of Payment and Settlement Systems Regulation, 2008; *(2)* Payment and Settlement Systems Regulations, 2008.

Board for Regulation and Supervision of Payment and Settlement System (BPSS)

A Committee of the Central Board of Directors of RBI has been constituted. BPSS exercises powers on behalf of RBI for regulation and supervision. In terms of Section 4 of the PSS Act, 2007 no person other than the Reserve Bank can operate or commence a payment system unless authorized by the Reserve Bank. Any person desirous of commencing or operating a payment system needs to apply for authorization under the PSS Act, 2007 (Section 5).

Settlement (RTGS) System and all other payment systems function on a net settlement basis.

Definition: Definition under Payment and Settlement Systems Act are as under,

a) "Bank" means—Schedule Bank, a post office savings bank; a banking company as defined in the Banking Regulation Act, 1949; a co-operative bank, and such other bank as the Reserve Bank may, by notification, specify for the purposes of this Act;

b) "Derivative" means an instrument, to be settled at a future date, whose value is derived from change in interest rate, foreign exchange rate, credit rating or credit index, price of securities (also called "underlying"), or any other underlying or a combination of more than one of them and includes interest rate swaps, forward rate agreements, foreign currency swaps, foreign currency rupee swaps, foreign currency options, foreign currency rupee options or any other instrument, as may be specified by the Reserve Bank from time to time;

c) "Electronic funds transfer" means any transfer of Short title, extent and commencement Definitions funds which is initiated by a person by way of instruction, authorisation or order to a bank to debit or credit an account maintained with that bank through electronic means and includes point of sale transfers; automated teller machine transactions, direct deposits or withdrawal of funds, transfers initiated by telephone, internet and, card payment;

d) "Gross" settlement system means a payment system in which each settlement of funds or securities occurs on the basis of separate or individual instructions;

e) "Netting" means the determination by the system provider of the amount of money or securities, due or payable or deliverable, as a result of setting off or adjusting, the payment obligations or delivery obligations among the system participants, including the claims and obligations arising out of the termination by the system provider, on the insolvency or dissolution or winding up of any system participant or such other circumstances as the system provider may specify in its rules or regulations or bye-laws (by whatever name called), of the transactions admitted for settlement at a future date so that only a net claim be demanded or a net obligation be owned;

f) "Payment instruction" means any instrument, authorisation or order in any form, including electronic means, to effect a payment,

   (i) By a person to a system participant; or

   (ii) By a system participant to another system parti-cipant;

g) "Payment obligation" means an indebtedness that is owned by one system participant to another system participant as a result of clearing or settlement of one or more payment instructions relating to funds, securities or foreign exchange or derivatives or other transactions;

h) "Payment system" means a system that enables payment to be effected between a payer and a beneficiary, involving clearing, payment or settlement service or all of them, but does not include a stock exchange;

i) "Settlement" means settlement of payment instructions and includes the settlement of securities, foreign exchange or derivatives or other transactions which involve payment obligations;

j) "System participant" means a bank or any other person participating in a payment system and includes the system provider;

k) "System provider" means a person who operates an authorised payment system.

Application Fee: A sum of ₹ 10,000/- is required to be submitted as application fee, which can be submitted by cash or cheque or payment order or demand draft or electronic fund transfer in favour of the Reserve Bank along with the application for authorisation.

If application seeking authorisation is rejected by RBI or approval is later on invoked by RBI, the applicant may approach Central Government against RBI within 30 days.

Are foreign entities allowed to operate a payment system in India?

The PSS Act 2007 does not prohibit foreign entities from operating a payment system in India and the Act does not discriminate/differentiate between foreign entities and domestic entities.

Duties of a System Provider

The PSS Act, 2007 lays down the duties of the system provider. The system provider is required to operate the payment system in accordance with the provisions of the Act and the Regulations, the terms and conditions of authorization and the directions given by the Reserve Bank from time to time.

The system provider is also required to act in accordance with the contract governing the relationship among the system participants and the rules and regulations which deal with the operation of the payment system.

The Act requires the system provider to disclose the terms and conditions including the charges, limitations of liability etc., under the payment system to the system participants.

The Act also requires the system provider to provide copies of all the rules and regulations governing the operation of the payment system and other relevant documents to the system participants.

The system provider is required to keep the documents and its contents, provided to it by the system participants, as confidential and is prohibited from disclosing the same, except in accordance with the provisions of law.

Settlement of disputes under the PSS Act

The Act lays down an elaborate mechanism for settlement of disputes between system participants in a payment system, between system participant and system provider and between system providers.

The Act requires the system provider to make provision in its rules or regulations for creation of a panel to decide disputes between system participants. Where any system participant is dissatisfied with the decision of the panel, or where disputes arises between system participant and system provider or between system providers, such disputes are required to be referred to the Reserve Bank for adjudication, whose decision shall be final and binding on the parties.

In cases where the Reserve Bank, in its capacity either as a system participant or system provider, is itself a party to the dispute, then there is a provision for referring such cases to the Central Government for adjudication. (Section 24 of Act)

Consequences of Dishonour of Electronic Fund Transfer (Section 25)

Dishonour of EFT due to insufficiency of funds in an account, is an offence, punishable with imprisonment (up to 2 years) or with fine (up to double the amount) or both, on similar conditions as in case of dishonour of a cheque under Negotiable Instruments Act 1881.

Penalties or Punitive Action

Under the PSS Act, 2007, operating a payment system without authorization, failure to comply with the terms of authorization, failure to produce statements, returns information or documents or providing false statement or information, disclosing prohibited information, non-compliance of directions of Reserve Bank violations of any of the provisions of the Act, Regulations, order, directions etc., are offences punishable for which Reserve Bank can initiate criminal prosecution. Reserve Bank is also empowered to impose fine for certain contraventions under the Act.

Netting and Settlement Finality

The PSS Act 2007 states that a settlement, will be final and irrevocable as soon as the money, securities, foreign exchange or derivatives or other transactions payable as a result of such settlement is determined, whether or not such money, securities or foreign exchange or other transactions is actually paid.

ELECTRONIC PAYMENT SYSTEMS

Access Criteria for Payment Systems: The revised access criteria came into force w.e.f. Oct 01, 2011. There are two sets of access criteria.

(1) For centralised payment systems (CPS) and

(2) For decentralised payment systems (DPS).

Access Criteria for CPC: The CPC include Real Time Gross Settlement (RTGS) System, National Electronic Fund Transfer (NEFT) system and National Electronic Clearing Service (NECS). RBI introduced the RTGS system in India with effect from 26th March 2004. The membership is open to all licensed banks. The access criteria are given below:

a) Minimum CRAR of 9% (latest balance sheet);

b) Net NPAs below 5% (latest balance sheet);

c) Minimum net-worth of ₹ 25 crore;

Criteria for Decentralised Payment Systems: The DPS include Clearing Houses at MICR centers (including Cheque Truncation System centers) and Electronic Clearing Service (ECS) including the Regional Electronic Clearing Service (RECS). The membership is open to all licensed banks. The access criteria are:

a) Minimum CRAR of 9% (latest balance sheet);

b) Net NPAs below 5% (latest balance sheet). (On Mar 15, 2012, RBI decided to grant automatic membership to entities which are direct participants of centralised payment systems like RTGS, NEFT & NECS).

TEST YOURSELF

1. Payment and Settlement Systems Act, 2007 (PSS Act, 2007) received the assent of the President on 20th December 2007 and it came into force with effect from:
   (a) 12th August 2007
   (b) 12th August 2008
   (c) 20th December 2007
   (d) 20th December 2008

2. Payment and Settlement Systems Act, 2007 extends to the:
   (a) Whole of India
   (b) Whole of India except state of J & K
   (c) Whole of India except states of North East region
   (d) None of the above

3. Which of the following is not a payment system under the PSS Act 2007?
   (a) Payment through bank clearing
   (b) RTGS
   (c) NEFT
   (d) Credit card operations

4. What is the application fee, which can be submitted in favour of the Reserve Bank along with the application for authorisation?
   (a) ₹ 10,000/-   (b) ₹ 20,000/-
   (c) ₹ 50,000/-   (d) ₹ 1,00,000/-

5. Who is the appellate authority for all applications made for authorisation under PSS Act?

(a) Governor of RBI   (b) President of India

(c) Central Government   (d) SEBI

6. If application seeking authorisation is rejected by RBI or approval is later on invoked by RBI, the applicant may approach Central Government against RBI within ___________.

(a) 15 days   (b) 30 days

(c) 60 days   (d) 90 days

7. Dishonour of EFT due to insufficiency of funds in an account, is an offence, punishable amount is:

(a) Up to 50% of the amount of cheque

(b) Up to 100% of the amount of cheque

(c) Up to 200% of the amount of cheque

(d) Up to 500% of the amount of cheque

8. Dishonour of EFT due to insufficiency of funds in an account, is an offence, punishable with imprisonment:

(a) Up to 1 year   (b) Up to 2 years

(c) Up to 3 years   (d) Up to 5 years

9. In term of RTGS, what does 'T' stands for:

(a) Technical   (b) Token

(c) Time   (d) Truncation

10. Which are the access criteria for CPC?

(a) Minimum CRAR of 9% (latest balance sheet)

(b) Net NPAs below 5% (latest balance sheet)

(c) Minimum net-worth of ₹ 25 crore

(d) All of the above

11. 'RTGS' in India started w.e.f. ___________.

(a) 1st April 2004   (b) 26th March 2004

(c) 1st April 2004   (d) 26th March 2005

12. What is the present settlement cycle for RTGS transaction?

(a) 2 hours   (b) 4 hours

(c) 6 hours   (d) 8 hours

13. Minimum size of transaction for RTGS:

(a) ₹ 50,000   (b) ₹ 1 lac

(c) ₹ 2 lac   (d) ₹ 5 lac

14. The DPS include Clearing Houses at MICR centers (including Cheque Truncation System centers) and Electronic Clearing Service (ECS) including the Regional Electronic Clearing Service (RECS). The membership is open to all licensed banks. The access criteria are:

(a) Minimum CRAR of 9% (latest balance sheet);

(b) Net NPAs below 5% (latest balance sheet). (On Mar 15, 2012, RBI decided to grant automatic membership to entities which are direct participants of centralised payment systems like RTGS, NEFT & NECS).

(c) Both of the above

(d) None of the above

15. The headquarter of SWIFT is located in:

(a) New York   (b) Belgium

(c) France   (d) Brazil

ANSWER

1	2	3	4	5	6	7	8	9	10
(b)	(a)	(d)	(a)	(c)	(b)	(c)	(b)	(c)	(d)

11	12	13	14	15
(b)	(a)	(c)	(c)	(b)

MODULE–D

COMMERCIAL LAWS WITH REFERENCE TO BANKING OPERATIONS

INDIAN CONTRACT ACT, 1872

INTRODUCTION

The Indian Contract Act, 1872 prescribes the law relating to contracts in India. It is one of the most important laws for banking, trade, commerce and industry in the country. It determines the circumstances in which promises made by the parties to a contract shall be legally binding and the enforcement of these rights and duties. This Act may be called be the Indian Contract Act, 1872. It is applicable to all the states of India except the state of Jammu and Kashmir.

OBJECTIVE

The objective of the Contract Act is to ensure that the rights and obligations arising out of a contract are honoured and that legal remedies are made available to an aggrieved party against the party failing to honour his part of agreement. The Indian Contract Act makes it obligatory that this is done and compels the defaulters to honour their commitments.

Key Components to form a contract as per the Contract Act:

○ When one person signifies to another his willingness to do or to abstain from doing any-thing, with a view to obtaining the assent of that other to such act or abstinence, he is said to make a proposal;

○ When a person to whom the proposal is made, signifies his assent thereto, the proposal is said to be accepted. A proposal, when accepted, becomes a promise;

○ The person making the proposal is called the "promisor", and the person accepting the proposal is called "promisee",

○ Every promise and every set of promises, forming the consideration for each other, is an agreement;

○ Promises which form the consideration or part of the consideration for each other, are called reciprocal promises;

○ An agreement enforceable by law is a contract;

○ An agreement which is enforceable by law at the option of one or more of the parties thereto, but not at the option of the other or others, is a voidable contract;

○ A contract which ceases to be enforceable by law becomes void when it ceases to be enforceable.

CONTRACT

As per Section 10 of Indian Contract Act 1872, "all agreements are contracts if they are made by the free consent of the parties, competent to contract, for a lawful consideration and with a lawful object and are not expressly declared to be void". In other words, all agreements are contracts and a contract has following important elements:

a) Parties should be competent to contract

b) Contract should be made with free consent

c) Consideration should be lawful

d) Contract should be for a lawful object

e) Contract should not be declared to be void.

Capacity to Contact

As per Section 11 of Indian Contract Act 1872, every person is competent to contract who is of the age of majority according to the law to which he is subject, and who is sound mind and is not disqualified from contracting by any law to which he is subject.

Revocation of Proposals and Acceptance: A proposal may be revoked at any time before the communication of its acceptance is complete as against the proposer, but not afterwards.

An acceptance may be revoked at any time before the communication of the acceptance is complete as against the acceptor, but no afterwards.

Free Consent: Free consent of the parties to a contract is required. A consent is said to be free when the parties agree to the same thing in the same sense.

Lawful Consideration: Consideration as per Section 2(d) means an act when at the desire of the promisor, the promisee does or abstains from doing or promises to do or abstains from doing something. A consideration to be lawful should not be forbidden by law, does not defeat the provisions of any law, is not fraudulent and is not immoral or opposed to public policy (saying to pay bribe).

Lawful Object: It means that the result of the agreement should not be forbidden by the law or violate the law or fraudulent or immoral or opposed to public policy (say an agreement to murder someone).

Minor's Contract: Minor is a person who has not attained the age of 18. An agreement made by minor is void *ab initio*. Hence, a minor is not liable to perform any promise made by him under an agreement. Guardian of a minor can enter into a contract on behalf of a minor.

CONTRACT OF INDEMNITY

Contract of Indemnity: As per Section 124 of Indian Contract Act 1872, a contract by which one party promises to save the other from loss caused to him by the contract of the promisor himself, or by the conduct of any other person, is called a "contract of indemnity". For example, A contracts to indemnify B against the consequences of any proceedings which C may take against B in respect of a certain sum of ₹ 10,000/-. This is a contract of indemnity.

Right of Indemnity-holder when Sued: The promisee in a contract of indemnity, acting within the scope of his authority, is entitled to recover from the promisor:

(1) All damages which he may be compelled to pay in any suit in respect of any matter to which the promise to indemnify applies;

(2) All costs which he may be compelled to pay in any such suit, if in bringing of defending it, he did not contravene the orders of the promisor, and acted as it would have been prudent for him to act in the absence of any contract of indemnity, or if the promisor authorised him to bring or defend the suit;

(3) All sums which he may have paid under the terms of any compromise of any such suit, if the compromise was not contract to the orders of the promisor, and was one which it would have been prudent for the promise to make in the absence of any contract of indemnity, or if the promisor authorised him to compromise the suit.

CONTRACT OF GUARANTEE

Contract of Guarantee: As per Section 126 of Indian Contract Act 1872, a "contract of guarantee" is a contract to perform the promise, or discharge the liability, of a third person in case of his default.

"Surety", "Principal Debtor" and "Creditor": The person who gives the guarantee is called the "surety", the person in respect of whose default the guarantee is given is called the "principal debtor", and the person to whom the guarantee is given is called the "creditor". A guarantee may be either oral or written.

Consideration for Guarantee: Anything done, or any promise made, for the benefit of the principal debtor, may be a sufficient consideration to the surety for giving the guarantee.

Bank Guarantee: A Bank guarantee is a promise from a bank that the liabilities of a debtor will be met in the event that debtor fails to fulfill your contractual obligations. It is a promise from a bank or other lending institution that if a particular borrower defaults on a loan, the bank will cover the loss.

Surety's Liability: The liability of the surety is co-extensive with that of the principal debtor, unless it is otherwise provided by the contract.

Continuing Guarantee: A guarantee which extends to a series of transaction, is called, a "continuing guarantee".

Revocation of Continuing Guarantee by Surety's Death: The death of the surety operates, in the absence of any contract to the contrary, as are vocation of a continuing guarantee, so far as regards future transactions.

Discharge of Surety by Variance in Terms of Contract: Any variance made without the surety's consent, in the terms of the contract between the principal debtor and the creditor, discharges the surety as to transactions subsequent to the variance.

Discharge of Surety by Release or Discharge of Principal Debtor: The surety is discharged by any contract between the creditor and the principal debtor, by which the principal debtor is released, or by any act or omission of the creditor, the legal consequence of which is the discharge of the principal debtor.

Creditor's Forbearance to Sue does not Discharge Surety: Mere forbearance on the part of the creditor to sue the principal debtor or to enforce any other remedy against him, dies not, in the absence of any provision in the guarantee to the contrary, discharge the surety.

Release of One Co-surety does not Discharge Other: Where there are co-sureties, a release by the creditor of one of them does not discharge the others neither does set free the surety so released from his responsibility to the other sureties.

Rights of Surety on Payment or Performance: Where a guaranteed debt has become due, or default of the principal debtor to perform a guaranteed duty has taken place, the surety upon payment or performance of all that he is liable for, is invested with all the rights which the creditor had against the principal debtor.

Surety's Right to Benefit of Creditor's Securities: A surety is entitled to the benefit of every security which the creditor has against the principal debtor at the time when the contract of suretyship entered into, whether the surety knows of the existence of such security or not; and if the creditor loses, or without the consent of the surety, parts with such security, the surety, the surety is discharged to the extent of the value of the security.

Guarantee Obtained by Misrepresentation, Invalid: Any guarantee which has been obtained by means of misrepresentation made by the creditor, is invalid. Any guarantee which the creditor has obtained by means of keeping silence as to material circumstances, is invalid.

Implied Promise to Indemnify Surety: In every contract of guarantee there is an implied promise by the principal debtor to indemnify the surety, and the surety is entitled to recover from the principal debtor whatever sum he has rightfully paid under the guarantee, but no sums which he has paid wrongfully.

Co-sureties Liable to Contribute Equally: Where two or more persons are co-sureties for the same debt and whether with or without the knowledge of each other the co-sureties are liable to pay each an equal share of the whole debt, or of that part of it which remains unpaid by the principal debtor.

Revocation of Continuing Guarantee: A continuing guarantee may at any time be revoked by the surety, as to future transactions, by notice to the creditor.

CONTRACT OF BAILMENT

Bailment: As per Section 148 of Indian Contract Act 1872, a "bailment" is the delivery of goods by one person to another for some purpose, upon a contract that they shall, when the purpose is accomplished, be returned or otherwise disposed of according to the direction of the person delivering them.

The person delivering the goods is called the "bailor". The person to whom they are delivered is called the "bailee".

Explanation: If a person already in possession of the goods of other contracts hold them as a bailee, he thereby becomes the bailee, and the owner becomes the bailor of such goods, although they may not have been delivered by way of bailment.

Delivery to Bailee: The delivery to be bailee may be made by doing anything which has the effect of putting the goods in the possession of the intended bailee or of any person authorised to hold them on his behalf.

Bailor's duty to Disclose faults in Goods Bailed: The bailor is bound to disclose to the bailee faults in the goods bailed:

a) of which the bailor is aware, and

b) which materially interfere with the use of them,

c) or expose the bailee to extraordinary risk; and

If he does not make such disclosure, he is responsible for damage arising to the bailee directly from such faults.

Care to be taken by Bailee: In all cases of bailment the bailee is bound to take as much care of the goods bailed to him as a man of ordinary prudence would, under similar circumstances, take of his own goods of the same bulk, quantity and value as the goods bailed.

Bailee when not liable for Loss, etc., of thing Bailed: The bailee, in the absence of any special contract, is not responsible for the loss, destruction or deterioration of the thing bailed, if he has taken the amount of care of it described in section 151.

Termination of Bailment by Bailee's Act Inconsistent with Conditions: A contract of bailment is voidable at the option of the bailor, if the bailee does any act with regard to the foods bailed, inconsistent with the conditions of the bailment.

Liability of Bailee making Unauthorised use of Goods Bailed: If the bailee makes any use of the goods bailed which is not according to the conditions of the bailment, he is liable to make compensation to the bailor for any damage arising to the goods from or during such use of them.

Return of Goods Bailed, on Expiration of time or an Accomplishment of Purpose: It is the duty of the bailee to return, or deliver according to the bailor's directions, the goods bailed, without demand, as soon as the time for which they were bailed has expired, or the purpose for which they were bailed has been accomplished.

Termination of Gratuitous Bailment by Death: A gratuitous bailment is terminated by the death either of the bailor or of the bailee.

Bailee's Lien: Where the bailee has, in accordance with the purpose of the bailment, rendered any service involving the exercise of labour or skill in respect of the goods bailed he has in the absence of a contract to the contrary, a right to retain such goods until he receives due remuneration for the services he has rendered in respect of them.

Bankers, factor, attorneys of a High Court and policy brokers may, in the absence of a contract to the contrary, retain as a security for a general balance of account, any goods bailed to them; but no other person have a right retain, as a security for which balance, goods, bailed to them, unless is a contract to that effect.

CONTRACT OF PLEDGE

Pledge: As per Section 172 of Indian Contract Act 1872, the bailment of goods as security for payment of a debt or performance of a promise is called "pledge".

The bailor is in this case called "pawnor". The bailee is called "pawnee".

Pawnee's Right of Retainer: The pawnee may retain the goods pledged, not only for payment of the debt or the performance of the promise, but for the interests of the debt, and all necessary expenses incurred by him in respect to the possession or for the preservation of the goods pledged. The pawnee is entitled to receive from the pawnor extraordinary expenses incurred by him for the preservation of the goods pledged.

Right where Pawnor makes Default: As per Section 176, if the pawnor makes default in payment of the debt, or performance, at the stipulated time, the pawnee may:

a) bring a suit against the pawnor upon the debt or promise and retain the goods pledged as a collateral security; or

b) He may sell the thing pledged, on giving the pawnor reasonable notice of the sale.

c) If the proceeds of such sale are less than the amount due in respect of the debt or promise,

the pawnor is still liable to pay the balance. If the proceeds of the sale are greater than the amount so due, the pawnee shall pay over the surplus to the pawnor.

Where person pledges goods in which he has only a limited interest, the pledge is valid to the extent of that interest.

Banker's Right and Other Dues: Bank's right of pledge prevails over any other dues including Govt. dues (Supreme Court: State of Bihar vs Bank of Bihar)"except workers' wages.

Duties of the Pledgee: To return the goods (along with accretion to goods if any) once the money is paid back by the pledger. To take that much care of the goods, which he would have been taking, had the goods belonged to him.

CONTRACT OF AGENCY

Agent and Principal: As per Section 182 of Indian Contract Act 1872, an "agent" is a person employed to do any act for another, or to represent another in dealing with third persons. The person for whom such act is done, or who is so represented, is called the "principal".

Who may Employ Agent: Any person who is of the age of majority according to the law to which he is subject, and who is of sound mind, may employ an agent.

Who may be an Agent: As between the principal and third persons, any person may become an agent, but no person who is not of the age of majority and sound mind can become an agent, so as to be responsible to the principal according to the provisions in that behalf herein contained.

Agent's Authority may be Expressed or Implied: An authority is said to be express when it is given by words spoken or written.

An authority is said to be implied when it is to be inferred from the circumstances of the case; and things spoken or written, or the ordinary course of dealing, may be accounted circumstances of the case.

For example: *A owns a shop in Patna, living himself in Kanpur, and visiting the shop occasionally. The shop is managed by B, and he is in the habit of ordering goods from C in the name of A for the purposes of the shop, and of paying for them out of A's funds with A's knowledge. B has an implied authority from A to order goods from C in the name of A for the purpose of the shop.*

Extent of Authority: An agent, having an authority to do an act, has authority to do every lawful thing which is necessary in order to do such act. An agent having an authority to carry on a business, has authority to do every lawful thing necessary for the purpose, or usually done in the course, of conducting such business.

For instance, *A is employed by B, residing in London, to recover at Chennai a debt due to B. A may adopt any legal process necessary for the purpose of recovering the debt, and may give a valid discharge for the same.*

Authority in an Emergency: An agent has authority, in an emergency, to do all such acts for the purpose of protecting his principal from loss and would be done by a person or ordinary prudence, in his own case, under similar circumstances.

For example: *A consigns goods to be at Calcutta, with direction to send them immediately to C, at Cuttack, may sell the goods at Calcutta, if they will not bear the journey to Cuttack without spoiling.*

Delegation by the Agent: An agent cannot lawfully employ another person to perform acts which he has undertaken to perform personally, unless by the ordinary custom of trade a sub-agent must, be employed.

Sub-Agent: A "sub-agent" is a person employed by, and acting under the control of, the original agent in the business of the agency.

Sub-agent Appointed without Authority: Where an agent, without having authority to do so, has appointed a person to act as a sub-agent, the agent is responsible for his acts both to the principal and to third person. The principal is not responsible for the acts of the person so employed, nor is that person responsible to the principal.

Acts without his Authority and Effect of Ratification: U/s 196, where acts are done by one person on behalf of another, but without his knowledge or authority, he may elect to ratify or to disown such acts. If he ratifies them, the same effects will follow as if they had been performed by his authority. Ratification may be express or may be implied in the conduct of the person on whose behalf the acts are done. Further, as per Section 199, a person ratifying any unauthorised act done on his behalf, ratifies the whole of the transaction.

Termination of Agency: U/s 201 an agency is terminated by the principal revoking his authority, or by the agent renouncing the business of the agency; or by the business of the agency being completed; or by either the principal or agent dying or becoming of unsound mind; or by the principal being adjudicated an insolvent.

Where Agency cannot-be Terminated: U/s 202 where the agent has himself an interest in the property which forms the subject-matter of the agency, the agency cannot, in the absence of an express contract, be terminated to the prejudice of such interest.

For example: *A consigns 1,000 bales of cotton to B, who has made advances to him on such cotton, and desires B to sell the cotton, and to repay himself out of the price the amount of his own advances. A cannot revoke this authority, nor is it terminated by his insanity or death.*

Revocation where Authority has been Partly Exercised: As per Section 204, the principal cannot revoke the authority given to his agent after the authority has been partly exercised, liability of principal arise from acts already done in the agency.

For example: *A authorises B to buy 1,000 bales of cotton on account of A, and to pay for it out of A's money remaining in B's hands. B buys 1,000 bales of cotton in A's name. A cannot revoke B's authority to pay for the cotton.*

Termination of Sub-agent's Authority: As per Section 210, the termination of the authority of an agent automatically terminates the authority of all sub-agents appointed by the agent.

Agent's duty in conducting Principal's Business: As per Section 211, an agent is bound to conduct the business of his principal according to the directions given by the principal. In the absence of any such directions, it is to be conducted according to the customs which prevails in doing business of the same kind at the place where the agent conducts such business. When the agent acts otherwise, he must make good the loss to his principal and if any profit accrues, he must account for it.

Agent dealing on his Own Account, in Business of Agency without Principal's Consent: If an agent deals on his own account in the business of the agency, without first obtaining the consent of his principal and acquainting him with all material circumstances which have come to his own knowledge on the subject, u/s 215, the principal may repudiate the transaction. Further u/s 216, where an agent, without the knowledge of his principal, deals in the business of the agency on his own account instead of on account to his principal, the principal is entitled to claim from the agent any benefit which may have resulted to him from the transaction.

Remuneration for Business Misconducted: As per Section 220, an agent who is guilty of misconduct in the business of the agency, is not entitled to any remuneration in respect of that part of the business which he has misconducted.

Agent to be Indemnified against Consequences of Acts done in Good Faith: U/s 223, where the agent does the act in good faith, the employer is liable to indemnify the agent against the consequences of that act.

For example: *A, a decree-holder and entitled to execution of B's goods requires the officer of the court to seize certain goods, representing them to be the goods of B. The officer seizes the goods, and is sued by C, the true owner of the goods. A is liable to indemnify the officer for the sum which he is compelled to pay to C, in consequence of obeying A's directions.*

Enforcement and Consequences of Agent's Contract with 3rd Parties: As per Section 226, the contracts entered into through an agent, and obligations arising from acts done by an agent, may be forced in the same manner, and will have the same legal consequences as if the contracts had been entered into the acts done by the principal in person.

When Agent Exceeds Authority: U/s 227, when an agent does more than he is authorised to do, and when the part of what he does, is within his authority and can be separated from the part which is beyond his authority, the principal is bound for that portion what he does within his authority.

Effect on Agreement of Misrepresentation or Fraud by Agent: As per Section 238, Mis-representations made or fraud committed, by agent have the same effect on agreements made by such agents as if such frauds had been committed by the principals.

For example, *A, being B's agent for the sale of goods, induces C to buy them by a misrepresentation, which he was not authorised by B to make. The contract is voidable, as between B and C, at the option of C.*

TEST YOURSELF

1. The Indian Contract Act, 1872 is applicable to:
   - (a) All the states of India,
   - (b) All the states of India, except the state of Jammu and Kashmir.
   - (c) All the states of India, except the state of Goa
   - (d) All the states of India, except the Union Territories

2. Key Components to form a contract as per the Contract Act are:
   - (a) When one person signifies to another his willingness to do or to abstain from doing anything, with a view to obtaining the assent of that other to such act or abstinence, he is said to make a proposal.
   - (b) When a person to whom the proposal is made, signifies his assent thereto, the proposal is said to be accepted. A proposal, when a accepted, becomes a promise.
   - (c) The person making the proposal is called the "promisor", and the person accepting the proposal is called "promisee", Promises which form the consideration or part of the consideration for each other, are called reciprocal promises; An agreement enforceable by law is a contract.
   - (d) All of the above

3. As per Indian Contract Act 1872, every promise and every set of promises, forming the consideration for each other, is _______.
   - (a) An agreement
   - (b) A consent
   - (c) A contract
   - (d) A promise

4. Which of the following is a valid contract?
   - (a) Consideration
   - (b) Free consent
   - (c) Proposal and acceptance
   - (d) All of the above

5. In which of the agreement is valid even without consideration?
   - (a) Agreement in writing and registered
   - (b) Agreement between parties standing in near relation to each other
   - (c) Agreement which is made out of natural love
   - (d) All of the above

6. As per Section 10 of Indian Contract Act 1872, all agreements are contract and a contract has following important elements:
   - (a) Parties should be competent to contract
   - (b) Contract should be made with free consent
   - (c) Consideration should be lawful, Contract should be for a lawful object
   - (d) All of the above

7. Who among the following not legally competent to enter into a contract?
   - (a) Person who has crossed the age of majority
   - (b) Person of a sound mind
   - (c) Person who is disqualified from entering into a contract by any law
   - (d) All of the above

8. Which of the following is a type of indemnity?
   - (a) Bank FD
   - (b) Mutual funds
   - (c) NSC
   - (d) Insurance policy

9. How many parties are there in guarantee?
   - (a) 2
   - (b) 3
   - (c) 4
   - (d) 5

10. In which of the following case the relation between the customer and bank is "Bailor and Bailee"?
 (a) Deposit account
 (b) SDV Locker
 (c) Safe Custody
 (d) Loan Account

11. Under pledge, the possession of the security is with:
 (a) Borrower   (b) Creditor
 (c) Debtor   (d) Third party

12. In case of pledge, the relationship between bank and borrower is:
 (a) Pawnor & Pawnee   (b) Pawnee & Pawnor
 (c) Pledgee & Pledger   (d) Both (b) & (c)

13. Which of the following statement is correct in respect of pledge?
 (a) The Pawnee can sell the goods if Pawnor fails to pay
 (b) The Pawnee can keep the goods even after the Pawnor has paid the dues
 (c) The Pawnee can sell the goods without giving notice to the Pawnor
 (d) All are correct

14. The usual form of agency contract is by way of:
 (a) Indemnity bond   (b) Power of Attorney
 (c) Both the above   (d) None of the above

15. Which of the following statements is correct in respect of agency contract?
 (a) Consideration is the most essential element in any contract of agency
 (b) Minor can be an agent
 (c) An agent can have a lien on the goods of the principal for the dues payable by the principal to the agent
 (d) An agent can employ another person to perform act which he has undertaken to perform personally

16. An agency can be terminated by:
 (a) Either the principal or agent dying
 (b) Either the principal or agent becoming of unsound mind
 (c) The Principal being adjudicated an insolvent
 (d) All of the above

17. A guarantee which extends to a series of transaction, is called, a ___________.
 (a) Continuing guarantee   (b) Absolute guarantee
 (c) Implied guarantee   (d) Regular guarantee

18. As per Section 148 of Indian Contract Act 1872, a "bailment" is the delivery of goods by one person to another for some purpose. The person delivering the goods is called the "_____________". The person to whom they are delivered is called the "_________".
 (a) Bailor, Bailee   (b) Bailee, Bailor
 (c) Creditor, Debtor   (d) Debtor, Creditor

19. The bailor is bound to disclose to the bailee which types of faults are there in the goods bailed:
 (a) of which the bailor is aware
 (b) which materially interfere with the use of them
 (c) or expose the bailee to extraordinary risk
 (d) All of the above

20. A Bank guarantee is a promise from a bank that the liabilities of a _______ will be met in the event that _____ fails to fulfill your contractual obligations. It is a promise from a bank or other lending institution that if a particular borrower defaults on a loan, the bank will cover the loss.
 (a) Creditor   (b) Debtor
 (c) Guarantor   (d) Lender

ANSWER

1	2	3	4	5	6	7	8	9	10
(b)	(d)	(a)	(d)	(d)	(d)	(c)	(d)	(b)	(c)
11	12	13	14	15	16	17	18	19	20
(b)	(d)	(a)	(b)	(c)	(d)	(a)	(a)	(d)	(b)

CHAPTER 30

THE SALE OF GOODS ACT, 1930

OBJECTIVE

The objective of the act is to provide knowledge about the contractual right and liabilities of the seller and the buyer in a contract for sale of goods. The goods are sold from owner to buyer for a certain price and at a given period of time.

INTRODUCTION

The Sale of Goods Act, 1930 is a kind of Indian Contract Act. It came into existence on 1 July 1930. Indian Sale of Goods Act 1930 is a Mercantile Law. Mercantile agent means an agent having authority either to sell goods, or to consign goods for the purposes of sale, or to buy goods, or to raise money on the security of goods. It is a contract whereby the seller transfers or agrees to transfer the property in the goods to the buyer for price.

It is applicable all over India, except Jammu and Kashmir.

Some Important Terms defined under the Sale of Goods Act

- ○ **"Buyer"** means a person who buys or agrees to buy goods.
- ○ **"Seller"** means a person who sells or agree to buy a goods.
- ○ **"Delivery"** means voluntary transfer of possession from one person to another.
- ○ **"Price"** means the money consideration for a sale of goods.
- ○ **"Goods"** means every kind of movable property (other than actionable claim and money) and includes:

- Stock and shares,
- Growing crops, grass,
- Things attached to or forming part of the land which are agreed to be served before sale or under the contract of sale.

- ○ **"Future Goods"** means the goods to be manufactured or produced or acquired by the seller after making the contract of sale.
- ○ **"Specific Goods"** means the goods identified and agreed upon at the time of contract of sell is made.
- ○ **"Mercantile Agent"** means an agent having authority either to sell goods, or to consign goods for the purposes of sale, or to buy goods, or to raise money on the security of goods.

Sale and Agreement to Sell

(1) A contract of sale of goods is a contract whereby the seller transfers or agrees to transfer the property in goods to the buyer for a price. There may be a contract of sale between one part-owner and another.

(2) A contract of sale may be absolute or conditional.

(3) Where under a contract of sale the property in the goods is transferred from the seller to the buyer, the contract is called a sale, but where the transfer of the property in the goods is to take place at a future time or subject to some condition thereafter to be fulfilled, the contract is called an agreement to sell.

(4) An agreement to sell becomes a sale when the time elapses or the conditions are fulfilled subject to which the property in the goods is to be transferred.

How Contract of Sale is Made (Sec 5)

A contract of sale is made by an offer to buy or sell goods for a price and the *acceptance* of such offer. The contract may provide for the immediate delivery of the goods or immediate payment of the price of both, or for the delivery or payment by installments, or that the delivery or payment or both shall be postponed. A contract of sale may be made in writing or by word of mouth, or partly in writing and partly by word of mouth or may be implied from the conduct of the parties.

Features of a Contract of Sale

1. It is bilateral contract involving two persons, the buyer and seller.
2. The consideration of a sale of goods must be in money, called the price payable for the transfer of goods. It cannot be a barter, where goods are exchanged for goods.
3. Sale is of movable property (stocks, vehicles etc.) and not of immovable property (land and building).
4. There is no particular form for the contract.
5. The contract may be oral or in writing.
6. The delivery of goods may be immediate or later on.
7. The payment for the goods may be immediate or later on.

As Certainment of Price (Sec 9)

The price in a contract of sale may be fixed by the contract or may be left to be fixed in manner thereby agreed or may be determined by the course of dealing between the parties. Where the price is not determined in accordance with the foregoing provisions, the buyer shall pay the seller a reasonable price. What is a reasonable price is a question of fact dependent on the circumstances of each particular case.

CONDITION AND WARRANTIES

As per Section 12, a stipulation in a contract of sale with reference to goods may be a condition or a warranty. Whether a stipulation *in a contract of sale* is a condition or a warranty depends in each case on the construction of the contract. A stipulation may actually be a condition, though called a warranty in the contract.

What is a Condition?

A condition is a stipulation essential to the main purpose of the contract. Its breach gives rise to a right to treat the contract as repudiated.

What is a Warranty?

A warranty is a stipulation collateral to the main purpose of the contract. Its breach gives rise to a claim for damages but not to a right to reject the goods and treat the contract as repudiated.

When condition to be treated as warranty (Sec 13):

(1) Where a contract of sale is subject to any condition to be fulfilled by the seller, the buyer may waive the condition or elect to treat the breach of the condition as a breach of warranty and not as a ground for treating the contract as repudiated.

(2) Where a contract of sale is not severable and the buyer has accepted the goods or part thereof, the breach of any condition to be fulfilled by the seller can only be treated as a breach of warranty and not as a ground for rejecting the goods and treating the contract as repudiated, unless there is a term of the contract, express or implied, to that effect.

Implied Conditions and Warranties

Title of the Seller (Sec 14): In a contract of sale there is:

(a) An implied condition on the part of the seller that, *in the case of a sale,* he has a right to sell the goods. In the case of an agreement to sell, he will have a right to sell the goods at the time when the property is to pass;

(b) An implied warranty that the buyer shall have and enjoy quiet possession of the goods;

(c) An implied warranty that the goods shall be free from any charge or encumbrance in favour of any third party not declared or known to the buyer before or at the time when the contract is made.

Sale by Description of Goods (Sec 15)

Where there is a contract for the sale of goods by description, there is an implied condition that the goods shall correspond with the description; and, if the sale is by sample, it is sufficient that the bulk of the goods correspond with the sample.

Quality or Fitness (Sec 16)

There is no implied warranty or condition as to the quality or fitness for any *particular purpose* of goods supplied under a contract of sale, except as follows:

(1) Where the buyer, expressly or by implication, makes known to the seller, the particular purpose for which the goods are required, so as to show that the buyer relies on the seller's skill or judgement, and the goods are of a description which it is in the course of the seller's business to supply, there is an implied condition that the goods shall be reasonably fit for such purpose.

In the case of a contract for the sale of a specified article under its patent or other trade name, there is no implied condition as its fitness for any particular purpose.

(2) Where goods are bought by description from a seller who deals in goods of that description (whether he is the manufacturer or producer or not), there is an implied condition that the goods shall be of merchantable quality. If the buyer has examined the goods, there shall be no implied condition as regards defects which such examination ought to have revealed.

Sale by Sample (Sec 17)

In the Case of a Contract for sale by sample there is an implied condition:

(a) That the bulk shall correspond with the sample in quality;

(b) That the buyer shall have a reasonable opportunity of comparing the bulk with the sample;

(c) That the goods shall be free from any defect, rendering them merchantable, which would not be apparent on reasonable examination of the sample.

EFFECT OF THE CONTRACT AS BETWEEN SELLER AND BUYER

Goods must be Ascertained (Sec 18)

Where there is a contract for the sale of ascertained goods, no property in the goods is transferred to the buyer unless and until the goods are ascertained.

Property Passes when Intended to Pass (Sec 19)

(1) Where there is a contract for the sale of specific or ascertained goods the property in them is transferred to the buyer at such time as the parties to the contract intend it to be transferred.

(2) For the purpose of ascertaining the intention of the parties regard shall be had to the terms of the contract, the conduct of the parties and the circumstances of the case.

(3) Unless a different intention appears, the rules contained in sections 20 to 24 are rules for ascertaining the intention of the parties as to the time at which the property in the goods is to pass to the buyer.

Specific Goods in a Deliverable State (Sec 20)

Where there is an unconditional contract for the sale of specific goods in a deliverable state, the property in the goods passes to the buyer when the contract is made, and it is immaterial whether the time of payment of the price or the time of delivery of the goods, or both, is postponed.

Specific Goods to be put into a Deliverable State (Sec 21)

Where there is a contract for the sale of specific goods and the seller is bound to do something to the goods for the purpose of putting them into a deliverable state, the property does not pass until such thing is done and the buyer has notice thereof.

Specific Goods in a Deliverable State, when the Seller has to do anything thereto in Order to Ascertain Price (Sec 22)

Where there is a contract for the sale of specific goods in a deliverable state, but the seller is bound to weigh, measure, test or do some other act or thing with reference to the goods for the purpose of ascertaining the price, the property does not pass until such act or thing is done and the buyer has notice thereof.

RIGHTS OF UNPAID SELLER AGAINST THE GOODS

Unpaid Seller Defined (Sec 46)

(1) The seller of goods is deemed to be an unpaid seller within the meaning of this Act—

(a) When the whole of the price has not been paid or tendered.

(b) When a bill of exchange or other negotiable instrument has been received as conditional payment, and the conditions on which it was received has not been fulfilled by reason of the dishonour of the instrument or otherwise.

(2) In this Chapter, the term "seller" includes any person who is in the position of a seller, as, for instance, an agent of the seller to whom the bill of lading has been endorsed, or a consignor or agent who has himself paid, or is directly responsible for, the price.

Rights of an Unpaid Seller (Sec 46)

1. Notwithstanding that the property in the goods may have passed to the buyer, the unpaid seller of goods, as such, has by implication of law—

(a) A lien on the goods for the price while he is in possession of them;

(b) In case of the insolvency of the buyer, a right of stopping the goods in transit after he has parted with the possession of them;

(c) A right of re-sale as limited by this Act.

2. Where the property in goods has not passed to the buyer, the unpaid seller has, in addition to his other remedies, a right of withholding delivery similar to and co-extensive with his rights of lien and stoppage in transit where the property has passed to the buyer.

Where the Property in Goods has not Passed to the Buyer

The unpaid seller has, in addition to his other remedies, a right of withholding delivery similar to and co-extensive with his rights of lien and stoppage in transit where the property has passed to the buyer.

Unpaid Seller's lien (Sec 47)

1. The unpaid seller of goods who is *in possession of them* is entitled to retain possession of them until payment or tender of the price, in the following cases, namely:
   (a) Where the goods have been sold without any stipulation as to credit;
   (b) Where the goods have been sold on credit, but the term of credit has expired;
   (c) Where the buyer becomes insolvent.
2. Further, the seller may exercise his right of lien notwithstanding that he is in possession of the goods as agent or bailee for the buyer.

Part Delivery (Sec 48)

Where an unpaid seller has made part delivery of the goods, he may exercise his right of lien on the remainder, unless such part delivery has been made under such circumstances as to show an agreement to waive the lien.

Termination of Lien (Sec 49)

1. The unpaid seller of goods loses his lien thereon—
   (a) When he delivers the goods to a carrier or other bailee for the purpose of transmission to the buyer without *reserving the right* of disposal of the goods;
   (b) When the buyer or his agent lawfully obtains possession of the goods;
   (c) By waiver thereof.
2. The unpaid seller of goods, having a lien thereon, does not lose his lien by reason only that he has obtained a decree for the price of the goods.

Right of Stoppage in Transit (Sec 50)

When the buyer of goods becomes insolvent, the unpaid seller who has parted with the possession of the goods has the right of stopping them in transit, that is to say, he may resume possession of the goods as long as they are in the course of transit, and may retain them until payment or tender of the price.

TEST YOURSELF

1. Documents of title to goods has been defined in:
   (a) NI Act
   (b) Sale of Goods Act
   (c) Indian Contract Act
   (d) Transfer of Property Act

2. The objective of the Sale of Goods Act is:
   (a) To provide knowledge about the contractual right and liabilities of the seller
   (b) To provide knowledge about the contractual right and liabilities the buyer in a contract for sale of goods
   (c) To define the 'Goods'
   (d) All of the above

3. Under the Sale of Goods Act, 'Goods' do not include:
   (a) Shares   (b) Stock
   (c) Actionable claims (d) Growing crops

4. Sale of Goods Act does not cover sale of which of the following?
   (a) Immovable property
   (b) Other movable goods
   (c) Stocks
   (d) All are covered

5. Which of the following means 'consideration' for Sale of Goods Act?
   (a) Shares   (b) Lien
   (c) Delivery   (d) Price

6. When the transfer of property is to occur some specific time in future and/or is to fulfilment of any condition, this type of contract/arrangement is referred to as:
   (a) Contract of future goods
   (b) Agreement of sale
   (c) Contract of specific goods
   (d) Sale contract

7. A mercantile agent means an agent having:
   (a) Authority to sell goods
   (b) Authority to consign goods for sale
   (c) Authority to buy goods
   (d) Any or all of the above

8. The contract relating to transfer of immovable property are governed by:
   (a) Transfer of property act
   (b) Sale of goods act
   (c) Indian contract act
   (d) Registration act

9. Which of the following is a 'Document of title of goods'?
   (a) Bill of lading
   (b) Warehouse receipt
   (c) Railway receipt
   (d) All of the above

10. The right to subrogation is available to:
    (a) Insurer   (b) Guarantor
    (c) Both of the above   (d) None of the above

11. In a contract of sale of goods which of the following is implied condition?
    (a) That the seller has a right to sell the goods
    (b) That the goods shall correspond with the description in case of sale of goods by description
    (c) That the buyer shall have an opportunity to compare the bulk with sample in case of a sale by sample
    (d) All of the above

12. The seller of goods is deemed to be an unpaid seller when the _______ has not been paid.

    (a) Price   (b) interest
    (c) damage   (d) penalty

13. There is no _______ as to the quality or fitness of goods for any particular purpose.
    (a) Implied condition
    (b) Implied warranty
    (c) Express condition
    (d) Express warranty

14. If the stipulation agreed to between the parties is essential to the main purpose of the contract, then such a stipulation is known as a:
    (a) Condition
    (b) Warranty
    (c) Implied condition
    (d) Guarantee

15. A _______ is a stipulation, collateral to the main purpose of contract.
    (a) Condition
    (b) Warranty
    (c) Implied condition
    (d) Guarantee

16. There is an implied condition on the part of the seller that he has a right to _______ the goods.
    (a) Use   (b) Sell
    (c) Retain   (d) Resell

ANSWER

1	2	3	4	5	6	7	8	9	10
(b)	(d)	(c)	(a)	(d)	(b)	(d)	(a)	(d)	(c)

11	12	13	14	15	16
(d)	(a)	(a)	(a)	(b)	(b)

INDIAN PARTNERSHIP ACT, 1932

INTRODUCTION

A partnership is an arrangement where parties, known as partners, agree to cooperate to advance their mutual interests. The partners in a partnership may be individuals, businesses, interest-based organizations, schools, governments or combinations. Organizations may partner to increase the likelihood of each achieving their mission and to amplify their reach. A partnership may result in issuing and holding equity or may be only governed by a contract.

The law relating to Partnership firms is codified in Indian Partnership Act 1932. This Act came into force on the 1st day of October, 1932, except Sec. 69 which came into force on the 1st day of October, 1933. It extends to the whole of India except the State of Jammu & Kashmir.

DEFINITION OF "PARTNERSHIP", "PARTNER", "FIRM" AND "FIRM NAME"

As per Sec. 4 of Partnership Act 1932, "Partnership" is the relation between persons who have agreed to share the profits of a business carried on by all or any of them acting for all. Persons who have entered into partnership with one another are called individually "partners" and collectively "a firm", and the name under which their business is carried on is called the "firm name".

Types of Partnership

Partnership may be classified as three types:

1. **Partnership at Will:** Where no provision is made by contract between the partners for the duration of their partnership, or for the determination of their partnership, the partnership is known as "Partnership at will". A partnership at will can be dissolved by any partner by giving notice in writing to all the other partners of his intention to dissolve the firm.

2. **Partnership for a Fixed Period:** When a partnership agreement is fixed for a period of time, it is known as a partnership for a fixed term. In this case, partnership comes to end automatically, when the period become over. However, the partners can continue to carry on business after the fixed period. In that case, the mutual rights and duties remain absolutely unaffected and the partnership is automatically transformed into a partnership at will.

3. **Particular Partnership:** The partnership which is entered into for completing a particular job or assignment taken up by two or more persons jointly and to share arising from the firm. Thus, a person may become a partner with another person in particular adventures or undertaking.

Number of Partners

As per Section 464 of The Companies Act 2013, Maximum number of partners can be up to 100 in a firm. (Earlier number of partners was restricted to 10 for banking business & 20 for other businesses as per Section 11 of The Companies Act 1956). Partnership is not a distinct legal person from the partners who have made partnership firm.

Joint Stock Company can become a partner in a firm and in such cases the banker needs to ensure that they are eligible to become partner. HUF cannot enter into a partnership as per Supreme Court judgement of 1998.

Minors Admitted to the Benefits of Partnership

As per Sec. 30 of The Companies Act 2013,

1) A person who is a minor according to the law to which he is subject may not be a partner in a firm, but with the consent of all the partners for the time being, he may be admitted to the benefits of partnership.

2) Such minor has a right to share of the property and profits of the firm as may be agreed upon, and he may have access to and inspect the accounts of the firm.

3) Such minors share is liable for the acts of the firm, but the minor is not personally liable for any such act.

4) **Minor Attaining Majority:** At any time within six months of his attaining majority, or of his obtaining knowledge that he had been admitted to the benefits of partnership, whichever date is later, such person may give public notice that he has elected to become or that he has elected not to become a partner in the firm, and such notice shall determine his position as regards the firm.

   Provided that, if he fails to give such notice, he shall become a partner in the firm on the expiry of the said six months.

General Duties of Partners

Partners are bound to carry on the business of the firm to the greatest common advantage, to be just and faithful to each other, and to render true accounts and full information of all things affecting the firm to any partner or his legal representative.

Duty to Indemnify for Loss caused by Fraud: Every partner shall indemnify the firm for any loss caused to it by his fraud in the conduct of the business of the firm.

Determination of Rights and Duties of Partners by Contract between the Partners: The partners of a firm can decide their mutual rights and duties from time to time with the consent of all the partners. Such contract may be expressed or may be implied by a course of dealing. Such contract may be varied by consent of all the partners, and such consent may be expressed or may be implied by a course of dealing.

The Conduct of the Business

Subject to a contract between the partners:

a) Every partner has a right to take part in the conduct of the business.

b) Every partner is bound to attend diligently to his duties in the conduct of the business.

c) Any difference arising as to ordinary matters connected with the business may be decided by a majority of the partners, and every partner shall have the right to express his opinion before the matter is decided, but no change may be made in the nature of the business without any consent of all the partners, and

d) Every partner has a right to have access to and to inspect any of the books of the firm.

Mutual Rights and Liabilities

Subject to a contract between the partners:

a) A partner is not entitled to receive remuneration for taking part in the conduct of the business;

b) The partners are entitled to share equally in the profits earned, and shall contribute equally to the losses sustained by the firm.

c) Where a partner is entitled to interest on the capital subscribed by him such interest shall be payable only out of profits.

d) A partner making, for the purposes of the business, any payment or advance beyond the amount of capital he has agreed to subscribe, is entitled to interest thereon at the rate of six per cent, per annum.

e) The firm shall indemnify a partner in respect of payments made and liabilities incurred by him—

   i) In the ordinary and proper conduct of the business, and

   ii) In doing such act, in an emergency, for the purpose of protecting the firm from loss as would be done by a person of ordinary prudence, in his own case, under similar circumstances.

f) Similarly, a partner shall indemnify the firm for any loss caused to it by his willful neglect in the conduct of the business of the firm.

The Property of the Firm

The property of the firm includes all property and rights and interests in property originally brought into the stock of the firm, or acquired, by purchase or otherwise, by or for the firm, or for the purposes and in the course of the business of the firm, and includes also the goodwill of the business.

Personal Profits Earned by Partners: If a partner derives any profit for himself from any transaction of the firm or from the use of the property or business connection of the firm or the firm name, he shall account for that profit and pay it to the firm. If a partner carries on any business of the same nature as and competing with that of the firm, he shall account for and pay to the firm all profits made by him in that business.

Right and Duties of Partners:

a) **After a Change in the Firm:** Where a change occurs in the constitution of a firm, the mutual rights and duties of the partners in the reconstituted firm remain the same as they were immediately before the change, as far as maybe,

b) **After the Expiry of the Term of the Firm:** Where a firm constituted for a fixed term continues to carry on business after the expiry of that term, the mutual rights and duties of the partners remain the same as they were before the expiry, so far as they may be consistent with the incidents of partnership at will, and

c) **Where Additional Undertakings are Carried out:** Where a firm constituted to carry out one or more adventures or undertakings carries out other adventures or undertakings, the mutual rights and duties of the partners in respect of the other adventures or undertakings are the same as those in respect of the original adventures or undertaking.

Partners to be Agent of the Firm

A partner is the agent of the firm for the purposes of the business of the firm. A partner can make the firm liable by his acts, if done in the name of the firm and in the ordinary course of business of the firm.

Implied Authority of Partner as Agent of the Firm: The act of a partner which is done to carry on, in the usual way, business of the kind carried on by the firm, binds the firm. The authority of a partner to bind the firm conferred by this section is called his "implied authority". The implied authority of a partner does not empower him to:

a) Submit a dispute relating to the business of the firm to arbitration;

b) Open a banking account on behalf of the firm in his own name;

c) Compromise or relinquish any claim or portion of a claim by the firm;

d) Withdraw a suit or proceeding filed on behalf of the firm;

e) Admit any liability in a suit or proceeding against the firm;

f) Acquire immovable property on behalf of the firm;

g) Transfer immovable property belonging to the firm; or

h) Enter into partnership on behalf of the firm.

Extension and Restriction of Partner's Implied Authority

The partners in a firm may, by contract between the partners, extend or restrict the implied authority of any partner. Any act done by a partner on behalf of the firm which falls within his implied authority binds the firm, unless the person with whom he is dealing knows of the restriction or does not know or believe that partner to be a partner.

Partner's Authority in an Emergency: A partner has authority, in an emergency, to do all such acts for the purpose of protecting the firm from loss as would be done by a person of ordinary prudence, in his own case, acting under similar circumstances, and such acts bind the firm.

Mode of doing act to Bind Firm: In order to bind a firm, an actor instrument done or executed by a partner or other person on behalf of the firm shall be done or executed in the firm name or in any other manner expressing or implying an intention to bind the firm.

Liability of a Partner for Acts of the Firm: Every partner is liable, jointly with all the other partners and also severally, for all acts of the firm done while he is a partner.

Liability of the firm for Wrongful Acts of a Partner: Whereby the wrongful act or omission of a partner acting in the ordinary course of the business of a firm, or with the authority, of his partners, loss or injury is caused to any third party, or any penalty is incurred, the firm is liable therefor to the same extent as the partner.

Liability of firm for Misapplication by Partners: Where:

a) A partner acting within his apparent authority receives money or property from a third party and misapplies it or,

b) A firm in the course of its business receives money or property from a thirty party, and the money or property is misapplied by any of the partners while it is in the custody of the firm. The firm is liable to make good the loss.

Retirement of a Partner

(1) A partner may retire—

    a) With the consent of all the other partners;

    b) In accordance with an express agreement by the partners; or

    c) Where the partnership is at will by giving notice in writing to all the other partners of his intention to retire;

(2) A retiring partner may be discharged from any liability to any third party for acts of the firm done before

his retirement by an agreement made by him with such third party and the partners of the reconstituted firm after he had knowledge of the retirement;

(3) Notwithstanding the retirement of a partner from a firm, he and the partners continue to be liable as partners to third parties for any act done by any of them which would have been an act of the firm if done before the retirement, until public notice is given of the retirement.

Dissolution of Firm

The dissolution of partnership between all the partners of a firm is called "dissolution of the firm". A firm can be dissolved through the following ways.

1. **Dissolution by Agreement:** A firm may be dissolved with the consent of all the partners or in accordance with a contract between the partners.

2. **Compulsory Dissolution:** A firm is dissolved,

   a) By the adjudication of all the partners or of all partners but one as insolvent or,

   b) By the happening of any event which makes it unlawful for the business of the firm to be carried on or for the partners to carry it on in partnership.

3. **Dissolution on the happening of Certain Contingencies:** Subject to contract between the partners a firm is dissolved—

   a) If constituted for a fixed term, by the expiry of that term;

   b) If constituted to carry out one or more adventures or undertakings by the completion thereof;

   c) By the death of a partner;

   d) By the adjudication of a partner as an insolvent.

4. **Dissolution by Notice of Partnership at Will:** Where the partnership is at will the firm may be dissolved by any partner giving notice in writing to all the other partners of his intention to dissolve the firm.

5. **Dissolution by the Court:** At the suit of a partner, the Court may dissolve a firm on any of the following grounds,

   a) That a partner has become of unsound mind;

   b) That a partner, other than the partner suing, has become in any way permanently incapable of performing his duties as partner.

   c) That the business of the firm cannot be carried on save at a loss.

   d) On any other ground which renders it just and equitable that the firm should be dissolved.

Liability for Acts of Partners done after Dissolution: Despite the dissolution of a firm, the partners continue to be liable as such to third parties for any act done by any of them which would have been an act of the firm if done before the dissolution, until public notice is given of the dissolution.

Registration of Firms

Application for registration of a firm may be effected at any time by sending by post or delivering to the registrar of the area in which any place of business of the firm is situated or proposed to be situated in the prescribed form.

As per latest guideline issued by RBI, for opening a bank account of a partnership firm, one certified copy of Registration Certificate and Partnership Deed of the firm shall be obtained compulsorily.

Effect of non-Registration:

1. No suit to enforce a right arising from a contract of or conferred by this Act shall be instituted in any court by or on behalf of any person suing as a partner in a firm against the firm or any person alleged to be or to have been a partner in the firm unless the firm is registered and the person suing is or has been shown in the Register of firms as a partner in the firm.

2. No suit to enforce a right arising from a contract shall be instituted in any court by or on behalf of a firm against any third party unless the firm is registered and the person suing are or have been shown in the Register of firm as partners in the firm.

3. The provisions of sub section (1) and (2) shall apply also to a claim of Set - off or other proceeding to enforce a right arising from a contract, but shall not affect:

   a) The enforcement of any right to sue for the dissolution of a firm or for accounts of a dissolved firm, or any right or power to realise the property of a dissolved firm or

   b) The powers of an official assignee, receiver of Court under the Presidency, towns insolvency Act 1909, or the Provincial insolvency Act, 1920, to realise the property of an insolvent partner.

Limited Liability Partnership (LLP)

A limited liability partnership (LLP) is a partnership in which some or all partners (depending on the jurisdiction) have limited liabilities. LLP is governed by limited liability partnership Act 2008.

An LLP has minimum two partners and shall have at least two individuals as designated partners having Designated Partners Identification Number (DPIN), at least one must be Indian resident and no limit on maximum number of Partners.

Liability is limited to the extent of his contribution in the LLP. A partner is not liable for another partner's misconduct or negligence, except in certain cases.

An LLP is a legal entity separate from its partner. The mutual rights and duties of the partners of the LLP and those of the LLP shall be governed by an agreement between the partners, subject to the provision of the act. Indian Partnership Act 1932 is not applicable for LLPs.

It has own assets in his name, sure and be sued. Since LLP contains element of both 'a corporate structure' as well as 'a partnership firm structure'. An LLP is called a hybrid between a company and a partnership.

It has perpetual succession (death of a partner does not affect the existence of LLP). Partners have a right to manage the business directly. Firms and companies can get themselves converted into LLPs. An LLP cannot raise fund from public.

Central Government shall have power to investigate the affairs of an LLP, if required, by appointment of competent inspector, for the purpose. The winding up of LLP may be either voluntary or by the National Company Law Tribunal (NCLT) under certain circumstances.

TEST YOURSELF

1. Partnership is _______ between persons who have agreed to share _______ of a business carried out by all or any of them acting for all.
   (a) Arrangement, profits
   (b) Relation, profit
   (c) Arrangement, profits & loss
   (d) Understanding, profit & loss

2. Where no provision is made by a contract between the partners for the duration of their partnership, such partnership is referred to as:
   (a) Particular partnership
   (b) Partnership at will
   (c) Fixed period partnership
   (d) Sleeping partnership

3. A partner may retire from a partnership firm:
   (a) With the consent of all partners
   (b) In accordance with an express agreement by the partners
   (c) By giving notice in writing to all other partners of intention to retire
   (d) By any one of the above methods

4. As per Company Act 2013, the maximum number of partners in a partnership firm permitted is:
   (a) 10 for banking business & 20 for others
   (b) 20 for banking business & 10 for others
   (c) 100 for all business
   (d) 50 for all business

5. Which is a correct statement?
   (a) Joint Stock Company can become a partner in a firm
   (b) HUF cannot enter into a partnership
   (c) Both are correct
   (d) None is correct

6. Which is a correct statement regarding LLP?
   (a) LLP is governed by limited liability partnership Act 2008
   (b) LLP cannot raise funds from public
   (c) LLP is a legal entity separate from its partner
   (d) All of the above

7. Which of the following is correct with regard of a partnership?
   (a) A firm is an association of person
   (b) A firm is not a legal entity
   (c) A firm is just like a private company
   (d) A firm is a separate entity from partners

8. A Partnership is formed for completion of a specific assignment/job. This is known as:
   (a) Particular partnership
   (b) Partnership at will
   (c) Fixed period partnership
   (d) Sleeping partnership

9. A partner of a firm commits a fraud with a 3rd party while working as partner for the firm. To the 3rd party, who is liable?
   (a) The partner who committed such fraud
   (b) Partnership firm
   (c) All the partners in their individual capacity
   (d) None of the above

10. A partner being agent of the firm, for the purpose of business carries authority which is called:
    (a) Absolute authority   (b) Collective authority
    (c) Implied authority   (d) Express Authority

11. A partner acted beyond his authority in an emergency situation and the firm suffers loss. Who is to make up this loss?
    (a) No one liable to a 3ʳᵈ party
    (b) Firm is liable
    (c) Firm is not liable, only concerned partner is liable
    (d) Both (b) & (c)

12. Which of the following statement is true with regard to relationship of minor in a partnership firm:
    (a) Minor cannot become a partner he can be admitted for benefits
    (b) Minor is entitled to property of the firm
    (c) Minor is entitled to the profit from the firm
    (d) All of the above

13. On attaining majority, the minor who is admitted for benefits, can decide about his status as partner within:
    (a) 6 months from date of majority
    (b) 6 months from date he comes to know that he was admitted for benefit
    (c) 6 months from date of his admission for benefits
    (d) Both (a) and (b), whichever is earlier

14. When a partner of a firm becomes insolvent and the firm is dissolved, this can be categorized which kind of dissolution:
    (a) By agreement
    (b) At will
    (c) Compulsory dissolution
    (d) Dissolution of happening of certain contingencies

15. In which of the following circumstance, the court can dissolve a firm?
    (a) Partner becoming of unsound mind
    (b) Business cannot be carried on except at a loss
    (c) A partner has transferred his interest to a 3ʳᵈ party
    (d) All of the above

16. In case of LLP, the liability of a partner is:
    (a) Unlimited
    (b) Limited to agreed contribution
    (c) Limited to extent of their personal net worth
    (d) Limited to the extent of their combined personal net worth

17. A partner has retired but failed to give a public notice. What is the status of his liability to the 3ʳᵈ parties?
    (a) He is not liable after retirement
    (b) He is not liable after retirement, where has given public notice
    (c) He is liable if a public notice is not given after retirement
    (d) Both (b) and (c)

18. If a firm is not registered firm, what are the disadvantages when compared to a registered one?
    (a) It cannot enforce its right through a court
    (b) It cannot enforce its right after obtaining consent of the court
    (c) It cannot enforce its right by obtaining consent of Registrar of firms
    (d) Both (a) and (c)

19. Your branch is maintaining a current account of a partnership firm and a stop payment instruction from a sleeping partner, who is not operating the account, is received. How would you deal with the request?
    (a) Instructions cannot be accepted
    (b) Instructions can be accepted if other partners agree
    (c) Instructions are acceptable and operations shall be stopped
    (d) None of the above

20. What would be the personal liability of a shareholder if a limited company is a partner in firm?
    (a) It would be equal to his share in the company
    (b) No personal liability
    (c) It would be to the full extent
    (d) It would be partial

ANSWER

1	2	3	4	5	6	7	8	9	10
(c)	(b)	(d)	(c)	(c)	(d)	(b)	(a)	(b)	(c)

11	12	13	14	15	16	17	18	19	20
(b)	(d)	(d)	(d)	(d)	(b)	(d)	(a)	(c)	(b)

DEFINITION AND FEATURES OF A COMPANY— DISTINCTION BETWEEN COMPANY AND PARTNERSHIP

INTRODUCTION

A company is a group of persons who have come together or who have contributed money for some common purpose and who have incorporated themselves into a distinct legal entity in the form of a company for that purpose. As per the provision of Company Act 2013 (implemented with effect from 1st April 2014), defines a Joint Stock Company is a legal person with perpetual entity & is distinct from its members. Supreme Court of India has held in the case of State Trading Corporation of India v/s CTO that a company cannot have the status of a citizen under the Constitution of India.

Definition of a Company

A company is an artificial person created by law. Section 3(1) of the Companies Act, 1956 defines a company as: "a company formed and registered under this Act or an existing Company". 'Existing Company' means a company formed and registered under any of the earlier Company Laws.

Features of a Company

A company as an entity has many distinct features which together make it a unique organization. The essential characteristics of a company are following:

a) **Registration:** A company has to be compulsory registered under the company Act 2013. Company registered under Companies Act, 1956 need not re-register.

b) **Separate Legal Entity:** Under Incorporation law, a company becomes a separate legal entity as compared to its members. The company is distinct and different from its members in law. It has its own seal and its own name, its assets and liabilities are separate and distinct from those of its members. It is capable of owning property, incurring debt, and borrowing money, employing people, having a bank account, entering into contracts and suing and being sued separately.

c) **Limited Liability:** The liability of the members of the company is limited to contribution to the assets of the company upto the face value of shares held by them. A member is liable to pay only the uncalled money due on shares held by him. If the assets of the firm are not sufficient to pay the liabilities of the firm, the creditors can force the partners to make good the deficit from their personal assets but this cannot be done in the case of a company once the members have paid all their dues towards the shares held by them in the company.

d) **Perpetual Succession:** An incorporated company never dies. A company does not cease to exist unless it is specifically wound up or the task for which it was formed has been completed. Membership of a company may keep on changing from time to time but that does not affect life of the company. Insolvency or Death of member does not affect the existence of the company.

e) **Separate Property:** A company is a distinct legal entity. The company's property is its own. A member cannot claim to be owner of the company's property during the existence of the company.

f) Transferability of Shares: Shares in a company are freely transferable, subject to certain conditions, such that no share-holder is permanently or necessarily wedded to a company. When a member transfers his shares to another person, the transferee steps into the shoes of the transferor and acquires all the rights of the transferor in respect of those shares.

g) Common Seal: A company is an artificial person and does not have a physical presence. Thus, it acts through its Board of Directors for carrying out its activities and entering into various agreements. Such contracts must be under the seal of the company, if any. As per Companies (Amendment) Act, 2015, Company Common Seal is not necessary, if other documents available during current account opening. The common seal, if any is the official signature of the company. The name of the company must be engraved on the common seal. Any document not bearing the seal of the company may not be accepted as authentic and may not have any legal force.

h) Capacity to Sue and Being Sued: A company can sue or be sued in its own name as distinct from its members.

i) Separate Management: A company is administered and managed by its managerial personnel i.e. the Board of Directors. The shareholders are simply the holders of the shares in the company and need not be necessarily the managers of the company.

j) One Share-One Vote: The principle of voting in a company is one share-one vote i.e. if a person has 10 shares, he has 10 votes in the company. This is in direct distinction to the voting principle of a co-operative society where the "One Member - One Vote" principle applies i.e. irrespective of the number of shares held, one member has only one vote.

Difference between a Partnership Firm and a Company

The following are the main distinctions between a partnership firm and a company:

(1) Registration: A company comes into existence only after its registration under the Companies Act, 1956. In case of partnership, the registration is not compulsory under Indian Partnership Act 1932. As per RBI instruction in July 2014, for opening of bank account of a partnership firm, Registration Certificate and Partnership Deed to be obtained compulsorily now.

(2) Legal Status: A company is a legal person and regarded by law as a single person. A partnership firm is a collection of individual. It does not have a separate legal existence different from its own partner.

(3) Minimum Number of Persons: The minimum number of persons required to form a company is two in case of private companies and seven in the case of public companies. In case of One Person Company only one person required. The minimum number of persons required to form a partnership firm is two.

(4) Maximum Number of Persons: A public company may have any number of members. In case of a private company the maximum number cannot be more than two hundred. As per the company Act 2013, the maximum number of partners can be one hundred (excluding minor) in a partnership firm. (Earlier it was ten for a banking business, twenty for the other business).

(5) Transferability: A shareholder can transfer his share without the consent of other shareholders. In case of partnership, a partner cannot transfer his share without the consent of other partners.

(6) Liability of Members: The liability of the members of a company is limited whereas liability of partners for debts of a firm is unlimited.

(7) Contractual Capacity: The shareholders of a company can enter into contract with the company and can be employees of the company. Partners can contract with other partners but not with firm as a whole.

(8) Length of Existence: The death or retirement of a partner dissolves the partnership. But company having legal existence can continue in spite of death and insolvency of the members. It has a perpetual existence.

(9) Statutory Obligations: A company is required to comply with various statutory obligations regarding management e.g.; filing balance sheet, maintaining prescribed registers. In case of partnership, there are no statutory obligations.

(10) Authority of Members: Management of a company vests in the hands of a few directors elected from amongst and by the shareholders. A shareholder has no say in the management. Whereas in the case of partnership all partners are entitled to share in the management of a firm. A partner is an agent of the firm and can bind it by his acts.

(11) Ownership of Property: The property of the company is owned by company itself and not its members as the company has a separate legal existence. The property of the firm is owned by the partners themselves and not by the firm.

(12) Distribution of Profits: Profits in case of a company can be distributed according to the provision of the articles by the directors but profits of a firm are distributed in agreed proportion or equally in absence of agreement among the partners.

(13) Audit: Audit in case of company is compulsory but in case of partnership firm it is not compulsory.

TEST YOURSELF

1. Which of the following is a correct statement?
   - (a) A company is a natural person
   - (b) A company is a corporate person
   - (c) A company is a legal person
   - (d) A company is a statutory person

2. Which of the following is not correct in regard to a company?
   - (a) A company is a citizen of India
   - (b) A company enjoys the rights of a natural person
   - (c) A company can enter into a legal contract, on its own
   - (d) A company takes birth through a process of law

3. The liability of a shareholder of the company is:
   - (a) Limited to the face value of the share, it is limited company
   - (b) Limited to the amount guaranteed by the shareholder, if it is a company limited by guarantee
   - (c) Unlimited, if it is unlimited liability company
   - (d) All of the above

4. A company formed and registered under any of the earlier Company Laws is called:
   - (a) Existing Company
   - (b) Statutory Company
   - (c) Govt. Company
   - (d) Holding Company

5. Find the correct statements:
   - (a) The liability of the members of a company is limited whereas liability of partners for debts of a firm is unlimited.
   - (b) A company is a legal person and regarded by law as a single person. A partnership firm is a collection of individuals.
   - (c) Audit in case of company is compulsory but in case of partnership firm it is not compulsory.
   - (d) All of the above

6. Find the correct statements:
   - (a) Minimum paid up share capital for private company is ₹ 1 lakh
   - (b) Minimum paid up share capital for public company is ₹ 5 lakh
   - (c) No minimum paid up share capital for private or public company is required now
   - (d) Company common seal is compulsory for opening of account

7. Which of the following documents contains the internal regulation of the company?
   - (a) Certificate of incorporation
   - (b) Article of association
   - (c) Memorandum of association
   - (d) Board resolution

8. Who issues certificate of incorporation in respect of a limited company?
   - (a) Ministry of corporate affairs
   - (b) Registrar of company
   - (c) Registrar of firms
   - (d) RBI

9. Find the correct statements:
   - (a) Directors are the actual owners of the company
   - (b) A company has to be compulsorily registered under the Companies Act 2013
   - (c) A company cannot enter into a legal contract, on its own
   - (d) If all members of the company die, then the company has to be wound up

10. Find the correct statements:
    - (a) A company can sue or be sued in its own name as distinct from its members.
    - (b) A company is administered and managed by its managerial personnel i.e. the Board of Directors.
    - (c) The principle of voting in a company is one share-one vote i.e. if a person has 10 shares, he has 10 votes in the company.
    - (d) All of the above

ANSWER

1	2	3	4	5	6	7	8	9	10
(c)	(a)	(d)	(a)	(d)	(c)	(c)	(b)	(b)	(d)

THE COMPANIES ACT, 1956

INTRODUCTION

The Companies Act 2013 is an Act of the Parliament of India which regulates incorporation of a company, responsibilities of a company, directors, and dissolution of a company. The 2013 Act is divided into 29 chapters containing 470 sections as against 658 Sections in the Companies Act, 1956 and has 7 schedules. The Act has replaced The Companies Act, 1956 (in a partial manner) after receiving the assent of the President of India on 29 August 2013. The Act came into force on 12 September 2013 with few changes like earlier private companies maximum number of member was 50 and now it will be 200. A new term of "one person company" is included in this act that will be a private company and with only 98 provisions of the Act notified. A total of another 184 sections came into force from 1st April 2014.

Recently the Companies (Amendment) Act, 2015 of Parliament received the assent of the President on the 25th May, 2015, and is hereby published for general information. It is an Act to amend the Companies Act, 2013. This Act may be called the Companies (Amendment) Act, 2015.

TYPES OF COMPANIES

There are various types of companies which can be formed under the Companies Act and they can classified on different basis.

(1) **Companies can be Classified in two types on the Basis of Incorporation:**

    I. **Statutory Company:** When a company is incorporated or created by a special act passed by either Central or State Legislature, It is called Statutory Company. It enjoys powers, right and privileges as laid down in the act. Example: RBI incorporated under RBI Act 1934, Food Corporation of India, etc.

    II. **Registered under either Companies Act, 1956 or Companies Act, 2013:** Such companies are incorporated and registered under the companies act.

(2) **Companies can be classified in three types on the basis of Liability:**

    I. **Company Limited by Shares:** A company limited by shares means a company having the liability of its members limited by the memorandum to the amount, if any, unpaid on the shares respectively held by them. In such companies, there is a share capital and each share has a fixed nominal value also known as the face value which the shareholder is bound to pay either at a time or installments. In other words, liability of the members of such a company is limited to the extent of amount unpaid on the shares.

    II. **Company Limited by Guarantee:** A company limited by guarantee means a company having the liability of its members limited by the memorandum of association to such amount as the members may respectively undertake to contribute to the assets of the company in the event of its being woundup. In other words, in such a company each member promises to pay a fixed sum of money in case of its winding up.

    III. **Company with Unlimited Liability:** Where the liability of the members of a company is unlimited it is known as an unlimited company. Every member of such a company is liable without any limit for his debts as in the case of a partnership firm in proportion to his interest in the company. If such a company has a share capital, it may be a public company or private company. An unlimited company must have article of association and it must state the number of members and the share capital (if any) with which it is proposed to be registered.

(3) **Companies can be Classified on the basis of Public Interest:** On the basis of public interest companies can be classified as under :

I. **Private Company:** Has shareholders with limited liability and its shares may not be offered to the general public. Shareholders of private companies limited by shares are often bound to offer the shares to their fellow shareholders prior to selling them to a third party. Private Limited Company having a no minimum paid-up share capital limitation now. (As per Companies (Amendment) Act, 2015, paid-up share capital of one lakh rupees or such higher paid-up share capital as may be prescribed is omitted now). It has minimum two members and maximum members restricted to two hundred and minimum two directors and no maximum number of directors is restricted.

II. **Public Company:** Public company means a company which is not a private company and has no minimum paid-up share capital limitation now (As per Companies (Amendment) Act, 2015, paid-up share capital of five lakh rupees or such higher paid-up share capital as may be prescribed is omitted now). Shares are offered to the public & are listed on stock exchange. Minimum seven members no limit of maximum number. Minimum 3 director maximum 15 director limit. Provided that a company may appoint more than fifteen directors after passing a special resolution. (As per Companies Act 2013, no Central Govt. permission required now). At least one woman director shall be on Board. Certificate of commencement of business is must to do any type of business.

III. **Government Company:** Government Company means any company in which not less than fifty one percent of paid-up share capital is held by the Central Government, or by any State Government, or partly by the Central Government and partly by one or more State Governments, and includes a company which is a subsidiary company of such a Government Company.

IV. **One Person Company:** The Companies Act 2013 introduces a new type of entity to the existing list i.e. apart from forming a public or private limited company, the act enables the formation of a new entity a 'one-person company' (OPC). An OPC means a company with only one person having a sole member [section 3(1) of 2013 Act]. OPC will be formed as a 'Private Limited Company'. Hence, minimum paid up capital will be ₹ 1,00,000/-. Memorandum of Association of such a company will mandatorily prescribe the name of the other person, who in the event of death or disability of the subscriber shall assume his position. An OPC can be formed only by an Indian Resident and Citizen.

V. **Foreign Company:** It means a company incorporated outside India and having a place of business in India whether by itself or through an agent, physically or through electronic mode and conduct any business activity in India in any other manner.

VI. **Existing Company:** A company which is established before the Company Act 1956 is called Existing Company.

VII. **Small Company:** It means a company, other than a public company, paid-up capital share of which does not exceed fifty lakh rupees or such higher amount as may be prescribed which shall not be more than fifty crore rupees or turnover of which as per its last profit and loss account does not exceed two crore rupees or such higher amount as may be prescribed which shall not be more than twenty crore rupees.

VIII. **Holding Company:** A company is known as the holding company of another company if it has control over another company.

IX. **Subsidiary Company:** A company is known as subsidiary of another company when control is exercised by the latter over the former called a subsidiary company. A company is to be deemed to be subsidiary company of another.

Important Documents in Relation to a Company

The promoters must make a decision regarding the type of company i.e. a public company or a private company or an unlimited company, and accordingly prepare the documents for incorporation of the company. In this connection the Memorandum and Articles of Association are crucial documents to be prepared.

(1) **Memorandum of Association of a Company:** No company can be registered under the Companies

Act, 2013 without the Memorandum of Association. It is a document of great significance as it embodies the fundamental rules regarding the constitution and scope of activities of a company. The Memorandum of Association of every company must contain the following clauses:

a) **Name Clause:** The name of the company is mentioned in the name clause. A public limited company must end with the word 'Limited' and a private limited company must end with the words 'Private Limited'. The company cannot have a name which in the opinion of the Central Government is undesirable. A name which is identical with or the nearly resembles the name of another company in existence will not be allowed. A company cannot use a name which is prohibited under the Names and Emblems (Prevention of Misuse) Act, 1950 or use a name suggestive of connection to Government or State patronage.

b) **Registered Office Clause:** The State in which the registered office of company is to be situated is mentioned in this clause. If it is not possible to state the exact location of the registered office, the company must state to provide the exact address either on the day on which commences its business or within 30 days from the date of incorporation of the company, whichever is earlier. Similarly, any change in the registered office must also be intimated to the Registrar of Companies within 30 days. The registered office of the company is the official address of the company where the statutory books and records must normally be kept. Every company must affix or paint its name and address of its registered office on the outside of the every office or place at which its activities are carried on in. The name must be written in one of the local languages and in English.

c) **Objective Clause:** This clause is the most important clause of the company. It specifies the activities which a company can carry on and which it cannot carry on. The company cannot carry on any activity which is not authorised by its Memorandum of Association. This clause must specify:

   i. Main objectives of the company to be pursued by the company on its incorporation objectives incidental or ancillary to the attainment of the main objects.

   ii. Other objectives of the company not included in above.

In case of the companies other than trading corporations whose objectives are not confined to one State, the States to whose territories the objectives of the company extend must be specified.

d) **Liability Clause:** A declaration that the liability of the members is limited in case of the company limited by the shares or guarantee must be given. The Memorandum of Association of a company limited by guarantee must also state that each member undertakes to contribute to the assets of the company such amount not exceeding specified amounts as may be required in the event of the liquidation of the company.

e) **Capital Clause:** The amount of share capital with which the company is to be registered divided into shares must be specified giving details of the number of shares and types of shares. A company cannot issue share capital greater than the maximum amount of share capital mentioned in this clause without altering the memorandum.

f) **Association Clause:** A declaration by the persons for subscribing to the memorandum that they desire to form into a company and agree to take the shares placed against their respective name must be given by the promoters.

(2) **Articles of Association:** The Articles of Association contain the rules and regulations for internal management of the company. The Articles of Association is nothing but a contract between the company and its members and also between the members themselves that they shall abide by the rules and regulations of internal management of the company specified in the Articles of Association. It specifies the rights and duties of the members and directors. The provisions of the Articles of Association must not be in conflict with the provisions of the Memorandum of Association. In case such a conflict arises, the Memorandum of Association will prevail.

Normally, every company has its own Articles of Association. However, if a company does not have its own Articles of Association, the model Articles of Association specified in Schedule I-Table A will apply. A company may adopt any of the model forms of Articles of Association, with or without modifications. The Articles of Association should be in any of the one form specified in the tables B, C, D and E of Schedule 1 to the Companies Act, 1956. Form in Table B is applicable in case of companies limited by the shares, form in Table C is applicable to the companies limited by guarantee and not having share capital, and form in Table D is applicable to company limited by guarantee and having a share capital whereas form in table E is applicable to unlimited companies. However, a private company must have its own Articles of Association.

The important items covered by the Articles of Association include powers, duties, rights and liabilities of Directors, powers, duties, rights and liabilities of members, rules for Meetings of the Company, Dividends, Borrowing powers of the company, Calls on shares, Transfer & transmission of shares, Forfeiture of shares, Voting powers of members, etc.

(3) Certificate of Incorporation: Once all the above documents have been filed and they are found to be in order, the Registrar of Companies will issue Certificate of Incorporation of the Company. This document is the birth certificate of the company and is proof of the existence of the company. Once, this certificate is issued, the company cannot cease its existence unless it is liquidated by order of the Court.

(4) Commencement of Business: A private company or a company having no share capital can commence its business immediately after it has been incorporated. However, Public company and other companies can commence their activities only after they have obtained Certificate of Commencement of Business.

(5) Company Common Seal: Common seal, if any of the company available should be embossed on bank's documents. As per RBI's instruction Company Common Seal is not necessary, if other documents available during current account opening.

As per Companies (Amendment) Act, 2015, the following proviso regarding Company Common Seal shall be inserted, namely:

"Provided that in case a company does not have a common seal, the authorisation under this sub-section shall be made by two directors or by a director and the Company Secretary, wherever the company has appointed a Company Secretary."

Doctrine of the Ultra-Vires

Any transaction which is outside the scope of the powers specified in the objects clause of the Memorandum of Association and are not reasonable incidentally or necessary to the attainment of objects, is ultra-vires the company and therefore void. No rights and liabilities on the part of the company arise out of such transactions and it is a nullity even if every member agrees to it.

Consequences of an ultra-vires Transaction:

1. The company cannot sue any person for enforcement of any of its rights.

2. No person can sue the company for enforcement of its rights.

3. The directors of the company may be held personally liable to outsiders for an ultra-vires However, the doctrine of ultra-vires does not apply in the following cases:
   a) If an act is ultra-vires of powers the directors but intra-vires of company, the company is liable.
   b) If an act is ultra-vires the articles of the company but it is intra-vires of the memorandum, the articles can be altered to rectify the error.
   c) If an act is within the powers of the company but is irregularly done, consent of the shareholders will validate it.
   d) Where there is ultra-vires borrowing by the company or it obtains delivery of the property under an ultra-vires contract, then the third party has no claim against the company on the basis of the loan but he has right to follow his money or property if it exist as it is and obtain an injunction from the Court restraining the company from parting with it provided that he intervenes before money is spent-on or the identity of the property is lost.

4. The subscriber of the money to a company under the ultra-vires contract has a right to make director personally liable.

Doctrine of Constructive Notice of Memorandum of Association & Articles of Association

Memorandum of Association and Articles of Association are registered with ROC, that cannot be inspected by any member of the public. (As per Companies (Amendment) Act, 2015, Provided that no person shall be entitled under section 399 to inspect or obtain copies of such resolutions). Hence while dealing with a company, any person is assumed to have notice of contents of Memorandum of Association and Articles of Association that is known as constructive notice of Memorandum of Association and Articles of Association.

The effect of this doctrine is that there is presumption that a person dealing with the company knows the contents and it stops the person from contending that he had no notice of the contents. The doctrine of constructive notice protects a company from outsiders as the outsiders are presumed to have notice of contents of Memorandum of Association and Articles of Association.

DOCTRINE OF INDOOR MANAGEMENT

The doctrine of indoor management saves the outsiders from the inside management. The person dealing with a company can presume that the company and its officials understand all the rules and regulations under which the company is to be managed. Hence the outsider is not bound to inquire into regularity of internal functioning of the company. Hence, the outsider would not be affected by any internal irregularity on the part of the company or its officials. This is known as doctrine of indoor management.

MEMBERS

Membership of a Company

As per Section 55 of The Companies Act 2013 "member", in relation to a company, means:

(i) The subscriber to the memorandum of the company who shall be deemed to have agreed to become member of the company, and on its registration, shall be entered as member in its register of members;

(ii) Every other person who agrees in writing to become a member of the company and whose name is entered in the register of members of the company;

(iii) Every person holding shares of the company and whose name is entered as a beneficial owner in the records of a depository.

Various Modes of Becoming a Member of a Company

One can become a member of a company by following modes:

❖ By subscription to Memorandum of Association;

❖ By getting shares allotted when company made an offer to issue such shares, including joint membership.

❖ By purchase of shares from market and getting them transferred in his name.

❖ By getting these shares as legal heirs, as part of the estate of a deceased shareholder.

Who can become a Member of a Company?

❖ **Individuals Including NRI:** Any person who is competent to contract including NRI can become member of a company;

❖ **Company:** A company, being a legal person it can become a member of another company provided it is so authorised by its Memorandum of Association;

❖ **Registered Society:** Registered society, registered under the Society act can hold share of a company;

❖ **Partnership Firm:** Since a partnership firm is not a legal person, it cannot buy any share of its own name and thus become a member of a company. The share have to be bought only in the name of the individual partners of the partnership firm even though such share constitute a part of the assets of the partnership firm.

❖ **Minor, Insolvent, Insane Persons:** These persons cannot become member of a company.

❖ **Fictitious Person:** A fictitious person (a person making application in a fictitious name) is punishable with imprisonment up to 5 years.

Cessation of Membership in a Company

The membership of a company cease in case of any of the following:

❖ When he transfers his share in the name of some other person or when he surrenders his shares, if such surrender is allowed;

❖ When his shares have been forfeited;

❖ When shares are sold in execution of a court decree;

❖ When withdrawal of the contract due to mis-representation in the prospectus;

❖ When he is adjudicated insolvent;

❖ When he expires (in that situation, the shares would be transferred in the name of legal heirs).

Register of Members for Shares and Debentures

Every company keeps a register of members that contains details about shareholders and enters following particulars:

❖ The name, address and the occupation of each member;

❖ The share held by each member, distinguishing each share by its member;

❖ The date in the register at which each person was entered as a member;

❖ The date in the register at which each person was ceased to be a member.

Closure of Register of Members

A company may close the register of members or the register of debenture holders or the register of other security holders for any period or periods not exceeding in the aggregate forty-five days in each year, but not exceeding thirty days at any one time, subject to giving of previous notice of at least seven days or such lesser period as may be specified by Securities and Exchange Board for listed companies or the companies which intend to get their securities listed, in such manner as may be prescribed.

Liability or Duties of Members

- ❖ If company is limited by shares, to the extent of unpaid amount of the shares;
- ❖ If the company is limited by guarantee, to the extent of guaranteed by the member;
- ❖ If it is unlimited company, the liability is to full extent of debts of the company.

Rights of Members

- ❖ Priority in new shares issued by the company;
- ❖ Right to transfer shares;
- ❖ Right to receive notice of meetings and voting rights;
- ❖ Right to receive copies of annual accounts;
- ❖ Right to inspect the register of members and copies of annual returns; (As per Companies (Amendment) Act, 2015, Provided that no person shall be entitled under section 399 to inspect or obtain copies of such resolutions).
- ❖ Right to apply to Company Law Board to call annual general meeting;
- ❖ Right to convene extra-ordinary general meeting;
- ❖ Right to file petition to the High Court to order winding up of the company;
- ❖ Right to receive dividends, if declared by the company;
- ❖ Right to participate in the distribution of asset in case of liquidation of the company.

DIRECTORS

Minimum Number of Directors: Minimum director for Public company -3, Private -2, and for OPC-1. Every public company (other than a deemed public company) must have at least three directors. Every other company must have at least two directors.

Maximum Number of Directors: No maximum number of directors is restricted for private company. A Public company can have a maximum number of fifteen directors and to increase this number, the approval of Central Government is required.

Board of Directors: The directors of a company collectively are referred to as the "Board of directors" or "Board". Only individuals can be appointed as directors. No body corporate, association or firm can be appointed director of a Company.

First Directors: In case the first directors are not appointed by the promoters of a company, subscribers of the memorandum who are individuals, shall be deemed to be the directors of the company, until the directors are duly appointed.

Resident Director: A company to have minimum one director who has stayed in India for minimum 182 days in previous calendar year.

Woman Director: At least one woman director shall be on Board.

Appointment of Directors and Proportion of those who are to Retire by Rotation

Unless articles provide for the retirement of all directors at every annual general meeting, at least two-thirds of the total number of directors of a public company, or of a private company which is subsidiary of a public company, must

(a) Retire by rotation

(b) Be appointed by the company in general meeting, except where otherwise provided by the Companies Act. The remaining directors in the case of any such company, and the directors generally in the case of a private company which is not a subsidiary of a public company, must also be appointed by the company in general meeting, unless otherwise provided in any regulations in the articles of the company.

Ascertainment of Directors Retiring by Rotation and Filling of Vacancies

At every annual general meeting of a public company, or a private company which is a subsidiary of a public company, one-third of the directors liable to retirement by rotation or if their number is not three or a multiple of three, then, the number nearest to one-third, shall retire from office. The directors to retire by rotation at every annual general meeting shall be those who have been longest in office since their last appointment, but as between persons who became directors on the same day, those who will have to retire is to be determined by lot, unless otherwise agreed to among themselves.

Right of Persons other than Retiring Directors to Stand for Directorship

A person who is not a retiring director shall, subject to the provisions of this Act, be eligible for appointment to the office of director at any general meeting, if he or some member intending to propose him has, given notice in writing to the company at its registered office of at least 14 days before the meeting, signifying his candidature for the office of director or the intention of such member to propose him as a candidate for that office along with a deposit of rupees five hundred refundable on successful election.

Right of Company to Increase or Reduce the Number of Directors

A company, at a general meeting may, by ordinary resolution, increase or reduce the number of its directors within the limits fixed in its articles.

Additional Directors

The Board of directors may appoint additional directors if such power is conferred on it by the articles of the company. Such additional directors shall hold office only up to the date of the next annual general meeting of the company.

Filling of Casual Vacancies Among Directors

In the case of a public company or a private company which is a subsidiary of a public company, if the office of any director appointed by the company in general meeting is vacated before his term of office will expire in the normal course, the resulting casual vacancy may, in default of and subject to any regulations in the articles of the company, be filled by the Board of directors at a meeting of the Board. Any person so appointed shall hold office only up to the date up to which the director in whose place he is appointed would have held office if it had not been vacated as aforesaid.

Alternate Director

The board of directors of a company may, if so authorised by its articles or by a resolution passed by the company in general meeting, appoint an alternate director to act for a director during his absence for a period of not less than three months from the state in which meetings of the board are ordinarily held. An alternate director so appointed shall not hold office for a period longer than the period for which the original director hold office and vacate office if and when the original director returns to the state in which meetings of the Board are ordinarily held.

Consent of Candidate for Directorship to be Filled with Registrar

A person shall not act as director of a company unless he has, by himself or by his agent authorised in writing, signed and filed with the Registrar, a consent in writing to act as such director within 30 days of his appointment.

Qualification Shares

These are the minimum number of shares a person must own, as provided in the articles of the company, in order to qualify to become a director of the company. Qualification shares must be acquired by a director within 2 months of his appointment.

The above provisions do not apply to a company not having a share capital; a private company; a company which was a private company before becoming a public company; or a prospectus issued by or on behalf of a company after the expiry of one year from the date on which the company was entitled to commerce business.

Disqualifications of Directors

A person shall not be capable of being appointed director of a company, if,

a) He has been found to be of unsound mind by a Court of competent jurisdiction and the finding is inforce;

b) He is an un-discharged insolvent;

c) he has applied to be adjudicated as an insolvent and his application is pending or he has been convicted by a court of any offence involving moral turpitude and sentenced in respect thereof to imprisonment for not less than six months, and a period of 5 years has not elapsed from the date of expiry of the sentence;

d) He has not paid any call in respect of shares of the company held by him, whether alone or jointly with others, and 6 months have elapsed from the last day fixed for the payment of the call;

e) An order disqualifying him for appointment as director has been passed by a court and is in force unless the leave of the court has been obtained for his appointment in pursuance of that section.

The Central Government may, by notification in the Official Gazette, remove:

i) The disqualification incurred by any person in virtue of clause (d) either generally or in relation to any company or companies specified in the notification; or

ii) The disqualification incurred by any person in virtue of clause (e)

A private company which is not a subsidiary of a public company may, by its articles, provide that a person shall be disqualified for appointment as a director on any grounds in addition to those specified above.

Maximum Number of Directorships

No person, after the commencement of this Act, shall hold office as a director, including any alternate directorship, in more than twenty companies at the same time. Provided that the maximum number of public companies in which a person can be appointed as a director shall not exceed ten. The members of the company may, by special resolution, specify any lesser number of companies in which a director of the company may act as directors.

Loan to Directors

No company shall, directly or indirectly, advance any loan, including any loan represented by a book debt, to any of its directors or to any other person in whom the director is interested or give any guarantee or provide any security in connection with any loan taken by him or such other person. However any loan or guarantee given by a company to its wholly owned subsidiary, or a guarantee extended to its subsidiary are exempted.

Removal of Directors

A company may, by ordinary resolution, remove a director (not being a director appointed by the Central Government in pursuance of section 408) before the expiry of his period of office.

A vacancy created by the removal of a director if he had been appointed by the company in general meeting or by the board in on a casual vacancy, be filled by the appointment of another director in his stead by the meeting at which he is removed, provided special notice of the intended appointment has been given. A director so appointed shall hold office until the date up to which his predecessor would have held office if he had not been removed as aforesaid. Qualified to act as such during the absence or incapacity of some other director.

Board Meeting

At least 7 days' notice is required to be given for a Board meeting. For a Meeting at shorter notice, at least one independent director shall be present at the meeting.

PROSPECTUS

A prospectus is any document that is described or is issued as a prospectus and includes any notice, circular, advertisement or other document, inviting deposit from the public or inviting offers from the public for subscription / purchase of shares or debenture of a body corporate. Private companies cannot issue prospectus as these cannot invite deposits nor they can offer shares to the public.

Where prospectus is not required to be issued:

- ❍ Where a person has entered into an underwriting agreement to purchase or subscribe the shares.
- ❍ Where shares are offered to existing shareholders or debenture holders only
- ❍ Where the offer, in all respects is uniform with the previously issued shares and debentures and these are listed on a recognized stock exchange.

Compliance with Respect to Prospectus:

a) **Time of Issue:** It can be issued only after incorporation of the company.

b) **Contents:** It should contain the mandatory provision that are to be stated in the prospectus.

c) **Date of Publication:** It must be dated and this ensures an evidence of date of publication.

d) **Signatures of Director:** Each person mentioned as director, must sign it.

e) **Application Form:** Every application should be accompanied by a copy of the prospectus.

f) **Statement by Experts:** A statement purporting to be made by an expert can be issued only if the company holds written consent of the expert and he has not withdrawn it.

g) **Registration of the Prospectus:** Before issue, it should be delivered to ROC for registration along with other documents.

Wrong Statements in the Prospectus

A person induced to buy shares or debentures on the faith of a statement in a prospectus which is untrue has twofold remedies:

a) **Against the Company:** To rescind the contract and claim damages.

b) **Against the Promoters:** The directors or person responsible would can be punished with fine or imprisonment or both.

REGISTRATION, MODIFICATION AND SATISFACTION OF CHARGE

U/s 77 of Companies Act 2013, every charge created by a company on its assets, shall be held void against the liquidator and any creditor of a company unless the prescribed particulars of the charge (together with copy of instrument, by which the charge in created) are filed with the Registrar, for registration within 30 days, after date of its creation. In case of charge created outside India, 30 days shall begin on receipt of instrument in India.

Delay in filing details for registration: The registrar can extend the period by 270 days. Beyond that, Central Govt. permission is required.

Certificate of Registration

The Registrar shall give a certificate of registration of any charge registered, stating the amount thereby secured. The certificate is conclusive evidence that requirement of registration has been fulfilled. Who is to file the particulars: It shall be the duty of a company to file the particulars of every charge but the registration of any such charge may also be effected on the application of any person interested therein.

Right to Inspect Copies of Instruments

The copies of the instruments creating charges shall not be available for inspection to any creditor or member of a company without fee, at their registered office. (As per Companies (Amendment) Act, 2015, Provided that no person shall be entitled under section 399 to inspect or obtain copies of such resolutions)

Search at the Office of ROC

As part of due diligence, a search can be carried out at the office of ROC before granting loan to a company, to ensure that the assets or securities offered, are not already charged to any other party.

TEST YOURSELF

1. Which of the following provisions of the Company Act 2013 was not defined in Company Act 1956:
   (a) Definition of listed company
   (b) Definition of one person company
   (c) Definition of existing company
   (d) None of the above

2. Minimum paid-up share capital of five lakh rupee for public company and one lakh rupee for private company or such higher paid-up share capital as may be prescribed is omitted now by:
   (a) Companies (Amendment) Act, 2015
   (b) Company Act, 2013
   (c) Companies (Amendment) Act, 2016
   (d) Company Act, 2015

3. Which of the following is not a feature of a joint stock company?
   (a) A company has perpetual succession
   (b) A company is a separate legal entity from its shareholders
   (c) A company is liquidated when majority of share-holders become insolvent
   (d) None of the above

4. The process of formation of a company is called:
   (a) Incorporation   (b) Dissolution
   (c) Creation   (d) Liquidation

5. The maximum number of shareholders that a private company must have:
   (a) 2   (b) 50
   (c) 200   (d) No limit

6. The minimum number of shareholders that a public company must have:
   (a) 2   (b) 7
   (c) 50   (d) No limit

7. The minimum and maximum number of shareholders that a government company must have:
   (a) Minimum 2 and Maximum 50
   (b) Minimum 7 and Maximum 200
   (c) Minimum no limit and Maximum 200
   (d) Minimum 7 and Maximum no limit

8. A company that is created by a Special Act enacted by the Parliament or State Assembly is called:
   (a) Public Limited Company
   (b) Statutory Company
   (c) Government Company
   (d) Registered Company

9. Which of the following falls under the category of a foreign company:
   (a) A company having place of business outside India
   (b) An Indian company having place of business outside India
   (c) A company incorporated outside India having business in India
   (d) A company incorporated outside India having business outside India

10. Which of the following companies can be called a Government Company:
    (a) Company having government shareholding of 51% of authorised capital
    (b) Company having government shareholding of 51% of paid up capital
    (c) Government shareholding may be of Central Govt. or State Govt. or both
    (d) Both (b) & (c)

11. The entire shareholding of a company is held by another company. The company holding the share capital is called:
    (a) Holding Company
    (b) Statutory Company
    (c) Subsidiary Company
    (d) Registered Company

12. The situation of ultra-vires arise due to violation of provision of which of the following document relating to a company?
    (a) Certificate of incorporation
    (b) Article of association
    (c) Memorandum of association
    (d) Board resolution

13. Who among of the following is competent to rectify an ultra-vires action of a company?
    (a) Registrar of Company
    (b) Company Law Board
    (c) Shareholders of the Company
    (d) None of the above

14. When a company changes the location of its registered office, the information is required to be sent to _____ within _____ days of such changes.
    (a) ROC, 45
    (b) Company Law Board, 30
    (c) ROC, 30
    (d) Shareholders, 45

15. Which of the following document is called document of outdoor management?
    (a) Certificate of incorporation
    (b) Article of association
    (c) Memorandum of association
    (d) Board resolution

16. A shareholder's right to receive new shares offered in case the company proposes to increase capital. The right is:
    (a) Statutory Right   (b) Proprietary Right
    (c) Moral Right   (d) Documentary Right

17. Which of the following companies cannot issue a prospectus?
    (a) Holding Company
    (b) Statutory Company
    (c) Subsidiary Company
    (d) Private Company

18. If the articles do not provide for retirement of all directors at every annual general meeting, how many directors would retire?
    (a) $1/4^{th}$ (b) ½
    (c) $1/3^{rd}$ (d) $2/3^{rd}$

19. When the directors are retired by rotation, which directors are to retire?
    (a) The directors having the longest period in office
    (b) The directors having the shortest period in office
    (c) The directors who are directed to retire by ROC
    (d) The directors who have not attended the meetings regularly

20. A person cannot act as a director unless he signs and files his consent with ROC within _________ of his appointment.
    (a) 15 days   (b) 30 days
    (c) 60 days   (d) 90 days

ANSWER

1	2	3	4	5	6	7	8	9	10
(b)	(a)	(c)	(a)	(c)	(b)	(d)	(b)	(c)	(d)

11	12	13	14	15	16	17	18	19	20
(a)	(c)	(d)	(c)	(b)	(a)	(d)	(d)	(a)	(b)

CHAPTER 34

FOREIGN EXCHANGE MANAGEMENT ACT, 1999

OBJECTIVE

The main objective of Foreign Exchange Regulation Act, 1973 (FERA) was conservation and proper utilization of the foreign exchange resources of the country. It also sought to control certain aspects of the conduct of business outside the country by Indian companies and in India by foreign companies. When a business enterprise imports goods from other countries, exports its products to them or makes investments abroad, it deals in foreign exchange. Foreign exchange means 'foreign currency' and includes deposits, credits and balances payable in any foreign currency and secondly drafts, travelers cheques, letters of credit or bills of exchange, expressed or drawn in Indian currency but payable in any foreign currency. The FERA has since been repealed.

The preamble to The Foreign Exchange Management Act, 1999 (FEMA) lays down the purpose of the Act is to consolidate and amend the law relating to foreign exchange with the objective of facilitating external trade and payments and for promoting the orderly development and maintenance of foreign exchange market in India.

INTRODUCTION

The Foreign Exchange Management Act, 1999 (FEMA) is an Act of the Parliament of India "to consolidate and amend the law relating to foreign exchange with the objective of facilitating external trade and payments and for promoting the orderly development and maintenance of foreign exchange market in India". It was passed in the winter session of Parliament in 1999, replacing the Foreign Exchange Regulation Act (FERA). This act makes offences related to foreign exchange civil offenses. It extends to the whole of India. It enabled a new foreign exchange management regime consistent with the emerging framework of the World Trade Organisation (WTO). It also paved the way for the introduction of the Prevention of Money Laundering Act, 2002.

DEFINITIONS

Definitions as per FEMA act are as under:

1. **"Authorised Person"** means any bank or any other person including an authorised money changer or dealer authorised under FEMA to deal in foreign exchange or foreign securities.

2. **"Authorised Officer"** means an officer of the Directorate of Enforcement authorised by the Central Government under FEMA.

3. **"Reserve Bank"** means the Reserve Bank of India constituted under RBI Act, 1934.

4. **"Capital Account Transaction"** means a transaction which alters the assets or liabilities, including contingent liabilities, outside India of persons resident in India or assets or liabilities in India of persons resident outside India.

5. **"Current Account Transaction"** means a transaction other than a capital account transaction and without prejudice to the generality of the foregoing such transaction includes:

   i) Payments due in connection with foreign trade, other current business, services, and short-term banking and credit facilities in the ordinary course of business;

ii) Payments due as interest on loans and as net income from investments;

iii) Remittances for living expenses of parents, spouse and children residing abroad; and

iv) Expenses in connection with foreign travel, education and medical care of parents, spouse and children.

6. "**Currency**" includes all currency notes, postal notes, postal orders, money orders, cheques, drafts, travellers cheques, letters of credit, bills of exchange and promissory notes, credit cards or such other similar instruments, as may be notified by the Reserve Bank.

7. "**Foreign Currency**" means any currency other than Indian currency.

8. "**Foreign Exchange**" means foreign currency and in addition of the foreign currency, it includes:
   i) Deposits, credits and balances payable in any foreign currency;
   ii) Drafts, travellers cheques, letters of credit or bills of exchange, expressed or drawn in Indian currency but payable in any foreign currency;
   iii) Drafts, travellers cheques, letters of credit or bills of exchange drawn by banks, institutions or persons outside India, but payable in Indian currency.

9. "**Foreign Security**" or "**Security**" means any security, in the form of shares, stocks, bonds, debentures or any other instrument denominated or expressed in foreign currency and includes securities expressed in foreign currency, but where redemption or any form of return such as interest or dividends is payable in Indian currency.

10. "**Import**", with its grammatical variations and cognate expressions, means bringing into India any goods or services.

11. "**Person**" is defined to include—
    i) An individual,
    ii) A Hindu Undivided Family,
    iii) A company,
    iv) A firm,
    v) An association of persons or a body of individuals, whether incorporated or not,
    vi) Every artificial juridical person, and
    vii) Any agency, office or branch owned or controlled by such person.

12. "**Person Resident in India**" means the following:
    i) A person residing in India for more than 182 days during the course of the preceding financial year but does not include:

(A) A person who has gone out of India or who stays outside India, in either case:
   (a) For or on taking up employment outside India, or
   (b) For carrying on outside India a business or vocation outside India, or
   (c) For any other purpose, in such circumstances as would indicate his intention to stay outside India for an uncertain period;

(B) A person who has come to or stays in India, in either case, otherwise than:
   (a) For or on taking up employment in India, or
   (b) For carrying on in India a business or vocation in India, or
   (c) For any other purpose, in such circumstances as would indicate his intention to stay in India for an uncertain period;

ii) Any person or corporate body registered or incorporated in India,

iii) An office, branch or agency in India owned or controlled by a person resident outside India,

iv) An office, branch or agency outside India owned or controlled by a person resident in India.

12. "**Person Resident Outside India**" means a person who is not resident in India.

13. "**Repatriate to India**" means bringing into India the realised foreign exchange and—
    i) The selling of such foreign exchange to an authorised person in India in exchange for rupees, or
    ii) The holding of realised amount in an account with an authorised person in India to the extent notified by the Reserve Bank, and includes use of the realised amount for discharge of a debt or liability denominated in foreign exchange and the expression "repatriation" shall be construed accordingly.

REGULATION AND MANAGEMENT OF FOREIGN EXCHANGE

Dealing in Foreign Exchange

A person has to obtain the general or special permission of the Reserve Bank to carry out the following activities:

(a) Deal in or transfer any foreign exchange or foreign security to any person other than an authorised person;

(b) Make any payment to any person resident outside India;

(c) Receive otherwise through an authorised person, any payment on behalf of any person resident outside India;

(d) Enter into any financial transaction in India as consideration of a right to acquire, any asset outside India by any person.

Holding of Foreign Exchange

No person resident in India shall acquire, hold, own, possess or transfer any foreign exchange, foreign security or any immovable property situated outside India, unless permitted by RBI.

Holding of Foreign Currency by Residents

A person resident in India may hold, own, transfer or invest in foreign currency, foreign security or any immovable property situated outside India if such currency, security or property was acquired, held or owned by such person when he was resident outside India or inherited from a person who was resident outside India.

Holding of Foreign Currency by non-Residents

A person resident outside India may hold, own, transfer or invest in Indian currency, security or any immovable property situated in India if such currency, security or property was acquired, held or owned by such person when he was resident in India or inherited from a person who was resident in India.

Current Account Transactions

Any person may sell or draw foreign exchange to or from an authorised person if such sale or draw is a current account transaction:

Provided that the Central Government may, in public interest and in consultation with the Reserve Bank, impose such reasonable restrictions for current account transactions as may be prescribed.

Capital Account Transactions

A transaction which alters the assets or liabilities, including contingent liabilities, outside India of a person resident in India or assets or liabilities in India of person resident outside India, is called capital account transaction. As per Section 6, any person may sell or draw foreign exchange to or from an authorised person for a capital account transaction. Reserve Bank may in consultation with the Central Government, specify:

(a) Any class or classes of capital account transactions which are permissible;

(b) The limit up to which foreign exchange shall be admissible for such transactions:

(c) Any class or classes of capital account transactions which are permissible;

(d) The limit up to which foreign exchange shall be admissible for such transactions:

Provided, Reserve Bank or the Central Government shall not impose any restriction on the draw of foreign exchange for payments due on account of amortization of loans or for depreciation of direct investments in the ordinary course of business transaction.

Restriction on Capital Account Transactions

Reserve Bank may, by regulations, prohibit, restrict or regulate the following:

(a) Transfer or issue of any foreign security by a person resident in India;

(b) Transfer or issue of any security by a person resident outside India;

(c) Transfer or issue of any security or foreign security by any branch, office or agency in India of a person resident outside India;

(d) Any borrowing or lending in foreign exchange in whatever form or by whatever name called;

(e) Any borrowing or lending in rupees in whatever form or by whatever name called between a person resident in India and a person resident outside India;

(f) Deposits between persons resident in India and persons resident outside India;

(g) Export, import or holding of currency or currency notes;

(h) Transfer of immovable property outside India, other than a lease not exceeding five years, by a person resident in India;

(i) Acquisition or transfer of immovable property in India, other than a lease not exceeding five years, by a person resident outside India;

(j) Giving of a guarantee or surety in respect of any debt, obligation or other liability incurred—

　i) By a person resident in India and owed to a person resident outside India; or

　ii) By a person resident outside India.

Reserve Bank's Powers to Issue Directions to Authorised Person (Section 11)

Reserve Bank, may give to the authorised persons, any direction in regard to making of payment or the doing or desist from doing any act relating to foreign exchange or foreign security, direct any authorised person to furnish such information, in such manner, as it deems fit.

Penalty on Authorized Person

Where any authorised person contravenes any direction given by the Reserve Bank under this Act or fails to file any return as directed by the Reserve Bank, the Reserve Bank may, after giving reasonable opportunity of being heard, impose on the authorised person a penalty which may extend to ₹ 10000 and in the case of continuing contravention with for every day during which such contravention continues.

Power of Reserve Bank to Inspect Authorised Person (Sec 12)

Reserve Bank may undertake an inspection of the business of any authorised person for the purpose of verifying the correctness of any statement, information or particulars furnished to the Reserve Bank, obtaining any information or particulars which such authorised person has failed to furnish on being called upon to do so.

CONTRAVENTION AND PENALTIES

Penalties (Sec 13)

If any person contravenes any provisions of this Act, or contravenes any rule, regulation, notification, direction or order issued in exercise of the powers under this Act, or contravenes any condition subject to which an authorisation is issued by the Reserve Bank, he shall, upon adjudication, be liable to a penalty up to *thrice the sum involved* in such contravention where such amount is quantifiable, or up to ₹ 2 lac where the amount is not quantifiable.

Such contravention is a continuing one, further penalty which may extend to ₹ 5000 for every day after the first day during which the contravention continues. If any person fails to make full payment of the penalty imposed on him under section 13 within a period of 90 days from the date on which the notice for payment of such penalty is served on him, he shall be liable to civil imprisonment u/s 14.

Power to Compound Contravention

U/s 15, any contravention under section 13 may, on an application made by the person committing such contravention, be compounded within 180 days from the date of receipt of application by the Director of Enforcement or such other officers of the Directorate of Enforcement and officers of the Reserve Bank as may be authorised in this behalf by the Central Government.

Adjudication and Appeal

U/s 16, Central Government may appoint officers of the Central Government, as the Adjudicating Authorities for holding an inquiry. Adjudicating Authority may direct the said person to furnish a bond or guarantee,

- ○ No Adjudicating Authority shall hold an enquiry except upon a complaint in writing made by any officer authorised by a general or special order by the Central Government. Adjudicating Authority shall have the powers of a civil court.
- ○ All proceedings before it shall be deemed to be judicial proceedings within the meaning of sections 193 and 228 of the Indian Penal Code.
- ○ Adjudicating Authority shall deal with the complaint to dispose of the complaint finally within one year from the date of receipt of the complaint.

Appellate Tribunal (Sec 18)

The Central Government shall establish an Appellate Tribunal to be known as the Appellate Tribunal for Foreign Exchange to hear appeals against the orders of the Adjudicating Authorities and the Special Director (Appeals). Appellate Tribunal shall consist of a Chairperson and such number of Members as the Central Government may deem fit.

Directorate of Enforcement

U/S 36, Central Government shall establish a Directorate of Enforcement with a Director and other officers. U/s 37, the Director of Enforcement and other officers of Enforcement, not below the rank of an Assistant Director, shall take up for investigation, the contravention referred to in section 13.

Empowering Other Officers

U/s 38, Central Government may authorise any officer of customs or any Central Excise Officer or any Police Officer or any other officer of the Central Government or a State Government to exercise such of the powers and discharge such of the duties of the Director of Enforcement or any other officer of Enforcement under this Act. The officers shall exercise the like powers which are conferred on the income-tax authorities under the Income Tax Act, 1961.

Power to Make Regulations

U/s 47, Reserve Bank may, make regulations to carry out the provisions of this Act and the rules made thereunder. Such regulations may provide for:

(a) The permissible classes of capital account transactions, the limits of admissibility of foreign exchange for such transactions, and the prohibition, restriction or regulation of certain capital account transactions under section 6;

(b) The manner and the form in which the declaration is to be furnished under clause (a) of sub-section (1) of section 7;

(c) The period within which and the manner of repatriation of foreign exchange under section 8;

(d) The limit up to which any person may possess foreign currency or foreign coins under clause;

(e) The class of persons and the limit up to which foreign currency account may be held or operated under clause;

(f) The limit up to which foreign exchange acquired may be exempted under clause (9) the limit up to which foreign exchange acquired may be retained under clause;

(h) Any other matter which is required to be, or may be, specified.

TEST YOURSELF

1. Under FEMA 1999, which of the following is included in the definition of authorised person:
   (a) A bank only
   (b) A bank or financial institution only
   (c) A bank, a financial institution, a money changer or dealer authorised by Govt.
   (d) A bank, a financial institution, a money changer or dealer authorised by RBI

2. What is the objective of FEMA 1999?
   1. Conservation of foreign currency
   2. To facilitate external trade and payment
   3. To promoter orderly development and maintenance of foreign exchange market in India.
   (a) 1 to 3 all   (b) 1 and 2 only
   (c) 2 and 3 only   (d) 1 and 3 only

3. Which of the following is a person as per Foreign Exchange Management Act, 1999?
   (a) An individual or HUF
   (b) A joint stock company or a partnership firm
   (c) An artificial judicial person
   (d) All of the above

4. The term repatriation to India, as per FEMA 1999 mean:
   (a) Bringing foreign exchange into India
   (b) Remitting foreign exchange outside India
   (c) Starting business in India by using foreign exchange funds
   (d) Any of the above

5. Which of the following is a "Person resident in India" means as per FEMA 1999?
   (a) A person residing in India for more than 182 days during the course of the preceding financial year
   (b) Any person or body corporate registered or incorporated in India
   (c) An office, branch or agency in India owned or controlled by a person resident outside India
   (d) Any of the above

6. "Foreign exchange" means foreign currency and in addition of the foreign currency, it includes:
   (a) Deposits, credits and balances payable in any foreign currency
   (b) Drafts, traveler cheques, letters of credit or bills of exchange, expressed or drawn in Indian currency but payable in any foreign currency
   (c) Drafts, traveler cheques, letters of credit or bills of exchange drawn by banks, institutions or persons outside India, but payable in Indian currency
   (d) Any of the above

7. For contravention of provision of FEMA, penalty can be levied _______ where amount is quantifiable:
   (a) Equal to the amount
   (b) Double the amount
   (c) Thrice the amount
   (d) Four times of amount

8. Such contravention is a continuing one, further penalty which may extend to _______ for every day after the first day during which the contravention continues.
   (a) ₹ 2000   (b) ₹ 5000
   (c) ₹ 10000   (d) No fixed amount

9. Which of the following transaction is not a current account transaction as per FEMA?
   (a) Payment for import of goods
   (b) Maintenance outward for expenses of children outside India
   (c) Purchase of office building by an Indian bank in London
   (d) Expenses in connection with foreign travel by an Indian resident

10. A foreign exchange transaction by which there may be a change in assets or liabilities outside India of person resident in India as per FEMA 1999, is called:
   (a) Capital account transaction
   (b) Foreign direct investment
   (c) Foreign currency transaction
   (d) Current account transaction

11. A foreign exchange transaction other than by which there may be a change in assets or liabilities outside India of a person resident in India as per FEMA 1999, is called:
   (a) Capital account transaction
   (b) Foreign direct investment
   (c) Foreign currency transaction
   (d) Current account transaction

12. As per FEMA 1999, foreign currency means:
   (a) A currency of a foreign country
   (b) A currency other than Indian currency
   (c) A currency approved as foreign currency by Govt. of India
   (d) A currency approved as foreign currency by RBI

13. U/S 36 of FEMA 1999, __________ shall establish a Directorate of Enforcement with a Director and other officers. U/s 37, the Director of Enforcement and other officers of Enforcement, not below the rank of an Assistant Director, shall take up for investigation, the contravention referred to in section 13:
   (a) Central Government
   (b) RBI
   (c) President of India
   (d) Minister of external affairs

14. As per FEMA 1999, no person resident in India shall acquire, hold, own, possess or transfer any foreign exchange, foreign security or any immovable property situated outside India, unless permitted by __________.
   (a) Central Government
   (b) RBI
   (c) President of India
   (d) Minister of external affairs

15. __________ may undertake an inspection of the business of any authorised person for the purpose of verifying the correctness of any statement, information or particulars furnished to the Reserve Bank.
   (a) Central Government
   (b) RBI
   (c) Director of Enforcement
   (d) Minister of External Affairs

ANSWER

1	2	3	4	5	6	7	8	9	10
(d)	(c)	(d)	(a)	(d)	(d)	(c)	(b)	(c)	(a)

11	12	13	14	15
(d)	(b)	(a)	(b)	(b)

TRANSFER OF PROPERTY ACT, 1882

BACKGROUND

Before the Transfer of Property Act came into existence in 1882, the transfers of immovable properties in India were governed by the principles of English law and equity. In the absence of any specific statutory provisions the courts had to fall back upon English law on real properties, sometimes forcing the courts to decide the disputes according to their own notions of justice and fair play, resulting in confused and conflicting case laws. To remedy these confusions and conflicts a Law Commission was appointed in England to prepare a Code of Substantive Law of Transfer of Properties in India. A draft Bill was prepared by this commission and was sent to India by Secretary of State for India. The Bill was introduced in the Legislative Council in 1877. The Bill was then referred to a select Committee and it was also sent to the Local governments for their comments. The Bill was redrafted on many points and referred to a third Law Commission.

INTRODUCTION

This Act may be called the Transfer of Property Act, 1882. It had come into force on the first day of July, 1882. It was amended in 2002. The amended act may be called the Transfer to Property (Amendment) Act, 2002. It is applicable all over India.

Sale of Immovable Property (Section 53)

Sale is a transfer of ownership in exchange for a price paid or promised or part-paid and part-promised. The sale of tangible immovable property for a consideration exceeding ₹ 100/- can be made only by a registered instrument. Delivery of tangible immovable property takes place when the seller places the buyer (or such person as directed by the buyer) in possession of the property.

"Transfer of Property" defined (Section 5)

In the following sections transfer of property means an Act by which a living person conveys property, in present or in future, to one or more other living persons, or to himself, [or to himself] and one or more other living persons; and to transfer property is to perform such Act.

What may be Transferred (Section 6)

Property of any kind may be transferred, except as otherwise provided by this Act or by any other law for the time being in force—

(a) The chance of an heir-apparent succeeding to an estate, the chance of a relation obtaining a legacy on the death of a kinsman, or any other mere possibility of a like nature, cannot be transferred;

(b) A mere right of re-entry for breach of a condition subsequent cannot be transferred to anyone except the owner of the property affected thereby.

Conditional Transfer (Section 25)

An interest created on a transfer of property and dependent upon a condition fails if the fulfilment of the condition is impossible, or is forbidden by law, or is of such a nature that, if permitted, it would defeat the provisions of any law, or is fraudulent, or involves or implies injury to the person or property of another, or the court regards it as immoral or opposed to public policy. For example A gives ₹ 500 to B on condition that he shall marry A's daughter C. At the date of the transfer C was dead. The transfer is void.

Transfer by Ostensible Owner (Section 41)

Where, with the consent, express or implied, of the persons interested in immovable property, a person is the ostensible owner of such property and transfers the same for consideration, the transfer shall not be voidable on the ground that the transferor was not authorised to make it. The transferee, after taking reasonable care to ascertain that the transferor had power to make the transfer, has acted in good faith.

Different types of Mortgage are as under:

Types of mortgage defined in Transfer of Property Act 1882 Section 58(b) to 58(g).

1. **Simple Mortgage: Sec. 58(b):** Where, without delivering possession of the mortgaged property, the mortgagor binds himself personally to pay the mortgage money, and agrees, expressly or impliedly, that, in the event of his failing to pay according to his contract, the mortgagee shall have a right to cause the mortgaged property to be sold and the proceeds of sale to be applied, so far as may be necessary, in payment of the mortgage-money, the transaction is called a simple mortgage and the mortgagee a simple mortgagee. Features of Simple mortgage are:

   ○ Mortgagee has no power to sell the property without court intervention.

   ○ Mortgagee has no right to get any payments out of the rents and produce of the mortgage property.

   ○ Mortgagee is not put in possession of the property.

   ○ Registration of the mortgage is compulsory if the principle amount secured is ₹ 100 and above.

   ○ Mortgagor is personally liable also.

2. **Mortgage by Conditional Sale: Sec. 58(c):** In this, the mortgagor ostensibly sells the mortgaged property on conditions that on default of payment of the mortgage money, the sale shall become absolute or on such payment being made, the sale shall become *void* or the buyer shall transfer the property to the seller. Features are as under:

   ○ Sale is ostensible and not real.

   ○ If money remains unpaid as per agreement, the sale becomes absolute. The mortgagee by applying to court can get decree in his favour

where after the mortgagor loses the right of redemption.

○ Mortgagee can sue for foreclosure.

○ No personal liability for repayment of the loan.

3. **Usufructuray Mortgage: Sec. 58(d):** Where the mortgagor delivers possession or expressly or by implication binds himself to deliver possession of the mortgaged property to the mortgagee, and authorizes him to retain such possession until payment of the mortgage-money, and to receive the rents and profits accruing from the property or any part of such rents and profits and to appropriate the same in lieu of interest, or in payment of the mortgage-money, or partly in lieu of interest or partly in payment of the mortgage money, the transaction is called an usufructuary mortgage and the mortgage an usufructuary mortgagee. Features are as under:

   ○ Mortgagee in actual legal possession of the property, till dues are repaid.

   ○ Mortgagee has the right to receive rents and profits accruing from the property.

   ○ No personal liability of the mortgager.

   ○ No time limit specified.

   ○ Sale in not allowed.

4. **English Mortgage. Sec. 58(e):** Where the mortgagor binds himself to repay the mortgage-money on a certain date, and transfers the mortgaged property absolutely to the mortgagee, but subject to a proviso that he will re-transfer it to the mortgagor upon payment of the mortgage-money as agreed, the transaction is called an English mortgage. Important features are:

   ○ Personal liability to pay on a specified date.

   ○ Absolute transfer of property to the mortgagee, subject to re-conveying (re-transfer) the property if the debt is repaid.

5. **Equitable Mortgage or Mortgage by Deposit of Title Deeds Sec. 58(f):** Where the mortgagor delivers (at notified places) to the mortgagee, the documents of title to immovable property with intention to create a security thereon to secure a loan. The transaction is not to be reduced to writing. In case of non-payment, the mortgagee can sue for sale but he cannot foreclose the mortgaged property. According to Section 58 (f) of Transfer of Property Act 1882, where a person delivers to a creditor or his agent documents of title to immovable property, with the intent to create a

security thereon, the transaction is called a mortgage by deposit of title deed. However the Act makes the provisions of this Section applicable only to Bombay, Calcutta, Madras and such other towns as may be notified by the State Governments by notification in the Official Gazette. Important features are:

○ Deposit can be made at Calcutta, Bombay and Madras or at places notified by State government only.

○ This territorial restriction does not affect the location of the property i.e. property can be located anywhere in India.

○ There should be deposit of title deed (preferably original) of the property with intention to secure a debt. U/s 96, the provisions which apply to a simple mortgage shall, so far as may be, apply to a mortgage by deposit of title-deeds.

6. **Anomalous Mortgage (Sec. 58g):** A mortgage which is not a simple mortgage, a mortgage by conditional sale, an usufructuary mortgage, an English mortgage or a mortgage by deposit of title deeds within the meaning of this section is called an anomalous mortgage.

Registration of Mortgage (Section 59)

Where the principal money secured is ₹ 100 or upwards, a mortgage other than a mortgage by deposit of title deeds can be effected only by a registered instrument signed by the mortgagor and attested by at least two witnesses. Where the principal money secured is less than ₹ 100, a mortgage may be effected either by a registered instrument signed and attested as aforesaid or (except in the case of a simple mortgage) by delivery of the property.

Right of Mortgagor to Redeem (Section 60)

At any time after the principal money has become due, the mortgagor has a right, on payment or tender, at a proper time and place, of the mortgage-money, to require the mortgagee:

(a) To deliver to the mortgagor the mortgage-deed and all documents relating to the mortgaged property which are in the possession or power of the mortgagee,

(b) Where the mortgagee is in possession of the mortgaged property, to deliver possession thereof to the mortgagor, and

(c) At the cost of the mortgagor either to re-transfer the mortgaged property to him or to such third person

as he may direct, or to execute and (where the mortgage has been effected by a registered instrument) to have registered an acknowledgement in writing that any right in derogation of his interest transferred to the mortgagee has been extinguished. The right conferred by this section has not been extinguished by the act of the parties or by decree of a court.

Right to Redeem Separately or Simultaneously (Section 60A)

A mortgagor who has executed two or more mortgages in favour of the same mortgagee shall, in the absence of a contract to the contrary, when the principal money of any two or more of the mortgages has become due, be entitled to redeem any one such mortgage separately, or any two or more of such mortgages together.

Obligation to Transfer to Third Party Instead of re-Transference to Mortgagor (Section 60A)

Mortgagor on payment of the debt, may require the mortgagee, instead of re-transferring the property, to assign the mortgage debt and transfer the mortgaged property to such third person as the mortgagor may direct; and the mortgagee shall be bound to assign and transfer accordingly. The provisions of this section do not apply in the case of a mortgagee who is or has been in possession.

Right to Inspection and Production of Documents (Section 60B)

A mortgagor, as long as his right of redemption subsists, shall be entitled at all reasonable times, at his request and at his own cost, and on payment of the mortgagee's cost and expenses in this behalf, to inspect and make copies or abstracts of, or extracts from, documents of title relating to the mortgaged property which are in the custody or power of the mortgagee.

Accession to Mortgaged Property (Section 63)

Where mortgaged property in possession of the mortgagee has, during the continuance of the mortgage, received any accession, the mortgagor, upon redemption shall, in the absence of a contract to the contrary, be entitled as against the mortgagee to such accession. Further, where mortgaged property in possession of the mortgagee has, during the continuance of the mortgage, been improved, the mortgagor, upon redemption, shall, in the absence of a contract to the contrary, be entitled to the improvement; and the mortgagor shall not, be liable to pay the cost thereof.

Renewal of Mortgaged Lease (Section 64)

Where mortgaged property is a lease, and the mortgagee obtains a renewal of the lease, the mortgagor, upon redemption, shall, in the absence of a contract by him to the contrary, have the benefit of the *new* lease.

Waste by Mortgagor in Possession (Section 66)

A mortgagor in possession of the mortgaged property is not liable to the mortgagee for allowing the property to deteriorate; but he must not commit any act which is destructive or permanently injurious thereto, if the security is insufficient or will be rendered insufficient by such act.

Right of Mortgagee to Foreclosure or Sale (Section 67)

In the absence of a contract to the contrary, the mortgagee has, at any time after the mortgage-money has become due to him, and before a decree has been made for the redemption of the mortgaged property, or the mortgage-money has been paid or deposited as hereinafter provided, a right to obtain from the court a decree that the mortgagor shall be absolutely debarred of his right to redeem the property, or a decree that the property be sold. A suit to obtain a decree that a mortgagor shall be absolutely debarred of his right to redeem the mortgaged property is called a suit for foreclosure.

Sale without Court Intervention (Section 69)

The Transfer of Property Act permits the mortgagee to sell the mortgaged property without the intervention of the court. Details of powers are as under:

Power of Sale when Valid:

(1) A mortgagee, or any person acting on his behalf, shall, subject to the provisions of this section have power to sell or concur in selling the mort-gaged property or any part thereof, in default of payment of the mortgage-money, without the intervention of the court, in the following cases and in no others, namely:

(a) Where the mortgage is an English mortgage, and neither the mortgagor nor the mortgagee is a Hindu, Muhammadan or Buddhist or a member of any other race, sect, tribe or class from time to time specified in this behalf by the State Government, in the Official Gazette;

(b) Where a power of sale without the intervention of the court is expressly conferred on the mortgagee by the mortgage-deed and the mortgagee is the Government;

(c) Where a power of sale without the intervention of the court is expressly conferred on the mortgagee by the mortgage-deed and the mortgaged property or any part thereof 8 was, on the date of the execution of the mortgage-deed, situated within the towns of Calcutta, Madras, Bombay, or in any other town or area which the State Government may, by notification in the Official Gazette, specify in this behalf.

(2) No such power shall be exercised unless and until—

(a) Notice in writing requiring payment of the principal money has been served on the mortgagor, or on one of several mortgagors, and default has been made in payment of the principal money, or of part thereof, for three months after such service; or

(b) Some interest under the mortgage amounting at least to five hundred rupees is in arrear and unpaid for three months after becoming due.

(3) When a sale has been made in professed exercise of such a power, the title of the purchaser shall not be impeachable on the ground that no case had arisen to authorise the sale, or that due notice was not given, or that the power was otherwise improperly or irregularly exercised; but any person indemnified by an unauthorised or improper or irregular exercise or the power shall have his remedy in damages against the person exercising the power.

(4) The money which is received by the mortgagee, arising from the sale, after discharge of prior encumbrances, if any, to which the sale is not made subject, or after payment into Court under section 57 of a sum to meet any prior encum-brance, shall, in the absence of a contract to the contrary, be held by him in trust to be applied by him, first, in payment of all costs, charges and expenses properly incurred by him as incident to the sale or any attempted sale; and, secondly, in discharge of the mortgage-money and costs and other money, if any, due under the mortgage; and the residue of the money so received shall be paid to the person entitled to the mortgaged property, or authorised to give receipts for the proceeds of the sale thereof.

Enforcement of Mortgages through Court

After the enactment of DRT Act 1993, recovery of debt due to bank and financial institution for dues ₹ 10 lakh and above only can be commenced in the DRT. For the total dues below ₹ 10 lakh, the bank has to file a civil suit for recovery of his dues by enforcement of the mortgage.

LEASES OF IMMOVABLE PROPERTY

Lease Defined (Section 105)

A lease of immovable property is a transfer of a right to enjoy such property, made for a certain time, express or implied, or in perpetuity, in consideration of a price paid or promised, or of money, a share of crops, service or any other thing of value, to be rendered periodically or on specified occasions to the transferor by the transferee, who accepts the transfer on such terms.

Lessor, Lessee, Premium and Rent Defined

The transferor is called the lessor, the transferee is called the lessee, the price is called the premium, and the money, share, service or other thing to be so rendered is called the rent.

Duration of Certain Leases in Absence of Written Contract or Local Usage (Section 106)

(1) In the absence of a contract or local law or usage to the contrary, a lease of immovable property for agricultural or manufacturing purposes shall be deemed to be a lease from year to year, terminable, on the part of either lessor or lessee, by six months' notice; and a lease of immovable property for any other purpose shall be deemed to be a lease from month to month, terminable, on the part of either lessor or lessee, by fifteen days' notice.

(2) Notwithstanding anything contained in any other law for the time being in force, the period mentioned in sub-section (1) shall commence from the date of receipt of notice.

(3) A notice under sub-section (1) shall not be deemed to be invalid merely because the period mentioned therein falls short of the period specified under that sub-section, where a suit or proceeding is filed after the expiry of the period mentioned in that sub-section.

(4) Every notice under sub-section (1) must be in writing, signed by or on behalf of the person giving it, and either be sent by post to the party who is intended to be bound by it or be tendered or delivered personally to such party, or to one of his family or servants at his residence, or (if such tender or delivery is not practicable) affixed to a conspicuous part of the property.

How are Leases Made? (Section 107)

A lease of immovable property from year to year, or for any term exceeding one year or reserving a yearly rent, can be made only by a registered instrument.

All other leases of immovable property may be made either by a registered instrument or by oral agreement accompanied by delivery of possession. Where a lease of immovable property is made by a registered instrument, such instrument or, where there are more instruments than one, each such instrument shall be executed by both the lessor and the lessee:

Provided that the State Government may from time to time, by notification in the Official Gazette, direct that leases of immovable property, other than leases from year to year, or for any term exceeding one year, or reserving a yearly rent, or any class of such leases, may be made by unregistered instrument or by oral agreement without delivery of possession.

TEST YOURSELF

1. Transfer of Property Act, 1882 was amended in:
   (a) 2001 (b) 2002
   (c) 2005 (d) 2008

2. Transfer of Property Act, 1882 is applicable to:
   (a) All the states of India
   (b) All the states of India, except the state of Jammu and Kashmir
   (c) All the states of India, except the state of Goa
   (d) All the states of India, except the Union Territories

3. Which of the following is defined under Transfer of Property Act, 1882?
   (a) Hypothecation
   (b) Pledge
   (c) Mortgage
   (d) All of the above

4. Mortgage is defined in:
   (a) Section 58(b) to 58(g) of Transfer of Property Act 1882
   (b) Section 57 of Transfer of Property Act 1882
   (c) Section 57 of Indian Contract Act
   (d) Section 58 of NI Act

5. Which of the mortgage is not required to be registered with the registrar of assurance?
   (a) English Mortgage
   (b) Equitable Mortgage
   (c) Simple Mortgage
   (d) Conditional Sale

6. In which of the mortgage, mortgagee cannot sell the property but loan can be recovered from income of the property?
(a) English Mortgage
(b) Equitable Mortgage
(c) Simple Mortgage
(d) Usufructuary Mortgage

7. For creation of equitable mortgage, which is the correct statement?
(a) An instrument in writing is necessary
(b) The mortgager will not sign any documents nor submit any memo in writing at the time of creation of mortgage
(c) Mortgage will be registered registrar of assurance
(d) Mortgage can be created at any place in India

8. In which of the mortgage, ownership transfers to the mortgagee?
(a) English Mortgage
(b) Equitable Mortgage
(c) Simple Mortgage
(d) Usufructuary Mortgage

9. In which of the mortgage, mortgager creates the mortgage by oral assent at any notified place in India in favour of the mortgagee?
(a) English Mortgage

(b) Equitable Mortgage
(c) Simple Mortgage
(d) Usufructuary Mortgage

10. Under Transfer of Property Act, in which type of the mortgage the mortgagee is authorised to receive rent and profits arising from the property?
(a) English Mortgage
(b) Equitable Mortgage
(c) Simple Mortgage
(d) Usufructuary Mortgage

11. In which type of the mortgage the mortgagor transfers the property absolutely to the mortgagee with condition of retransfer to mortgagor upon repayment of the mortgage money?
(a) English Mortgage
(b) Equitable Mortgage
(c) Simple Mortgage
(d) Usufructuary Mortgage

12. The power of sale without court intervention is available in case of:
(a) English Mortgage
(b) Equitable Mortgage
(c) Simple Mortgage
(d) Usufructuary Mortgage

ANSWER

1	2	3	4	5	6	7	8	9	10
(b)	(a)	(c)	(a)	(b)	(d)	(b)	(a)	(b)	(d)

11	12
(a)	(a)

CHAPTER 36

THE RIGHT TO INFORMATION ACT, 2005

OBJECTIVE

The basic object of the Right to Information Act is to empower the citizens, to promote transparency and accountability in the working of the Government, and public authority. The act helps to mitigate the corruption, and to enhance people's participation in democratic process, so that our democracy work for the people in a real sense. The act equipped the citizens to keep necessary vigil on the instruments of governance and make the government more accountable to the governed. Implication of the Act is a big step towards making the citizens informed about the activities of the Government.

INTRODUCTION

This law was passed by Parliament on 15 June 2005 and came into force on 12 October 2005. The Act covers the whole of India except Jammu and Kashmir, where J&K Right to Information Act 2009 is in force. This law is very comprehensive and covers almost all matters of governance. This Law has a wide reach, being applicable to Government at all levels—Union, State and Local as well as to the recipients of substantial government funds.

What is Information?

Information is any material in any form. It includes records, documents, memos, e-mails, opinions, advices, press releases, circulars, orders, logbooks, contracts, reports, papers, samples, models, data material held in any electronic form. It also includes information relating to any private body which can be accessed by the public authority under any law for the time being in force.

Who is a Public Authority?

a) A "public authority" is any authority or body or institution of self-government established or constituted by or under the Constitution; or by any other law made by the Parliament or a State Legislature; or by notification issued or order made by the Central Government or a State Government.

b) The bodies owned, controlled or substantially financed by the Central Government or a State Government are also public authorities.

c) A Non-Government organisation substantially financed by the Central Government or a State Government also fall within the definition of public authority. The substantial financing by the Central Government or a State Government may be direct or indirect. The Act does not define substantial financing.

d) Various courts/Information Commissions have been deciding on this issue on case to case basis, depending upon the merits of each case.

Public Information Officer

Public authorities have designated some of its officers as Public Information Officers. They are responsible to give information to a person who seeks information under the RTI Act.

Assistant Public Information Officer

These are the officers at sub-divisional level to whom a person can give his RTI application or appeal. These officers send the application or appeal to the Public Information Officer of the public authority or the concerned appellate authority. An Assistant Public Information Officer is not responsible to supply the information.

Right to Information under the Act:

- ❍ A citizen has a right to seek such information from a public authority which is held by the public authority or which is held under its control.
- ❍ A citizen has a right to inspection of a work, documents and records; taking notes, extracts or certified copies of documents or records; and taking certified samples of material held by the public authority or held under the control of the public authority.
- ❍ A citizen has a right to obtain information from a public authority in the form of diskettes, floppies, tapes, video cassettes or in any other electronic mode or through print-outs provided such information is already stored in a computer or in any other device.
- ❍ The information to the applicant should ordinarily be provided in the form in which it is sought. However, if the supply of information sought in a particular form would disproportionately divert the resources of the public authority or may cause harm to the safety or preservation of the records, supply of information in that form may be denied.
- ❍ In some cases, the applicants expect the Public Information Officer to give information in some particular proforma devised by them on the plea that they have a right to get information in the form in which it is sought. It need be noted that the provision in the Act simply means that if the information is sought in the form of photocopy, it shall be provided in the form of photocopy, or if it is sought in the form of a floppy or in any other electronic mode, it shall be provided in that form, subject to the conditions given in the Act. It does not mean that the PIO shall re-shape the information.

Supply of Information to Associations etc.

The Act gives the right to information only to the citizens of India. It does not make provision for giving information to Corporations, Associations, Companies etc. which are legal entities/persons, but not citizens. However, if an application is made by an employee or office-bearer of any Corporation, Association, Company, NGO etc. indicating his name and such employee/office bearer is a citizen of India, information may be supplied to him/her.

Fee for Seeking Information

A citizen who desires to seek some information from a public authority is required to send, along with the application, a demand draft or a bankers cheque or an Indian Postal Order of ₹ 10/- (Rupees ten), payable to the Accounts Officer of the public authority as fee prescribed for seeking information. The payment of fee can also be made by way of cash to the public authority or to the Assistant Public Information Officer, against a proper receipt. The payment of fee to the Central Ministries/departments can also be made online through internet banking of State Bank of India or through Master/ Visa Debit/credit cards.

The applicant may also be required to pay further fee towards the cost of providing the information, details of which shall be intimated to the applicant by the PIO as prescribed by the Right to Information Rules, 2012. Rates of fee as prescribed in the Rules are given below:

(a) Rupees two (₹ 2/-) for each page (in A-3 or smaller size paper);

(b) Actual cost or price of a photocopy in larger size paper;

(c) Actual cost or price for samples or models;

(d) Rupees fifty (₹ 50/-) per diskette or floppy; and

(e) Price fixed for a publication or rupees two per page of photocopy for extracts from the publication.

A citizen has a right to inspect the records of a public authority. For inspection of records, the public authority shall charge no fee for the first hour. But a fee of rupees five (₹ 5/-) for each subsequent hour (or fraction thereof) shall be charged.

If the applicant belongs to the below poverty line (BPL) category, he is not required to pay any fee. However, he should submit a proof in support of his claim as belonging to the below poverty line category.

Format of Application

There is no prescribed format of application for seeking information. The application can be made on plain paper. The applicant should mention the address at which the information is required to be sent. The information seeker is not required to give reasons for seeking information.

Information Exempted From Disclosure

The Act lists certain categories of information that is exempted from disclosure. These include:

a) Information, disclosure of which would prejudicially affect the sovereignty and integrity of India, the security, strategic, scientific or economic interest of the State, relation with foreign state or lead to incitement of an offence.

b) information which has been expressly forbidden to be published by any court of law or tribunal or the disclosure of which may constitute contempt of court.

c) Information, the disclosure of which would cause a breach of privilege of Parliament or State Legislature; or

d) Cabinet papers including records of deliberations of the Council of Ministers, secretaries and other officers subject to the conditions given in provision to clause (i) of sub-section (1) of Section 8 of the Act.

e) Information, the disclosure of which would endanger the life or physical safety of any person or identify the source of information or assistance given in confidence for law enforcement or security purposes.

f) Information which would impede the process of investigation or apprehension or prosecution of offenders.

g) Information received in confidence from foreign government.

In respect of item listed at (a), (c), and (d), the information if relating to any event which occurred or happened 20 years before the date on which the request is made shall be provided to the person making a request.

Record Retention Schedule and the Act

The Act does not require the public authorities to retain records for indefinite period. The records need to be retained as per the record retention schedule applicable to the concerned public authority.

Assistance Available to the Applicant

If a person is unable to make a request in writing, he may seek the help of the Public Information Officer to write his application and the Public Information Officer should render him reasonable assistance.

Time Period for Supply of Information

In normal course, information to an applicant shall be supplied within 30 days from the receipt of application by the public authority. If information sought concerns the life or liberty of a person, it shall be supplied within 48 hours.

Appeals

If an applicant is not supplied information within the prescribed time of thirty days or 48 hours, as the case may be, or is not satisfied with the information furnished to him, he may prefer an appeal to the first appellate authority who is an officer senior in rank to the Public Information Officer. Such an appeal should be filed within a period of 30 days from the date on which the limit of 30 days of supply of information is expired or from the date on which the information or decision of the Public Information Officer is received. The appellate authority of the public authority shall dispose of the appeal within a period of 30 days or in exceptional cases within 45 days of the receipt of the appeal.

If the first appellate authority fails to pass an order on the appeal within the prescribed period or if the appellant is not satisfied with the order of the first appellate authority, he may prefer a second appeal with the Information Commission within 90 days from the date on which the decision should have been made by the first appellate authority or was actually received by the appellant.

Complaints

If any person is unable to submit a request to a Public Information Officer either by reason that such an officer has not been appointed by the concerned public authority; or the Assistant Public Information Officer has refused to accept his or her application or appeal for forwarding the same to the Public Information Officer or the appellate authority, as the case may be; or he has been refused access to any information requested by him under the RTI Act; or he has not been given a response to a request for information within the time limit specified in the Act; or he has been required to pay an amount of fee which he considers unreasonable; or he believes that he has been given incomplete, misleading or false information, he can make a complaint to the Information Commission.

Imposition of Penalty

An applicant under the act has a right to appeal to the Information Commission and also to make complaint to the commission. The Information Commission has power to impose a penalty of ₹ 250/- each day information is furnished subject to the condition that the total amount of such penalty shall not exceed ₹ 25000/-. Where the Information Commission at the time of deciding any complaint or appeal is of the opinion that the Public Information Officer has without any reasonable cause, refused to receive an application for information or has not furnished information within the time specified or malafidely denied the request for information or knowingly given incorrect, incomplete or misleading information or destroyed information, it shall impose a penalty.

The Public Information Officer shall, however, be given a reasonable opportunity of being heard before any penalty is imposed on him.

Third Party Information

Third party in relation to the Act means a person other than the citizen making a request for information. The definition of third party includes a public authority other than the public authority to which the request has been made.

Disclosure of Third Party Information

Information including commercial confidence, trade secrets or intellectual property, the disclosure of which would harm the competitive position of a third party, is exempt from disclosure. Such information should not be disclosed unless the competent authority is satisfied that larger public interest warrants the disclosure of such information.

RTI ONLINE

Department of Personnel & Training has launched a web portal namely RTI online with URL www.rtionline.gov.in for all Central Ministries/Departments. This is a facility for the Indian citizens to file RTI applications and first appeals online to all Central Ministries/Departments. The prescribed RTI fees can also be paid online. Reply to the RTI applications and first appeals received online can also be given online by the respective PIOs/FAAs.

Compilation of OMs and notifications on RTI

Department of Personnel and Training has launched an online compilation of its office memorandums and notifications on Right to Information Act, 2005, with topic based search facility. This compilation is available on the website of the Department namely www. persmin.nic.in and is beneficial to all the stakeholders.

For Public Authorities

Public authorities are the repository of information which the citizens have a right to access under the Right to Information Act, 2005. The Act casts important obligations public authorities so as to facilitate the citizens of the country to access the information held under their control.

Maintenance and Computerisation of Records

Proper management of records is of utmost importance for effective implementation of the provisions of the Act. A public authority should, therefore, maintain all its records properly. It should ensure that the records are duly catalogued and indexed in such a manner and form that it may facilitate the right to information.

Protection for Work Done in Good Faith

Section 21 of the act provides that no suit, prosecution or other legal proceeding shall lie against any person for anything which is in good faith done or intended to be done under the act or any rule made thereunder. A Public Information Officer should, however, note that it would be his responsibility to prove that his action was in good faith.

TEST YOURSELF

1. Right to Information Act came into force on:
   - (a) 12 October, 2004
   - (b) 12 October, 2005
   - (c) 12 October, 2006
   - (d) 12 October, 2007

2. Which of the following is not true regarding Right to Information Act?
   - (a) The Act covers the whole of India except Jammu and Kashmir
   - (b) The Act covers the whole of India except Union Territories
   - (c) In the state of J&K Right to Information Act 2009 is in force
   - (d) None of the above

3. Under the Right to Information Act, a citizen of India can demand which type of Information?
   - (a) Records, documents, memos
   - (b) e-mails, press releases, circulars
   - (c) Advices, data material held in any electronic form
   - (d) All of the above

4. Which of the following is not true regarding Public authority?
   - (a) Any authority or body or institution of self-government established or constituted by or under the Constitution; or by any other law made by the Parliament or a State Legislature; or by notification issued or order made by the Central Government or a State Government.
   - (b) The bodies owned, controlled or substantially financed by the Central Government or a State Government are also public authorities.
   - (c) A Non-Government organisation substantially financed by the Central Government or a State Government also fall within the definition of public authority. The substantial financing by the Central Government or a State Government may be direct or indirect. The Act does not define substantial financing.
   - (d) None of the above

5. A citizen has a right to obtain information from a public authority in the form of ____.
   - (a) Diskettes, floppies, tapes,
   - (b) video cassettes or in any other electronic mode
   - (c) Throughprint-outs of the information
   - (d) All of the above

6. Which of the following is not true regarding application fee under Right to Information Act?
   (a) It is free for all
   (b) ₹ 10 for an application
   (c) No fee for BPL category
   (d) All of the above

7. The applicant may also be required to pay further fee towards the cost of providing the information. Which is not true?
   (a) Rupees two (₹ 2/-) for each page (in A-3 or smaller size paper)
   (b) Rupees five (₹ 5/-) for each page price of a photocopy in larger size paper
   (c) Rupees fifty (₹50/-) per diskette or floppy
   (d) None of the above

8. Under RTI Act, the applicant has right to:
   (a) Inspection of work, documents and records
   (b) Take extracts & copy of documents
   (c) Obtain information in CD/floppies
   (d) All of the above

9. Under RTI Act, who can get information from public authorities?
   (a) Any Indian resident of India
   (b) Any legal person of India
   (c) Any Indian citizen
   (d) Any person

10. Under RTI Act, each organisations will have __________ to provide this information who is to route the requests to the relevant department.
   (a) Information officer
   (b) Public information authority
   (c) Public information officer
   (d) Information authority

11. Under RTI Act, the Central Information Commission is headed by __________ to receive complaints if the PIO does not provide correct and timely information.
   (a) Chief Vigilance Commissioner
   (b) Chief Information Commissioner
   (c) President of India
   (d) Chief Justice of Supreme Court

12. In normal course, information to an applicant shall be supplied within __________ days from the receipt of application by the public authority.
   (a) 15   (b) 21
   (c) 30   (d) 45

13. Under RTI Act, if information sought concerns the life or liberty of a person, it shall be supplied within __________?
   (a) 48 hours   (b) 72 hours
   (c) 5 days   (d) 15 days

14. An applicant under the act has a right to appeal to the Information Commission and also to make complaint to the commission. The Information Commission has power to impose a penalty of __________ each day information is furnished subject to the condition that the total amount of such penalty shall not exceed ₹ 25000/-.
   (a) ₹ 100/-   (b) ₹ 200/-
   (c) ₹ 250/-   (d) ₹ 500/-

15. If an applicant is not supplied information within the prescribed time, an appeal should be filed within a period of _______ days from the date on which the limit of 30 days of supply of information is expired or from the date on which the information or decision of the Public Information Officer is received.
   (a) 15   (b) 21
   (c) 30   (d) 45

16. Appeal with CIC is supposed to be disposed of within maximum period of:
   (a) 30   (b) 45
   (c) 60   (d) 90

ANSWER

1	2	3	4	5	6	7	8	9	10
(b)	(b)	(d)	(d)	(d)	(a)	(b)	(d)	(c)	(c)

11	12	13	14	15	16
(b)	(c)	(a)	(c)	(c)	(b)

THE PREVENTION OF MONEY LAUNDERING ACT, 2002

INTRODUCTION

Banks were advised to follow certain customer identification procedure for opening of accounts and monitoring transactions of a suspicious nature for the purpose of reporting it to appropriate authority. The Prevention of Money Laundering Act (PMLA), 2002 is an Act of the Parliament of India enacted in January, 2003. The Act along with the Rules framed has come into force with effect from 1st July, 2005. PMLA (Amendment) Act, 2012 as passed by Lok Sabha on 29th November, 2012 has come into force from 15th February 2013. PMLA 2002 extends to the whole of India.

The Prevention of Money Laundering (Maintenance of Records) Rules 2005 have been amended vide Gazette Notification dated 1st June 2017 by Ministry of Finance.

OBJECTIVE

The objectives of the Act are as under:

a) To prevent banks from being used, intentionally or unintentionally, by criminals for Money Laundering or terrorist financing activities.

b) To enable banks to know/understand their customer and their financial dealings better.

c) To put in place a proper control mechanism for detecting and reporting suspicious transactions in accordance with the statutory and regulatory provisions.

d) To enhance method for fraud Prevention.

e) To ensure compliance with guidelines issued by the regulators including FIU-IND & RBI.

Obligation under PML Act 2002

PML Act 2002 places certain obligations on every banking company, financial institution and intermediary, which include:

I. Appointment of Principal Officers. The Principal Officer shall be responsible for ensuring compliance, monitoring transactions, and sharing and reporting information as required under the law/regulations. The name, designation and address of the Principal Officer shall be communicated to the FIU-IND.

II. A "Designated Director" shall be nominated by the Board. The name, designation and address of the Designated Director shall be communicated to the FIU-IND.

III. Maintaining record of prescribed transactions.

IV. Furnishing information of transaction to the specified authority.

V. Verifying & maintaining record of the identity of its clients.

VI. Preserving records for 5 years from the date of each transaction between bank & clients or for 5 years after business relationship ended.

Definition of Money Laundering

Sec.3 of PML Act defines 'money laundering' as: "whosoever directly or indirectly attempts to indulge or knowingly assists or knowingly is a party or is actually involved in any process or activity connected with the proceeds of crime and projecting it as untainted property shall be guilty of the offence of money-laundering". In India AML activities are monitored by FIU-IND as per PML Act. Any act or attempted act to conceal or disguise the identity of illegally obtained proceeds so that they appear to have originated from legitimate sources.

In other words, it is the process used by criminals through which they make "dirty" money appear "clean."

Punishment for Money Laundering

Punishment for non-adherence of the Act would be rigorous imprisonment for not less than 3 years but up to 7 years. If in case of offences done under Narcotic Drugs and Psychotropic Substance Act 1985 the maximum punishment may extend to 10 years.

Stages of Money Laundering

The money laundering cycle can be broken down into three distinct stages; however, it is important to remember that money laundering is a single process. The stages of money laundering include the:

○ **Placement:** Entry of funds in to the system at this stage, the launderer inserts the dirty money into a legitimate financial institution.

○ **Layering:** Making a series of transactions to distance fund from the point of entry. Layering involves sending the money through various financial transactions to change its form and make it difficult to know.

○ **Integration**: At the integration stage, the money re-enters the mainstream economy in legitimate-looking form. It appears to come from a legal transaction.

Other ways of Money Laundering

Various ways of money laundering are as under:

○ **Smurfing:** In banks, large cash transactions require reporting. To avoid such reporting, large deposits are divided into multiple smaller transactions. After deposit, the smurfer purchases drafts at other places which is deposited into other accounts.

○ **Front Companies:** Front companies are used to place and layer illicit proceeds. A front company can be used to protect a parent company, thus concealing illegal activities.

○ **Shell Company:** Shell companies are anonymous corporate structures that provide for anonymous ownership. These companies have various combination of nominee directors and ownership of stock by bearer shares. They do not have commercial manufacturing business.

○ **Black Salaries:** A company may have unregistered employees without a written contract and pay them cash salaries. Dirty money might be used to pay them.

Maintenance of KYC Documents and Preservation Period

PML Act and Rules cast certain obligations on the banks/FIs in regard to maintenance, preservation and reporting of customer account information. Banks/FIs are, therefore, advised to go through the provisions of the PMLA, 2002 and the Rules notified there under and take all steps considered necessary to ensure compliance with the requirements of the Act.

Maintenance of Records of Transactions

Banks/FIs should introduce a system of maintaining proper record of transactions prescribed under Rule 3 of Prevention of Money Laundering (Maintenance of Records) Rules, 2005 (PML Rules, 2005), as mentioned below:

(i) All cash transactions of the value of more than Rupees Ten Lakhs or its equivalent in foreign currency.

(ii) Series of all cash transactions individually valued below Rupees Ten Lakhs, or its equivalent in foreign currency which are that have taken place within a month and the monthly aggregate which exceeds rupees ten lakhs or its equivalent in foreign currency. It is clarified that for determining 'integrally connected transactions' 'all accounts of the same customer' should be taken into account.

(iii) All transactions involving receipts by non-profit organisations of value more than rupees ten lakhs or its equivalent in foreign currency [Ref: Government of India Notification dated November 12, 2009- Rule 3, sub-rule (1) clause (BA) of PML Rules].

(iv) All cash transactions, where forged or counterfeit currency notes or bank notes have been used as genuine and where any forgery of a valuable security or a document has taken place facilitating the transaction.

(v) All suspicious transactions, whether or not in cash, made as mentioned in the Rules.

Banks/FIs are required to maintain all necessary information in respect of transactions prescribed under PML Rule 3 so as to permit reconstruction of individual transaction, including the following information:

(i) The nature of the transactions;

(ii) The amount of the transaction and the currency in which it was denominated;

(iii) The date on which the transaction was conducted; and

(iv) The parties to the transaction.

PRESERVATION OF RECORDS

Banks/FIs should take appropriate steps to evolve a system for proper maintenance and preservation of account information in a manner that allows data to be retrieved easily and quickly whenever required or when requested by the competent authorities :

(i) In terms of PML Amendment Act 2012, banks/FIs should maintain for at least five years from the date of transaction between the bank/FI and the client, all necessary records of transactions, both domestic or international, which will permit reconstruction of individual transactions (including the amounts and types of currency involved, if any) so as to provide, if necessary, evidence for prosecution of persons involved in criminal activity.

(ii) Banks/FIs should ensure that records pertaining to the identification of the customers and their address (e.g. copies of documents like passports, identity cards, driving licenses, PAN card, utility bills, etc.) obtained while opening the account and during the course of business relationship, are properly preserved for at least five years after the business relationship is ended as required under Rule 10 of the Rules *ibid*. The identification of records and transaction data should be made available to the competent authorities upon request.

(iii) Banks/FIs may maintain records of the identity of their clients, and records in respect of transactions referred to in Rule 3 in hard or soft format.

(iv) As mentioned in this Master Circular, banks/FIs are required to pay special attention to all complex, unusual large transactions and all unusual patterns of transactions, which have no apparent economic or visible lawful purpose. It is further clarified that the background including all documents/office records/memorandums pertaining to such transactions and purpose thereof should, as far as possible, be examined and the findings at branch as well as Principal Officer Level should be properly recorded. Such records and related documents should be made available to help auditors to scrutinize the transactions and also to Reserve Bank/other relevant authorities. These records are required to be preserved for five years as is required under PMLA, 2002.

Customer Identification Procedure (CIP)

Customer identification means undertaking client due diligence measures while commencing an account-based relationship including identifying and verifying the customer and the beneficial owner on the basis of one of the Officially Valid Documents (OVDs). Banks/FIs need to obtain sufficient information to establish, to their satisfaction, the identity of each new customer, whether regular or occasional, and the purpose of the intended nature of the banking relationship.

"Officially Valid Document" (OVD)

The officially valid documents will serve the purpose for both identification of customer and also the address proof of customer.

'Officially Valid Document' (OVD) definition amended vide Gazette Notification dated 1st June 2017 by Ministry of Finance – the Permanent Account Number (PAN) Card; and the letter issued by the Unique Identification Authority of India have been removed from this definition. Now, these five documents are considered as officially valid documents:

1. Passport (within validity)

2. Driving License (within validity)

3. Voter's Identity Card

4. Job Card issued by NREGA

5. The letter issued by the National Population Register containing details of name, address or any other document as notified by the Central Government in consultation with the Regulator.

The Government has since amended the Prevention of Money Laundering (Maintenance of Records) Rules, 2005 providing additional relaxations for the purpose of proof of address in addition to the relaxations in proof of identity under 'simplified measures' as contained in paragraph 2(d) of PML Rules. Thus, for the limited purpose of proof of address the following additional documents are deemed to be OVDs under 'simplified measures' for 'Low Risk Customer'.

1. Utility bill which is not more than two months old of any service provider (electricity, telephone, post-paid mobile phone, piped gas, water bill);

2. Property or Municipal Tax receipt;

3. Bank account or Post Office savings bank account statement;

4. Pension or family pension payment orders (PPOs) issued to retired employees by Government Departments or Public Sector Undertakings, if they contain the address;

5. Letter of allotment of accommodation from employer issued by State or Central Government departments, statutory or regulatory bodies, and public sector undertakings, scheduled commercial banks, financial institutions and listed companies. Similarly, leave and license agreements with such employers allotting official accommodation; and

6. Documents issued by Government departments of foreign jurisdictions and letters issued by Foreign Embassy or Mission in India.

E-KYC

In order to reduce the risk of identity fraud, document forgery & paperless KYC verification, Unique Identification Authority of India (UIDAI) has launched its E-KYC service. The E-KYC service is accepted as a valid process for KYC verification under PMLA. While using E-KYC service of UIDAI, the individual user has to authorize the UIDAI, by explicit consent, to release his/her identity/ address through biometric authentication to the bank branch. The UIDAI then release the data name, age, gender, and photograph of the individual to bank. E-Aadhaar downloaded from UIDAI website may be accepted as an officially valid document.

CUSTOMER DUE DILIGENCE (CDD)

Customer Due Diligence (CDD) means identifying and verifying the customer and the beneficial owner using 'Officially Valid Documents' as a 'proof of identity' and a 'proof of address'.

Documents needed for Verification of Various types of Clients:

1. **Individuals:** Where the client is an individual, who is eligible to be enrolled for an Aadhaar number, he shall for the purpose of sub-rule (1) submit to the reporting entity—

   (a) The Aadhaar number issued by the Unique Identification Authority of India; and

   (b) The Permanent Account Number or Form No. 60 as defined in Income-tax Rules, 1962,

   And such other documents including in respect of the nature of business and financial status of the client as may be required by the reporting entity:

   Provided that where an Aadhaar number has not been assigned to a client, the client shall furnish proof of application of enrolment for Aadhaar and in case the Permanent Account Number is not submitted, one certified copy of an 'officially valid document' shall be submitted.

   a) One certified copy of an 'officially valid document' containing of his identity & address

   b) One recent photograph

   Notwithstanding anything contained in sub-rules, an individual who desires to open a small account in a banking company may be allowed to open such an account on production of a self-attested photograph and affixation of signature or thumb print, as the case may be, on the form for opening the account:

   Provided that the designated officer of the banking company, while opening the small account, certifies under his signature that the person opening the account has affixed his signature or thump print, as the case may be, in his presence.

2. **Company:**
   a) Certificate of incorporation;
   b) Memorandum and Articles of Association;
   c) A resolution from the Board of Directors
   d) Aadhaar numbers; and
   e) Permanent Account Numbers or Form 60 as defined in the Income-tax Rules, 1962.

3. **Partnership Firm:**
   a) Registration certificate;
   b) Partnership deed; and
   c) Aadhaar numbers; and
   d) Permanent Account Numbers or Form 60 as defined in the Income-tax Rules, 1962.

4. **Trust Documents:**
   a) Registration certificate;
   b) Trust deed;
   c) Aadhaar numbers; and
   d) Permanent Account Numbers or Form 60 as defined in the Income-tax Rules, 1962.

5. **Association of Persons:**
   a) Resolution of the managing body of such association or body of individuals;
   b) Power of attorney granted to him to transact on its behalf;
   c) Aadhaar numbers; and
   d) Permanent Account Numbers or Form 60 as defined in the Income-tax Rules, 1962.

   Information as may be required by the banking company or the financial institution or the intermediary to collectively establish the legal existence of such an association or body of individuals.

TEST YOURSELF

1. The Prevention of Money Laundering Act 2002 along with the Rules framed has come into force with effect from ___________.
   (a) 1st Jan, 2003
   (b) 1st July, 2004
   (c) 1st July, 2005
   (d) 1st Jan, 2005

2. The Prevention of Money Laundering Act 2002 extends to the ________.
   (a) Whole of India
   (b) Whole of India except Union Territories
   (c) Whole of India except Jammu and Kashmir
   (d) Whole of India except state of Goa

3. The objective of the PMLA 2002 is:
   (a) To prevent banks from being used, intentionally or unintentionally, by criminals for Money Laundering or terrorist financing activities.
   (b) To enable banks to know/understand their customer and their financial dealings better.
   (c) To enhance method for Fraud Prevention and to ensure compliance with guidelines issued by the regulators including FIU-IND & RBI.
   (d) All of the above

4. PML Act 2002 places certain obligation on every banking company, financial institution and inter-mediary, which include:
   (a) Appointment of Principal Officers. The Principal Officer shall be responsible for ensuring compliance, monitoring transactions, and sharing and reporting information as required under the law/regulations. The name, designation and address of the Principal Officer shall be communicated to the FIU-IND.
   (b) A "Designated Director" shall be nominated by the Board. The name, designation and address of the Designated Director shall be comm-unicated to the FIU-IND. Maintaining record of prescribed transactions.
   (c) Verifying & maintaining record of the identity of its clients.
   (d) All of the above

5. As per PML Act 2002, preserving records for __________ from the date of each transaction between bank & clients or for 5 years after business relationship ended, is obligator.
   (a) 3 years   (b) 5 years
   (c) 8 years   (d) 10 years

6. Which of the following is **not** correct statement as per PMLA 2002?
   (a) Sec.3 of PML Act defines 'money laundering.'
   (b) In India Money Laundering activities are moni-tored by FIU-IND.
   (c) Money Laundering is the process used by criminals through which they make "clean" money appear "dirty."
   (d) Money Laundering is defined as 'Any act or attempted act to conceal or disguise the identity of illegally obtained proceeds so that they appear to have originated from legitimate sources.'

7. Punishment for non-adherence of the Act would be rigorous imprisonment for not less than ________ years but up to ______ years. If in case of offences done under Narcotic Drugs and Psychotropic Substance Act 1985 the maximum punishment may extend to 10 years.
   (a) 3, 5   (b) 3, 7
   (c) 5, 7   (d) 5, 10

8. Punishment for non-adherence of the Act would be rigorous imprisonment, if in case of offences done under Narcotic Drugs and Psychotropic Substance Act 1985 the maximum punishment may extend to __________.
   (a) 10 years   (b) 15 years
   (c) 12 years   (d) 8 years

9. The money laundering cycle can be broken down into three distinct stages; the correct stages of money laundering are the:
   (a) Placement: Integration : Layering
   (b) Layering: Placement : Integration:
   (c) Placement: Layering : Integration
   (d) Integration: Layering : Placement

10. At the ________ stage, the money re-enters the mainstream economy in legitimate-looking form. It appears to come from a legal transaction.
    (a) Placement
    (b) Integration
    (c) Layering
    (d) Smurfing

11. In banks, large cash transactions require reporting. To avoid such reporting, large deposits are divided into multiple smaller transactions. This process of money laundering is called:
    (a) Placement   (b) Integration
    (c) Layering   (d) Smurfing

12. All cash transactions of the value of more than __________ or its equivalent in foreign currency are covered by the Act.
(a) 5 lac
(b) 10 lac
(c) 20 lac
(d) 50 lac

13. 'Officially Valid Document' (OVD) definition amended vide Gazette Notification dated 1st June 2017 by Ministry of Finance–the ______; and the letter issued by the ______ have been removed from this definition.
(a) Permanent Account Number (PAN) Card, Unique Identification Authority of India (Aadhaar)
(b) Driving license, Passport
(c) Voter id card, Ration card
(d) PAN card, Passport

14. Which of the documents required compulsorily for opening of a Partnership Firm account?
(a) Registration certificate
(b) Partnership deed
(c) Aadhaar numbers; and Permanent Account Numbers or Form 60
(d) All of the above

15. Banks/FIs should introduce a system of maintaining proper record of transactions prescribed under Rule 3 of PML Rules, 2005. Those records are:
(a) All cash transactions of the value of more than Rupees Ten Lakhs or its equivalent in foreign currency; and Series of all cash transactions individually valued below Rupees Ten Lakhs, or its equivalent in foreign currency which have taken place within a month and the monthly aggregate which exceeds rupees ten lakhs or its equivalent in foreign currency.
(b) All transactions involving receipts by non-profit organisations of value more than rupees ten lakhs or its equivalent in foreign currency.
(c) All cash transactions, where forged or counterfeit currency notes or bank notes have been used as genuine and where any forgery of a valuable security or a document has taken place facilitating the transaction.
(d) All of the above

ANSWER

1	2	3	4	5	6	7	8	9	10
(c)	(a)	(d)	(d)	(b)	(c)	(b)	(a)	(c)	(b)

11	12	13	14	15
(d)	(b)	(a)	(d)	(d)

INFORMATION TECHNOLOGY ACT, 2000

BACKGROUND

The General Assembly of the United Nations passed a resolution in 1997 adopting the Model Law on Electronic Commerce adopted by the United Nations Commission on International Trade Law. The said resolution recommends inter alia that all States give favourable consideration to the said Model Law when they enact or revise their laws, in view of the need for uniformity of the law applicable to alternatives to paper-cased methods of communication and storage of information. Therefore, it is considered necessary to give effect to the said resolution and to promote efficient delivery of Government services by means of reliable electronic records.

INTRODUCTION

An Act to provide legal recognition for transactions carried out by means of electronic data interchange and other means of electronic communication, commonly referred to as "electronic commerce", which involve the use of alternatives to paper-based methods of communication and storage of information, to facilitate electronic filing of documents with the Government agencies and further to amend the Indian Penal Code, the Indian Evidence Act, 1872, the Banker's Books Evidence Act, 1891 and the Reserve Bank of India Act, 1934 and for matters connected therewith or incidental thereto.

The Act was passed by Parliament in May 2000. The Act aims to provide the legal infrastructure for e-commerce in India. It was amended with some modification in 2008. It shall extend to the whole of India and, it applies also to any offence or contravention thereunder committed outside India by any person.

Definitions

In this Act, unless the context otherwise requires:

1. **"Access"** with its grammatical variations and cognate expressions means gaining entry into, instructing or communicating with the logical, arithmetical, or memory function resources of a computer, computer system or computer network.

2. **"Addressee"** means a person who is intended by the originator to receive the electronic record but does not include any intermediary.

3. **"Adjudicating Officer"** means an adjudicating officer appointed under subsection (1) of section 46.

4. **"Affixing Digital Signature"** with its grammatical variations and cognate expressions means adoption of any methodology or procedure by a person for the purpose of authenticating an electronic record by means of digital signature.

5. **"Appropriate Government"** means as respects any matter,
   1) enumerated in List-II of the Seventh Schedule to the Constitution;
   2) relating to any State Law enacted under List-III of the Seventh Schedule to the Constitution, the State Government and in any other case, the Central Government.

6. **"Asymmetric Crypto System"** means a system of a secure key pair consisting of a private key for creating a digital signature and a public key to verify the digital signature.

7. **"Certifying Authority"** means a person who has been granted a licence to issue a digital signature Certificate under section 24.

8. **"Certification Practice Statement"** means a statement issued by a Certifying Authority to specify the practices that the Certifying Authority employs in issuing Digital Signature Certificates.

9. **"Computer"** means any electronic magnetic, optical or other high-speed data processing device or system which performs logical, arithmetic, and memory functions by manipulations of electronic, magnetic or optical impulses, and includes all input, output, processing, storage, computers software, or communication facilities which are connected or related to the computer in a computer system or computer network.

10. **"Computer Network"** means the interconnection of one or more computers through,

    (i) The use of satellite, microwave, terrestrial line or other communication media; and

    (ii) Terminals or a complex consisting of two or more interconnected computers whether or not the interconnection is continuously maintained.

11. **"Computer Resource"** means computer, computer system, computer network, data, computer data base or software.

12. **"Computer System"** means a device or collection of devices, including input and output support devices and excluding calculators which are not programmable and capable of being used in conjunction with external files, which contain computer programmes, electronic instructions, input data and output data, that performs logic, arithmetic, data storage and retrieval, communication control and other functions.

13. **"Controller"** means the Controller of Certifying Authorities appointed under sub-section (l) of section 17.

14. **"Cyber Appellate Tribunal"** means the Cyber Regulations Appellate Tribunal established under sub section (1) of section 48.

15. **"Data"** means a representation of information, knowledge, facts, concepts or instructions which are being prepared or have been prepared in a formalized manner, and is intended to be processed, is being processed or has been processed in a computer system or computer network, and may be in any form (including computer printouts magnetic or optical storage media, punched cards, punched tapes) or stored internally in the memory of the computer.

16. **"Digital Signature"** means authentication of any electronic record by a subscriber by means of an electronic method or procedure in accordance with the provisions of section 3;

17. **"Digital Signature Certificate"** means a Digital Signature Certificate issued under subsection (4) of section 35.

18. **"Electronic Form"** with reference to information means any information generated, sent, received or stored in media, magnetic, optical, computer memory, micro film, computer generated micro fiche or similar device.

19. **"Electronic Gazette"** means the Official Gazette published in the electronic form.

20. **"Electronic Record"** means data, record or data generated, image or sound stored, received or sent in an electronic form or micro film or computer generated micro fiche.

21. **"Function"**, in relation to a computer, includes logic, control arithmetical process, deletion, storage and retrieval and communication or telecommunication from or within a computer.

22. **"Information"** includes data, text, images, sound, voice, codes, computer programmes, software and databases or micro film or computer generated micro film.

23. **"Intermediary"** with respect to any particular electronic message means any person who on behalf of another person receives, stores or transmits that message or provides any service with respect to that message.

24. **"Key Pair"**, in an asymmetric crypto system, means a private key and its mathematically related public key, which are so related that the public key can verify a digital signature created by the private key.

25. **"Law"** includes any Act of Parliament or of a State Legislature, Ordinances promulgated by the President or a Governor, as the case may be. Regulations made by the President under article 240, Bills enacted as President's Act under sub-clause (a) of clause (1) of article 357 of the Constitution and includes rules, regulations, byelaws and orders issued or made thereunder.

26. **"Licence"** means a licence granted to a Certifying Authority under section 24.

27. **"Originator"** means a person who sends, generates, stores or transmits any electronic message or causes any electronic message to be sent, generated, stored or transmitted to any other person but does not include an intermediary.

28. **"Prescribed"** means prescribed by rules made under this Act.

29. **"Private Key"** means the key of a key pair used to create a digital signature.

30. **"Public Key"** means the key of a key pair used to verify a digital signature and listed in the Digital Signature Certificate.

31. **"Secure System"** means computer hardware, software, and procedure that—

    I. Are reasonably secure from unauthorised access and misuse;

    II. Provide a reasonable level of reliability and correct operation;

    III. Are reasonably suited to performing the intended functions; and

    IV. Adhere to generally accepted security procedures.

32. **"Security Procedure"** means the security procedure prescribed under section 16 by the Central Government.

33. **"Subscriber"** means a person in whose name the Digital Signature Certificate is issued.

34. **"Verify"** in relation to a digital signature, electronic record or public key, with its grammatical variations and cognate expressions means to determine whether—

    (a) The initial electronic record was affixed with the digital signature by the use of private key corresponding to the public key of the subscriber;

    (b) The initial electronic record is retained intact or has been altered since such electronic record was so affixed with the digital signature.

Digital Signature

Any subscriber may authenticate an electronic record by affixing his digital signature. The authentication of the electronic record shall be effected by the use of asymmetric crypto system and hash function which envelop and transform the initial electronic record into another electronic record.

ELECTRONIC GOVERNANCE

Legal Recognition of Electronic Records

Where any law provides that information or any other matter shall be in writing or in the typewritten or printed form, then, such requirement shall be deemed to have been satisfied if such information or matter is—

    (a) Rendered or made available in an electronic form; and

    (b) Accessible so as to be usable for a subsequent reference.

Legal Recognition of Digital Signatures

Where any law provides that information or any other matter shall be authenticated by affixing the signature or any document shall be signed or bear the signature of any person such requirement shall be deemed to have been satisfied, if such information or matter is authenticated by means of digital signature.

REGULATION OF CERTIFYING AUTHORITIES

1. The Central Government may, appoint a Controller of Certifying Authorities and may also appoint such number of Deputy Controllers and Assistant Controllers as it deems fit.

2. The Controller may perform all or any of the following functions, namely:

    (a) Exercising supervision over the activities of the Certifying Authorities;

    (b) Certifying public keys of the Certifying Authorities;

    (c) Laying down the standards to be maintained by the Certifying Authorities;

    (d) Specifying the qualifications and experience which employees of the Certifying Authorities should possess;

    (e) Specifying the conditions subject to which the Certifying Authorities shall conduct their business;

    (f) Specifying the contents of written, printed or visual material and advertisements that may be distributed or used in respect of a Digital Signature Certificate and the Public Key;

    (g) Specifying the form and content of a Digital Signature Certificate and the key.

3. Controller may recognise any foreign Certifying Authority as a Certifying Authority for the purposes of this Act.

4. The Controller shall be the repository of all Digital Signature Certificates issued under this Act.

DIGITAL SIGNATURE CERTIFICATES

1. Any person may make an application to the Certifying Authority for the issue of a Digital Signature Certificate along with fee not exceeding twenty five thousand rupees.

2. No Digital Signature Certificate shall be granted unless the Certifying Authority is satisfied that,

(a) The applicant holds the private key corresponding to the public key to be listed in the Digital Signature Certificate;

(b) The applicant holds a private key, which is capable of creating a digital signature;

(c) The public key to be listed in the certificate can be used to verify a digital signature affixed by the private key held by the applicant.

DUTIES OF SUBSCRIBERS

1. Where any Digital Signature Certificate, the public key of which corresponds to the private key of that subscriber which is to be listed in the Digital Signature Certificate has been accepted by a subscriber, then, the subscriber shall generate the key pair by applying the security procedure.

2. Every subscriber shall exercise reasonable care to retain control of the private key corresponding to the public key listed in his Digital Signature Certificate and take all steps to prevent its disclosure to a person not authorised to affix the digital signature of the subscriber.

PENALTIES AND ADJUDICATION

Computer related Offences

As per section 66 of IT Act, if any person, dishonestly or fraudulently, does any act referred to in section 43, he shall be punishable with imprisonment for a term which may extend to three years or with fine which may extend to five lakh rupees or with both.

If any person without permission of the owner—

I. Accesses or secures access to such computer, computer system or computer network;

II. Downloads, copies or extracts any data, computer data base or information from such computer, computer system or computer network;

III. Introduces any computer contaminant or computer virus into any computer, computer system or computer network;

IV. Damages any computer, computer system, data, residing in such computer system; disrupts any computer system;

V. Disrupts or causes disruption of any computer, computer system or computer network;

VI. Denies access to any person authorised to access any computer system by any means:

He shall be liable to pay damages by way of compensation not exceeding one crore rupees to the person so affected.

The Central Government shall, appoint any officer not below the rank of a Director to the Government of India to be an adjudicating officer for holding an inquiry regarding contravention of any provision of the Act. The said adjudicating officer has been given the power of a Civil Court.

TEST YOURSELF

1. Information Technology Act was enacted in the year:
   (a) 2000
   (b) 2001
   (c) 2002
   (d) 2003

2. Which of the following is not correct in respect of digital signature?
   (a) It is authentication of an electronic record by means of electronic method or procedure
   (b) It is a pair of keys under a system known as Asymmetric Crypto System
   (c) It is a scanned copy of manual signature
   (d) None of the above

3. The term Cyber Law stands for which of the following?
   (a) The law governing cyber cafe establishments only
   (b) The law governing in-house computer activities
   (c) The law relating to various aspects of information technology
   (d) Any of the above

4. Banking records in an electronic form shall be treated ________ records under the provision of _______.
   (a) Valid, NI Act
   (b) Valid, IT Act 2000
   (c) Invalid, BR Act
   (d) Valid, IT Act 1961

5. Where an information needs to be authenticated by affixing electronic authentication, this requirement shall be deemed to have been fulfilled if authentication is by way of:
   (a) Confirmation through email
   (b) Digital signature
   (c) Confirmation in any manner
   (d) Any of the above

6. What is the minimum time period for which the electronic records are to be preserved?

(a) Till they are available in a computer system

(b) As per rules of physical records unless modified

(c) There are no need for maintenance of such records

(d) All of the above

7. Where rules are published both in paper form and electronic form, the date of publication of will be date of _____________ publication of such matter in any form.

(a) First
(b) Last
(c) Paper
(d) Electronic

8. Which of the following actions of a person can be included as part of the legal definition of computer crime?

(a) Securing access to computer or computer system

(b) Download, copy or extraction of data from a computer system

(c) Introduction of computer virus or causing denial to access to any person authorised to access the computer system

(d) All of the above

9. Which of the following actions of a person can be included as part of the legal definition of computer crime?

(a) Damage a computer system

(b) Disruption of network of computers

(c) Providing assistance to another person to get access to a computer system

(d) None of the above

10. Within the meaning of computer crime, a set of instructions that is designed to modify, destroy, record, transmit data or program residing within a computer is called:

(a) Computer Virus
(b) Computer Contaminant

(c) Computer hacking

(d) All of the above

11. Penal provision for data theft under section 66 of IT Act 2000 are:

(a) Fine up to ₹ 2 Lac and/ or imprisonment up to 3 years

(b) Fine up to ₹ 2 Lac and/ or imprisonment up to 5 years

(c) Fine up to ₹ 5 Lac and/ or imprisonment up to 3 years

(d) Fine up to ₹ 5 Lac and/ or imprisonment up to 2 years

12. Online frauds or crimes committed on or through internet network are referred to as:

(a) Internet fraud
(b) Electronic crime
(c) Cyber-crime
(d) Online crime

13. IT Act 2000 extends to:

(a) Whole India

(b) Whole India except J&K

(c) Whole India except Union Territory

(d) Whole India except state of Goa

14. For unauthorised access, virus and malicious code or denial of service, what is the penalty under section 43 of IT Act?

(a) Up to ₹ 1 lac
(b) Up to ₹ 10 lac
(c) Up to ₹ 50 lac
(d) Up to ₹ 100 lac

15. The Act was passed by Parliament in May 2000. The Act aims to provide the legal infrastructure for e-commerce in India. It was amended with some modification in _________.

(a) 2005
(b) 2008
(c) 2010
(d) 2012

ANSWER

1	2	3	4	5	6	7	8	9	10
(a)	(c)	(c)	(b)	(b)	(b)	(a)	(d)	(d)	(b)

11	12	13	14	15
(a)	(c)	(a)	(d)	(b)

MOCK TEST

Legal & Regulatory Aspects of Banking

MOCK TEST-1

1. A minor who was admitted to the benefits of partnership has become major. Within how much period, he has to decide to remain partner in the firm or not?
   (a) within 1 month of attaining majority
   (b) within 3 months of knowing that he is the partner in the firm
   (c) within 6 months of attaining majority or 6 months of knowing that he is the partner in the firm whichever is later
   (d) within 1 month of attaining majority or 3 months of knowing that he is the partner in the firm whichever is later.

2. If on a cheque words "Account Payee" is written between two parallel lines or with the name of a bank, then:
   (a) The cheque cannot be endorsed
   (b) The cheque can be endorsed
   (c) Endorsee will have better title than endorser
   (d) Endorser will have better title than endorsee

3. The Limitation period for filing case in case of dishonour of cheque due to insufficient funds is:
   (a) 1 month from the date of cause of action
   (b) 3 month from the date of cause of action
   (c) 6 month from the date of cause of action
   (d) No time limit

4. Objectives for which a company has been formed are given in:
   (a) Article of Association
   (b) Memorandum of Association
   (c) Certificate of incorporation
   (d) Board Resolution

5. Direct Impact of increase in CRR is:
   (a) Controlling Liquidity
   (b) Regulate Interest
   (c) Control Financing
   (d) Control Inflation

6. Grace Period is allowed in the case of:
   (a) Demand Bills   (b) D P Note
   (c) Usance Bills   (d) All the above

7. Banking regulation Act 1949 was enacted with the objective of:
   (a) Creating banking companies
   (b) Accepting of deposits' and leading
   (c) Regulating banking business
   (d) Regulating the companies

8. RBI functions under the general superintendence and directions of:
   (a) Central govt
   (b) Governor RBI
   (c) Central Board of Directors of RBI
   (d) All of the above

9. As per section 11 of BR Act, foreign banks are required to deposit certain percentage of their annual profit with RBI, what is the percentage?
   (a) 10   (b) 20
   (c) 25   (d) 30

10. Banking companies are permitted:
    (a) Only ordinary share
    (b) Only Equity Share
    (c) Preference share
    (d) Both (a) and (b)

11. A banking company is prohibited from entering into any commitment for granting any loans or advances to or on behalf of a director if the said director is _______ for the firm/company.
    (a) Partner   (b) Manager
    (c) Guarantor   (d) Any of the above

12. Banks have to transfer at least ___% out of ___ to a reserve fund, u/s 17(1) of BR Act.
    (a) 20%, Profits
    (b) 20%, Profits before tax
    (c) 25%, Profits before dividend
    (d) 20%, Profits before dividend

13. Non-scheduled banks have to maintain cash reserve u/s _______ of banking regulation Act at _______ % of demand and time liabilities.
    (a) 18, 5%   (b) 42, 3%
    (c) 18, 3%   (d) 24, 25%

14. If a bank intends to amalgamate with the other bank, which of the following is not correct to meet the objective:
    (a) A scheme of amalgamation would be prepared
    (b) Draft scheme to be approved by the shareholders of both the banks
    (c) Notice has to be given to majority of shareholder
    (d) Scheme has to be approved by RBI

15. Central Govt. can order amalgamation of two banking companies for which of the following:
    (a) The powers are as per Section 396 of companies Act
    (b) The powers are vested as per Section 36 of BR Act
    (c) The powers can be exercised in consultation with RBI
    (d) Both (a) and (c)

16. What is meant by the term 'moratorium' in the context of a bank:
    (a) Stopping the bank to accept fresh deposits
    (b) Stop further lending by the bank
    (c) Stop the bank to make payment to depositors and discharge other obligations
    (d) Stop the bank to do any kind of banking business

17. For opening branches by co-operative banks, the application to RBI is required to be routed through:
    (a) State Govt.   (b) Central Govt.
    (c) SLBC of the state   (d) NABARD

18. Which of the following appoints Chairman of RRB?
    (a) Reserve Bank   (b) Sponsor Bank
    (c) Central Govt.   (d) State Govt.

19. RRB may operate:
    (a) A district
    (b) Notified area
    (c) Whole state
    (d) Anywhere in India

20. Which is not correct about limited liability partner-ship (LLP)?
    (a) LLP is governed by limited liability partnership Act 2008.
    (b) Minimum 3 designated partner and no limit on maximum number of Partners.
    (c) LLP is a legal entity separate from its partner.
    (d) LLP cannot raise fund from public.

21. Which is not necessary for financing a Private Company?
    (a) Memorandum of Association
    (b) Article of Association
    (c) Certificate of commencement of business
    (d) Board resolution

22. A company is known as the __________ of another company if it has control over another company.
    (a) Holding company
    (b) Existing company
    (c) Other company
    (d) Foreign company

23. Usually short-term loans are repayable within:
    (a) 3 moths   (b) 6 moths
    (c) 12 months   (d) 36 months

24. Which is not an un-secured loan?
    (a) Bill finance   (b) Credit card
    (c) Clean Personal loan (d) Small Education loan

25. Financing against stock and book debt, banks are generally provides:
    (a) Over draft   (b) Cash credit
    (c) Term loan   (d) Bill finance

26. Right of indemnity-holder is defined in:
    (a) Section 125 of the Indian Contract Act 1872
    (b) Section 124 of the Indian Contract Act 1872
    (c) Section 124 of the NI Act 1881
    (d) Section 125 of the Companies Act 2013

27. Indemnifier's liability in a contract of indemnity is:
    (a) Primary   (b) Secondary
    (c) Subsisting   (d) None of these

28. Under deferred payment guarantee, the liability of the bank is:
    (a) Primary   (b) Secondary
    (c) As per contract term (d) All of the above

29. Claim period in a guarantee is ______ than the validity period.
    (a) Same
    (b) Longer
    (c) Shorter
    (d) Depends upon terms of guarantee

30. The letter of credit where packing or anticipatory credit is available against the LC is called:
    (a) Transferable LC   (b) Red clause LC
    (c) Back to back LC   (d) Revolving LC

31. Transferable letter of credit can be transferred:
    (a) Any number of times
    (b) only once
    (c) 2 times
    (d) As per instruction of issuer

32. When a seller undertakes to make the goods available for export, at his factory, such arrangement is called:
    (a) Ex-works   (b) FOB
    (c) CIF   (d) CFR

33. Back to back letter of credit means:
  (a) A revolving credit
  (b) Another credit behind the credit issued
  (c) Issuance of another credit on the security of the original letter of credit
  (d) LC which is backed by a tangible security

34. A bill of exchange is not supported by any documents of title of goods is called:
  (a) Demand documentary bill
  (b) Clean bill
  (c) Usance documentary bill
  (d) Incomplete bill

35. If in a bill of exchange, time of payment is not mentioned, it is:
  (a) Payable on demand   (b) Invalid bill
  (c) Incomplete bill   (d) Not negotiable

36. Noting or protesting is compulsory in case of:
  (a) Foreign bill
  (b) Inland bill
  (c) Accommodation bill
  (d) Usance bill of exchange

37. A bill is presented to drawee. What is the period during which he is to give his acceptance?
  (a) 3 days including holidays
  (b) 3 days excluding holidays
  (c) 48 hours including holidays
  (d) 48 hours excluding holidays

38. Which of the following value of LIC policy is taken while taking as a security?
  (a) Maturity value   (b) Face value
  (c) Surrender value   (d) Insured value

39. Advance against shares can be made if shares are:
  (a) In physical form
  (b) Party paid shares
  (c) Fully paid shares
  (d) All of the above

40. _________ arises in relation to transaction of sales of goods, with government and public sector undertaking.
  (a) Supply bills
  (b) Accommodation bills
  (c) Trust receipts
  (d) Inspection notes

41. Which of the mortgage is not required to be registered with the registrar of assurance?
  (a) English Mortgage
  (b) Equitable Mortgage
  (c) Simple Mortgage
  (d) Conditional sale

42. In which of the mortgage, mortgagee cannot sale the property but loan can be recovered from income of the property?
  (a) English Mortgage
  (b) Equitable Mortgage
  (c) Simple Mortgage
  (d) Usufructuary Mortgage

43. _________ is the right of a debtor to take into account a debt owing to him by a creditor, when claiming a debt due from him to the creditor.
  (a) Set-off   (b) Lien
  (c) Pledge   (d) Assignment

44. _________ is that lien which confers the right to retain that particular commodity in respect of which the particular debt arose.
  (a) Negative lien   (b) General lien
  (c) Particular lien   (d) Banker's lien

45. Bank grants a loan against the security of goods relating to a firm, which kind of charge on goods can be created?
  (a) Pledge   (b) Hypothecation
  (c) Assignment   (d) Either (a) or (b)

46. The person to whom the possession of goods is transferred is called:
  (a) Transferee   (b) Bailee
  (c) Beneficiary   (d) Bailor

47. Charge created by company shall be registered with:
  (a) Registrar of Assurance
  (b) Registrar of firms
  (c) Registrar of companies
  (d) CERSAI

48. Under Companies Act a charge includes:
  (a) Mortgage   (b) Bill of Exchange
  (c) Promissory Note   (d) Letter of Credit

49. A cheque is presented for payment, amount of cheque stated in words and figure differs. What is the proper course of action as per NI Act?
  (a) After making alteration, it can be paid
  (b) Lesser amount can be paid
  (c) Cheque cannot be paid
  (d) As per section 18, amount stated in the words can be paid

50. As per section 129 of NI Act, the paying banker will not get protection:
  (a) If banker makes payment of a cheque crossed generally, otherwise than to the banker
  (b) Crossed special, otherwise than to the banker
  (c) Either (a) or (b)
  (d) Both (a) & (b)

51. If mutilated cheque is presented for payment, what should be the action of a paying banker?
(a) Cheque must be return unpaid
(b) Cheque may be paid, when it is accidental, the banker should get the drawer's confirmation before honouring it.
(c) If it is intentional, banker should refuse payment with mark 'mutilated cheque' or 'mutilation required confirmation'
(d) Both (b) and (c) are correct

52. A cheque is in favour of a Trust. The trustee wants to deposit this cheque in his personal account. The collecting bank:
(a) Must be collected in Trust account only
(b) Need not enquire before its collection
(c) May be collected in personal account if Trustee request
(d) Should know the customer is enough

53. A current account customer of your branch deposited a cheque on 22 May 2018, dated 10 September 2017, issued by Ministry of Rural Development for collection. Find the correct statement.
(a) Its validity can be 6 months
(b) Its validity is forever till paid
(c) Cannot be collected as validity period of cheque is limited to 3 months as per RBI directive
(d) It can be collected any time

54. As a collecting banker, you receive an un-crossed cheque for collection. What should you do?
(a) You may request the customer to cross the cheque
(b) The bank may itself cross the cheque
(c) You may send un-crossed cheque if customer title is beyond any doubt
(d) Either 'a' or 'b'

55. The Presiding Officer of DRAT is called:
(a) Chairman
(b) Chairperson
(c) President
(d) Judge

56. Presiding Officer of DRT is to be appointed by notification of the Central Government for _________ or he attains the age of _________ .
(a) 5 years, 62 years
(b) 5 years, 65 years
(c) 3 years, 62 years
(d) 3 years, 65 years

57. For filing appeal at DRAT against DRT, 50% of the amount to be deposited by the appellant. Provided that the Appellate Tribunal may, reduce the amount to be deposited by such amount which shall not be less than _______ of the amount of such debt so due.
(a) 40%
(b) 25%
(c) 10%
(d) Nil

58. Any person aggrieved by order passed by DRT may appeal to DRAT within _______ of order received.
(a) 15 days
(b) 30 days
(c) 45 days
(d) 60 days

59. Where registration of a securitisation company is cancelled, what are the provision of appeal?
(a) Appeal to Company Law Board within 30 days
(b) Appeal to ROC within 45 days
(c) Appeal to Central Govt. within 30 days
(d) No appeal is available

60. When the securitisation company fails to realize the securitized assets, the qualified institutional buyers holding _______% of total value of the security receipts can force the securitisation company for a particular decision.
(a) 75
(b) 60
(c) 50
(d) 25

62. Powers available to Securitisation Company can be exercised by it as per guideline framed by _______ only.
(a) RBI
(b) SEBI
(c) RoC
(d) Central Registry

62. What is the maximum period allowed to a securitisation company for recovery of reconstructed financial assets?
(a) 2 years
(b) 3 years
(c) 4 years
(d) 5 years

63. Direction issued by RBI under the provision of SARF-AESI Act 2002 are _______ on the parties concerned and have _______ effect.
(a) Binding, Moral
(b) Compulsory, Statutory
(c) Binding, Statutory
(d) Binding, Compulsory

64. How much time is given to the borrower to make the payment of the dues under the provision of SARFAESI Act 2002, before taking possession of the assets?
(a) 60 days
(b) 50 days
(c) 45 days
(d) 30 days

65. The Banking Ombudsman may award compensation not exceeding _________ to the complainant for mental agony and harassment.
(a) ₹ 1 lac
(b) ₹ 5 lac
(c) ₹ 10 lac
(d) ₹ 20 lac

66. Appeal against the order of banking ombudsman may be filed by a bank only with the prior sanction of the __________ or any other officer of equal rank.
    (a) Chairman
    (b) MD or CEO
    (c) ED
    (d) Any of the above

67. Customer and bank have to send acceptance of the award within ________ of date of receipt of the award.
    (a) 15 days
    (b) 30 days
    (c) 60 days
    (d) 90 days

68. 'The Bankers' Books Evidence Act' was passed in the year ________. It extends to the whole of India except the State of __________.
    (a) 1891, Jammu and Kashmir
    (b) 1991, Jammu and Kashmir
    (c) 1891, Tamil Nadu
    (d) 1991, Tamil Nadu

69. Which of the following is part of banker's book under 'The Bankers' Books Evidence Act'?
    (1) Ledgers
    (2) Day books
    (3) Cash book
    (4) Account book
    (a) 1 to 4 all
    (b) 1 to 3 only
    (c) 2, 3, 4 only
    (d) 3 and 4 only

70. Award of the Lok Adalat has the status of order of:
    (a) Civil Court
    (b) High Court
    (c) Supreme Court
    (d) District Collector

71. Lok Adalats are supposed to be guided by the principal of:
    (a) Justice
    (b) Equity and fair play
    (c) Legal Principles
    (d) All of the above

72. Under the Legal Services Authorities Act, which is the correct statements?
    (a) The award (decision) made by the Lok Adalats is deemed to be a decree of a High Court
    (b) The award is final but not binding on all parties
    (c) No appeal against such an award lies before any court of law
    (d) Any of the above

73. Which is the correct statement about COPRA?
    (a) A simple written complaint in duplicate with full name and address of opposite party narrating facts of the complaint along with copies of the supporting documents required.
    (b) Prescribed Court Fee is charged.

    (c) Engaging of Lawyer is necessary.
    (d) All of the above

74. The terms 'goods' as per COPRA means which of the following:
    (a) Movable and immovable property
    (b) Actionable claim
    (c) Goods as stated in Indian Contract Act
    (d) Goods as stated in Sale of Goods Act

75. Consumer can file his complaint in which the following consumer forum?
    (a) District Forum
    (b) State Commission
    (c) National Commission
    (d) All of the above

76. Which is the correct statement about consumer forums?
    (a) Complaint can be filed at District Forum, if claim does not exceed ₹ 20 lakh.
    (b) Complaint can be filed at State Commission, if claim does not exceed ₹ 20 lakh but up to ₹ 50 lac
    (c) Complaint can be filed at National Commission, if claim exceeds ₹ 50 lakh
    (d) All of the above

77. Limitation period for right of foreclosure by a mortgage is ________ years from the date when money become due.
    (a) 3
    (b) 12
    (c) 30
    (d) No limitation period

78. In which of the following the limitation period is 3 years?
    (a) Foreclosure of a mortgage
    (b) Enforcing payments of money secured by a mortgage
    (c) For specific performance of a contract
    (d) Money secured by Demand Promissory Note

79. In which of the following the limitation period is not 3 years?
    (a) Equitable Mortgage
    (b) Demand Promissory Note
    (c) Agreement of hypothecation of movable assets
    (d) All of the above

80. A PAN is a ________ character alphanumeric number allotted by the Income Tax Deptt, to a taxpayer who is eligible to file the income tax return.
    (a) 5
    (b) 7
    (c) 9
    (d) 10

81. IT Act rule 114B has made it mandatory PAN (Form 60/61 in the absence of PAN) for the certain banking transaction.
    (a) An application for issuing Credit/Debit card;
    (b) Opening of Demat Account;
    (c) Deposit/payment of cash exceeding ₹ 50,000/- day;
    (d) All of the above

82. Originally, it had 137 Section. Five Section were added in 1988, and again five Section were added during December 2002. At present it has ___________.
    (a) 147 Sections and 17 Chapters
    (b) 149 Sections and 17 Chapters
    (c) 149 Sections and 18 Chapters
    (d) 147 Sections and 18 Chapters

83. The Negotiable Instruments Act extends to the:
    (a) Whole of India, except the state of J & K
    (b) Whole of India, except NE state
    (c) Whole of India
    (d) Whole of India, except the state of Tamil Nadu

84. According to Section 13 (a) of the Act, Negotiable Instruments means:
    (a) Promissory Note (PN),
    (b) Bill of Exchange (BOE)
    (c) Cheque
    (d) All of the above

85. Bill of exchange is defined under which section of the NI Act?
    (a) Section 4   (b) Section 5
    (c) Section 6   (d) Section 7

86. If application seeking authorisation is rejected by RBI or approval is later on invoked by RBI, the applicant approach Central Government against RBI within:
    (a) 15 days   (b) 30 days.
    (c) 60 days   (d) 90 days

87. Dishonour of EFT due to insufficiency of funds in an account, is an offence, punishable amount is:
    (a) Up to 50% of the amount of cheque
    (b) Up to 100% of the amount of cheque
    (c) Up to 200% of the amount of cheque
    (d) Up to 500% of the amount of cheque

88. As per Section 10 of Indian Contract Act 1872, all agreements are contract and a contract has following important elements:
    (a) Parties should be competent to contract
    (b) Contract should be made with free consent

(c) Consideration should be lawful, contract should be for a lawful object
(d) All of the above

89. Who among the following not legally competent to enter into a contract?
    (a) Person who has crossed the age of majority
    (b) Person of a sound mind
    (c) Person who is disqualified from entering into a contract by any law
    (d) All of the above

90. Which of the following is a type of indemnity?
    (a) Bank FD   (b) Mutual funds
    (c) NSC   (d) Insurance policy

91. Which of the following means 'consideration' for Sale of Goods Act?
    (a) Shares   (b) Lien
    (c) Delivery   (d) Price

92. When the transfer of property is to occur some specific time in future and/or is to fulfilment of any condition, this type of contract/arrangement is referred to as:
    (a) Contract of future goods
    (b) Agreement of sale
    (c) Contract of specific goods
    (d) Sale contract

93. A partner may retire from a partnership firm:
    (a) With the consent of all partners
    (b) In accordance with an express agreement by the partners
    (c) By giving notice in writing to all other partners of intention to retire
    (d) By any one of the above methods

94. As per Company Act 2013, The maximum number of partners in a partnership firm permitted is:
    (a) 10 for banking business & 20 for others
    (b) 20 for banking business & 10 for others
    (c) 100 for all business
    (d) 50 for all business

95. Minimum paid-up share capital of five lakh rupee for public company and one lakh rupee for private company or such higher paid-up share capital as may be prescribed is omitted now by:
    (a) Companies (Amendment) Act, 2015
    (b) Company Act 2013
    (c) Companies (Amendment) Act, 2016
    (d) Company Act 2015

96. Which of the following is not a feature of a joint stock company?
    (a) A company has perpetual succession

(b) A company is a separate legal entity from its shareholders

(c) A company is liquidated when majority of shareholders become insolvent

(d) None of the above

97. The process of formation of a company is called:
   (a) Incorporation
   (b) Dissolution
   (c) Creation
   (d) Liquidation

98. The term repatriation to India, as per FEMA 1999 means:
   (a) Bringing foreign exchange into India
   (b) Remitting foreign exchange outside India
   (c) Starting business in India by using foreign exchange funds
   (d) Any of the above

99. Which of the following is not true regarding application fee under Right to Information Act?
   (a) It is free for all
   (b) ₹ 10 for an application
   (c) No fee for BPL category
   (d) All of the above

100. The applicant may also be required to pay further fee towards the cost of providing the information. Which is not true?
   (a) Rupees two (₹ 2/-) for each page (in A-3 or smaller size paper);
   (b) Rupees five (₹ 5/-) for each page price of a photocopy in larger size paper;
   (c) Rupees fifty (₹ 50/-) per diskette or floppy;
   (d) None of the above

ANSWER

1	2	3	4	5	6	7	8	9	10
(c)	(a)	(a)	(b)	(a)	(c)	(c)	(c)	(a)	(d)
11	12	13	14	15	16	17	18	19	20
(d)	(d)	(c)	(c)	(d)	(c)	(d)	(b)	(b)	(b)
21	22	23	24	25	26	27	28	29	30
(a)	(a)	(c)	(a)	(b)	(a)	(a)	(a)	(b)	(b)
31	32	33	34	35	36	37	38	39	40
(b)	(a)	(c)	(b)	(a)	(a)	(d)	(c)	(c)	(a)
41	42	43	44	45	46	47	48	49	50
(b)	(d)	(a)	(c)	(d)	(b)	(a)	(a)	(d)	(d)
51	52	53	54	55	56	57	58	59	60
(d)	(a)	(c)	(d)	(b)	(a)	(b)	(c)	(c)	(a)
61	62	63	64	65	66	67	68	69	70
(a)	(d)	(c)	(a)	(a)	(d)	(b)	(a)	(a)	(a)
71	72	73	74	75	76	77	78	79	80
(d)	(c)	(a)	(d)	(d)	(a)	(c)	(d)	(a)	(d)
81	82	83	84	85	86	87	88	89	90
(d)	(a)	(c)	(d)	(b)	(b)	(c)	(d)	(c)	(d)
91	92	93	94	95	96	97	98	99	100
(d)	(b)	(d)	(c)	(a)	(c)	(a)	(a)	(a)	(b)

MOCK TEST-2

1. As per section 5 (b) of Banking Regulation Act, which of the following is not an important element of the definition of banking?
   (a) Acceptance of deposit from public
   (b) Issuance of ATM for withdrawal of deposit amount
   (c) Acceptance of deposit for the purpose of lending
   (d) Acceptance of deposit for investment

2. As per section 5 (b) of Banking Regulation Act, the amount deposited by the public can be withdrawn by way of:
   (a) Cheque
   (b) Draft
   (c) Otherwise
   (d) All of the above

3. Each bank in its name must include, which of the following words under the provision of banking regulation Act?
   (a) Bank
   (b) Banking company
   (c) Banking
   (d) Any of the above

4. Minimum paid up capital for banking company incorporated outside India, operating in India:
   (a) ₹ 15 lakh
   (b) ₹ 20 lakh
   (c) ₹ 15 lakh & ₹ 20 lakh both, depending upon the place of business
   (d) None of these

5. For Indian banking company, minimum paid up capital and reserves if operating in a single state are:
   (a) ₹ 1 lakh
   (b) ₹ 2 lakh
   (c) ₹ 5 lakh
   (d) ₹ 10 lakh

6. Shifting of a bank's branch does not require permission if the shifting is in the same:
   (a) State
   (b) Town or village
   (c) District
   (d) No permission requires at all

7. Which of the following actions are required to be taken by the bank in connection with unclaimed deposit:
   (a) Annual return is required to be submitted to RBI
   (b) Annual return is to be prepared as on Dec 31 for submission to RBI
   (c) Annual return is to be submitted within 30 days of end of each calendar year
   (d) All the above

8. Section 45 ZA of BR Act deals with each aspect of banking operations:
   (a) Rules regarding preservation of records
   (b) Rules regarding return of paid instruments to customers
   (c) Rules regarding registration of nomination in deposit account
   (d) Rules regarding nomination in safe deposit locker

9. For nomination in case of articles in safe custody, under which of the following, the legal provisions are contained:
   (a) Section 45 C of BR Act
   (b) Section 24 of BR Act
   (c) Section 45 ZC of BR Act
   (d) Section 45 ZD of BR Act

10. On the basis of inspection report of a bank, if central Govt. decides to take stern action such as prohibition of acceptance of fresh deposits, what it is required to do?
    (a) Give opportunity to the bank
    (b) Can impose additional terms and condition
    (c) Can publish the report
    (d) All the above

11. Who among the following are not the members of Board of financial Supervision?
    (a) Governor RBI
    (b) Dy. Governors
    (c) 2 directors from local Boards of RBI
    (d) 4 directors from Central Board of RBI

12. Which of the following functions are not carried by Board for Financial Supervision?
    (a) Inspection of banks
    (b) Supervision of banks
    (c) Any other function notified by the central govt.
    (d) All the above

13. For opening of branches by co-operative banks, the application to RBI is required to be routed through:
(a) State Govt.
(b) Central Govt.
(c) SLBC of the state
(d) NABARD

14. Which of the following appoints Chairman of RRB?
(a) Reserve Bank
(b) Sponsor Bank
(c) Central Govt.
(d) State Govt.

15. Which is not correct about limited liability partnership (LLP)?
(a) LLP is governed by limited liability partnership Act 2008.
(b) Minimum 3 designated partner and no limit on maximum number of Partners.
(c) LLP is a legal entity separate from its partner.
(d) LLP cannot raise fund from public.

16. Which is not necessary for financing a Private Company?
(a) Memorandum of Association
(b) Article of Association
(c) Certificate of commencement of business
(d) Board resolution

17. A company is known as the _________ of another company if it has control over another company.
(a) Holding company
(b) Existing company
(c) Other company
(d) Foreign company

18. Which is a correct statement regarding export finance?
(a) Bank finance for both Pre Shipment/packing credit & Post Shipment credit advances
(b) Packing credit facilitates to the exporter for purchase raw materials and produce goods
(c) In the Post Shipment credit advances, maximum period prescribed for realization of export proceeds is 12 month from date of shipment
(d) All of the above

19. Which is a correct statement regarding letter of credit?
(a) It is issued by bank on request of the exporter
(b) As per UCPDC 600, all LC is irrevocable
(c) It is a non-fund credit facility
(d) All of the above

20. Limitation period for filing a suit in term loan is _________ years from date of default of installments.
(a) 1
(b) 2
(c) 3
(d) 5

21. The risk covered in a contract of indemnity is called:
(a) A subsisting risk
(b) A matured risk
(c) A contingent risk
(d) A settlement risk

22. Which of the following is a contract of indemnity?
(a) Obtaining loan from a bank
(b) Giving guarantee for a loan
(c) Opening a bank account with a bank
(d) Settlement of deceased accounts

23. As per RBI guideline in 2014 minimum claim period to be mentioned in the bank guarantee is _______ Limitation clause as to time and amount.
(a) 1 moths
(b) 3 moths
(c) 6 moths
(d) 1 year

24. When a guarantee is invoked by the beneficiary, normally court can grant stay on encashment when:
(a) Beneficiary does not state the reason for invocation
(b) Applicant approaches the court for stay
(c) Bank certifies that the invocation is not proper
(d) When there is element of fraud

25. If a guarantee is invoked by the beneficiary, the payment is made by the bank when:
(a) Beneficiary brings order from competent court
(b) Beneficiary makes demand on the bank
(c) Bank obtains consent of the applicant
(d) Sufficient balance is available in the account of applicant

26. Who is entitled to receive the payment on delivering of documents stipulated in a LC?
(a) Beneficiary
(b) Negotiating bank
(c) Advising Bank
(d) Confirming bank

27. Which is the role of Negotiating Bank?
(a) The bank that hands over the LC to the beneficiary
(b) Negotiates documents delivered to bank by beneficiary of LC
(c) The bank that opens the LC
(d) None of the above

28. Which is the role of Reimbursing Bank?
(a) It reimburse the payment to the seller
(b) It reimburse the payment to the applicant bank
(c) It reimburse the payment to the advising bank
(d) It reimburse the payment to the negotiating bank

29. The letter of credit where documents are paid immediately are called:
(a) Sight credit
(b) Usance credit
(c) Revocable credit
(d) Demand credit

30. The letter of credit where packing or anticipatory credit is available against the LC is called:
(a) Transferable LC
(b) Red clause LC
(c) Back to back LC
(d) Revolving LC

31. Transferable letter of credit can be transferred:
    (a) Any number of times
    (b) Only once
    (c) 2 times
    (d) As per instruction of issuer

32. When a seller undertakes to make the goods available for export, at his factory, such arrangement is called:
    (a) Ex-works   (b) FOB
    (c) CIF   (d) CFR

33. In case of 'Bill purchase' or 'Bill discounting', bankers becomes:
    (a) Holder   (b) Holder in due course
    (c) Possessor   (d) Negotiator

34. A bill of exchange is not supported by any documents of title of goods is called:
    (a) Demand documentary bill
    (b) Clean bill
    (c) Usance documentary bill
    (d) Incomplete bill

35. If a bill of exchange, time of payment is not mentioned, it is:
    (a) Payable on demand
    (b) Invalid bill
    (c) Incomplete bill
    (d) Not negotiable

36. Which is not a character of a good security?
    (a) The security should have encumbrance or liability.
    (b) The security should be easily marketable.
    (c) The value of security should be easily ascertainable.
    (d) The security should not be liable to wide price fluctuation.

37. Which is an a attributes of a good security?
    (a) The security should be easily and freely transferable.
    (b) The security should be durable.
    (c) The security should be easily transportable.
    (d) All of the above

38. In case of hypothecation, the borrower can:
    (a) Take goods out of godown and use them
    (b) Keep new goods inside the godown in place of old ones
    (c) Sell the goods hypothecated and replenish the stock
    (d) All of the above

39. Bank grants a loan against the security of goods relating to a firm, which kind of charge on goods can be created?
    (a) Pledge   (b) Hypothecation
    (c) Assignment   (d) Either (a) or (b)

40. The person to whom the possession of goods is transferred is called:
    (a) Transferee   (b) Bailee
    (c) Beneficiary   (d) Bailor

41. Creation of charge by the borrowers on various kinds of securities/assets means:
    (a) Creation of a right in favour of the bank.
    (b) The ownership is not transferred in favour of the creditor normally
    (b) The ownership is transferred in favour of the creditor in case of English Mortgage
    (d) All of the above

42. The term that institutions will have a "Pari Passu charge" over the assets means:
    (a) This term is usually used in case of consortium lending.
    (b) In case of such lending, a number of banks or financial institutions join together to lend to a single borrower in an agreed ratio against some common securities.
    (c) The lenders are entitled to have equal rights over the assets as per the agreed share.
    (d) All of the above

43. If a cheque is lost, a customer is bound to inform about the lost cheque to:
    (a) Payee   (b) Endorsee
    (c) Drawee Bank   (d) Collecting bank

44. If one of the signature is forged in case of jointly operated account, who is liable?
    (a) Only the customer
    (b) Only the paying bank
    (c) Both customer and banker
    (d) None

45. The collecting banker need not satisfy himself that all the endorsements on the cheque are regular.
    (a) True   (b) False

46. When a banker receives information that a cheque for collection is lost, the banker should:
    (a) Inform the drawer
    (b) Inform the drawee
    (c) Inform to RBI
    (d) Exercise due caution while collecting the cheque

47. The duties of collecting banker to claim protection has been laid down in:
    (a) NI Act
    (b) Indian Contract Act
    (c) RBI Act
    (d) Banking Regulation Act

48. Which of the following actions of a person can be included as part of the legal definition of computer crime?
(a) Securing access to computer or computer system
(b) Download, copy or extraction of data from a computer system
(c) Introduction of computer virus or causing denial to access to any person authorised to access the computer system
(d) All of the above

49. Which of the following actions of a person can be included as part of the legal definition of computer crime?
(a) Damage a computer system
(b) Disruption of network of computers
(c) Providing assistance to another person to get access to a computer system
(d) None of the above

50. At the _______ stage, the money re-enters the mainstream economy in legitimate-looking form. It appears to come from a legal transaction.
(a) Placement   (b) Integration
(c) Layering   (d) Smurfing

51. In banks, large cash transaction requires reporting. To avoid such reporting, large deposits are divided into multiple smaller transactions. This process of money laundering is called:
(a) Placement   (b) Integration
(c) Layering   (d) Smurfing

52. Which of the following is not true regarding Right to Information Act?
(a) The Act covers the whole of India except Jammu and Kashmir
(b) The Act covers the whole of India except Union Territories
(c) In the state of J&K Right to Information Act 2009 is in force
(d) None of the above

53. Under the Right to Information Act, a citizen of India can demand which type of Information?
(a) Records, documents, memos
(b) e-mails, press releases, circulars
(c) Advices, data material held in any electronic form.
(d) All of the above

54. Which of the following is defined under Transfer of Property Act, 1882?
(a) Hypothecation
(b) Pledge
(c) Mortgage
(d) All of the above

55. Mortgage is defined in:
(a) Section 58 (b) to 58 (g) of Transfer of Property Act 1882
(b) Section 57 of Transfer of Property Act 1882
(c) Section 57 of Indian Contract act
(d) Section 58 of NI act

56. "Foreign exchange" means foreign currency and in addition of the foreign currency, it includes:
(a) Deposits, credits and balances payable in any foreign currency
(b) Drafts, traveler cheques, letters of credit or bills of exchange, expressed or drawn in Indian currency but payable in any foreign currency
(c) Drafts, traveler cheques, letters of credit or bills of exchange drawn by banks, institutions or persons outside India, but payable in Indian currency
(d) Any of the above

57. For contravention of provision of FEMA, penalty can be levied _______ where amount is quantifiable.
(a) Equal to the amount
(b) Double the amount
(c) Thrice the amount
(d) Four times of amount

58. If the articles do not provide for retirement of all directors at every annual general meeting, how many directors would retire?
(a) $1/4^{th}$ (b) ½
(c) $1/3^{rd}$ (d) $2/3^{rd}$

59. When the directors are retired by rotation, which directors are to retire?
(a) The directors having the longest period in office
(b) The directors having the shortest period in office
(c) The directors who are directed to retire by ROC
(d) The directors who have not attended the meetings regularly

60. A person cannot act as a director unless he signs and files his consent with ROC within _______ of his appointment.
(a) 15 days   (b) 30 days
(c) 60 days   (d) 90 days

61. Which of the following is a correct statement?
(a) A company is a natural person
(b) A company is a corporate person
(c) A company is a legal person
(d) A company is a statutory person

62. Which of the following statement is true with regard to relationship of minor in a partnership firm?
(a) Minor cannot become a partner, he can be admitted for benefits

(b) Minor is entitled to property of the firm

(c) Minor is entitled to the profit from the firm

(d) All of the above

63. On attaining majority, the minor who is admitted for benefits, can decide about his status as partner within:

(a) 6 months from date of majority

(b) 6 months from date he comes to know that he was admitted for benefit

(c) 6 months from date of his admission for benefits

(d) Both (a) and (b), whichever is earlier

64. When a partner of a firm becomes insolvent and the firm is dissolved, this can be categorized in which kind of dissolution?

(a) By agreement

(b) At will

(c) Compulsory dissolution

(d) Dissolution of happening of certain contingencies

65. A _________ is a stipulation, collateral to the main purpose of contract.

(a) Condition   (b) Warranty

(c) Implied condition   (d) Guarantee

66. There is an implied condition on the part of the seller that he has a right to ______ the goods.

(a) Use   (b) Sell

(c) Retain   (d) Resell

67. As per Section 148 of Indian Contract Act 1872, a "bailment" is the delivery of goods by one person to another for some purpose. The person delivering the goods is called the "_______". The person to whom they are delivered is called the "________".

(a) Bailor, Bailee   (b) Bailee, Bailor

(c) Creditor, Debtor   (d) Debtor, Creditor

68. The bailor is bound to disclose to the bailee which types of faults in the goods bailed:

(a) Of which the bailor is aware

(b) Which materially interfere with the use of them

(c) Or expose the bailee to extraordinary risk

(d) All of the above

69. Which of the followings are advantage of the buyer or importer?

(a) No cash advance payment has to be made to the seller

(b) Possibility to stipulate favourable terms and condition to protect his interest

(c) Shipment schedule ensured

(d) All of the above

70. In an Appellate Tribunal and a Tribunal who shall be deemed to be public servants within the meaning of section 21 of the Indian Penal Code.

(a) The Chairperson of an Appellate Tribunal

(b) The Presiding Officer of a Tribunal

(c) The Recovery Officer

(d) All of the above

71. The objective of enactment of DRT Act is:

(a) For expeditious adjudication and recovery of debts due to banks and financial institutions.

(b) To increase capital in banks and financial institutions

(c) To meet the international standard of recovery

(d) All of the above

72. DRT Act does not cover the loans due to which of the following:

(a) Commercial banks

(b) Financial institution

(c) NBFC

(d) None of the above

73. When offer of sale of property is accepted by the purchaser and secured creditor, the purchaser has to immediately deposit _____% of the offer price.

(a) 10   (b) 20

(c) 25   (d) 50

74. On sale of the immovable property as security by the creditor, which of the following document is executed?

(a) Sale certificate

(b) Sale agreement

(c) Sale deed

(d) Conveyance certificate

75. How much time is given to the borrower to make the payment of the dues under the provision of SARFAESI Act 2002, before taking possession of the assets?

(a) 60 days   (b) 50 days

(c) 45 days   (d) 30 days

76. Under the provision of SARFAESI Act 2002, which among the following is a borrower?

(a) A person who has obtained financial assistance from bank

(b) A person who has created mortgage or any other charge over assets

(c) A person who has given guarantee

(d) All of the above

77. Appeal against the order of banking ombudsman may be filed by a bank only with the prior sanction of the ______________ or any other officer of equal rank.

(a) Chairman   (b) MD or CEO

(c) ED   (d) Any of the above

78. Customer and bank have to send acceptance of the award within _____ of date of receipt of the award.
(a) 15 days   (b) 30 days
(c) 60 days   (d) 90 days

79. Bank is to implement the award within _______ from the date of receipt of the acceptance from the complainant and intimate compliance to the Banking Ombudsman.
(a) One month
(b) Three month
(c) Six month
(d) Decided by Banking Ombudsman

80. Unless the court otherwise directs, bank officer cannot be compelled to produce original books to prove any Banker's Books contents when copy is produced.
(a) True   (b) False

81. Award of the Lok-Adalat has the status of order of:
(a) Civil Court   (b) High Court
(c) Supreme Court   (d) District Collector

82. Lok-Adalats are supposed to be guided by the principal of:
(a) Justice   (b) Equity and fair play
(c) Legal Principles   (d) All of the above

83. Under Consumer Protection Act, the Central Government has established a council known as:
(a) National Commission
(b) State Commission
(c) Central Consumer Protection Council
(d) All of the above

84. Who acts as the chairman of State Consumer Protection Council?
(a) The Minister-In-charge of the Consumer Affairs in the Central Government
(b) The Minister-In-charge of the Consumer Affairs in the State Government
(c) Secretary of the Consumer Affairs in the State Government
(d) Chief Justice of High Court

85. Who makes the appointment of the member of District Forum?
(a) Supreme Court   (b) High court
(c) State Govt.   (d) Central Govt.

86. Which of the following instance give rise to fresh period of limitation?
(a) Acknowledgement of liability by the borrower before expiry of limitation
(b) Part payment of debt by the borrower or his duly authorised agent on his behalf before expiry of limitation

(c) Both of the above
(d) None of the above

87. The limitation period for guarantor starts from:
(a) From the date of execution of deed of guarantee
(b) From the date of execution of D.P. Note by the borrower
(c) From the date of notice of demand given to the guarantor by the bank
(d) There is no limitation for guarantor

88. GST is an indirect tax which was introduced in India on _____ and was applicable throughout India.
(a) 1 July 2016   (b) 1 June 2017
(c) 1 July 2017   (d) 1 Sept. 2017

89. The Constitution of India has given the power to the Central Government to levy a tax on any income other than agricultural income, which is defined in _____ of the Income Tax Act, 1961.
(a) Section 10(1)   (b) Section 11(1)
(c) Section 10(2)   (d) Section 11(1)

90. A PAN is a _______ character alphanumeric number allotted by the Income Tax Department, to a tax-payer who is eligible to file the income tax return.
(a) 5   (b) 7
(c) 9   (d) 10

91. IT Act rule 114B has made it mandatory PAN (Form 60/61 in the absence of PAN) for the certain banking transaction.
(a) An application for issuing Credit/Debit card;
(b) Opening of Demat Account;
(c) Deposit/payment of cash exceeding ₹ 50,000 per day;
(d) All the above

92. If a cheque is payable to Anil or order and Anil only signs on a back of the instrument, such a chain is:
(a) Partial endorsement
(b) Blank endorsement
(c) Full endorsement
(d) Conditional endorsement

93. Who can cross a cheque?
(a) Drawer of the cheque
(b) Holder of the cheque
(c) A banker who receive the cheque for collection
(d) All of the above

94. What constitutes special crossing?
(a) Drawing two parallel transverse lines on the face of the cheque
(b) Writing a/c payee only on the face of the cheque
(c) Drawing two parallel transverse lines on the face of the cheque and writing the name of the bank in between

(d) Writing the words not negotiable on the face of the cheque

95. What is the application fee, which can be submitted in favour of the Reserve Bank along with the application for authorisation?
(a) ₹ 10,000/-
(b) ₹ 20,000/-
(c) ₹ 50,000/-
(d) ₹ 100,000/-

96. Who is the appellate authority for all application made for authorisation under Payment and Settlement Systems (PSS) Act?
(a) Governor of RBI
(b) President of India
(c) Central Government
(d) SEBI

97. Guarantees are defined in:
(a) Section 125 of Indian Contract Act 1872
(b) Section 126 of Indian Contract Act 1872
(c) Section 125 of Transfer of Property Act 1882
(d) Section 126 of NI Act 1881

98. Which of the mortgage is not required to be registered with the registrar of assurance?
(a) English Mortgage
(b) Equitable Mortgage
(c) Simple Mortgage
(d) Conditional sale

99. The bank is considered to be Pawnee in case of which of the following securities?
(a) Stocks of goods
(b) Shares
(c) Immovable property
(d) debenture

100. A loan which is granted for both buying capital assets and to meet working capital requirements is called _______.
(a) Bridge loans
(b) Composite loan
(c) Credit card
(d) Bill finance

ANSWER

1	2	3	4	5	6	7	8	9	10
(b)	(d)	(d)	(c)	(a)	(b)	(d)	(c)	(c)	(d)
11	**12**	**13**	**14**	**15**	**16**	**17**	**18**	**19**	**20**
(c)	(d)	(d)	(b)	(b)	(c)	(a)	(d)	(a)	(c)
21	**22**	**23**	**24**	**25**	**26**	**27**	**28**	**29**	**30**
(c)	(d)	(d)	(d)	(b)	(a)	(b)	(d)	(a)	(b)
31	**32**	**33**	**34**	**35**	**36**	**37**	**38**	**39**	**40**
(b)	(a)	(b)	(b)	(a)	(a)	(d)	(d)	(d)	(b)
41	**42**	**43**	**44**	**45**	**46**	**47**	**48**	**49**	**50**
(d)	(d)	(c)	(b)	(b)	(d)	(a)	(d)	(d)	(b)
51	**52**	**53**	**54**	**55**	**56**	**57**	**58**	**59**	**60**
(d)	(b)	(d)	(c)	(a)	(d)	(c)	(d)	(a)	(b)
61	**62**	**63**	**64**	**65**	**66**	**67**	**68**	**69**	**70**
(c)	(d)	(d)	(d)	(b)	(b)	(a)	(b)	(d)	(d)
71	**72**	**73**	**74**	**75**	**76**	**77**	**78**	**79**	**80**
(a)	(c)	(c)	(a)	(a)	(d)	(d)	(b)	(a)	(a)
81	**82**	**83**	**84**	**85**	**86**	**87**	**88**	**89**	**90**
(a)	(d)	(c)	(b)	(c)	(c)	(c)	(c)	(a)	(d)
91	**92**	**93**	**94**	**95**	**96**	**97**	**98**	**99**	**100**
(d)	(b)	(d)	(c)	(a)	(c)	(b)	(b)	(a)	(b)

www.ingramcontent.com/pod-product-compliance
Lightning Source LLC
LaVergne TN
LVHW080605200726
843509LV00007B/245